Justice for the Poor?

Justice *for the* Poor?
Social Justice in the Old Testament in Concept and Practice

Walter J. Houston

CASCADE *Books* · Eugene, Oregon

JUSTICE FOR THE POOR?

Social Justice in the Old Testament in Concept and Practice

Copyright © 2020 Walter J. Houston. All rights reserved. Except for brief quotations in critical publications or reviews, no part of this book may be reproduced in any manner without prior written permission from the publisher. Write: Permissions, Wipf and Stock Publishers, 199 W. 8th Ave., Suite 3, Eugene, OR 97401.

Cascade Books
An Imprint of Wipf and Stock Publishers
199 W. 8th Ave., Suite 3
Eugene, OR 97401

www.wipfandstock.com

PAPERBACK ISBN: 978-1-5326-4600-3
HARDCOVER ISBN: 978-1-5326-4601-0
EBOOK ISBN: 978-1-5326-4602-7

Cataloguing-in-Publication data:

Names: Houston, Walter J., author.

Title: Justice for the poor? : social justice in the Old Testament in concept and practice / by Walter J. Houston.

Description: Eugene, OR: Cascade Books, 2020 | Includes bibliographical references and index.

Identifiers: ISBN 978-1-5326-4600-3 (paperback) | ISBN 978-1-5326-4601-0 (hardcover) | ISBN 978-1-5326-4602-7 (ebook)

Subjects: LCSH: Social justice—Biblical teaching | Bible.—Old Testament—Criticism, interpretation, etc. | Social justice | Justice—Biblical teaching

Classification: BS1199.J8 H68 2020 (print) | BS1199.J8 (ebook)

Manufactured in the U.S.A.   03/05/20

To
The Society for Old Testament Study
in recognition of the honour of election
to their Presidency for the year 2020

Contents

Acknowledgments | x
Abbreviations | xii
Introduction | xvi

Chapter 1: "Justice and Right": Biblical Ethics and the Regulation of Capitalism | 1

Chapter 2: "You Shall Open Your Hand to Your Needy Brother": Ideology and Moral Formation in Deut 15:1–18 | 17

Chapter 3: The King's Preferential Option for the Poor: Rhetoric, Ideology, and Ethics in Psalm 72 | 35

Chapter 4: What's Just about the Jubilee? Ideological and Ethical Reflections on Leviticus 25 | 58

Chapter 5: The Role of the Poor in Proverbs | 73

Chapter 6: Was There a Social Crisis in the Eighth Century? | 85

Chapter 7: Exit the Oppressed Peasant? Rethinking the Background of Social Criticism in the Prophets | 105

Chapter 8: Corvée in the Kingdom of Israel: Israelites, "Canaanites," and Cultural Memory | 120

Chapter 9: The Scribe and His Class: Ben Sira on Rich and Poor | 133

Chapter 10: Doing Justice: The Phrase "Justice and Right" in the Hebrew Bible | 150

Chapter 11: The Psalms of YHWH's Kingship: The Divine King Executes Royal Justice | 181

Chapter 12: "To Share Your Bread with the Hungry": Justice or Charity? | 191

Chapter 13: Justice and Violence in the Priestly Utopia: Reflections on Genesis 1 and 6–9 in the Shadow of the Environmental Crisis | 201

Bibliography | 215
Author Index | 233
Subject Index | 237
Ancient Document Index | 241

Acknowledgments

The sources of the chapters in this book are as follows. Where permission for their republication was required, I am grateful for the permissions of the respective publishers as named below. Where the title is given, it has been altered as printed in this volume.

Chapter 1. "Justice and Righteousness: Biblical Ethics and the Regulation of Capitalism." *De Ethica* 2/3 (2015): Futures of Capitalism 7–21. http://www.de-ethica.com/archive/articles/v2/i3/a04/de_ethica_15v2i3a04.pdf. This is an open-source journal.

Chapter 2. *The Bible in Ethics: The Second Sheffield Colloquium*, edited by John Rogerson, Margaret Davies and M. Daniel Carroll R., 296–314. JSOTS 207. Sheffield, UK: Sheffield Academic Press, 1995.

Chapter 3. *Biblical Interpretation* 7 (1999) 341–67. Koninklijke Brill NV, Leiden.

Chapter 4. *Studies in Christian Ethics* 14 (2001) 34–47. https://doi.org/10.1177/095394680101400104 Sage Publications Ltd.

Chapter 5. *Reading from Right to Left: Essays on the Hebrew Bible in Honour of David J. A. Clines*, edited by J. Cheryl Exum and H. G. M. Williamson, 229–40. JSOTS 373. Sheffield, UK: Sheffield Academic Press, 2003.

Chapter 6. *In Search of Pre-Exilic Israel: Proceedings of the Oxford Old Testament Seminar*, edited by John Day, 130–49. JSOTS 406. London: T. & T. Clark, 2004.

Chapter 7. *Prophecy and Prophets in Ancient Israel: Proceedings of the Oxford Old Testament Seminar*, edited by John Day, 101–16. LHBOTS 531. London: T. & T. Clark, 2010.

Chapter 8. *Journal for the Study of the Old Testament* 43/1 (2018) 29–44. https://doi.org/10.1177/0309089215692183 Sage Publications Ltd.

Chapter 9. *Writing the Bible: Scribes, Scribalism and Script*, edited by Philip R. Davies and Thomas Römer, 108–23. BibleWorld. Durham: Acumen, 2013.

Chapter 10. "Doing Justice: The Ideology, Theology and Distribution in the Hebrew Bible of משפט וצדקה." *Zeitschrift für Altorientalische und Biblische Rechtsgeschichte* 22 (2017) 13–38. Otto Harrassowitz GmbH & Co KG.

Chapter 11. Previously unpublished.

Chapter 12. *Scripture as Social Discourse: Social Scientific Perspectives on Early Jewish and Christian Writings*, edited by Jessica Keady, Todd Klutz and Casey Strine, 71–81. London: T. & T. Clark, 2018.

Chapter 13. "Justice and Violence in the Priestly Utopia." *Bible and Justice: Ancient Texts, Modern Challenges*, edited by Matthew J. M. Coomber, 93–105. London: Equinox, 2011.

In addition I am grateful to Bloomsbury Publishing Plc for permission to reproduce Figure A from "Shaping the Psalter: A Consideration of Editorial Linkage in the Book of Psalms," by Gerald H. Wilson. In *The Shape and Shaping of the Psalter*, edited by J. Clinton McCann Jr., 72–82. JSOTS 159. Sheffield, UK: Sheffield Academic Press, 1993.

Abbreviations

This list does not include well-known abbreviations such as those of Bible versions or American states.

AB	Anchor Bible
ABD	*Anchor Bible Dictionary* (see bibliography)
ATD	Altes Testament Deutsch
BAR	British Archaeological Reports
BASOR	*Bulletin of the American Schools of Oriental Research*
BBB	Bonner Biblische Beiträge
BBET	Beiträge zur biblische Exegese und Theologie
BEATAJ	Beiträge zur Erforschung des Alten Testaments und des antiken Judentum
BETL	Bibliotheca ephemeridum theologicarum lovaniensium
BHS	*Biblia Hebraica Stuttgartensia*
BHTh	Beiträge zur historischen Theologie
BibInt	*Biblical Interpretation*
BJRL	*Bulletin of the John Rylands Library*
BJS	Brown Judaic Studies
BKAT	Biblischer Kommentar, Altes Testament
BWANT	Beiträge zur Wissenschaft vom Alten und Neuen Testament
BZAW	Beihefte zur Zeitschrift für die alttestamentliche Wissenschaft
BZNW	Beihefte zur Zeitschrift der neutestamentlichen Wissenschaft
CB OTS	Coniectanea Biblica, Old Testament Series

CBET	Contributions to Biblical Exegesis and Theology
CD	Barth, *Church Dogmatics* (see bibliography)
DCH	*Dictionary of Classical Hebrew* (see bibliography)
EvTh	*Evangelische Theologie*
FAT	Forschungen zum Alten Testament
HKAT	Handkommentar zum Alten Testament
HThKAT	Herders Theologischer Kommentar zum Alten Testament
HUCA	*Hebrew Union College Annual*
ICC	International Critical Commentary
IEJ	*Israel Exploration Journal*
JAJ	*Journal of Ancient Judaism*
JBL	*Journal of Biblical Literature*
JNES	*Journal of Near Eastern Studies*
JPS	Jewish Publication Society of America
JR	*Journal of Religion*
JSOT	*Journal for the Study of the Old Testament*
JSOTS	Journal for the Study of the Old Testament Supplement Series
JTS	*Journal of Theological Studies*
LCL	Loeb Classical Library
LHBOTS	Library of Hebrew Bible/Old Testament Studies
MT	Masoretic Text
NCB	New Century Bible
NCBC	New Century Bible Commentary
NICOT	New International Commentary on the Old Testament
OBO	Orbis biblicus et orientalis
OTG	Old Testament Guides
OTL	Old Testament Library
OTS	*Oudtestamentische Studien*
PEQ	*Palestine Exploration Quarterly*
PG	*Patrologia Graeca*
RB	*Revue biblique*
SBLDS	SBL Dissertation Series

SBS	Stuttgarter Bibelstudien
SJOT	*Scandinavian Journal of the Old Testament*
SVT	Supplements to Vetus Testamentum
SWBA	Social World of Biblical Antiquity
ThZ	*Theologische Zeitschrift*
UF	*Ugarit-Forschungen*
VT	*Vetus Testamentum*
WBC	Word Biblical Commentary
WMANT	Wissenschaftliche Monographien zum Alten und Neuen Testament
WUNT	Wissenschaftliche Untersuchungen zum Neuen Testament
ZAR	*Zeitschrift für altorientalische und biblische Rechtsgeschichte*
ZAW	*Zeitschrift für die alttestamentliche Wissenschaft*
ZDPV	*Zeitschrift des Deutschen Palästina-Vereins*

Introduction

"There is no record of civilization that is not at the same time a record of barbarism"—Walter Benjamin.¹ The building of cities and monuments, the creation of even the smallest state, requires the subjection of one person to another, and very often leads to the exploitation of the efforts of one to the advantage of the other. If this has been one of the main drivers of human history since the Neolithic, the attempt to fight back against barbarism and in favor of justice has driven in the opposite direction. And foremost in these efforts in most societies have been adherents of their religious traditions, since the ideal must embrace ideal relations between people. Thus it is that the Jewish scriptures that Christians know as the Old Testament exhibit in many places denunciations of injustice, teaching in ways of justice, laws to execute justice, and praise of God as a God of justice.

Almost from the start of my career as a scholar of the Old Testament² I have sought to explore the significance of its texts for the social and political, as well as religious, life of the modern world; and central to this exploration has been the question of social justice. In this I am hardly unique among scholars of my discipline; there is a massive, wide-ranging, and valuable body of work drawing out the significance of these texts for the struggle for justice in contemporary society, especially in recent decades. I nevertheless

---

1. I have been unable to locate the source of this well-known quotation.

2. I use here the traditional Christian designation, rather than "Hebrew Bible" or any other expression, for two main reasons. One is that I include the deuterocanonical writings in my study (see chapter 9 here), so that the designation "Hebrew Bible" would not cover the subject. The other and more important is that it is precisely as Christian scripture, accepted as such along with the New Testament by the church, and read and reflected on by Christians, that these writings are significant for me as a Christian. However, as a scholar of those writings, I refer in a number of places in the individual chapters to "the Hebrew Bible."

came fairly early in my study of the matter to the view that I was able to make a distinctive contribution to this body of work. I believe like everyone who writes on the issue that faithful readers of the Old Testament, Jewish or Christian, will find its words challenging some aspect, at least, of their own society, political arrangements, or political economy. But I took the view that these texts could only be understood correctly as words emerging from a specific social situation in the past, spoken or written by a representative of a specific social group, which could well be concerned largely for its own advantage; but that nevertheless the situation might compel them to give voice to a view transcending the situation and their own advantage, which could still have relevance for our own day. I do not need to go in more detail into this hermeneutical proposal at this point, as readers will find ample discussions in the early parts of chapters 1, 2, 3, and 5 in particular, as well as in my book *Contending for Justice*.

An important stimulus to my work was the invitation in 1985 to join a group of biblical scholars brought together under the auspices, initially, of the former British Council of Churches, to offer guidance on various aspects of present-day society from a biblical point of view, and later developing into an independent group commissioning work from among its members under the names of, first "Scripture, Theology and Society," and later "Bible and Society Group." As related in the preface to *Contending for Justice*, I contributed papers on various topics to our annual meetings, material from some of which has eventually found its way into this book. I am very grateful to all my colleagues in this group and to all that I heard there.

But the germ of much that was in that book and this one lay in the lectures that I was invited to give to the Vacation Term for Biblical Study at Oxford in 1994. These formed much of the basis for *Contending for Justice*, as the material was developed over the following twelve years, and much of it worked up into three articles published in journals and collections of essays, which were then taken up, with one other, into that book, which was published in 2006, with a revised edition two years later.

The volume before you has a close relationship to that book. The material here is of diverse origins. There are, first, the four essays just referred to that were taken up into *Contending for Justice*, mostly in an abbreviated as well as revised form, here chapters 2 to 5. I debated with myself whether to republish these in their original form, and eventually decided to do so, reflecting that some readers might welcome the opportunity to view them all together in a form that reflects the original circumstances and impulses behind their publication. Another two (chapters 6 and 7) were presented as papers during my work on the book, the first before its first publication and the second between the publications of the first and second editions. They closely reflect work that I was doing on the book at the time. The other seven were originally presented and published at various times after I had finished work on the second edition. Chapter 8, although published and even written some years later, seeks to prove a hypothesis suggested in *Contending for Justice*, and chapter 9 repairs a notable omission in *Contending*. The remaining five essays are less closely related to that book, but, except for chapter 13, they are dependent on it at various points.

The Individual Essays

I hesitated for some time over what order I should put the essays in. The first and most obvious choice was to present them in chronological succession, and, even as it is, it will be seen that there is a broad chronological order, with some notable deviations. Eventually I decided that for a reader reading through the book some deviations from chronology would help them to make connections and to understand the context from which I was writing. The sharpest of these deviations is that I have placed at the beginning as chapter 1, before the earliest essay, a version of a relatively recent lecture, given at the University of Winchester, England, in 2014, at a conference, "Futures of Capitalism," organized by my friend and former student Neil Messer, and published online in 2016 (it is dated 2015 but it did not actually appear till the following year). I have several reasons for this. It is the most adapted to a general audience of any of the essays, and so, I think, the easiest read. It starts with a precise delineation of the social and economic circumstances to which it responds. Most of the essays include reflection on the present-day relevance of the theme, but more usually towards the end than the beginning. I judge that any reader who reads that first will thus be easily drawn into the book and will be clear from the beginning about the present-day concerns that are the context of all the essays. (Chapter 13 stands apart in this respect: see further below.) Further, it makes connections with many of the following items, so that it should form a readable and provocative introduction to the whole issue.

Chapter 2 is the earliest publication in the book. Worked up from one of my lectures to the Vacation Term in 1994, it was presented to the then Scripture, Theology, and Society group the following year (I think) before being read a few weeks later at the second Sheffield Colloquium on the Bible in Ethics at the University of Sheffield and published later the same year, 1995, along with the other papers read at the colloquium. Parts were included in slightly revised form in two chapters of *Contending*. It includes my first discussion of the problem of ideological texts, laying down the main lines of the hermeneutics that I attempt to follow in all my publications on this subject, before launching into a detailed study of Deut 15:1-11 and 12-18, and ends with brief reflections on law, consent, liberty, and the formation of community.

Chapter 3's origins also go back to the Vacation Term lectures, and even further back to talks given to lay groups, but it reached something like its present form through being read as an academic paper to the staff and graduate seminar of the (lamentably) former Department of Biblical Studies at the University of Sheffield in 1998, and later to the Ehrhardt Seminar in the Department of Religions and Theology at the University of Manchester. It was accepted by Cheryl Exum as a contribution to *BibInt*,[3] and published in 1999. Parts were included in two chapters of *Contending*. In its original published form the study of "rhetoric, ideology, and ethics" in Psalm 72 is preceded by a brief discussion on the use of the Old Testament for reflection on Christian social ethics, and concluded with thoughts on the relevance of the psalm for political theology. It also includes my first discussion of the question whether Judean kings ever took seriously the responsibility focused on by the psalm to do justice by the poor, which I take up again in chapter 10. This is probably the most cited of all these essays, and because of the way databases work those concerned with Psalm 72 are more likely to cite it from *Biblical Interpretation* than from *Contending*. I hope that its republication here will therefore prove useful.

Continuing with the papers behind *Contending* in chronological order, the study of the Jubilee legislation in chapter 4 took shape in a paper read to a meeting of the Society for the Study of Christian Ethics in Oxford in 2000, and according to the Society's practice it was published in their journal *Christian Ethics* the following year. It appeared in a revised form in one chapter of *Contending*. Its opening paragraph makes a link to the campaign current at the time for the cancellation of unrepayable debts owed by highly indebted poor countries, which was known as Jubilee 2000. Was it right to appropriate that name? The blunt question is asked: what kind of justice does Lev 25 offer, and for whom?

The last of the papers taken up in *Contending* is chapter 5, which was written in response to an invitation to contribute to a Festschrift for David Clines (his first), published as *Reading from Right to Left* in 2003. But before that it was read to the Society for Old Testament Study at their summer meeting in Dublin in 2002. This paper addresses the question of class perhaps more sharply than any of the others. It is essentially a critique of the view,

---

3. For names of journals, see the list of abbreviations, or the acknowledgments, where they are given in full.

which still survives (see only chapter 9!), that the wisdom writers blame the poor for their own poverty. The section on Proverbs in *Contending* addresses wider questions, and so though much of the essay was incorporated in it, this specific argument is omitted. This republication should therefore again prove useful to those pursuing a particular question.

The Oxford Old Testament Seminar, of which I was a member from 2000 to 2008, arranged from time to time for a series of papers to be given on a particular theme, which were then published as a collection through the efforts of my colleague John Day. Chapters 6 and 7 each originated in this way. Chapter 6 was my contribution to the series "In Search of Pre-Exilic Israel," and was given as a paper to the seminar in or around 2003, before the whole series was published under the same title in 2004. It reflects the work I had been doing on the social background to the texts studied in *Contending*, embodied in that book's second chapter, but with a more strongly historical focus. The theoretical question addressed in it, as distinct from the historical one expressed in the title, was to what extent social distress was a result of exploitation of the poor by the ruling class, rather than broader social dysfunction.

Shortly after the publication of the first edition of *Contending*, Avraham Faust, whom I did not know at the time, sent me on his own initiative a collection of articles by himself, and it was my reading of these articles and my later conversations with Avi himself that led to my revision of the book, particularly of my account of the social background. Chapter 7, originating in a paper contributed to another series, "Prophecy and the Prophets," at the Oxford seminar in 2007–8, my last year at Oxford, before the publication of the revised edition, is a critical examination of Faust's hypothesis that the pre-exilic prophets were responding to social distress not in the countryside but in the cities. It was eventually published with other papers from the series in 2010.

Chapter 8 is another that is out of chronological order, placed here next to the two other chapters on the historical background of the texts studied in *Contending*. I had suggested there that in the kingdom of Israel forced labor was demanded from the non-Israelite ("Canaanite") population, while ethnic Israelites were spared. I repeated this hypothesis in my Old Testament Guide to Amos in 2015.[4] I realized that this hypothesis could not be allowed to stand without substantial argument, so I wrote a paper that I read at the meeting of the European Association of Biblical Studies (EABS) in Leuven in July 2016, developed further and submitted to *JSOT*. After some delay, it was published in 2018.

---

4. Houston, *Contending*, 39; *Amos*, 61.

In 2009, after I had retired and moved back to the north of England, making the University of Manchester my academic base, one of the regular colloquia between Manchester biblical scholars, along with some from Sheffield, and those at Lausanne (with Geneva) took place at Lausanne, and I was invited by the kindness of George Brooke, then Rylands Professor of Biblical Criticism at Manchester, and chair of the Ehrhardt Seminar, to join the Manchester contingent. The stated theme was "Scribes and Scribalism." I took the opportunity to repair an omission in *Contending for Justice* by studying the book of Sirach (Ecclesiasticus), avowedly the work of the scribe Ben Sira, from the same point of view and with the same hermeneutical method as I did with texts in *Contending*. All the papers read at the colloquium were eventually published as a book in 2013, and mine appears here as chapter 9.

The longest chapter in this book is chapter 10, and it has a correspondingly complicated history. I was invited by Susanne Gillmayr-Bucher to contribute a paper at the meeting in Vienna in July 2014 of the EABS, to their research group on "The Production of Authoritative Books in Persian-Period Judah." The theme was "Ṣedaqa and Torah in Postexilic Discourse." I found the yoking of these two incommensurable terms awkward, but took the opportunity to read a paper on a puzzle that had been exercising me for a little time: why the expression *mishpat utsedaqa*,[5] "justice and right," which includes one of these terms, is so rare in the Torah while being very common in the prophets and the Psalms. Later I expanded the paper considerably, to discuss the usage of the expression in every part of the Hebrew Bible, read it to the Ehrhardt Seminar in 2015, and submitted it in final form to the German annual *ZAR*, where it appeared in 2017. The paper covers in one way or another the entire range of types of contexts that deal with the theme of justice in the Old Testament.

I have placed immediately after this chapter, because it pivots on the same Hebrew expression, an unpublished paper that I read at the meeting of the International Organization for the Study of the Old Testament in Aberdeen in August 2019, here revised and expanded. This chapter 11, with the section of chapter 10 dealing with the justice of God, makes connections with the chapter of *Contending for Justice* on the same topic, and asks how belief in God's justice may function in believing communities.

Chapter 12 takes a different approach from all the previous chapters, viewing concepts of justice in their evolution through time from the monarchic to the late Second Temple period, in the light of theories from economic anthropology. It was written for, and read at, the meeting of the

---

5. See chapter 1, 4–5.

Manchester-Lausanne colloquium of 2014 in Manchester, which had the theme of social-scientific perspectives on early Jewish and Christian writings, and then at the meeting of the Society of Biblical Literature later the same year at San Diego. The publication of the colloquium proceedings was excessively delayed; they only emerged in 2018.

The last chapter in the book appears to have a different theme and to be addressed to a different present-day situation from the rest, and for that reason it has been placed at the end, but also because it points forward to the most urgent and difficult task of our time. But its difference from the rest is only apparent. For it is the same desires for wealth and power, the same unequal distribution of wealth and power, and, today, the same system of capitalist accumulation indicted in chapter 1, that is responsible for the destruction of the environment as well as for social injustice; while in biblical texts such as Psalm 72 social justice and the fertility of the earth are seen as intimately bound up together. The article was read at a conference in Sheffield in 2008 on "Bible and Justice," and the proceedings were published in 2011. In it, I reach back to my earliest substantial contribution to biblical study, at the Oxford Biblical Studies Conference of 1978, exactly thirty years before the one in Sheffield. That was published, but is not included here. It has been overtaken by events—for example, although it has a strong sense of urgency, there is no mention of climate change.

Matters of Presentation

Broadly speaking, the essays are printed here in their original wording. They have not been subjected to any extensive updating or revision. However, errors have been corrected (those that I was aware of, that is!), here and there stylistic improvements have been made, and of course spelling and other aspects have been made to conform to Wipf and Stock house style: in particular, where references were in the text, they have been moved to the footnotes. Three of the chapters have had their titles slightly changed (see the acknowledgments). A limited degree of updating has been carried out in the footnotes: there are references to later literature, and in particular I have created as thorough a network of cross-references between the essays as I can, always to the relevant chapter, and often to the page. References in the original essays to earlier essays that are now in this book have been changed to references to the appropriate chapter and page. Details of the original publications will be found in the acknowledgments, not in the bibliography. Additions to the footnotes, other than references and foreign-language quotations (see below) moved from the text, have been placed in square brackets.

Most of the essays included here were originally read as papers to academic gatherings of biblical scholars and published in academic journals or collections of academic papers. Hebrew was often left untranslated. There were also untranslated quotations in modern languages. There are only three chapters (1, 4, and 13) that originally had a somewhat wider audience. But I am conscious that, to quote Wipf and Stock's style guide, books published under the Cascade Books imprint "combine academic rigor with wide appeal and readability." I have therefore made considerable efforts to smooth away obstacles such as untranslated Hebrew from the path of the non-specialist reader. Much Hebrew (and Greek in chapter 9) has been transferred to the footnotes; I have not thought it necessary to make the footnotes equally readable in the same way. Where Hebrew needs to be quoted in the text, usually single words or phrases, I have paired the word in Hebrew script with an informal transliteration, not using diacritical marks, so that any reader can see the approximate pronunciation, and given a translation except where the same word or phrase occurs repeatedly in the same context.[6] I have only used a formal scholarly transliteration when quoting words in ancient languages other than Hebrew or Greek (Akkadian, and once Egyptian).

Thanks

I cannot conclude this introduction without expressing my appreciation to everyone who has in any way contributed to the work presented here. I must first thank my audiences. Every one of these chapters was first read as a paper before an audience before appearing in print, and was followed by often lively discussion. Particular thanks go to those who suggested ideas for improvement; occasional mentions of individuals may be found in the footnotes. More persons than I can name were involved in the original publications of the essays, but one or two are named above. The late John Rogerson is much more significant to me than as the lead editor of the volume in which what is now chapter 2 was published. It was he who got our group of contextual biblical scholars going again as Bible and Society Group when it seemed that it had folded, and his personal friendship and encouragement maintained my own interest in the project. I miss him. For the present publication I owe thanks to Matthew Wimer of Wipf and Stock, who accepted it for Cascade Books, to my editor Robin Parry, who has been unfailingly helpful, and to those involved in the book's production.

---

6. Hebrew script is not used in chapter 1, and elsewhere where the same word or phrase is repeated, I have often only repeated the transliteration.

Finally, as ever, I am grateful to my wife Fleur for her interest and encouragement at moments when I tired of the task of converting thirteen essays with disparate styles into a book. The bibliography will reveal that her contribution to this work was academic as well as personal.

Chapter 1

"Justice and Right"

Biblical Ethics and the Regulation of Capitalism

(2015)

Capitalism Regulated and Unregulated

It has long been recognized that the constant tendency of industrial capitalism, if unrestrained and unregulated, is to enable the enrichment of the capitalist through the impoverishment of those who provide labor to the enterprise. Marx thought that this would lead to a crisis for capitalism in that workers would be increasingly unable to afford the goods that they themselves had made. This has not happened for a number of reasons, among them being that capitalism has needed to operate restrained by the collective action of the workforce in their unions and regulated in a variety of directions by the power of the state. The capitalist system that outperformed the socialist economy of Eastern Europe between the Second World War and the fall of the Berlin Wall was far from a pure unmixed capitalism. Most advanced countries included an extensive public sector and a welfare system and had pay and conditions regulated by the state; however, they depended heavily on cheap imports produced by impoverished workers in the so-called Third World.

But modern globalized and increasingly unregulated capitalism has increased inequality dramatically both on the national and the global level. Absolute poverty has not necessarily grown worse (although in some places it has), it is rather that the relationships between people in different economic circumstances, different classes, and different countries have become more openly exploitative. It is difficult to be unaware that our pensions and our T-shirts are bought at the expense of poorly paid and poorly protected workers in other parts of the world; or that our offices are cleaned and our sandwiches sold by an army of underpaid part-time workers, many of them immigrants; and that many of their employers are hugely wealthy.

The question arises: what kind of regulation does this system demand? That depends on what the aims of the regulator are, whether to achieve greater efficiency, to eliminate fraud and corruption, to ease the alleged burden of red tape, or perhaps to encourage investment. The choice of such aims is an ethical choice. One of the mystifications thrown up on this subject is the pretense that such decisions are purely practical, and even unavoidable. Those of us of a certain age in the UK may remember TINA, "there is no alternative" to the neo-liberal reforms introduced under the Thatcher government; a rhetorical topos (also used more recently) that concealed the fact that policy-makers were choosing between alternatives, and doing so according to specific ethical beliefs. Policy choices can and should be assessed ethically.

The Old Testament as an Ethical Source

In this paper I shall describe one of the sources of Christian thought on social ethics, showing that it does have relevance to the issue of policy in a capitalist economy. That source is the Bible, and specifically the Old Testament or Hebrew Bible. I am not assuming that Christian thought is to be derived exclusively from the Bible, nor that everything found in the Bible on this subject is to be accepted. I am assuming at least that Christians will want to take much of it seriously, and also hoping that non-Christians will find it of interest and worthy of reflection. There are of course immense differences between the society and economy of ancient Israel and that of modern capitalist countries. In particular, nothing like modern capitalism existed: wealth was accumulated for conspicuous consumption and for storage, not normally for productive investment.[1] For some, this puts the Bible entirely out of court as a serious source for ethics in the modern world. See, for example, Cyril Rodd's *Glimpses of a Strange Land*, whose title sums up his view of Old Testament ethics. However, philosophers as well as theologians go on reading old texts and finding value in them. Consider, for example, Michael Sandel's use of Aristotle in a popular work on justice.[2] How is this possible?

J. W. Rogerson argues that "while many of the Bible's precepts cannot be applied directly to today's world . . . a process of moral discernment

---

1. For a recent study of the economic structures of ancient Israel, see Boer, *Sacred Economy*.

2. Sandel, *Justice*, 184–207.

and action within them can be recognized." This process of discernment, he suggests, is the example to be followed by modern readers, rather than the individual commands.[3] For example, Deut 15:12–18, directing slaves to be released after six years, which interpreted literally might be thought of as authorizing the institution of slavery, exemplifies what Rogerson calls a "structure of grace," that "allows graciousness and compassion to function in human relationship" and implicitly condemns slavery.[4]

Hans-Georg Gadamer offers his concept of the "merging of horizons."[5] The reading and understanding of a work of the past, especially if the reader stands in the same tradition, involves the reader in seeing the world within the horizon of that work, so that its horizon and the reader's perspective merge. The value of this idea is that it enables an understanding of how readers naturally pick up ideas and carry them forward into their own horizon, by grasping what is the same within the two horizons in the midst of the obvious differences. In my own discussions of the issue, I have emphasized the importance of the imagination in this process alongside the intellectual comprehension of the work.[6] Whatever the character and genre of the text being read, it is a work of the imagination, in many cases calling into being an imaginary world infused by the justice of God—for example, in Leviticus 25, an Israel governed by the law of the Jubilee—that challenges the injustice of the world as it exists, and to which the reader's imagination may respond by reflecting on its expression of justice in contrast with injustice in the modern world. It must be understood, and will be evident in the following discussion, that ethical texts in the Old Testament do not describe the society of Israel as it really was, but challenge a reality that in many respects failed to meet their standards. This is as true of legal and wisdom texts as of prophecy. An ideological text that legitimizes the king's rule by praising his alleged justice (Psalm 72) may be read as challenging him to be just, and thus, in the merging of horizons, our modern rulers also.[7]

To express my findings in a single sentence: there is a widespread assumption in the Hebrew Bible that *the state has an obligation to exercise its power on behalf of the most vulnerable*. While the concern of the Bible for the poor is generally recognized, it is perhaps less widely realized that many texts presume the existence of a specific obligation of the state, in the person of the king, to protect the poor from exploitation. The social system reflected in the

---

3. Rogerson, *According to the Scriptures*, 80.
4. Rogerson, *According to the Scriptures*, 81–82.
5. Gadamer, *Truth and Method*, 302–5.
6. Houston, *Justice—the Biblical Challenge*, 13–14.
7. Houston, *Contending*, 139–50, and chapter 3 below, 54–56.

biblical writings was, like ours, sharply unequal, though our historical information is too limited for us to able to measure its inequality statistically. It is sufficient to note that many texts of the Hebrew Bible that deal with economic affairs speak of the relationships between rich and poor; or of the duties owed by the addressees of the texts, presumably at least comfortably off, to the poor and to other vulnerable people, often expressed as "the widow, the fatherless, and the stranger [that is, the resident alien]."

"Justice and Righteousness" as a Virtue of God and the Obligation of the King[8]

There is a phrase that appears in many Hebrew Bible texts, especially in the prophets and the Psalms, that is conventionally translated as "justice (or 'judgment' in older translations[9]) and righteousness," in Hebrew *mishpat u tsedaqa* (or less often in the reverse order); in poetic texts the two elements are often divided between the two halves of the poetic line, e.g., "Let justice roll down like water, and righteousness like an ever-flowing stream" (Amos 5:24);[10] "I looked for justice and found bloodshed, for righteousness, and heard a cry" (Isa 5:7). Rather than indicating two distinct characteristics, it is widely agreed that this phrase expresses a single idea by the use of two words grammatically coordinated. This is often referred to as a hendiadys, but this is an inaccurate use of this technical term.[11]

It is has been pointed out that in so-called "synonymous parallelism," where the two halves of a poetic line correspond to each other, as in the Amos and Isaiah texts quoted above, the second half tends to intensify the effect of the first, or to make it more precise, to disambiguate it.[12] This effect may apply to individual words as well as to the half-line as a whole. Now each of the key words *mishpat* and *tsedaqa* has a wide range of meanings. They are by no means synonyms, but their semantic ranges overlap at certain points. *mishpat* may mean rule, judgment, justice, custom, law, legal decision, and more. The range of meaning of *tsedaqa* is even wider, covering right order, just conduct, generosity, prosperity, victory, to name a few of its connotations. Pairing *mishpat* with *tsedaqa* makes it clear it is a question of *right* or *just* rule, laws, or customs. Since *mishpat* generally precedes *tsedaqa*,

---

8. [For more detail, see below, chapter 3.]

9. [And in Alter's recent version *The Hebrew Bible*.]

10. [According to most versions. For a detailed argument for a different translation, see Houston, "Folly at Bethel."]

11. Fowler, *Modern English Usage*, 245. See below in chapter 10, 151–52.

12. Alter, *Biblical Poetry*, 3–26 and passim.

it also conversely excludes most of the senses of the latter: the semantic field is narrowed to the sphere of social and political relationships. What applies to the poetic line may also apply to the two words as a single expression. Taken together, they refer to God's just ordering of the world, and in the human realm to just and generous social and political relationships, or what we would call social justice, and the legal, political, and religious means by which they may be ensured.[13] One may say that the ethical content of the expression is carried principally by *tsedaqa*. This is conventionally translated as "righteousness"; but I prefer the rendering "right" or "the right," except where it appears to denote a personal characteristic.

Several examples show that "justice and right" is understood both as a gift of God and as the responsibility of the ruler. It is presented as a characteristic of God and God's governance of the world in, e.g., Ps 33:5, "He loves righteousness and justice: the faithful love of YHWH fills the earth," or 89:14, "Right[14] and justice are the foundation of your throne." God's "justice and right" can be bestowed on human society. "Give to the king your justice,[15] O God, and your righteousness to the king's son" (Ps 72:1) is the prayer of the Psalmist. According to 2 Sam 8:15, "David did justice and right for all his people." The Queen of Sheba tells Solomon, "Blessed be the LORD your God, who has . . . made you king to do justice and right" (1 Kgs 10:9). The expression is used in the book of Isaiah more often than in any other book, and on a number of occasions it refers to the expectation of an ideal king of the near or remote future; the quality is not to be found in the present corrupt times (Isa 1:21; 5:7). The prophecy "To us a child is born, to us a son is given" includes the words "There shall be endless peace for the throne of David and his kingdom. He will establish and uphold it in justice and right from this time forth and for evermore. The zeal of the Lord of hosts will achieve this" (Isa 9:7 [6 in the Hebrew]). If, as in the texts from Amos and Isaiah 5 that I quoted earlier, there is no reference to the ruler, we can nevertheless assume that it is the ruler who would normally be seen to have the responsibility for supplying what in these cases is found to be lacking, as the societies in view were monarchical—the king is referred to later in Amos (7:9–11), and very often in Isaiah.

---

13. Miranda, *Marx and the Bible*, 93 and 107, nn. 35–38; Weinfeld, *Social Justice*, 25–44.

14. Here *tsedeq* rather than *tsedaqa*, but a difference in meaning is unlikely.

15. [Those who know the text will realize that the noun here in the Hebrew text is plural, "judgments," but in the Greek it is singular. Very likely the Greek translators were assimilating it to the well-known phrase, but in any case the allusion is clear.]

"Justice and Right" as the Protection of the Poor

But what is the content of "justice and right"? Jeremiah makes this clear in his incisive criticism of king Jehoiakim's use of forced labor on his private projects. He asserts that his father Josiah in contrast "did justice and right . . . he judged the cause of the humble and needy" (Jer 22:15–16).

Amos and Psalm 72 express the same idea with great clarity. Amos complains that certain Israelites—there can be hardly any doubt that the ruling elite are intended—"have turned justice into poison, and the fruit of right into wormwood" (Amos 6:12). What he means by this can be seen from his accusations of specific wrongdoings. "They sell the innocent for silver, and the needy for a pair of sandals . . . they lie down on garments taken in distraint" (Amos 2:6, 8); "you cows of Bashan on the hill of Samaria, who exploit the poor and oppress the needy" (4:1); "you tax[16] the poor, and raise a grain levy on them" (5:11); "they oppress the innocent and take bribes, and turn aside the needy in the gate" (5:12); even the fraudulent selling of grain in 8:5–6, which might be expected to affect everyone, is said to be aimed at "buying poor people for money, and the needy for a pair of sandals," an echo of 2:6. What is meant by turning justice to poison, and right to wormwood, is the oppression of the poor, economically, legally, and through the tax system. The issues are debt, slavery, and violence, issues intimately connected with each other.[17]

In Psalm 72,[18] the king who is prayed for is to "judge" or "rule your people with righteousness, and your poor [or humble] with justice" (v. 2). The emphasis on the poor is continued in v. 4: "May he give judgment for [or "deliver"] the poor of the people, rescue the children of the needy, and crush the exploiter." Then after a series of rather far-fetched petitions for the long life and far-extended rule of the king, the prayer returns to the theme of the protection of the poor.

> For he rescues the destitute who cries out, and the poor [or humble], and the one who has no helper,
> he has compassion on the poor and the needy, and saves the lives of the needy.
> From oppression and violence he redeems their lives, and precious is their blood in his sight. (Ps 72:12–14).

---

16. [See Paul, *Amos*, 172–73.]
17. See Graeber, *Debt*.
18. See chapter 3, [and Houston, *Contending*, 139–50.]

The text asserts that the king is entitled to world-wide rule by virtue of his care for and protection of the poor,[19] which is also God's concern, as several psalms assert (Pss 12:5; 18:27; 35:10; 76:9), and thus clarifies what is meant by the divine justice and righteousness with which he is endowed. It evokes a picture of oppressive and even violent class relationships, which it is the king's duty to suppress, rescuing the poor from oppression by "crushing" those responsible. The kind of practices that are in view here can be deduced from Amos and other texts: they center on the abuse of patronage, the abuse of taxes, the subversion of the legal system, and especially the manipulation of credit: as in many other places and periods, landowners and creditors imposed oppressive rates of interest and foreclosed on security to bring poor people with unpayable debts into a dependent relationship with them, as slaves or possibly as sharecroppers.[20] It has been objected that no one would bother to enrich themselves by exploiting the poor, who have no wealth to seize.[21] But even the destitute have labor to make use of, and the relatively poor do have some property and are numerous by comparison with the wealthy, and have in fact been the victims of such behavior throughout history.

This psalm, which was undoubtedly produced in the service of the dynasty, is ideological in the sense that it presents the action the king takes on behalf of the poor, which is likely to have been rather infrequent, as motivated by his care for them rather than by his own interest in suppressing rival centers of power by "crushing the oppressor." It also conceals the contribution of the monarchical system to the impoverishment of the poor. But because every ideology strives to be recognized as universal and incontestable truth, it must incorporate generally current ethical views and worldviews.[22] In this case, it builds on a tradition of venerable antiquity in the ancient Near East.

The King as the Promoter of Justice

The king's self-presentation as promoter of justice and protector of the poor can be traced back to the mid-third millennium BCE in Mesopotamia, or the better part of two thousand years before the composition of this psalm. There is extensive evidence showing that in many ancient states the claim of the monarch to repress exploitation, cancel debts, and in general rebalance inequalities was not merely propaganda—though it was that—but was implemented,

---

19. Chapter 3, 41–43.
20. Graeber, *Debt*, 73–88.
21. Guillaume, *Land, Credit and Crisis*.
22. Houston, *Contending*, 13–14; chapter 3 below, 36–37.

however inadequately.[23] Weinfeld documents in detail the array of royal decrees issued by many of the Mesopotamian monarchs, typically announcing the establishment of "justice" (*misharum*) and/or "freedom" (*andurarum*).[24] Evidence of these decrees comes especially from the Old Babylonian dynasty (c. 1800–1550 BCE), but according to Weinfeld it extends from the middle of the third to the end of the first millennium BCE. The content of the decrees includes *inter alia* the reunion of families, presumably after family members had been taken into debt bondage[25] ("To the mother he restored her children, and to the children their mother"; cf. Lev 25:10, "Everyone shall return to their holding and to their family"); liberation from forced labor, liberation from imprisonment for non-payment of debts and taxes, and even for crimes; protection of widows and orphans from exploitation; remission of arrears of taxes; remission of debts, signified by the breaking of the tablets on which the contracts were written, and with that the release of debtors from debt bondage.[26] It is likely, as Weinfeld suggests, that the remission of debts also involved the return of mortgaged land that had been foreclosed on.[27] That these decrees were actually implemented is shown by the fact that attempts were made in contracts to nullify their effect.[28]

While Weinfeld identifies the royal commitment to justice with these decrees of *misharum* and *andurarum*, Jackson argues that the king's judicial activity is equally important, either in person or through appointed judges.[29] Weinfeld understands "justice and righteousness" as modifying by decree the harsh effects of positive law applied by the judges, for example the requirement to repay debts in full or accept the forfeiture of persons or land pledged in security. Jackson in contrast and more plausibly argues that judges acted according to custom and generally accepted understandings of justice, possibly influenced by royal decrees, while the so-called law codes both in Mesopotamia and in the Bible embody ideals of justice previously implied in the royal exercise of "justice and right." Unlike the decrees, which were infrequent, often issued on a new king's accession, but on only a few subsequent occasions during his reign, the hearing of cases in the courts was a continuous activity.

23. Weinfeld, *Social Justice*; Jackson, "Justice and Righteousness"; Charpin, "Le 'bon pasteur.'"

24. Weinfeld, *Social Justice*, 75–96.

25. Weinfeld, *Social Justice*, 78–79.

26. Weinfeld, *Social Justice*, 90.

27. Weinfeld, *Social Justice*, 95.

28. Weinfeld, *Social Justice*, 78; Jackson, "Justice and Righteousness," 236, n. 69.

29. Jackson, "Justice and Righteousness," 244–47; cf. Charpin, "Le 'bon pasteur," 110–13.

This royal administrative activity presented itself, by the use of such Akkadian expressions as *kittum u misharum*, "truth and justice" (corresponding to the Hebrew *mishpat utsedaqa*), as establishing true justice, offering relief to poorer or less powerful members of the community, or to cities or other communities held to deserve privileges,[30] from the demands of creditors or of the tax-collector, reversing the flow of resources and power to the already rich and powerful, and in general giving "freedom" (*andurarum*) to the citizens. In reality, as Boer points out, debts were cancelled partially and selectively, and the effect was "to shift labor from one type of dependency to another"; not to free them, but to put them "back into their previous status."[31]

It may be asked what evidence there is that kings of Israel and Judah really stood in this tradition and actually instituted any such measures at all.[32] There is little direct evidence for it. Only one specific example of a liberative decree is given in the Hebrew Bible: the release of debt slaves in Jerusalem instituted by covenant by king Zedekiah during the Babylonian siege in 589–87 BCE (Jer 34:8–22). This was in unusual circumstances and was said to have been almost immediately reversed. Otherwise, Weinfeld can refer to the fact that David (tenth century; 2 Sam 8:15) and Josiah (c. 640–609 BCE; Jer 22:15–16) are said to have "done justice and right,"[33] but the reliability of the sources may be questioned. However, it may be argued that self-interest would have inclined kings to cut their rivals for wealth and influence down to size, and that the promulgation of edicts of "justice and righteousness" would at the same time have enabled them to gain favor with those burdened with debt or otherwise financially embarrassed.[34] Later, when Judah was under foreign rule, we find Nehemiah as governor doing just this, according to his own account in Nehemiah 5, attacking his aristocratic opponents for their rapacity in making loans at interest (presumably high interest) to the peasantry, and obliging them to return forfeited security, and thus surely gaining favor with the majority of the population.[35]

But the important thing for us is not whether the ideal of the just king was often or ever realized, or how inextricably it was associated at the time with the royal ideology and propaganda, but the existence and canonization in Scripture of the ideal itself. According to this, the definition of the

30. Weinfeld, *Social Justice*, 97–132.
31. Boer, *Sacred Economy*, 160, quoting the decree of Lipit-Ishtar.
32. Chapter 3, 47–53; Houston, *Contending*, 143–45.
33. Weinfeld, *Social Justice*, 45–48, 54–55.
34. Chapter 3, 52–53; Houston, *Contending*, 145–47.
35. Gottwald, "Expropriators."

just society turns out to be, not merely one where the rich do not oppress the poor, but one where exploitative practices are actively repressed. As I have indicated, the ideal functions as a challenge to state authorities both then and now, wherever the text is taken seriously, to take measures to ensure that this is so.

It must be recognized that there was no question of making any permanent difference to the distribution of power and resources in the community. There was no suggestion that a more equal society, one where there were no rich or poor, would be better. Charpin emphasizes that in Mesopotamia (and it is likely that the same applied in ancient Israel) justice was not connected with anything similar to our idea of "social progress," but was rather to be found in the past.

> For the ancient Mesopotamians, the ideal of justice is found, in contrast, at the point of origin: all injustice is basically thought of as a *disorder* . . . the royal measures of *misharum* are . . . measures to restore the former order that has been disturbed. The rules of the game were not changed, they simply proceeded to a new deal.[36]

The use of the expression "a new deal" recalls, whether intentionally or not, its use in the politics of the twentieth century: appropriately so, since the measures under that name taken by the Roosevelt administration in the USA were, like the *misharum* decrees of the kings of Babylon, intended to restore a degree of social justice and equilibrium without fundamentally altering the social order. But this weakness of the ideal, as we may see it, enhances its relevance to the question of the regulation of our admittedly unequal economy.

Transformations of the Tradition

However ineffective this tradition was in practice, its canonization in the Hebrew Bible as a moral ideal has had immense influence, leading to a particular concern for the poor within the Christian moral tradition, which in every period, including that of capitalism, has contributed to the demands made by the church of political leaders. In the biblical tradition, however, it undergoes certain transformations in the exilic and Second Temple period,

---

36. Charpin, "Le 'bon pasteur,'" 113. My translation; emphasis in the original. ("Pour les anciens Mésopotamiens, l'idéal de la justice se situe au contraire aux origines: toute injustice est fondamentalement conçue comme un *désordre* . . . les mesures royales de *misharum* sont . . . des mesures de restauration de l'ordre ancien perturbé. Les règles du jeu n'étaient pas changées, on procédait seulement à une nouvelle donne.")

as its implementation depends on the existence of a state authority.[37] In the course of the first millennium the Israelite people saw their independent states invaded and annexed by foreign powers, and they came under the rule of a succession of imperialisms: Assyrian, Babylonian, Persian, Macedonian, and Roman. In these conditions, how was this concern for the oppression of the poor to be expressed? To a large extent, those oppressing the poor were precisely the foreign rulers whose power could not be challenged, and in any case no institutions any longer existed to exercise "justice and right."

Many post-exilic texts, however, continue to use the expression in its original sense referring to the royal prerogative, either looking back to the monarchic period, as in Ezek 45:9 (Ezekiel, like other prophets, finds "justice and right" lacking where it should have been found), or looking forward to an eschatological expression of just kingship, as in Jer 23:5 and 33:15, and Isa 32:1 (perhaps also in Isa 9:7, depending on one's view of the book's editorial history). Others, as pre-exilic texts already did, use it of a general social ideal, which like royal justice can be seen as a gift of God: Isa 32:16; 33:5; 56:1; 58:2 (nations, like kings, can and must "do justice and right"); 59:8–9, 14; Ps 99:4.

But we also find the expression transferred to describe the justice required of the private individual in a position of power, in a way probably not found in earlier writing, as in Ezek 18:5–9: "When a man is just [the gendered language corresponds to the reality of the society] and does justice and right," followed by a list of things such a man does and does not do, including "he does not oppress anyone, returns the debtor's pledge and does not exploit, gives his bread to the hungry and clothes the naked, does not lend at interest . . ." (vv. 7–8a).[38] In other words, "justice and right" is here the behavior of those who do not engage in the kind of conduct that might have made them the targets of a king's campaign of justice. In context, the three generations of individuals symbolize successive generations of the nation, but there is no reason to suppose that the characterization of individual conduct is not intended realistically, despite its schematic nature. The expression also clearly characterizes individual conduct in some late psalms (Pss 36:7; 37:6; 106:3; 119:121), and in the wisdom literature: Prov 1:3; 2:9; 16:8; 21:3; Job 29:14. Weinfeld connects the individual usage with the absence of "kings and leaders" during the exile.[39] But the usage continues into much later times, when, if there were still no native kings, there were certainly leaders. The fact is, it is precisely leaders, at least in

---

37. [See below, chapters 10 and 12.]
38. Cf. Houston, *Contending*, 100–105.
39. Weinfeld, *Social Justice*, 221.

a general and local sense, to whom these words apply. The addressees of these texts belong to a relatively small class of power holders. Weinfeld and others use the word "democratization" of this usage;[40] but it implies, rather, a hierarchical conception of moral duty, in which there are some who "do (or do not do) justice and right" and others, the majority, who benefit from it, or suffer from its absence.

The expression occurs only once (Gen 18:19) in the Torah, the first five books of the Old Testament and the principal source of Jewish law, which was probably edited in the Persian period. The text appears to concern an individual, but as the individual is Abraham, and the text concerns his responsibility to teach his children and family "right and justice," it can be seen as expressing the entire nation's responsibility for justice. Some of the provisions of the Torah embody this collective responsibility, as we shall see, yet neither they nor any of the more frequent injunctions to individual responsibility[41] are introduced with this expression. I have suggested that the reason why the expression "justice and right" is mostly avoided in the editing of the Torah is because of its association with the defunct monarchy and hierarchical relationships in general.[42] The Torah presents its ideal Israel as a society of equals, free of hierarchies among adult males, despite the fact of inequality that it presupposes.

Community Solidarity in the Torah

There are a small number of laws that provide for collective action in favor of the poor or the solidarity of the community. They include the jubilee law in Lev 25:8-22, which prohibits the permanent alienation of agricultural land, and the law in Deut 15:1-3, which ordains the cancellation of debts every seven years. These texts have two key points in common.

Firstly, they image the national community as a family, by referring to fellow-Israelites, or rather to the male heads of family among them, as "brothers," thus implying an underlying equality despite existing class division.[43] The laws and the exhortations that follow them up refer to the fellow-Israelite about fifteen times as "your brother"[44] (Lev 25:25, 30, 35, 39, 46, 47, 48; Deut 15:2, 3, 7, 9, 11, etc.). The national community is seen in the guise of a family. The bond between its members is personal; the motive

---

40. Weinfeld, *Social Justice*, 216.
41. For a detailed survey, see Baker, *Tight Fists*, 223-304.
42. Chapter 10, 177-78.
43. Chapter 2, 25-28.
44. A usage obscured in inclusive-language translations such as the NRSV.

for compassionate action is expressed in Deut 15:7–11 in particular in emotional terms, with the use of what has been called "somatic" language, referring to parts of the body: "a wicked thought in your heart"; "lest your eye be evil"; "do not let your heart be grudging"; "open your hand."[45] This response cannot be forced, it arises from a heart that acknowledges its natural and covenantal bond with its neighbor. Secondly, there is no indication what authority is to be responsible for enforcing the laws; they are addressed to the people as a whole, who are exhorted to put the law into effect. This is also true of the law providing for the tithes of every third year to be stored as a food bank for propertyless and vulnerable residents, "the Levite . . . the resident foreigner, the orphan and the widow" (Deut 14:28–29). An effort was made to enforce these laws, except perhaps the jubilee; the year of release was recognized, but its provisions were evaded.

What we have here, in my judgment, are versions of older administrative decrees cancelling debts or reversing the alienation of property, which could in monarchic times have been enforced by the royal bureaucracy, but are now cut free from the essential enforcement mechanism. It would seem that the editors of the Torah, after the fall of the monarchy, wished to assert the essential equality and solidarity of full members of the community (meaning in those days male family heads), a tradition probably reaching back to the tribal village of the monarchic and earlier periods, and to recognize the responsibility to protect the poor as a community responsibility. But they were unable because of the loss of independence to make any provision for enforcement. Like the tradition of "justice and right," these texts constitute a challenge to any society where they are read and regarded as in any sense authoritative. The challenge they present is this: if ancient scribes could imagine institutions whereby the freedom and independence of small farmers and other poor people could be protected from the depredations of creditors, can we, in our more complex society and economy, achieve it in reality? Can we indeed reimagine our own contemporary societies as families of brothers and sisters? Many would suggest that the high levels of migration around the world make this too difficult. The question is whether, even without that, the cultural and imaginative resources to attain this shift in perception are any longer accessible.

Charity as Justice?

Subsequently, especially in the period after the composition of most Hebrew biblical literature, the expression "justice and right" falls out of use,

---

45. Hamilton, *Social Justice*, 31–34.

and *tsedaqa*, "right," on its own comes to mean "almsgiving," or what we would call "charity": giving one's bread to the hungry and clothing the naked, as in Ezekiel 18.[46] In those parts of the book of Sirach (Ecclesiasticus) that are preserved in the original Hebrew, *tsedaqa* occurs several times, and on each occasion it is translated in the Greek of the translation in which the whole book is known to us with the word *eleemosune*, "charity" or a "work of compassion" (Sir 3:14, 30; 7:10; 12:3; 16:14). The context shows in each place that this translation is appropriate. We can assume that in several places where *eleemosune* occurs without any preserved Hebrew counterpart, the Hebrew was *tsedaqa*. This includes, for example, Sir 29:8, "But be patient with a lowly person, and do not keep them waiting for your charity." The context here is significant: the next line says "Give a poor person help for the sake of the commandment." The reference to the commandment implies that charity is an obligation; it is not voluntary, even though precisely who is helped and how is a matter of choice.[47] It is thus an expression of justice. In the book of Tobit, which is only preserved in Greek, the word *eleemosune* occurs repeatedly, referring to Tobit's good works, and it is probable that it usually represents *tsedaqa*.[48]

Thus, there is no sharp distinction between charity and justice in biblical thought. To give alms is to exercise justice. But it is not all that justice requires. "Charity" does not in itself make any difference to the class structure of any society, and is even more limited in its impact than the Babylonian *misharum* edicts would have been. The compassionate rich remain rich and the compassionate poor remain poor, as Deut 15:11 admits: "the poor shall not cease out of the land." In ancient class societies, both the exercise of royal power and individual charity are attempts based on hierarchy to right the imbalances arising out of hierarchy, so that their effects were limited.

Yet for unequal access to power and wealth modern capitalist society, especially in the USA and the UK, cannot claim to be superior. The ideas generated by these ancient societies remain relevant, and I would suggest are capable of being concretely expressed in today's world. Indeed, it is not so long, as I suggested at the start of this paper, since ideas like them were taken for granted in most developed democratic countries, and it is doubtful whether more than a relatively small number of influential theorists and political and commercial actors, especially in the US and the UK, have ever truly abandoned them.

---

46. See chapter 12. For a study of the theological understanding of charity mostly in post-biblical works, see Anderson, *Charity*.

47. Chapter 9, 145. See also Houston, *Contending*, 132–34, and Gregory, *Signet Ring*.

48. See Anderson, *Charity*, 19 and passim.

Keys to Intervention

Certainly, the presence of these traditions in some of the earliest documents lying at the root of the Jewish and Christian traditions (the ancient horizon), may inspire readers within modern horizons to formulate criteria for state intervention in the economy on at least two fronts.

First, kings were supposed to intervene to defend the poor from exploitation. Whatever other aims state intervention may have, it cannot claim the authority of the biblical tradition unless it places the defense of the poor and other vulnerable groups—the disabled, the asylum seeker—at the top of the list. In modern conditions, that would include setting a minimum wage, and making it a living wage, controlling working people's rights and conditions, and taking action on an international level to ensure that employers can find no workers anywhere without similar protections; furthermore, on the side of consumption, enabling adequate housing to be available at reasonable cost even to the poorest.

Secondly, the community of Israel is understood as a family, bound together by the bonds of feeling. But all such bonds are dissolved in the advance of capitalism. *The Communist Manifesto* asserted in 1848: "The bourgeoisie . . . has left remaining no other bond between man and man than naked self-interest, than callous 'cash payment.'"[49] This was perhaps only half true when it was written. In the past thirty years it has become more and more true. One of the functions of the state, I would suggest, is to maintain and strengthen such bonds, and thus to prevent capitalism from wreaking the extreme of depersonalization, in part by social security systems that recognize and support the personality and dignity of all. But this is, as I have suggested above, a cultural even more than an economic issue.

The Present Situation

At the present time, so far from fulfilling these functions, states that have the resources to correct extreme inequality, but are unable to see the relationships between their citizens in any but the terms of the cash nexus, are engaged in dismantling protections and hollowing out welfare states, aided and abetted by international bodies such as the IMF and the EU. International trade treaties now regularly include a provision (so-called Investor-State Dispute Settlement) enabling companies to appeal in a closed hearing against any social or environmental protections in a country where they are

---

49. Marx and Engels, *Communist Manifesto*, 5–6.

investing that they perceive to put them at a disadvantage.[50] Such provisions present the risk of leveling down such protections to the lowest level offered by any party to the treaty.

In the UK today the screwing down of social security, the severe cuts in the funding of social services, especially through cuts to the support of local government, and the failure to control housing costs, are removing support for the personality and dignity of the poor, especially the disabled and learning-impaired,[51] and asylum seekers.[52] That anyone here should have to rely on food banks to survive is a sign that what, according to the Bible, is the test of a just society is no longer being applied. People resort to food banks very often because their welfare benefits have been suspended for (often trivial and unintentional) failures to fulfill conditions, which strongly suggests a lack of respect, or even contempt, for the dignity of the poor (even perhaps the only temporarily poor).[53]

In an article otherwise quite relaxed about disparities of wealth, the columnist Simon Jenkins says,

> There are many causes of Lombard Street being rich and Benefits Street poor. But the widening of the gap must in part be caused by the actions or inactions of the state. . . . There will always be rich and poor, but the actions of the state should not be what makes the rich obscenely rich and the poor obscenely poor.[54]

He is right. The modern state, immensely more powerful and with far more resources than ancient kingdoms, is in a good position to reverse the impoverishing and demeaning effects of modern capitalism, but is utterly failing to do so. The alternative, of course, is that the impoverished and demeaned do it for themselves. This was of course Marx's solution. But it may have also been what Occupy Wall Street was about. And it may indeed be that only such self-help measures can effect the cultural change that is demanded alongside the economic, restoring the sense of solidarity in society and enabling the poor to look the rich in the eye.

---

50. Jones, "TTIP deal."
51. Belgrave, "Work Capability Assessments."
52. Houston, *You Shall Love the Stranger*.
53. Butler, "Benefit Sanctions."
54. Jenkins, "Budget 2014."

Chapter 2

"You Shall Open Your Hand to Your Needy Brother"

Ideology and Moral Formation in Deut 15:1–18

(1995)

1. The Problem of Ideology

AMONG THOSE WHO HAVE reflected on the significance of the Bible for the struggle for justice for the poor in our world varied positions may be identified. What one might call the classical liberation theology approach treats the Bible as a witness to a God who is on the side of the poor.[1] Others, like Itumeleng Mosala,[2] see it as a document of social struggles with analogies in the modern world, and in large part the work of elites who benefited from the exploitation of the poor, and whose work can be seen as the ideological defense of their own position. Middle-class black theologians, Mosala contends, have been betrayed by their uncritical acceptance of the dominant theological ideology into proclaiming this document of conflicting interests as "the Word of God" and taking the words of oppressors for the voice of liberation.

Mosala is surely correct in this: that the Bible is a social product reflecting the views and interests of groups within society and their views of reality. And the mere fact that it is a written product perpetuated by institutional means suggests that these groups must have been in ruling and influential positions in society. If the voice of God does indeed address the Bible's reader—and I for one believe that it does—it is not from above or outside of the social struggle, but from within it, and it must be sought for and discerned among the conflicting human voices to be heard within the Bible's pages.

1. E.g., Miranda, *Marx and the Bible*.
2. Mosala, *Biblical Hermeneutics*.

However, if the Bible is the work of social elites, and if such elites profited by the exploitation of the poor, how comes it that there is such strong sympathy for the poor in the Bible, denunciations of oppression and legal measures in their favor—sufficient even for Mosala to detect sympathetic voices there, and for Miranda, who does not use the "Word of God" language, to see it as a book that is essentially on the side of the poor?

It is, of course, true that individuals may speak and act in ways that are contrary to their class or individual interests. This is particularly true of people who are not closely involved in the economic activities of their class, and can stand back from them to criticize them. Academics are more likely than bankers to criticize the way the economy is organized. In the Hebrew Bible, the prophetic collections may have originated fairly close to the governmental and temple elites; but to a large extent they functioned as their conscience. However, this does not explain why such material, originating perhaps in the conscience of an individual, should be preserved and disseminated by social groups whose interests were threatened by them, even when framed, as Mosala shows Micah is, by material more acceptable to them.[3]

There are a number of possible answers. One, which applies to much of the prophetic material, is that the denunciation of the oppressive practices of long-dead elites was perfectly safe for their descendants. "The word of the LORD which came to Micah of Moresheth in the days of Jotham, Ahaz, and Hezekiah" was no threat to the leaders of the Second Temple community and could indeed sustain their reputation if they were seen to be interested in disseminating it.

Another answer is given by Marvin Chaney.[4] It is that the elite was riven into factions, as usually happens throughout history in societies of a similar type. Three of the nineteen kings of Judah after Solomon died by assassination; and the throne of Israel was constantly in contention. It was always open to these factions to bolster their power by appealing to the peasants against the outrageous exploitation being practiced—by the other side! Nehemiah 5 is a vivid example of this. In a similar way, it would frequently have been to the advantage of the kings to get the better of their rivals by appearing before the public as the defenders of the poor, whatever exploitative activities they themselves may have been guilty of. This was particularly so as there was an immensely ancient tradition that one of the king's prime functions was as protector of the poor against the oppressor.

Although these answers are partly true, they do not go deep enough. The historian and political philosopher Michael Walzer discusses a related

---

3. Mosala, *Biblical Hermeneutics,* 101–53.
4. Chaney, "Debt Easement."

question: from where do social critics get the moral standards that they use to criticize their own society?[5] The answer is, they get them from the traditions of their own culture, largely disseminated by intellectuals in the service of its ruling elites. And if it seems strange that such people should provide the ammunition for their own critics, it is very easily explained. Walzer turns to Marxist writers, particularly to Gramsci with his theory of hegemony; that is, the informal leadership of one class over others. The class that claims to direct society must, in order to make good their claim, present themselves as guardians of the common interest. They have to set standards for themselves.

> ... they have to make a case for the ideas they are defending among men and women who have ideas of their own. "The fact of hegemony," Gramsci argues, "presupposes that one takes into account the interests and tendencies of the groups over which hegemony will be exercised, and it also presupposes a certain equilibrium, that is to say that the hegemonic groups will make some sacrifices of a corporate nature."[6]

In other words, any enduring ideological expression of the leadership of a class in society will always carry with it concessions to the subordinate classes, and in particular will contain moral ideas that are acceptable to them. It is essential to any ideology that it should claim to be universally and unquestionably true, a claim that cannot be made good if it contradicts fundamental moral ideas of the people. But this carries the consequence that the leadership of the dominant group may be criticized and contested in the light of its own ideology if it fails to act in accordance with such ideas.

In the case of the Bible and ancient Israel, these ideas are theological as well as moral. Psalm 72 is a simple example.[7] The aim of the psalm is to support the monarchy by presenting it as divinely legitimated, but in order to do so effectively it must present the king as the defender of the poor. Once such ideas are in the public domain they become a standard by which the ruler is to be judged, and a mirror in which the ugliness of the sheer pursuit of self-interest can be revealed to the perpetrator.

Thus I would accept the contention that the Bible's ideas and language of social theology and morality originate in social contexts and serve social ends; but I would contend that knowing this enables us to discriminate among them, not to reject them wholesale, and to recognize those whose

---

5. Walzer, *Interpretation*, 40–42. I am grateful to Raymond Plant for drawing my attention to this work.

6. Walzer, *Interpretation*, 41, quoting from Mouffe, "Hegemony and Ideology," 181.

7. [See chapter 3.]

roots are deeper than the needs of the moment and the hegemonic class. These cannot be falsified by the uses to which they are put. As readers we may take a critical attitude to such uses, but we may allow the ideas to criticize our society to the extent to which they are applicable.

I should like to apply this double approach to the texts concerned with social welfare and reform in the Torah. Within this corpus there can be no doubt that the Deuteronomic code is the most consistently concerned with the poor and with marginal groups in society, and as an expression of that concern chapter 15, vv. 1–18, takes a central place. The chapter has been the subject recently of a detailed study focused on its ideas of social justice,[8] but this does not address the questions I have been raising.

The task is both important and difficult. It is important because there are relatively few passages in the Hebrew Bible that express an ideal for society, as distinct from giving moral instruction or condemning injustice. It is difficult because it is probably impossible to discover the historical background of any part of the Torah with any assurance, and because there is no consensus even about the original function or purpose of the codes. I make no assumptions here about the historical background of Deuteronomy (though towards the end of the essay I make some suggestions).[9] It is less important, as well as more difficult, to establish this than to establish the social world of the text—the relations of classes (and other groups, e.g., genders) that it *assumes*, the conception of ideal relations that it inculcates—and this is primarily what I shall be aiming at.

As for the function of the law-codes, the wise confess themselves at a loss. It would seem sensible to read them as expressing at least moral teaching and instruction in the principles of justice. There would then be no difficulty in reading "casuistic laws" (impersonal law stating what is be done "when/if" so-and-so happens) and apodictic material (direct moral instruction) alongside each other—as they tend to stand—or in

8. Hamilton, *Social Justice*.

9. The view closely associating at least the kernel of the book with Josiah's reform measures described in 2 Kings 23 is still the most popular, and supports the reconstruction, from a politically critical and liberationist standpoint, of Nakanose (*Josiah's Passover*, 87–91, 104–11), who sees Josiah's measures as aimed at concentrating as many as possible of the rural surpluses in the hands of the Jerusalem elites. Nakanose, however, overlooks those elements of the constitutional sketch of Deut 12–18 that restrict royal power and the centralization of surpluses, and strangely interprets the *consumption* of the passover and the first- and second-year tithes by the producer and his household at the chosen place as a *redistribution* of these surpluses to the elites. Crüsemann ("'damit er dich segne,'" 86–92 [cf. now *The Torah*, 212–24]) sees the book as proposing to restrict the royal demands on the rural economy and to appeal to the free peasantry; this would make the book much less closely linked with the royal leadership. The analysis of chapter 15 that I go on to propose would fit better with Crüsemann's view.

understanding a mixture of decree, casuistic law, and moral appeal such as we have in Deuteronomy 15.

Whether the chapter was intended as practical reform, to express an ideal, or to encourage good conduct in society is far from clear in the first instance. I hope that my analysis will shed some light on it. But what is beyond dispute is the fact that material of this kind is governed by, and serves to express, an ideal of social justice.

A peaceful and well-ordered society is, of course, to the advantage of any ruling power, whether native, as in the time of Josiah, or foreign, as in the Persian period. And that means a society in which economic and social relationships are acceptable to most of its members. Hence the emphasis on the welfare of the poor in all the codes. What matters, however, in this regard, is not the objective degree of exploitation—that is, the quantity of surplus transferred from the producer to the lord or creditor—but the degree of *perceived* justice or injustice; and that depends on the moral traditions of the people, built up over centuries, in part by intellectuals who may be seen as in the service of the ruling class—prophets, priests, and psalmists—and in part coming from older tribal traditions of village communities.

The difference is illustrated by Kippenberg[10] with the example of the land-reform decree of the former Communist government of Afghanistan in 1978. It was not dissimilar from those laws freeing the peasant from the power of the landlord which were welcomed by French, Russian, and Chinese peasants with open arms, and which played a very important part in the early success of the respective revolutions in those countries. In Afghanistan, the decree raised great resentment, and played a significant part in the failure of the revolution there. Why? Because in the tribal society of Afghanistan, peasants do not perceive their landlords as exploiters but as protectors: their rent is reckoned to be fair exchange for a guarantee of protection from bandits, the tribe over the hill or, nowadays, rival guerrilla armies, and for help in bad times.[11]

Kippenberg comments that the Marxist definition of exploitation as an objective fact ignores what the patron contributes to the relationship between himself and his client, which is unquantifiable, but may make all the difference between the perception of a relationship as legitimate and as illegitimate. "Legitimacy is called into question if the conditions of exchange

---

10. Kippenberg, "Entlassung."

11. [In fact, the position was not so simple. The land reform came as part of a package including such offences against tradition as the abolition of bride price. The measures "took no account at all of the complexities of Afghan society and the interlocking economic and social relationships on which it depended" (Ewans, *Afghanistan*, 191).]

deteriorate for the dependents,"[12] and this occurs particularly when they are threatened with proletarianization (that is, with ceasing to be independent producers), or with enslavement. It is important to bear this in mind when we contemplate the apparently very limited degree of social justice offered by Deuteronomy 15: no equality, no abolition of slavery, and the poor commended to the voluntary charity of the well-to-do.

But, it may be asked, does the opinion of the poor matter in relation to Deuteronomy 15? Surely its audience, its implied or ideal reader, is the well-to-do: those who use slaves, can give loans, and have the money for hand-outs. Such a person is the "you" who is addressed throughout. This has frequently been observed, most recently by Hamilton.[13] However, it is not quite as simple as that. At various points on the campus of Sheffield University a notice has been placed that says: "For your safety this area is subject to closed-circuit television surveillance." Now, to whom is this notice addressed? It is couched in the second person, so there should be no difficulty: it is you and me, the respectable citizens who are in need of protection. "For your safety" a benevolent university administration has installed this protection. But this can hardly be the whole truth. It is no doubt useful for you and me to have this assurance: but it must be far more important for others to have the warning that it implies. Are not the true addressees of this text the enemies of society who lurk in the shadows to carry out their nefarious plans against us and who may be deterred by being warned that they are under observation?

Just as a warning to the evildoer is implied by that overt assurance to the potential victim, so inversely Deuteronomy 15, by its overt warnings and exhortations of the potential oppressor, may imply an assurance to the poor and the potential victim: "Don't worry, God is on your side and things are being ordered in your favor." Thus, as the text nevertheless leaves the well-to-do in earthly control, it fulfills the conditions of hegemonic ideology: it has something for everyone.

2. Background

Deuteronomy's attack on Judean social problems in this chapter is aimed at their roots: it is targeted at the problems of secured credit (vv. 1–11) and debt-slavery (vv. 12–18). As Kippenberg has shown, the formation of ancient class societies was achieved mainly through the use of surplus wealth to offer credit to peasants in difficulty on the security of their land and of

12. Kippenberg, "Entlassung," 75.
13. Hamilton, *Social Justice*, 137.

persons; that is, generally the security of their own children. The forfeiture of the pledges led to the steady drift of peasants into landlessness and their families into bondage. This process can be illustrated from Neh 5:1–5,[14] and is indirectly attested in the prophetic literature in such a text as Amos 2:6, which may suggest that creditors in Israel, like those in early Greece and Rome, were entitled to seize the debtor's own person if he or she defaulted. (Second Kings 4:1 may be compared.) We have here a process that, if left unchecked, would certainly lead to the breakdown of anything recognizable as legitimate, just relationships between poor and rich.

Against this process, Deuteronomy is able to appeal in the first place to local agrarian institutions. The "Year of Release" or sabbath year (Exod 23:10–11) is referred to in v. 1: the same verb, שמט/*shamat*, "let go," is used as in Exodus, though with a different object. Deuteronomy does not mention the fallow; but if it was observed in the way attested in the Second Temple period, the fallow would be a time of stringency when relief might be needed. Another, in all probability old, custom that is taken up is the golden handshake for the released bondservant (vv. 13–14). David Daube notes the allusion to it in Exod 3:21–22: "you shall not go out empty"—the Israelites are to trick the Egyptians into giving them what should be theirs by right.[15] And, in general, the reliance on the generosity of the better-off members of the community must have been characteristic of a healthily functioning local community in ancient Judah. The main difficulty with which this writer is faced is that the old customs depended on community solidarity, which the new situation had corroded.

Secondly, there are two older laws, one at the basis of each of the two sections. It is easily seen that vv. 12, 16–17, repeat Exod 21:2, 5–6, with modification. Verse 2, though not found elsewhere, is also an older law, as is shown by its formulation in the third person in distinction from the uniform second person around it.[16]

What does Deuteronomy do with these laws?

3. The Year of Release, Deut 15:1–11

Verse 2, the basic law taken up by the Deuteronomic author, requires a remission of debts. It assumes loans are normally for the relief of poverty, and without regular relief are likely to lead to distress. This verse has occasioned

---

14. cf. Kippenberg, *Religion*, 54–62.
15. Daube, *Exodus Pattern*, 55–61.
16. Seitz, *Redaktionsgeschichtliche Studien*, 167–68; followed by Mayes, *Deuteronomy*, 248.

much difficulty, and the text has been brought into question.[17] However, in my view the traditional translation "every creditor [lit. lord of a loan of his hand] shall remit what he has lent to his neighbor" is correct.

But what is meant by "remission"? Is it a one-year suspension of the creditor's right to repayment or the cancellation of the debt?[18] The arguments are rather finely balanced. The presumption of v. 9, that lenders might be put off by the approach of the year of release, may be thought "evidently more forcible" if a cancellation is meant.[19] However, the weight of this consideration depends on the usual term of loans of this kind. If, as seems likely, repayment would normally be expected within the year (i.e., by the next harvest), then even a year's suspension would be a serious deterrent to lending, though not as serious as a cancellation. A further argument for assuming a cancellation is that we have plenty of comparative material requiring the cancellation of debts, among them the *mīšarum* edicts of the kings of the

---

17. The most detailed recent discussion is in Chirichigno (*Debt-Slavery*, 263–75). It may make the text easier to insert משה את after בעל (see BHS and Merendino, *Deuteronomische Gesetz*, 108–9). But a more significant question is whether ב נשה (hiph.) here means "lend to" or "hold on pledge against," and whether (ידו) משה means "debt" or "pledge" (this is the only place where the noun appears). Does the sentence mean "every creditor must give up what he has lent his neighbor" (Driver, *Deuteronomy*, 175; RSV; Craigie, *Deuteronomy*, 234) or ". . . return the pledge he holds against his neighbor" (North, "*Yād*"; NEB; REB; Mayes, *Deuteronomy*, 248; Hamilton, *Social Justice*, 17; NRSV is ambiguous)? (For further interpretations, see Chirichigno, *Debt-Slavery*, 265–68.) This is partly tied up with the question whether cancellation or suspension is meant. To return the pledge would amount to cancelling the debt (probably: contra North); the issue is less clear if the sense is "remit the debt." The case was argued by North in relation to the widespread practice of handing over a pledge (e.g., a child of the debtor) at the time the loan was made. However, that is not a conclusive argument (and Chirichigno [ibid., 270] denies that Deuteronomy envisages the taking of persons or land on pledge). The phrase in v. 3, אשר יהיה לך את־אחיך, on the other hand, is difficult to reconcile with North's view: "that which is yours (which is) with your brother" must mean the loan, not a pledge (so Chirichigno [ibid., 271]), and North's view can only be supported by the forced interpretation "*from* your brother." The question of cancellation or suspension, therefore, seems to be left open so far as this factor is concerned.

18. Jewish tradition as far back as we can go has taken it in the sense of cancellation (Philo, *De Septenario* 8; *M. Sheb.* 10.1; cf. Driver, *Deuteronomy*, 179; Neh 10:32 uses the perhaps stronger verb נטש [from Exod 23:11], which points in the same direction), and critical opinion has shifted towards this view in the twentieth century (for the nineteenth see Driver, *Deuteronomy*, 179–80, who hesitantly marks the beginning of the switch); of recent commentators only Craigie (*Deuteronomy*, 236) maintains the older view [together now with McConville, *Deuteronomy*, 259, and Veijola, *5. Buch Mose*, 312–13]. For a detailed discussion see Chirichigno, *Debt-Slavery*, 272–75.

19. Driver, *Deuteronomy*, 179.

Old Babylonian dynasty,[20] and revolutionary measures in the Greek states,[21] but none ordaining a temporary suspension. Against this it has to be said that all the examples of debt-cancellation we know of are irregular events, and the idea of a regular, periodic cancellation is as unexampled as that of a moratorium. While a one-off measure, which would have taken creditors by surprise, could be a very effective measure of relief, perhaps retarding, if not reversing, progress towards a class-divided society, a periodic measure could be prepared for and neutralized in advance by the owners of capital. If observed in the spirit intended by Deuteronomy, such a measure would have a strong egalitarian effect; but how could that be achieved?

We must therefore choose between an interpretation that reads the law as a modest measure of relief consequent on the observance of the fallow year,[22] and one that takes it as a profoundly egalitarian measure verging on the utopian in its impracticality. The decisive argument is that of Jewish tradition, which is unanimous for cancellation from an early period; and this is also consonant with the tone of the Deuteronomic passage, which expounds the necessary conditions of a just society and not simply what can be practically achieved. In Judah around the turn of the eras, though the law was technically in force, it was deprived of effect by a legal device, the prozbul *(M. Sheb.* 10.3). The problem of creditors' unwillingness to let the law have full effect is dealt with in vv. 7–11.

The first modification of this law that comes to our attention is the use of the word אחיו/*ahiw* in v. 2: literally, "he shall not press his neighbor *and his brother.*"[23] It is clear that the second word explicates the first, and "your brother," as the term for the person for whom the subject of the text must have concern, is typical of the Deuteronomic code: from this point on, it is used repeatedly, especially in social justice contexts. In chapter 15 it appears six times: vv. 2, 3, 7, 9, 11, 12. It is normally in the second person, "*your* brother"; the use of the third person in v. 2 shows that the author is deliberately adding to an older formulation. "Neighbor" (רע/*rea*) seems to be the older term, used in the Decalogue and the Covenant Code, and only here do the two appear alongside each other in this sense.[24] Lothar Perlitt

---

20. F. R. Kraus, *Ein Edikt*, "Ein Edikt"; J. J. Finkelstein, "The Edict"; cf. Epsztein, *Social Justice*, 12–14; Hamilton, *Social Justice*, 48–53[; and esp. now Weinfeld, *Social Justice*, 25–56].

21. Solon's σεισαχθεία (Aristotle, Ἀθηναίων Πολιτεία 6.1), for example.

22. Craigie, *Deuteronomy*, 236.

23. The Samaritan text omits "and."

24. Hamilton, *Social Justice*, 37.

has devoted an article to the usage of "your brother" in Deuteronomy, and much of what I have to say about it is indebted to this.[25]

What does this usage imply? First, a summary of its occurrences in this chapter. It occurs once in v. 3, where it is contrasted with "a foreigner" (cf. 17:15; 23:21). In the passage vv. 7-11 it appears thrice, invariably referring to the poor community member towards whom generosity is required. In v. 12 we have "when your brother, a Hebrew or a Hebrew woman [this is the literal translation!], sells himself [or "is sold"] to you." Compare this with Exod 21:2: "When you buy a Hebrew slave." The awkwardness of the expression in Deuteronomy arises from the concern to bring in two special points: to designate the slave as a "brother" and to make it clear that the law extends to women.

Despite this, the first thing obviously implied is that the object of concern is, ideally, a man, even though the text in v. 12 emphasizes that the law applies equally to men and women, and even though widows are likely to have been prominent among the recipients of charitable loans. The patriarchal character of Israelite society is, as ever, reflected in the use of language.[26]

Next, does v. 3 imply that only the true-born Israelite is worthy of just treatment, as opposed to the foreigner? There is a contrast with the foreigner, but not a chauvinistic one: the contrast is with נכרי/*nokri*, "foreigner," not גר/*ger*, "resident alien," and it has often been thought that the exception is intended to exclude commercial loans from the operation of the law. The *ger* has the same claim on Israel's concern as the Israelite, as 24:14 shows. Perlitt argues that the three passages that contrast the "brother" with the foreigner belong to a later stratum, and that the usage does not have a background in the idea of the blood relationship of all the members of the people, which has no interest for Deuteronomy.[27] To this we shall return.

Perlitt lays stress above all on the word's emotional coloring, which emerges very strongly in its concentration in vv. 7-11. The coloring is so much stronger than that of "neighbor," and this makes it appropriate to use where a strong ethical appeal is to be made to help and protect the needy. "The (national) community of brothers arises out of the claim on the individual Israelite to see and treat his neighbor as a brother."[28] It is a more

25. Perlitt, "Ein einzig Volk."

26. Hamilton manages to obscure this by translating את consistently as "kin." This also loses the emotional coloring of "brother." The NRSV's "member of the community" is equally unsatisfactory in both respects, but has the advantage over "kin" of not misleading the reader over its referent.

27. Perlitt, "Ein einzig Volk," 42, 50-51.

28. Perlitt, "Ein einzig Volk," 37. Quotations from this essay are given in my own translations.

emotional and indeed a more religious way of saying "your neighbor," a way that appeals more deeply to the heart; a way of expressing "the common humanity of those who together live out of the liberating love of God."[29] The appeal to brotherhood is not the result of the natural relationship of all Israelites: the relation of all Israelites as brothers (and sisters) is the result of the law's appeal to treat each other as such.

But is Perlitt right in arguing that it is not an extension of the older cultural ideal of responsibility within the extended family or clan?[30] It is true that Deuteronomy hardly ever refers to this (the law of Levirate marriage might be an exception [25:5–10], and implicitly the reference to blood-vengeance in 19:6); and 13:6–11 (Heb. 7–12) makes it uncompromisingly plain that the Israelite has a higher loyalty even than that to his immediate family and his literal brothers. Perlitt may be exaggerating in saying that Deuteronomy does not know of any division of the people into families and lineages;[31] but it is an illuminating exaggeration. Whereas in the Holiness Code's "welfare" provisions in Leviticus 25, the particular responsibility of the lineage or clan is provided for in the institution of "redemption" (v. 25), this is, strikingly, not true of Deuteronomy 15, where responsibility is defined solely in terms of the "brother," meaning the fellow-citizen in general. It is certainly one of the major objects of the book to promote national loyalty above local and family feeling, and in a passage like chapter 13 this works in a decidedly totalitarian way.

But all of this does not disprove that Deuteronomy is intending to depict the relationship between members of the national community as if it were an extended family or clan; indeed, it rather tends to confirm it. The text uses language that recalls the requirements of clan redemption. It also recalls the pragmatic fact that inequalities arose within the lineage because of the way in which this institution worked, tending to concentrate wealth within the senior branches and render the junior ones dependent on them.[32] But it extends and deepens the import of the language of "brotherhood" in two ways: by extending its range to the nation as a whole, and by implicitly pleading that "brothers," whatever their degree of blood relationship, should genuinely act as brothers; that is, with generosity, not with hard-heartedness.

It cannot therefore be sufficient to define the stress of "your brother" in purely emotional and ethical terms. It does have emotional weight, and it is used to argue for an ethical stance, but it does that in part because it defines

---

29. Perlitt, "Ein einzig Volk," 42.
30. Perlitt, "Ein einzig Volk," 50–51.
31. Perlitt, "Ein einzig Volk," 51.
32. Kippenberg, *Religion*, 33–41; cf. Crüsemann, "'damit er dich segne,'" 93.

the nation in the image of the kin-group and redefines responsibility to kin as responsibility for fellow-nationals. Thus, the idea of brotherhood, ethically central to this chapter, can be seen as the expression in a new context of a very old idea of community in which it defines the responsibility of people to those who, in the typical tribal village inhabited by members of one or a few "clans,"³³ would be both neighbors and relatives. Its practical expression would in most situations be very similar, even in the new situation.

Verses 4–6 are a theological reflection that if Israel were truly obedient measures like this would not be required because there would be no poor.³⁴ Many scholars have attributed vv. 4–6 to a redactional layer on stylistic grounds.³⁵ There is a consensus that the "commandment" here referred to (v. 5) means the Deuteronomic code as a whole.³⁶ This consensus is ignored (not rebutted!) by Hamilton; this enables him to integrate this passage into the rhetoric of the chapter.³⁷ But the contradiction with v. 11, "the poor will never cease out of the land," has frequently been noted. There have been various attempts to overcome it. Thus Craigie interprets this passage as a possibility "contingent on the completeness of Israel's obedience," while v. 11 is "a more realistic appraisal."³⁸ For Hamilton, vv. 4–6 represent the consequence of obedience, like v. 10b, while v. 11a expresses the situation that makes the law necessary.

But it is Lohfink's view that is of particular interest for us.³⁹ According to him, the whole passage partakes of the "utopian" character often attributed to vv. 4–6. It sees poverty as a very temporary state arising quite naturally from, say, a bad harvest, which is instantly eliminated by the generosity of those who have not been affected to the same extent: so v. 11 means "people will always be falling into poverty," and v. 4 means "but there will be no *class* of poor people," provided that the command of generosity is heeded. It is an attractive view, but in the end I do not find it convincing. The consistent use throughout vv. 7–11 of the term אביון/*evyon*, "poor," usually as a noun, suggests a person with this constant characteristic, and its use elsewhere points in that direction also. To express the idea in Hebrew of someone temporarily falling into financial straits one would expect a verb, as we find in Lev

---

33. משפחות in Hebrew.
34. So Driver, *Deuteronomy*, 175–76.
35. E.g., Seitz, *Redaktionsgeschichtliche Studien*, 169; Mayes, *Deuteronomy*, 248.
36. E.g., REB, "these commandments"; NRSV, "this entire commandment"; Craigie, *Deuteronomy*, 234, "the whole of this code of law."
37. Hamilton, *Social Justice*, 15–16.
38. Craigie, *Deuteronomy*, 237.
39. Lohfink, "Poverty," 47.

25:35, "if your brother *falls into difficulty* and becomes dependent on you" (NRSV adapted).[40] Moreover, as we shall shortly see, v. 12 assumes that poor people are going to continue to have to go as far as selling their children into slavery to get out of difficulties.

Therefore, despite all these considerations, we must say that there is a contradiction, and it is more than formal: the utopianism of vv. 4–6 contrasts with the realism of vv. 7–11, and is undermined by it.

The realism of vv. 7–11 is seen in its highlighting in v. 9 of the potential ineffectiveness of the law. It would choke off credit in the year or two leading up to the year of release. The way the text deals with the problem is not to introduce a refinement in the law but to call for a generosity going beyond the demands of the law, and to appeal to concern and compassion. Give loans anyway, whether you expect them back or not! It is not your advantage you should be concerned with, but your brother's need.

There are several points to note here. First, the repeated use of "your brother," more concentrated in this passage than anywhere else in Deuteronomy. Secondly, Hamilton notes the repeated strategic use of "somatic" vocabulary—"hand" and "heart" and "eye": open your hand, let there not be a villainous thought in your heart, let your eye not be evil.[41] This concentration of terms for parts of the body, closest of all things to us, as our brother or sister is closest of all people, intensifies the emotional power of the rhetoric.

Thirdly, there is a religious appeal. It is of two kinds: the stick and the carrot, the threat and the promise. In v. 9 we have the threat of the poor man's appeal to God, as in the Covenant Code (Exod 22:22, 26–27). Verse 10 is more characteristic of Deuteronomy: the promise of blessing if the command of generosity is heeded; this refers to this specific commandment, not like vv. 4–6, which refers to all in general. There is no question here of a rule that can be enforced. This is an appeal straight to the heart. As Perlitt says of it, "it gets love moving."[42] The text presents this as the only way of counteracting the deterrent effect of the law, quite correctly if one grants the basic, and indeed quite realistic, premise in v. 11: there will always be poor in the land. However, one finds oneself asking, if the well-to-do could be counted on to respond to such an appeal, what need would there have been for the debt-remission law in the first place, and if not, what use would it have been?

---

40. וכי ימוך אחיך ומטה ידו עמך
41. Hamilton, *Social Justice*, 31–34.
42. Perlitt, "Ein einzig Volk," 33: ". . . *macht man der Liebe Beine.*"

In other words, the text, by its premise in v. 11, presumes the continued existence of inequalities and of the patron-client relationship.[43] There will be poor, and there will be others who will be in a position to help them. The fundamental relation of dependence is not abolished by the law or by the circumstances that it presumes. If we had temporarily to reckon with such a revolution through vv. 4–6, we are rapidly disabused. Yet it is precisely this part of the text, vv. 7–11, that most urgently insists on the transformation of relationships between the dependent and those on whom they depend. As Hamilton puts it, the text places dependents "at the center of society, not at the margins," indeed, with the power to call down the wrath of God upon the hardhearted and close-fisted. Above all, it makes them members of one family. No social revolution is assumed, but there is a call for a moral revolution to transform the relationships within society, and make perceived exploitation impossible.

A further point may be made. Deuteronomy may accept that the poor will not cease from the land, but it does not accept the continued existence of the rich as an exploiting class, and as Crüsemann argues, many of the social provisions would undermine the power of the capital-city elite.[44] The class appealed to appear to be well-to-do farmers. They could be seen as the "people of the land" of 2 Kings, or in a later period as the "citizens" of the "citizen-temple community" (*Bürgertempelgemeinde*) of Weinberg's thesis.[45] This could be a simple (too simple?) ideological deception: the ruling classes to whom the intellectual elite who composed the book are responsible appear in the guise of benevolent fellow-citizens. But, on Crüsemann's showing, it would seem more likely that the free peasantry are, in Gramscian terms, the class aiming at hegemony under the leadership of the Deuteronomists.[46]

These conclusions are confirmed when we turn to the second section, on the release of debt-slaves.

---

43. Although the relationship in Judean society may not have the same customary and legal character as the *clientela* at Rome, it seems reasonable, following Kippenberg (*Religion*, 22), to use the same terms for a relationship that is functionally analogous. (Kippenberg refers to Gellner and Waterbury, *Patrons and Clients*.)

44. Crüsemann, "'damit er dich segne,'" 86–92.

45. Weinberg, *Citizen-Temple Community*.

46. Nakanose (*Josiah's Passover*, 110–11) maintains that Josiah's reform offered advantages to the proletarianized poor while exploiting the free peasants. If so, it can hardly have had much to do with Deuteronomy, which plainly appeals to the voluntary support of the free peasants as a leading class.

4. Slave Release

The text here accepts that debtors are going to continue to sell family members into bondage to pay off debts.[47] In view of the use of the verb מכר/*makar*, "sell," this seems more likely to be the situation than the offering of persons on pledge (though it could also be creditors who are envisaged as selling forfeit debtors). If the text envisages the taking of persons as surety, this has already been covered in v. 2.[48] The old law (Exod 21:2–6) requiring the release of bondservants after six years' service is modified in three directions.[49]

First, it is to apply equally to women (vv. 12, 17b; against Exod 21:7–11).[50] This is achieved by simple and rather awkward additions to the older text. The addition of "or a Hebrew woman"[51] in v. 12 implies that women are members of the community in the same "brotherly" sense.

Secondly, all implications are dropped that the master can control the slave's personal life (e.g., by giving a bondsman a wife who remains the master's property [Exod 21:4]).

Thirdly, on release, the freed slave should receive a generous share of the master's own agricultural wealth (vv. 13–14).

This law also is brought home to the hearer by personal appeal to feeling for the "brother" (or sister!). Even at the expense of stylistic smoothness, "your brother" is added in v. 12. The "slave" is actually a brother! Where all are brothers, there can be no masters and slaves. The contract is not one of slavery, but of the sale of one's labor for a fixed term.

Verses 13–15 may have put an old custom into words, but it could be enforced only by the pressure of public opinion, and where that failed, by appeal to "brotherly" feeling. It is not an enforceable rule, but again relies on generosity that goes beyond the law. And like vv. 7–11, this responds to an inadequacy in the law. It was not sufficient to provide for a fixed term of service: for released bondservants would have no recourse but to return to

---

47. Chirichigno, *Debt-Slavery*, 221–23.
48. Cf. Kippenberg, "Entlassung," 80.
49. [Van Seters (*Law Book*) argues the reverse of the normal assumption that this passage is dependent on Exod 21. But it is clear that Deut 15:12 must be dependent on an older law, because of the use of the term עברי, which only occurs here in Deuteronomy, and because of the awkward opening, which points to the addition of material (Houston, *Contending*, 187, n. 80).]
50. Jackson ("Ideas of Law," 198) may be correct in maintaining that for literary reasons the case of a female sold for non-sexual services is passed over in Exod 21:2–11: but the fact remains that the text fails to make it clear that she is entitled to be released after six years like a male slave.
51. או העבריה

their families, which, with an extra mouth to feed, would be left in no better position than before. If they brought with them a substantial addition to their resources that might make all the difference.

Here the prime religious appeal is very pertinent: the master is reminded that his own current prosperity is due solely to the divine blessing (v. 14), and further to "remember that you were a slave in Egypt and YHWH your God redeemed you" (v. 15). This underlines that all are in the same boat: there can be no class divisions where everyone is a freed slave and all owe their liberty and prosperity to God. The point is essentially the same as with the language of "brotherhood." Also implied here may be an appeal to the imitation of God. The God whom the master serves is one who releases slaves! How can the servant of this God do less with his own servants?

Thus in this section, in an even more marked way than with the year of release, the institutional structure of dependency is retained, but the expectation is that it will be transformed by a new understanding of social relationships.

5. Conclusion

It is painfully easy to deconstruct this chapter. The social and moral assumptions pull in opposite directions. The "prozbul" is able to thwart the fundamental intention of the law of Deut 15:2 because nothing had been done between Deuteronomy's time and his to conform society in practical terms to Deuteronomy's moral rhetoric, and Deuteronomy itself did not require it. To rely on personal generosity and goodwill was, surely, to rely on precisely that quality in social life whose absence had caused the social grievances in the first place. Yet Deuteronomy's appeals are not simply appeals to individual generosity. When they are read in context we see that they are attempts to re-create a sense of community.

The appeal to brotherly generosity is bound up with the inadequacy of the law in the narrower sense to achieve a real change in social relationships. Was this just a failure in the specific measures offered? Does it not rather reflect a general problem in achieving and preserving social justice? The problem is this: that legal and institutional changes, even revolutionary ones, are not enough by themselves. They must be accompanied by the personal and communal commitment to their intention that Deuteronomy calls for. And that can only be achieved by moral education, by the influence of a recognized moral tradition.

In the search for social justice, no people can do without such a moral tradition—and that is part of the point Walzer is making in the book I referred to earlier. Whatever the inadequacies of Deuteronomy's institutional contribution, its renewal of the sense of community of Israelite tribal society in a national context is a profound contribution to the kind of moral tradition that any society aiming to be just requires; and it is there waiting to be picked up by anyone—social critic, reformer, revolutionary—bold enough to take it seriously, even against the social implications of the Deuteronomic context. The evidence is that it was picked up very quickly by the compilers of the Holiness Code, who use the "your brother" language five times in Leviticus 25.

And it is surely not irrelevant to modern society. The French revolution proclaimed as its goal "liberty, equality, and fraternity." The history of the last two hundred years has been largely one of the promotion by rival political forces of liberty and equality. Fraternity has been forgotten, yet one might argue that it is the glue without which the other two must inevitably fall apart and appear, as they do, to be rivals. Mark Chapman reminds me that fraternity was a significant ideal of the Christian Socialists of the nineteenth century in England. Others object that in an age when we are conscious of the frequent oppressiveness [especially to women] and dysfunction of the family, an image drawn from the family is not attractive. This may well be true for modern Western societies: members of the Colloquium in which this paper was read whose sphere of work lay largely in the Third World had no objection. In Western societies, words such as "solidarity" or "community" may well need to be substituted.

The point, however, remains. To achieve equality, or something approaching equality, must mean the restriction of my liberty; that is, I must be coerced, *unless* I recognize my poorer fellow-citizen as a brother or sister or fellow community member.[52] Conversely, as those of us in the UK, along with many others, have learned with brutal clarity over recent decades, the cry of liberty must result in increasing inequality, unless, once more, we deepen the sense of community which we have instead seen eroded. We need to learn that we belong together. We could do worse than learn it from Deuteronomy.

I would argue that in the long run a people's moral tradition must be supported by a religious tradition. What vitiated the socialist experiment in Russia and led to the horrors of the Gulag Archipelago was not only the

---

52. [In *Contending* (Houston, *Contending*, 189), I quote Tawney (*Equality*, 166): "Freedom . . . is not only compatible with conditions in which all men are fellow-servants, but would find in such conditions its most perfect expression. What it excludes is a society where only some are servants, while others are masters." Setting aside the gendered language characteristic of Tawney's time, this is an admirable expression of the ideal of "fraternity."]

distortion of morality but the contemptuous rejection of religion. At a minimum, we need to accept that the world is structured in such a way that justice is possible and will result in happiness for the society that truly lives by it. And that, of course, is Deuteronomy's ground-bass: "because of this YHWH your God will bless you in all your works and all you undertake." Beyond that, Deuteronomy maintains that the God who guarantees blessing is a just God who is concerned for the poor, and will hear their cry and deliver them as he delivered Israel from oppression. To act justly is to imitate YHWH.

Chapter 3

The King's Preferential Option for the Poor

Rhetoric, Ideology, and Ethics in Psalm 72

(1999)

THIS ARTICLE IS AN exercise towards the development of a book-length work, accessible, I hope, to a larger readership, in which my purpose is to examine the value and limitations of the Hebrew Bible as a resource for a Christian understanding of social justice.[1] Many of my dialogue partners in this work have made clear their social and political commitments, and it is incumbent on me to do the same. I regard myself as a participant in the struggle beginning in my country to repair the damage done by eighteen years of enriching the comfortable at the expense of the poor. This struggle demands more than glib generalizations about fairness and compassion. Any attempt to create a fairer society or a fairer world demands a clear conception of what we mean by "fair," what is required by social justice.

The social ethics of Christians have frequently been inspired, both theoretically and practically, by the texts on social ethics that can be found in abundance in the Hebrew Bible. Of course, the literary products of another and in many respects very different society will not supply us with programs or blueprints for our own. On the other hand, the attempt to boil them down to "moral principles" rarely results in more than banality. Ethical ideas in the Hebrew Bible are invariably the products of concrete situations, frequently ones of conflict, oppression, or struggle, and cannot be distilled from those situations without loss.

---

1. I am grateful to Northern College for granting me sabbatical leave for a semester, during which most of the work for this article was done. Versions of it have been read to the Graduate Seminar of Sheffield University's Department of Biblical Studies and to the Ehrhardt Seminar in the Department of Religions and Theology in the University of Manchester.

But it will no longer do to claim to see everywhere in the Bible the God who is on the side of the poor, as liberation theology has tended to do. This has been effectively criticized by Itumeleng Mosala.[2] Writing in the South African situation, he had seen how the Bible could be, and was, used to justify apartheid. And it is to his credit that he has discerned that this was not because white South Africans were uniquely unscrupulous in twisting the meaning of the Bible, but because the Bible itself in many ways does actually justify oppression, most relevantly in the story of the "Conquest." To Mosala, with his historical-materialist viewpoint, this is because the biblical documents are social products, "signifying practices" of particular social classes, mostly dominant ones, with their particular agenda and stake in the situation. Thus it is that concrete efforts to apply so-called "biblical principles" in society have not always had happy results.

It is my intention to respond to the challenge posed by the materialist interpretation of the Bible practised by Mosala, Gottwald,[3] and others. I am unable to treat texts on this subject as disembodied texts for whose meaning the reader is solely responsible, as much recent literary criticism has suggested. In these texts someone is trying to persuade me of something. It actually matters that I can identify what they are trying to persuade me of, and how, and, most importantly, why they want me to believe what they are saying. As Terry Eagleton suggests, a criticism that is open about its political agenda needs to see speaking and writing in essentially the same way as the classical science of rhetoric: not as mere textual objects, but "as forms of *activity* inseparable from the wider social relations between writers and readers, orators and audiences, and as largely unintelligible outside the social purposes and conditions in which they were embedded."[4]

Thus I begin by understanding the text as rhetoric, as discourse of persuasion, and observing how it is structured and pointed to achieve its persuasive ends. As all persuasion is based on power and tends to conceal what it does not want the audience to know, this inevitably leads to an understanding of the discourse as ideological, as expressing a partial view of the world supporting the power of a class or institution.

The next step is to recognize that the plausibility of any discourse—essential to its persuasive effect—depends on its inclusion of ideas, especially moral and theological ideas, which are common ground between speaker and audience, between dominant and oppressed classes. I have given some

---

2. Mosala, *Biblical Hermeneutics*.
3. E.g., Gottwald, "Social Class and Ideology in Isaiah 40–55."
4. Eagleton, *Literary Theory*, 206.

attention to this in an earlier essay.[5] It is not simply a question of the oppressed classes being induced to internalize the dominant ideology; as we shall see, the moral ideas in Psalm 72 have the potential to undermine the psalm's ideology. When the ideological superstructure does not fit the moral foundation, we need not accept the whole package, but can disentangle the foundation. Here, I am convinced, it does indeed reveal the God who is on the side of the poor.[6] Thus from this point on this essay falls into three parts: rhetoric, ideology, and ethics.

Rhetoric

Psalm 72 is clearly a text of great importance for any understanding of social justice in the Old Testament. Of all the recognized royal psalms it is the only one that makes social justice a significant theme. Just how important it is in the text we shall shortly see. David Jobling has contributed a substantial essay on the psalm as part of his study of "Deconstruction and the Political Analysis of Biblical Texts." His approach is not dissimilar to mine, and I shall be using some of his more interesting suggestions. The actual text I, like Jobling, shall interpret is Ps 72:1–17; vv. 18–19 are the doxology that concludes Book II of the Psalter, and v. 20 is its colophon.

As I have suggested, the rhetorical understanding of discourse views it as a transaction between a speaker and an audience. When discourse becomes text, it may of course acquire new audiences and provoke new reactions. But even in the original speech situation, the matter is not straightforward, for a discourse formally and explicitly addressed to one audience may be overheard by another, and indeed may be intended to be overheard, so that the implied audience is wider than the stated audience.[7]

Psalm 72 is an example of this. The audience is explicitly stated in the first word: it is God; and the rhetoric of the psalm may be effectively interpreted as a plea to God. But to leave it at that would be to miss the unmistakable message that it sends to human hearers, specifically to the subjects of the king on whose behalf the prayer is uttered. However, in the last analysis we

---

5. Above, chapter 2.

6. In his work on Micah, Mosala (*Biblical Hermeneutics*, 101–53) finds fragments of material that represent a viewpoint close to that of the oppressed classes. But his strategy is not the same as mine. He does not explain what function these fragments have in the rhetoric of the book as a whole, which is clearly created by the dominant class, or even why they are there at all. I, on the other hand, see nothing in Psalm 72 that does not originate from the dominant class, but will try to show that its own rhetoric is at odds with itself.

7. See above, p. 22.

cannot omit the king himself from those who are to hear and reflect on these words. I shall return to this point in the last part of the paper.

The speaker is anonymous, in fact invisible. There is no use of the first person anywhere in the text. The speaker is as faceless as the omniscient narrator of Hebrew narrative. It therefore becomes a delicate question to decide whom the speaker represents. For Gunkel,[8] the poet, though a *Hofdichter*, a court poet, identifies himself with the wretched poor of vv. 2, 4, 12–14, and this has some plausibility; however, both tradition and socio-cultural probability would suggest that this psalm, like others, represents how the dynasty itself wished to be understood.

Traditional exegesis makes no bones about this. The reference to Solomon in the title, combined with the implication in the colophon that it is among the "prayers of David," appears to suggest that in the view of the editors of the Psalter, the psalm should be understood as David's prayer for his son. Calvin follows this understanding, with the refinement that David passed on the gist to Solomon, who gave it poetic form.[9] There is in fact every probability that prayers for the king uttered in the royal temple had royal approval and expressed dynastic policy.[10]

One essential point in understanding the rhetoric of this text is far from unambiguous, that is, whether it is a prayer or a prophecy. All the older and more traditional versions translate the ubiquitous "imperfect" (prefix conjugation) verbs as futures: the LXX, the Vulgate, the KJV, the RV, and, more recently, in great part, the NIV and the JB. Most modern translations, however, as well as most modern commentators, make them largely wishes ("may he judge," etc.), with the important exception that the verbs in vv. 12–14, which stand in the shadow of the word כי/*ki* at the beginning of v. 12, must be understood as indicative. Whether this means "for" or "when," it does not make sense to follow it with verbs of wishing.[11]

---

8. *Psalmen*, 305.

9. Calvin, *Commentary on the Psalms*, 255.

10. Another possibility that I do not rule out, but do not explore here, is that the psalm belongs to the Second Temple and is a prayer for the Persian king; that might explain the lack of Davidic and Zion language. [Krusche, *Königtum*, 192–94, dates it in the mid Persian period at the earliest, on the grounds of literary connections and alleged Aramaisms, but as a purely messianic text, and yet regards it as a prayer. It is unclear to me what sense a prayer on behalf of a *future* king makes.]

11. I do not understand Schwantes' argument (*Das Recht der Armen*, 186) that, because of their connection with vv. 8–11, the verbs in 12–14 must be understood as jussives. [Zenger (in Hossfeld and Zenger, *Psalmen 51–100*, 304) takes כי as an emphatic particle, "Ja," and thus translates the verbs as subjunctives, "may he rescue," etc. But there is no parallel for using כי in this way before volitive verbs in Hebrew.]

Since the first verb is an imperative, and the address is to God, there is surely a presumption in favor of the latter understanding, that the psalm is a prayer. But under the influence, no doubt, of the conception of the psalm as a messianic prophecy, some verbs have been spelt as indicatives in the course of transmission; and it is unquestionably this prophetic conception that has accounted for the futures in traditional versions.[12]

Considered as text, then, the psalm needs to be understood both as a prayer for the reigning king and as a prophecy of a future king. The latter is unquestionably important for my subject, but this article is confined to the first aspect, apart from a few remarks at the end.[13]

How is the prayer structured? Some commentators complain of a lack of clarity in the structure, and repetitiousness[14]—a cue to look for structures that depend on repetition. Roughly speaking, the topics follow one another as follows:[15]

1–4	Just rule
5	Longevity
6–7	Fertility of the land
8–11	Universal rule
12–14	Just rule
15	Universal rule; prayer for the king
16	Fertility of the land
17	Longevity, prayer

---

12. Verbs spelt as indicatives, where there are distinct forms for indicative and jussive, include ידין (v. 2) and יושיע (v. 4), as well as in vv. 12–14. These are indeed outnumbered by jussive forms in vv. 8 (וירד), 15 (ויחי), 16 and 17 (יהי), and even in v. 13 (יחס). The last example gives the clue to understanding this variety. Originally the psalm would have been written without even the limited amount of plene spelling found in the MT; as so often happens, one example remains. An exception to this would be the verbs ending in ה, where the final vowel would have been indicated; its absence in the three cases mentioned shows that the jussive was intended. When *matres lectionis* were introduced for inner vowels, they were added in the two cases in vv. 2 and 4, as well as in cases where there is no distinction of mood.

13. [See now Houston, *Contending*, 153–60.]

14. E.g., Gunkel, *Psalmen*, 308; Kraus, *Psalms*, 76.

15. [There are varying proposals for the structure of the psalm. I mention Broyles, "Redeeming King," 35, because his proposal is relevant to the theme of this chapter: there are three strophes, vv. 1–3, 4–11, and 12–17, and the theme of the poor begins each of them.]

Verses 5–17 look to me like a palistrophic structure, with vv. 1–4 as a prologue sounding the main theme. But this theme is also that of the central panel of the palistrophe, though it is there treated somewhat differently. In two ways, therefore, the theme of the king's just rule emerges as structurally dominant.[16] [17]

H. H. Schmid has shown how ancient Near Eastern conceptions of the world, not least in the Hebrew Bible, are governed by the concept of justice as an inclusive term for world order, in the maintenance of which the king plays a key role.[18] This idea clearly governs the presentation of the prayer in vv. 1–4, especially in v. 3. However, central to this order in this psalm, and certainly in these verses, is justice for the poor, their deliverance from exploitation. Weinfeld[19] argues that the expression משפט וצדקה/*mishpat u tsedaqa*, "justice and right," is a hendiadys meaning roughly what we understand by social justice, more specifically measures put in hand by kings or high officials to remedy the effects of oppression. It is reasonable to consider the use of the two roots in vv. 1–2 here as variations on this well-known expression. The splitting of a phrase between the two halves of a bicolon in Hebrew poetry is common enough to cause no difficulty.[20] The development of the theme in v. 4 supports this: God's "justice and righteousness" are to be exhibited specifically in the king's action in defense of the poor against oppression. Prosperity for the people in general (v. 3) is included here as an aspect of the divine צדקה/*tsedaqa*, and is developed further in vv. 6–7, 16. But the central divine gift, from which the implied reader is

---

16. In v. 5, read ויאריך for ייראוך with LXX and most commentators: MT offers irrelevance. Weinfeld (*Social Justice*, 51–53) argues that the original reading, in line with a widespread ancient Near Eastern idea, was יראוהו עם שמש, "they will see him (he will appear to them) as the sun," and that this was deliberately altered by scribes into the present MT to avoid blasphemy. But there is no evidence for the alleged original, and the contention that prayer for the king himself does not appear before v. 17 is hardly correct.

17. Jobling ("Deconstruction and the Political Analysis of Biblical Texts," 101), seeing v. 7 as a climax, divides the psalm into two parts, vv. 1–7 and 8–17, and understands the king's justice as playing a different role in the two parts.

18. Schmid, *Gerechtigkeit*. [See below, chapter 10, 167–68.]

19. Weinfeld, *Social Justice*, 25–44. [See also now at length chapter 10 below.]

20. The use of the plural משפטיך, if that is the correct reading (LXX and Peshitta read the singular), might refer to God's "judgments" (cf. Exod 21:1), which would provide models for the king's exercise of social justice. If this is correct, it suggests that Weinfeld's almost exclusive understanding of "justice and righteousness" as established by decree should be enlarged to include the king's judicial function. See further on this below, 46. The use in v. 2 of the masculine צדק/*tsedeq* in place of צדקה/*tsedaqa* is unlikely to imply a major difference in sense, especially as this verse explicitly speaks of "judging"—that is, acting on the side of—the poor.

to understand that all else flows, is that of justice, the defense of the poor against their oppressors.

The prayer proceeds to a number of petitions that would appear to be of more personal interest to the king, though as we see from other royal psalms they are an essential part of the ideology: petitions for his everlasting and universal rule take up four verses continuously in vv. 8–11. Clearly persuasion is needed if God is to grant such blessings. I employ here an idea from classical rhetoric that seems sufficiently general to be applicable to a persuasive text from any culture.

Aristotle in his *Rhetoric* divides the "proofs," or persuasive elements, of rhetoric into three types: *logos* or rational argument; *pathos* or emotion; and *ethos*, which is the personal character of the speaker.[21] The last of these is irrelevant here, as the speaker is anonymous. Rational argument appears here primarily in the כי/*ki* of v. 12. There are two possible ways to understand this. Either it means "for," assigning a reason or motive (so most versions and commentators), or it means "when" or "if."[22] If it is the former, the assurance that the king intends to act to deliver the poor from oppression serves as motivation for allowing him to rule over all nations. The form of argument is what Aristotle calls an "enthymeme," an informal syllogism with the minor premise (2 below) suppressed. Set out in full, the syllogism would run:

1. The king will deliver the poor from oppression.

2. (Kings who deliver the poor from oppression should have universal rule.)

3. Therefore, the king should have universal rule.

The suppressed minor premise will be in due course essential to my argument.

Dahood sees vv. 12–14 as the long protasis of a conditional sentence; the apodosis is introduced with v. 15: "If he delivers the poor man when he cries . . . then let him live and be given the gold of Sheba." Clearly, because of the palistrophic structure, there is no essential difference in the rhetorical effect of these two constructions.

Pathos, or emotion, also plays a significant role in the rhetoric. I would identify it at two main points. In v. 2, the people which the king is to judge is called "your people," and in the parallel colon the poor are (more unusually) "your poor." God is thus reminded of his personal connection with the

---

21. Aristotle, *Rhetoric*, 16–17.
22. So Dahood, *Psalms 51–100*, 182.

king's subjects. The second person suffixes echo those in v. 1: his personal commitment to the people of Israel requires him to bestow the gift of righteousness on their king for their sake. Remarkably for a royal psalm, the king is not called "your king" or "your anointed."

The other main locus of emotive language is in vv. 12–14, which we have already seen to be also both structurally and logically the center of the argument. The comparatively restrained language of vv. 1–4 is here heightened in several ways. The poor man[23] is here "crying out," and he "has no one to help." The king not merely helps him, but does so through "taking pity on him"; the verb is defined by Milton Schwantes as "pity marked by distress, tears, and personal sympathy."[24] He saves, not simply "the poor," but "*the lives* of the poor," with which the phrase in the next verse "precious is their blood in his eyes" coheres: their very lives are in danger from their unfeeling oppressors; they suffer from חמס/*hamas*, the strongest of Hebrew words for oppression, with its connotations of violence and rapine.[25] The final verb in the section is יגאל/*yigʾal*, "he redeems." This verb גאל/*gaʾal*, though it is in a sense a synonym of הושיע/*hoshiaʿ*, "he saved," הציל/*hitsil*, "he rescued," and so on, has its distinct connotations. As גאל/*goʾel* the king takes the place of the family redeemer whom "he who has no helper" is without. The climax is the unique and deeply affecting "precious is their blood in his eyes."

This emotive heightening of the language underlines the seriousness of the king's concern; the hearers—God or the king's subjects—are thus persuaded to take it seriously and so to accept more easily the claim to dominion that the prayer embodies.

The main rhetorical device by which this plea or claim is urged is hyperbole. The prayer is for a rule unlimited in both time and space. As far as time is concerned, the words can hardly be taken literally of a single king; but, to quote Jobling:[26]

---

23. Phyllis Bird ("Poor Man or Poor Woman") points out that when "the poor" are mentioned in the Hebrew Bible, it is always the poor *man* who is in question. Social justice texts tend to treat separately the plight of impoverished full citizens, all of course adult males—these are "the poor"—and that of non-citizens such as widows and orphans and aliens, who may well be poor but are vulnerable for different reasons. It would be fair to say that for the writers of the Hebrew Bible these raise less disturbing issues than impoverished or landless male family heads. It agrees with this analysis that Psalm 72 does not mention widows and orphans. (I am grateful to Cheryl Exum for drawing this article to my attention.)

24. My translation. Schwantes, *Recht der Armen*, 187: חוס is "das betrübte, zu Tränen bewegte, persönlich mitleidende Erbarmen."

25. Pons, *L'oppression*, 30–38.

26. Jobling, "Deconstruction," 100.

whether through hyperbolic rhetoric about the present king, or more "realistically" in terms of royal succession or the king's lasting reputation (v. 17a), it is the same permanence of the system of monarchy which is evoked. Time is treated as seamless, as beginningless and endless; nothing preceded the system, or is to follow it.... Part of the point of the "nations" theme, perhaps, is to make a corresponding statement about space. The monarchical system has no "inside" or "outside"; "all nations" (vv. 11, 17) are within it.

Thus, the impression that is imposed upon the overhearer is that the monarchy is a universal system.

One can sum up the impression that the psalm leaves upon the unsuspicious listener in three broad statements:

1. Monarchy is a universal, divinely authorized system, which sustains the fertility, peace, and order of the land.
2. The king's chief concern is to act on behalf of the poor against their oppressors.
3. It is this concern for the poor that entitles him to reign.

It is worth noting that this third point, which will be our ultimate concern, is confirmed in other royal psalms.[27] Psalm 45:7 says to the king "you love righteousness and hate injustice, *therefore* God your God has anointed you with the oil of joy above your companions," that is, marked you out among your companions. Psalm 101 (cf. Ps 18:20–25) exemplifies the genre of the "negative confession," used by the king at the Babylonian *akitu* festival; possibly it was used at a similar ceremony of renewal of the king's office. The main emphasis is on the character of the people the king has around him ("in my house," vv. 2, 7). A large number of moral terms are used, and not all can be connected directly with conduct towards the poor; but the reference to משפט/*mishpat* in v. 1, which here must mean "justice," should be taken with the assertion in v. 8, "I shall destroy all the wicked (רשעי/*rish'e*) of the land." As José Miranda has observed, רשע/*rasha'*, usually translated "wicked," is regularly contrasted with צדיק/*tsaddiq*, "just," and therefore should be translated "unjust."[28]

---

27. Cf. Jobling, "Deconstruction," 108.
28. Miranda, *Marx and the Bible*, 96–97.

Ideology

The Marxist critic Fredric Jameson[29] offers a theory of literary criticism, which Jobling attempts to use in the essay to which I have referred. According to this theory, the contradictions in the class position from which a text emerges should manifest themselves in a contradiction within the text itself. Jobling finds such a contradiction in the different roles that, as he sees it, the king's justice plays in vv. 1–7 and in vv. 8–17. In vv. 1–7, he sees "a perpetual motion machine generated somehow from within; God gives the king his justice, the king brings the people peace and prosperity, and the people offer prayer to God that he will give the king his justice . . ." and so on. The king is "drawn into the sphere of divine righteousness."[30] But in vv. 8–17 "the theme of the king's justice . . . has been withdrawn from the perpetual motion machine, to become the machine's motor. From being part of a permanent, inevitable system, it has become a condition for the working of the rest of the system."[31] "The king's righteousness is his own achievement, on which his position depends," rather than being the gift of God.[32] This same contradiction is manifest in the uncertainty in Davidic covenant texts whether the covenant is unconditional or not: Jobling contrasts Ps 89:30–33 with Ps 132:12.[33]

I believe Jobling has mis-stated this contradiction and given it undue weight. He speaks of a cause-and-effect relationship between the king's justice and the functioning of the monarchic system; but my study of the rhetoric of the psalm has shown that the כי/*ki* in v. 12, taken as "for," does not introduce a cause, but a motivation: a reason for God to maintain the king in office. God's apparent absence from the second part of the psalm is only apparent: since he is being addressed, he continues to be part of the system projected. He is asked to grant the king worldwide dominion, on the grounds that his justice deserves it; it is not a natural consequence. The paradox that remains, that the king's justice can at the same time be a gift of God and worthy of reward, is a paradox inherent in ethical theism generally rather than specific to a political ideology. Both statements in their different ways make the same point: that the king's justice, his concern for the poor, is the one thing that matters.

The contradiction that concerns me far more is the moral contradiction between praying that the king may protect the poor from oppression and that he may receive tribute from the nations, for tribute is oppressive.

---

29. Jameson, *Political Unconscious*.
30. Jobling, "Deconstruction," 102, 108.
31. Jobling, "Deconstruction," 103.
32. Jobling, "Deconstruction," 108.
33. Jobling, "Deconstruction," 109.

It may be levied on kings, but the burden eventually falls upon those in the system who cannot shift it on to anyone else: the peasants. Second Kings 15:19–20 illustrates this very well: Pul's 1000 talents are raised by a fifty-shekel levy on the גברי־חיל/*gibbore-hayil*, literally "mighty men of worth," of the kingdom. Since, at 3000 shekels to the talent,[34] there must have been 60,000 of these, it is clear that NRSV's "the wealthy" is an unlikely translation; if the figures are anywhere near correct, we are speaking of all free landholders, however small.[35] Of course, the contradiction is not apparent to those who share the text's ideology; for in this, it is the poor of the people who are to be protected, and foreign nations are fair game. Yet this only raises the contradiction in another form. Is the monarchy really universal, that is, a universal benefit, or is it not? The truth of the matter is, of course, that it barely controls Judah, let alone Sheba and Seba and territories beyond the sea. What tribute there is has to be raised from the king's home territory, from the people to whom the text asserts that his presence is a guarantee of justice, peace, and prosperity. The concealment of this fact is the most obvious distortion of the truth that this text commits.

Are we therefore to say that it is all simply propaganda, lies, and deceit? That the monarchy was knee-deep in the exploitation of the people and was thoroughly identified with the class interests of the exploiters? That if they threw up the odd smokescreen, claiming that they were concerned for the poor, it is hardly something to be taken seriously?

We shall see that there is truth in this, but the truth as usual is rather more complicated. Ideology is never simply lies: it is a partial, and partisan, view of the truth, and it has to be plausible to its consumers. The consumers of ideology always extend beyond the class of its producers, unless society is held together by nothing but sheer force. And the plausibility of this ideology depends in large part on expectation. All our knowledge of the ancient Near East shows that kings were expected to do justice, to protect the poor and oppressed, and there is some substantial evidence to show that at least some of them tried to do so, consequently that the language of our text in this regard was likely to raise serious expectations.

Moshe Weinfeld has undertaken a very detailed study of the theme of social justice in Israel and the ancient Near East, primarily as an activity, or a claim to activity, of kings, and for documentation I need only refer to his book.[36] Certain points emerging from the survey should be underlined here. First, there is the antiquity and continuity of this theme and its wide

---

34. Exod 38:25–26; *ABD* 6: 905.
35. [See further below, chapter 6, 95–97.]
36. Weinfeld, *Social Justice*.

geographical spread. Although it can be traced back at least to Uru-inimgina (Uru-KA-gina) of Lagash in 2360 BCE, and the richest evidence for decrees of *mīšarum* is found in the Old Babylonian period,[37] it extends to the Neo-Assyrian period, and into the West, where the rebuke addressed to King Keret in the Ugaritic epic is expressed in terms very reminiscent of the Hebrew Bible.[38] Most importantly, evidence exists to show that the theme was not always mere propaganda, for frequently in Mesopotamia contracts are found showing that the king's decrees of liberation have to be taken into account as factors affecting the transaction.[39]

It should be added here that the king's activity in establishing social justice was not solely by means of decrees, which is the impression given by Weinfeld. The king's regular judicial activities, in which he responded to appeals and petitions, often, as in 2 Kgs 8:3–6, restoring property, or defending the rights of *personae miserae*, were not only at least as important as his liberative decrees, which were infrequent, but may have been the context in which the ideas of justice expressed in the decrees were developed. An inspection of the Mesopotamian law codes (so-called) will show that they contain and were very likely intended to exemplify principles of justice. Bernard Jackson, in a response to Weinfeld,[40] suggests that, contrary to Weinfeld's assumption that the justice of decree tempered a purely positive law administered by the courts, the courts themselves were expected to operate according to unwritten ideas of equity, and that it is difficult to draw a sharp line between the king's administrative and judicial functions.[41]

Can it be shown that expectations that the king would act in support of justice and specifically in support of the poor were common currency in Israel and Judah, and, more particularly, that their kings did take specific administrative action on behalf of the poor?

There is no question about the expectations. Jeremiah's attack on Jehoiakim (Jer 22:13–19), for example, is particularly specific and scathing. Jehoiakim has not only not defended the poor against oppression, he has done a lot of oppressing on his own account. The text defines the proper function of the king in very similar words to our psalm: "your father ate and drank and did justice and righteousness; he defended the cause of the poor and needy."

---

37. Weinfeld, *Social Justice, passim*. For texts, see F. R. Kraus, *Königliche Verfügungen*.
38. Gibson, *Canaanite Myths*, 101–2.
39. Weinfeld, *Social Justice*, 78, 94.
40. Jackson, "Justice and Righteousness."
41. [See below, chapter 10, 161–64, for greater detail.] I am grateful to Professor Jackson for giving me a copy of his article when it was in press, and also to Loveday Alexander who had earlier pointed out to me the importance of the king's judicial function.

Proverbs 31:1–9, from a different literary tradition, is equally forthright, and almost verbally identical, in defining the proper task of a king.

What about the reality? Can it be shown that Judean kings (let us confine ourselves to the dynasty on whose behalf this text was probably produced) did engage in specific judicial and administrative activity on behalf of the exploited in their kingdom? The Deuteronomistic History (Joshua to Kings) is clearly uninterested in the subject, and has preserved virtually no information on it.[42] We need not conclude, as Frick does, that this lack of interest reflects the dynasty's own ideology. The assumption that the History is dynastic propaganda is insecure, to say the least. The prophetic texts have relatively few explicit references to kings, and they are mostly sharply critical.

Weinfeld, however, is in no doubt about the matter, citing not only the Jeremianic text about Josiah, but first of all the statement in 2 Sam 8:15 that David "established justice and righteousness for all his people."[43] According to Weinfeld, this refers to acts similar to the *mīšarum* acts of the Old Babylonian kings, and occurs, he assures us, "in an official document whose authenticity is not to be doubted."[44] It is hard to see why not; but in any case, if so, we have the dynasty testifying on its own behalf as in the psalm.[45] Jeremiah's evidence is more independent, yet doubt must be aroused by the fact that the book emerges from the Deuteronomistic school, which was also responsible for the praise of Josiah in 2 Kings. Jeremiah was supported by the family of Shaphan, which was close to Josiah and probably out of favor under Jehoiakim, so that *parti pris* may be detected.

The only specific liberative decree of which we are informed from this dynasty is the liberation of Hebrew slaves under Zedekiah, narrated in Jer 34:8–11. This act of liberation, effected by covenant, is described as a דרור/ *deror*, the word that also describes the intention of the Jubilee proclamation in Leviticus 25, and the proclamation of the anointed figure in Isaiah 61, and is probably derived from the Akkadian *andurārum*.[46] Terms drawn from the law in Deut 15:12–18 and that in Lev 25:39–46 appear in the rendition of the decree in vv. 8–9, but Chavel has shown that these are likely to be scribal

---

42. Frick, "*Cui Bono?*"
43. Weinfeld, *Social Justice*, 45–56; cf. Weinfeld, *Deuteronomy*, 153–55.
44. Weinfeld, *Social Justice*, 46.
45. Weinfeld had earlier (*Deuteronomy*, 154, esp. n. 3) argued that all the Judean kings who are said in Kings to have done right in the eyes of Yahweh must also have issued such decrees. This is not repeated in *Social Justice*: has Weinfeld realized how precarious such an argument must be?
46. Lemche, "*andurārum* and *mīšarum*," 22. [But see now my argument against this in chapter 10, 161, n. 50.]

expansions.[47] It appears to be an isolated act rather than part of a wider ranging liberation, and its motives can only be guessed at.[48]

It can be argued that the parallels in vocabulary, theme, and intention between the liberative measures in the Torah (the debt release of Deuteronomy 15 and the Jubilee of Leviticus 25), Mesopotamian royal measures, and this act of Zedekiah's, suggest that the Torah measures have a background in occasional acts of the Davidic dynasty.[49] This is plausible, but the evidence is highly indirect. On the other hand, if we can place the dynasty within the socio-economic formation of monarchic Judah, as our argument in any case requires, we can derive an a priori argument that it was certainly to the advantage of the dynasty to act to reduce the power of rich exploiters who were not directly within its own control, whether or not it actually did so.

Gottwald has argued that monarchic Israel was an example of what he calls the "tributary mode of production," and this idea has been taken up by followers such as Chaney and Mosala; independently it has been pursued by liberation theologians such as François Houtart.[50] For those unfamiliar with Marxist terminology, the notion of "mode of production" should be briefly explained. This expression denotes the way in which classes in society are differently related to the means of production: for example, in the capitalist mode of production, the means of production are owned and controlled by the bourgeoisie, who pay wages to the proletariat to use them to engage in production. A mode of production is an abstraction; no actually existing society exhibits one mode in its purity. Thus in societies that might be called capitalist, independent farmers and tradesmen and state-owned enterprises exist alongside the dominant capitalist enterprises. It is also not a purely economic idea, although the "base" of society is seen as the economy, since it embraces the social and political relationships of classes.

---

47. Chavel, "'Let My People Go!'"

48. Chavel ("'Let My People Go!'" 71–73) reviews the various suggestions. The idea that the intention was to conscript the slaves into the defense forces has certain limited classical analogies [see Weinfeld, *Social Justice*, 152, n.1; Jackson, "Justice and Righteousness," 239, n. 79]. But, as Chavel shows, there are too many possibilities to be certain.

49. Weinfeld (*Social Justice*, 173) apparently believes they originated with Moses, but the above case has been argued by Lemche ("Manumission," 56–57) and by Kaufman ("Social Welfare Systems," 281). Lemche argues from the use of דרור that the practice was derived from the Assyrian overlords in the seventh century. [See also below, 174–75.]

50. Gottwald, "Social Class as an Analytic and Hermeneutical Category," 5–9 (24–28 in reprint); Chaney, "Systemic Study"; Mosala, *Biblical Hermeneutics*, 103–18; Houtart, *Religion* (not seen by me).

What Gottwald calls the tributary mode of production is more usually referred to in Marxist literature as the Asiatic mode of production, since Marx described it mainly with reference to large Asian states such as China and India. The basic features of the system, as summarized by Melotti,[51] are:

1. There is no fully developed private ownership of land. The crown lays claim to the entire territory, and there is no clear distinction between tax and rent.

2. The base of the system is a large number of self-sufficient village communities, who work the land in an autonomous fashion, but are compelled to hand over surpluses to state representatives in the form of taxes/rents in kind or cash, or in labor on state projects.

3. The central power's role is the commanding one. The main exploiting class, who live off the labor of the peasants, is the state bureaucracy. The main weakness of the system is the tendency for these officials to carve out independent spheres of power by means of corrupt practices.

The concept corresponds fairly closely to non-Marxist economic historians' notion of the "redistributive economy," in which goods are redistributed by the state from the producers to the state's supporters. In such an economy, private property and the market are only weakly developed.[52] In arguing that the socio-economic formation of monarchic Israel and Judah conformed broadly to this type, that is, that the primary burden on the peasants was state exactions and the exploiting class primarily state officials, Gottwald and his school place considerable weight on the descriptions of Solomon's administration in 1 Kings 4–5.[53] But these surely ought to be treated with reserve. They certainly date from a time long after Solomon's,[54] and they share one characteristic with Psalm 72, in that their object is to magnify the glory of Solomon. Their own ideological character is brought out by the irony that in magnifying Solomon's glory they only succeed in exaggerating the exploitative character of his rule.

---

51. Melotti, *Marx and the Third World*, 54.
52. Cf. Carney, *Economics of Antiquity*, 25.
53. E.g., Chaney, "Systemic Study."
54. The expression עבר הנהר in 1 Kgs 5:4 (EVV 4:24), which only makes sense from a viewpoint east of the Euphrates, clearly derives from the Aramaic name of the Levantine Persian satrapy עבר נהרא (Ezra 4:10, etc.; the identical Hebrew expression to that in 1 Kgs 5:4 appears in Ezra 8:36, Neh 2:17 etc.; it occurs elsewhere, e.g., Josh 24:2, with the sense "*east* of the River"). There is no reason to assume (with Gray, *Kings*, 137) that the verse is interpolated.

Nevertheless, there is no reason to doubt that monarchic rule was exploitative, and that state officials were in the forefront of those fleecing the peasants. Isaiah includes שׂרים/*sarim*, "officials," among those "grinding the faces of the poor" (Isa 3:14–15), and the culprits in Isa 10:1–3 who "make iniquitous decrees" in order to despoil widows and orphans are undoubtedly state officials. Micah accuses the "heads of Jacob and rulers of the house of Israel" of chopping the people up "like meat in a cauldron" (Mic 3:1–3), and of "building Zion with blood and Jerusalem with wrong" (v. 10). We have virtually no information about taxes, and the passages quoted may rather refer to illegal and corrupt exactions, or to officials exploiting their position to engage in moneylending and foreclosure. We have already seen Jeremiah accusing Jehoiakim of misusing the corvée for private building projects, so that corruption did not stop at the royal house itself.[55] Archaeology demonstrates the great extent of the crown lands in late eighth-century Judah.[56]

Nevertheless, I am unconvinced of the value of the concept of the tributary mode of production for illuminating the socio-economic formation of monarchic Judah. Jobling suspects that Israel was simply too small a territory to effectively impose such a system.[57] Rainer Kessler[58] has some sharp criticisms of the idea, noting first that Marx himself did not include "the Jews" under the heading of the Asiatic mode of production, but rather lists them along with Rome and the Greeks as examples of the "ancient" mode of production, in which the basis is the private ownership of land by the citizens, and its heritability.[59] Now Marx's opinion may not be thought relevant to historicity (though avowed historical materialists like Gottwald or Mosala ought to be aware of it, one would have thought); but, as Kessler points out, there are quite a number of cultural features in ancient Israel and Judah that are much more appropriate to this type of formation than to the Asiatic mode of production. There are also economic features, such as the widespread use of cash, for example for making loans to the impoverished (Exod 22:25 [Heb. 24]).[60]

Cultural features include the inheritance of land within families. The existence of a communal form of landholding in early Israel has been widely suspected,[61] but if it ever existed it has left very few traces in the Hebrew

---

55. Cf. Kessler, *Staat und Gesellschaft*.
56. Zwickel, "Wirtschaftliche Grundlagen."
57. Jobling, "Deconstruction," 121–22.
58. Kessler, "Frühkapitalismus," 421–22.
59. Marx, *Ökonomische Manuskripte*, 383; *Grundrisse*, 476.
60. [But this probably only became widespread in the Second Temple period.]
61. E.g., Henrey, "Land Tenure"; Dybdahl, *Israelite Village Land Tenure*; Osgood,

Bible; the references to land division by lot in Mic 2:5, Amos 7:17, and Ps 16:5-6 need not refer to a regular redivision, and still less to a comprehensive one.[62] The Deuteronomic evidence is particularly important here, for while Deuteronomy innovates in some respects, what it takes for granted is likely to be current custom. Deuteronomy 21:15-17 assumes that the firstborn son should inherit "a double portion." Whether this means double any other son's share,[63] or double everyone else's shares put together, that is, two-thirds of the estate whatever the number of brothers,[64] it is a differential that in time would lead to the concentration of wealth in the senior line of a family, and the impoverishment of the others. Further, the institution of the גאלה/ge'ulla, the redemption of property within the family,[65] was likely to have a similar effect, as Kippenberg has pointed out.[66] Based as it was on a conception of land as a family (hardly a communal) possession, its practical effect would be to concentrate property further within the wealthiest branch, and make the others dependent on it.

All this would be expected to lead to a position in which there were powerful local figures in each community, and of course this is precisely what we find: references to the "elders" of local communities are very frequent in Deuteronomy and common enough elsewhere. Hebrew narrative takes for granted the existence of powerful and wealthy local figures like Boaz or the Shunemite in the Elisha stories. Naturally these stories could have originated in the post-monarchic period, but it seems unlikely that the culture could have changed so radically. Further, the fathers of at least three of the Judean queen mothers cited in the archival material of Kings (2 Kgs 12:1; 22:1;

"Early Israelite Society," 282-85. Kippenberg, "Typik," 35-36, interprets the usual texts along with ones from classical literature to hypothesize the existence of such a form at an early stage over the whole Mediterranean area; by the eighth century (he suggests) the family lots had come to be regarded as permanently heritable. But societies so widely separated in origins and in space should not be bundled together in this way. Lemche (*Early Israel*, 196-98) usefully discusses the question in relation to the present-day *muša'* system in Arab villages.

62. Wright (*God's People in God's Land*, 66-70) sufficiently demonstrates the improbability of the idea, though his arguments do not necessarily have any bearing on the situation before the monarchy. Cf. Alt, "Micha 2.1-5."

63. Driver, *Deuteronomy*, 246.

64. Mayes, *Deuteronomy*, 304, referring to Zech 13:8.

65. Lev 25:24-25: note that this does not provide that the *go'el* should return the property to the original seller; cf. Jer 32:6-12, Ruth 4—in both these cases the impoverished family member sells directly to the *go'el*. Lemche (*Early Israel*, 198) is surely misled in suggesting that the גאלה supports the hypothesis of the existence of a *muša'*-like system during the monarchy: the latter redistributes land within the village; the former keeps it within the lineage.

66. Kippenberg, *Religion und Klassenbildung*, 34.

23:31; 24:18) seem to be provincial Judeans, suggesting that the dynasty felt the need of making alliances with local families. The narrative of 2 Kgs 21:24; 23:30 attributes the influence in the succession of Josiah and Jehoahaz to "the people of the land" (עַם הָאָרֶץ/'am ha'arets). It is possible that this refers to a group with a provincial power base;[67] and both kings, significantly, have provincial Judean mothers. We note that, along with the officials, Isa 3:15 accuses the "elders" of YHWH's people of exploitation of the poor; and the comprehensive indictment for oppression of various estates of Judean society in Ezek 22:23–31 gives a special place to "the people of the land" (v. 29; cf. Jer 34:19). Oppression in Judean society was not a monopoly of the official class. This is the conclusion of the very detailed examination by Kessler in his book on state and society in Judah.[68]

All this points not to a society of weak egalitarian peasant communes under the lordship of a powerful state, but to a relatively powerful state forced to share power with the wealthy members of unequal and socially divided village communities. All who have addressed this question refer to the growth of latifundia denounced in Isa 5:8 and Mic 2:1–5.[69] While it is quite likely that many of these were created by officials on the make, rather than by local elders, their very existence represents the growth of a power that could eventually threaten the power of the monarchy. This perhaps throws a new light on the origin of those "anti-monarchical" passages such as 1 Sam 8:10–18, which Crüsemann[70] took to represent feeling in the early years of the monarchy. If one asks Crüsemann's question about the interests represented by such feeling, one finds an equally satisfactory *Sitz im Leben* in the last years of the monarchy. Of course the monarchy was exploitative: that is the supreme fact that the psalm distorts. But those who most keenly resented this exploitation were in all probability not the poor, whose immediate exploiters were much closer to home, but the well-to-do who possessed the wherewithal of which the dynasty could avail itself.

It now becomes clear how much it was in the interests of the monarchy itself to repress the exploitation of the poor by wealthy local elites;

---

67. Cf. Oded, "Judah and the Exile," 456–58. Seitz, *Theology in Conflict*, 42–71, re-examines the question and notes that the "people of the land" operate in Jerusalem in all the references to them in Kings: his conclusion is that they are elements of the rural population forced to migrate to the capital by invasion or for other reasons. In that case, I suppose, their influence may not have been aristocratic, as is most often assumed, but more like that of the *sansculottes* in the French Revolution.

68. Kessler, *Staat und Gesellschaft*, 118; cf. also Fleischer, *Menschenverkäufer*, 287–97.

69. See also Premnath, "Latifundialization." [But see chapter 7 below (116–18), where I question the reality of latifundia in the proper sense.]

70. Crüsemann, *Widerstand*, esp. 122–27.

for in doing so they were cutting down to size dangerous threats to their own power.[71] This is not a contradiction to the policy I alluded to above of making alliances with the local elites. One policy or the other could be followed at a particular time according to convenience. We should also note the prevalence of faction in Judean politics at the center, exemplified by the fact that three kings of Judah were assassinated in court intrigues. Chaney concludes that Judean kings would have wished to gain support in such conflicts by easing conditions for the peasantry.[72] It would clearly have been as much in the interests of the dynasty to gain support from the masses as to suppress rival centers of power.

Thus our analysis gives a certain a priori plausibility to the hypothesis that social measures in the Torah like the debt-release and the Jubilee could have originated in occasional royal decrees. It does seem likely that the Judean monarchy sometimes acted in the ways suggested by Ps 72:1–4, 12–14. We have no way of knowing how consistent a policy it was. What is absent from the text is any recognition that it was the king's interest, and not solely his concern, that motivated his attempts to defend the poor.

I have thus identified two main points at which the text mystifies the true relationships between the king and his subjects. Its pathos draws attention away from the interest of the king in controlling rival centers of power. And the king's own exploitative activities are displaced on to foreign nations, so that he appears exclusively beneficent to his own people.

Jobling suggests that the kings were operating with a borrowed ideology more appropriate to a genuine Asiatic mode of production like Egypt's or in Mesopotamia.[73] Even if so, a text like this must certainly have served a purpose in inflating the king's dignity among his entourage and the powerful men of the kingdom. It is a truly ideological text that harmonizes the king's interests with those of his poor subjects. However, it does not give that utopian picture of a society without class division that Jameson suggests an ideological text will tend to do.[74] Rather, in suppressing the interests of the king and his court it gives the impression that *shalom* arises from the alliance of the king with the poor against the exploiting class.

---

71. Jobling ("Deconstruction," 121) points to the importance of such action by the central power in true "Asiatic" polities. Compare Scouflaire's interpretation ("Le pouvoir en Mésopotamie") of a number of royal measures in the Old Babylonian period as moves against the merchants (*tamkaru*) as a rival center of power.

72. Chaney, "Debt Easement."

73. Jobling. "Deconstruction," 116.

74. Jameson, *Political Unconscious*, 286–91.

Ethics

While the psalm may have succeeded in harmonizing the interests of the poor with those of the king, it is able to do this only by making an unmistakable, if unspoken, moral point in the logic and pathos of its rhetoric: that the legitimacy of the king's claim to rule is dependent on his justice and his compassion for the poor. This is not incompatible with the doctrine of the Royal Psalms more generally that the king's legitimacy derives from his divine appointment. For to rule by divine appointment is to rule in order to implement the divine will, which is justice; and the first verse of the psalm implies that such justice is unattainable otherwise than by God's gift. One may compare Calvin on v. 1;[75] or more recently Brueggemann: "The king is to do what Yahweh as king proposes to do . . . faithful kingship mediates Yahweh's sovereignty . . . in the . . . transformation of public power in the interest of communal well-being."[76] The implication of vv. 12–14 is, further, that the king's compassion is pleasing to God.

But though this text's doctrine of legitimacy is not incompatible with the more general one, it has the potential to undermine it. In a text like Psalm 89 the Davidic covenant is eternal and unconditional (Ps 89:18–38 [17–37]). If the king fails to observe YHWH's commandments, he will be punished, but his throne will not be removed. The absolute authority of the king is unalterable, because it depends on a divine decree, which is by definition unchallengeable. Psalm 72 enables us to penetrate into the inner motivation of this divine decree, to understand its purpose and the circumstances in which it may truly be regarded as implemented. A king who is not just, who does not care for the poor, who does not allow the prayer for God's righteousness to be fulfilled in himself, is not in reality God's king. By replacing the formal requirement of divine election with the material requirement of justice, this text effectively demolishes the doctrine of the divine right of kings.[77]

It thus becomes possible to envisage the king himself as an appropriate audience for the text. A text intended to validate his rule becomes, because of its ethical foundation, a warning or challenge to it when treated as a *Fürstenspiegel*, "prince's mirror." It is possible to suppose that the policy and behavior of certain kings could actually have been influenced by such a text, and that the policy of defense of the poor against oppression, which was in any case in their own interests, may have been strengthened by genuine

---

75. Calvin, *Psalms*, 256.

76. Brueggemann, *Theology of the Old Testament*, 612.

77. Jobling ("Deconstruction," 108–09) sees that this text (and, e.g., Pss 101; 18:20–24; 132:12) threatens the assurance of the Davidic covenant, but does not quite draw my conclusion.

conviction. And be it noted, this comes about when an ideological text is compelled to bow to public opinion or religious tradition, to include as justification for the power of the ruler a traditional conception of how rulers ought to use their power.

It is scarcely surprising that with such texts in front of them some of the pioneers of Christian political theology were able to assert that against an unjust (and therefore Godless) sovereign rebellion is legitimate.[78] They were able to read this text not as ideological legitimation of the current governing power, but as a theological standard by which to test the legitimacy of any. So may we.

Another way of looking at it is to understand the psalm, like other works of the imagination, in line with Gadamer's hermeneutic, as creating a "world" into which the reader may enter, and whose horizon may then become fused with that of our own.[79] But not all works are susceptible to such *Horizontverschmelzung*, "merging of horizons." Clearly Psalm 72 is not like an escapist novel, blotting out the real world of greedy officials, extravagant courts, and compromised rulers but not having any relation to it. The world it creates does have a relation to the real world, and as a work of literature it enables us to see that world in a new light.

But is that light false or true? Does it lull us into saying, "Well, that's all right then, the king (or president or prime minister, or whoever may hold rule in our own society) is God's justice minister, and they will do the best they can for the poor," when he or she is doing nothing of the sort? Or does it rather startle us into saying, "That is what a state that truly embodied the rule of God would be like. Is the state I live under in any way like it, and if not, what am I prepared to do about it?" The imaginative world for one prepared to take it seriously creates possibilities that did not exist on earth before. We still read it as (partially) contrary to reality, but as challenging and thereby changing reality, rather than simply concealing or distorting it.

It is at this point that the prophetic or messianic reading of the text, which as we have seen is present already in the traditional Hebrew text, as well as being expressed by the versions and in traditional exegesis, becomes relevant. The ideology of those who looked for a messianic king and shaped the text to express their longing would need as careful examination as we have in this article given to the ideology of those who created the text. Does the desire simply reflect the frustration of an erstwhile ruling elite that rule had effectively passed to others, or does it rather reflect a longing for justice

---

78. [O'Donovan and O'Donovan, *Irenaeus to Grotius*, 281–82 (John of Salisbury), and esp. 695–701 (John Ponet).]

79. Gadamer, *Truth and Method*, 269–74. See above, chapter 1, 3.

itself in the face of the failure of all existing governments to provide it? In either case the emphasis of the text on justice for the poor makes it clear that the messianic community must be a community of justice. Here the study of this text would need to merge into the study of such unambiguously messianic texts as Isa 11:1–9.[80]

At all events, Psalm 72 still challenges rulers to heed its call: that authority is only valid when based on care for the poor; that the humblest have first claim on state resources of power and money; that unless they defend the oppressed and repress the oppressor, they have no claim to any of the privileges that go with authority. It is a challenge never likely to be out of date. Few if any societies beyond the simple tribal stage have succeeded in eliminating inequality and exercise of authority. To relegate social justice to "after the revolution" is in most cases to deny its possibility altogether.

Nevertheless, we must also recognize the limitations of the picture of justice projected by this text. In the first place, justice is here an act of the king who protects his subjects. He delivers them when they cry, but he remains in control. He decides when justice has been breached, and how it is to be restored. There is no hint, even elsewhere in the Hebrew Bible, of the idea that the poor might, to use a phrase from liberation theology, become subjects of their own history, defend themselves against exploitation and create a non-hierarchical society.

Secondly, the frequent use of the phrase "social reform" to describe Mesopotamian *mīšarum* decrees and the like, is rightly queried by D. O. Edzard,[81] and his query would also be relevant to the corresponding measures in the Torah and to anything implied by this text. These measures are limited to repairing the inroads made by the powerful upon the rights of the weak: cancelling debts, returning property, liberating debt-slaves. The language of the psalm gives no hint of anything beyond this. "Crushing" the oppressor may safely be listed in the repertoire of the text's hyperbole. The idea that justice might require a permanent change in relationships between classes or in the distribution of wealth is not apparent. Dominique Charpin's comment on Mesopotamia applies here: "The rules of the game were not changed; they simply proceeded to a new deal."[82] The expression "a new deal" is peculiarly appropriate, whether Charpin intended the allusion or not. For the conception behind Roosevelt's measures in the 1930s is the same as the *mīšarum* and the same as the ideal of justice

---

80. See *Contending*, 153–60.

81. Edzard, "'Soziale Reformen,'" 145.

82. "Les règles du jeu n'étaient pas changées, on procédait seulement à une nouvelle donne." Charpin, "Le 'bon pasteur,'" 113. My translation.

in Psalm 72: to give the poor a fresh start without changing the economic system or upsetting the social order.

Charpin points out that injustice in Mesopotamia was always conceived as disorder, and justice was a return to origins, not a progress toward a future goal. This text shares the same fundamental ideology. משפט/*mishpat*, "justice," and שלום/*shalom*, "peace," depend on the divine blessing of צדקה/*tsedaqa*, "righteousness," upon the present order, indeed the present ruler. Whether we find elsewhere in the Hebrew Bible the idea that true justice might involve an end to the present order and present rulers is a question that requires further investigation.

Chapter 4

What's Just about the Jubilee?

Ideological and Ethical Reflections on Leviticus 25

(2001)

Introduction

IT IS AN EXTRAORDINARY fact that a Hebrew word from a single chapter of the Hebrew Bible should have become accepted as the slogan, the iconic designation of a modern secular movement, Jubilee 2000.[1] The movement admittedly depends on much motivating and supportive energy from Christian sources, and in the choice and reception of its name we may perhaps see the influence of radical Christian theologians, whose imagination for many years has been seized by the Jubilee as the symbol *par excellence* of the social justice inculcated by the Old Testament. It is this general function rather any specific idea in Leviticus 25 that is important in the choice. After all, Leviticus 25 makes no explicit reference at all to the remission of debts, unlike Deuteronomy 15. Moreover, Deuteronomy 15 makes the uncomfortable admission (v. 11) that "the poor you shall have with you always"; whereas Tim Gorringe, for example,[2] can assume that the restoration of alienated property mandated by the Jubilee law "does away with poverty altogether," and he lays emphasis on "the denial of absolute ownership rights to any individual on the grounds that the land belonged to God."[3] The Jubilee sets clear limits to the operation of the market, and offers the appealing vision of a repeated return to a primitive equality, every fifty years sweeping away the distortions of human community introduced and multiplied over

---

1. [This was an international movement campaigning for the partial remission of the national debts of heavily indebted poor countries.]

2. Gorringe, *Capital*, 117.

3. Gorringe, *Capital*, 116.

time. It offers to the wretched of the earth a fresh start symbolized by the round figure of fifty years—or two thousand.

The welcome given to the Jubilee as an icon of justice has not gone unchallenged among Christian theologians. Such points as the following have frequently been made. The Jubilee presupposes that the economic omelet can be unscrambled every fifty years. The chapter assumes that people could be induced to act in ways contrary to their own economic interest. There is no evidence that the Jubilee was ever implemented, and indeed every reason to suppose that it could not be. For whatever benefits there might be in an occasional economic shake-up, if potential financiers knew in advance that it was coming, they would be encouraged to prepare for it by choking off credit in the last ten years or so of the cycle, so that the end for those in financial straits would be worse than the beginning. The passage bears all the hallmarks of the dreamy academic theorizing of a priestly caste cocooned by tithes and perks from the necessity of earning their living, and quite out of touch with the real world. What is the point of nailing such utopian colors to our mast? After all, economists in support of Jubilee 2000 have very practical and scarcely revolutionary, let alone utopian, ideas of how the global economy should be working.

My object in this chapter is to study the text of Leviticus 25 anew to tell whether and to what extent it deserves its status as an icon of justice. Its impracticality is a serious issue, but not the only one. Unless we accept that superficial and unexamined readings are adequate for this purpose, we cannot avoid the questions that have to be asked about any text that claims, or is claimed, to mediate justice: what kind of justice does it offer and to whom; whose interests are represented by the text; what understanding of the social world does it embody, and how close is that to anything we might recognize? The question "what's just about the Jubilee?" is not an ironic or rhetorical one, but a perfectly genuine inquiry. It is obvious that Leviticus 25 sets out a social ideal that can be understood as one of justice, though words in that semantic field are, interestingly enough, not used in the text. The question is, *what kind* of justice and *for whom?*

Genre

How we should go about answering the question depends very much on how we understand the genre of the text. In the past, the instructional material in the Pentateuch has generally been seen as law in a sense close to what we mean by that word in our culture: statutes laid down for implementation to the letter by constituted authorities and courts: positive law. The dismissal of the jubilee as utopian in part depends on this understanding: if law that the text apparently requires to be faithfully observed (v. 18) is not capable of being observed, it apparently has no point.

However, the closest analogues to this material in the ancient Near Eastern environment suggest rather different conclusions. Leviticus 25 is a composition consisting of two halves related in content but stylistically inconsistent. Verses 2–22 ("A") are mainly in the style of a decree: it mandates the community to take certain measures that have a universal effect. Verses 23–55 ("B"), on the other hand, is set out as a series of laws (so-called casuistic laws), detailing the way in which individuals should behave in particular situations.[4]

Both these types of material are paralleled in the ancient Near East. To take the latter type first, in Mesopotamia not only legal codes such as Hammurabi's but also working legal documents, case records, contracts, wills, etc., are preserved in great quantity, and it is recognized that rarely if ever do the working documents refer to the codes. It seems that the codes operate rather as a teaching resource than as statutes. And Jackson has argued that the same applies to the way in which the biblical codes work. Where instructions are given specifically to judges (e.g., Deut 16:18–19), they are not told to apply a written code.[5] In part the codes are intended as "self-executing" rules, not applied by a court but by the parties themselves;[6] in part they are didactic in intention, teaching standards of justice that may be applied by analogy.

Mesopotamian records also include administrative decrees, such as the decrees known as *mīšarum* decrees, decrees of equity. These typically provide for the remission of debts, the release of slaves, the return of security for debts, and the remission of taxes: in a word, everything provided for by the jubilee law.[7] Now, it is clear that unlike the codes, the decrees were intended to be observed *ad litteram*, and so far as the king could enforce it, they were: we hear of royal commissioners in different places who broke contract tablets and heard appeals against particular decisions. But there are two major differences between the jubilee law and the *mīšarum* decrees. The first is obvious and has frequently been observed.

---

4. [The situations are widely understood as being three successive stages of destitution for an indebted peasant proprietor, the last two at the same stage: Chirichigno, *Debt-Slavery*, 323–43; Milgrom, *Leviticus 21–27*, 2191–92; Lefebvre, *Jubilé*, 176, 246–83.]

5. Jackson, "Ideas of Law," 187–88.

6. [See now Jackson, *Wisdom-Laws*.]

7. Weinfeld, *Social Justice*, is largely devoted to detailed comparison between these decrees and the biblical laws of social justice.

The *mišarum* decrees were issued unexpectedly, at irregular intervals, to be applied immediately. No one could anticipate such a decree and discount it. By contrast, the jubilee is ordained to occur at regular intervals, which can be calculated. The owners of property and credit can allow for it in advance, and nullify its effect. It is in this feature especially that the "utopian" character of the law is seen to lie.

The second difference is equally obvious but not referred to nearly so often. It is that while a royal decree is impersonal and enforced by royal officers, the jubilee law is addressed to the nation in the second person and enforced solely by the covenantal justice of YHWH, as set out in the following chapter. But the effect of this is entirely retrospective: it is activated by the obedience or disobedience of Israel. Nothing either here or anywhere else in the Pentateuchal legislation makes it clear whose responsibility it might be to implement such laws on behalf of the nation. The plain implication of the second-person formulation is that implementation was everyone's responsibility. The text, it may be suggested, projects a narrative ideal of justice rather than mandating a specific administrative procedure.

We may say that the jubilee law is like a royal decree in its universal scope, but in effect it is rather different. It is a standard of justice, a call to do justice. Its object is not to administer but to persuade, and in its interpretation canons of rhetoric are more significant than those of law.

Table: The Rhetorical Structure of the Text

Section A: the decree	2b–22
1) the sabbath year	2b–7
2) the jubilee	8–22
sanctify the fiftieth year and proclaim liberation: everyone shall return	8–10
digression linking with sabbath year	11–12
resumption: everyone shall return	13
consequence of the jubilee for sale of land: do not take advantage	14
explication	15–16
resumption: do not take advantage	17a
theological motivation: obey my commands!	17b–19
appendix: a problem	20–22

Section B: casuistic laws	23–55	
1) redemption of property before the jubilee	23–34	
principle: no permanent sale: the land is mine		23–24
main law		25
subcase a		26–27
subcase b		28
exemption: walled cities		29–30
villages and Levites' cities not exempt		31–34
2) responsibility to impoverished fellow-citizens	35–38	
main statement		35–37
theological motivation		38
3) sale of a person to an Israelite: don't treat as a slave	39–46	
main statement		39–41
theological motivation		42
addendum: aliens can be chattel slaves		43–46
4) sale of a person to an alien, redemption required	47–55	
main statement		47–52
default: not to be treated as a slave; to be released at the jubilee		53–54
theological motivation		55

Rhetorical Structure

This is set out in the table. Each of the five subsections, that is section A and the four laws of section B, is supported by a theological motivation. The first law in section B, that concerning the redemption of land, uniquely has its motivation placed at the beginning rather than the end. The paragraph division in the NRSV, for example, might suggest vv. 23–24 are the motivating conclusion to the law of jubilee proper (section A). In fact, it is the statement of principle that is placed before the law on redemption of land. The effect is to create a bridge between the two main sections, since both jubilee and redemption are mechanisms that prevent the permanent sale of land, and also to highlight it in its position at a pivotal point of the text.

    Note how the points where there is the greatest likelihood of injustice creeping into the system are emphasized by warnings to "fear your God" (vv. 17, 36). Here it is non-family members who have the responsibility, whereas for redemption it is the nearest male relative who must act, and he may reasonably be expected to see it as in his own interests to do so.

The structure of theological motivations projects a vision of the land of Israel and its law as part of a divine, cosmic system of justice.[8] Both land and people belong to YHWH, the people having been rescued from slavery in Egypt to become his slaves or his tenants, in two different but not incompatible metaphors. It is the divine master, patron, landlord, who commands just and compassionate conduct. If Israel so acts, then the land will co-operate with them and produce its bounty. If they rebel, it will rebel against them, and they will lose it.

The accusation of impracticality leveled against the law is relativized once we accept that the object is to teach justice rather than to enforce detailed regulations. If that object is not achieved, no legislation, no matter how ingenious, will achieve a just society. For the impracticality is not a matter of physical impossibility but of motivation: the allegedly "natural" response to the approach of the jubilee will defeat its object. Although Leviticus 25 does not explicitly acknowledge the problem, its persuasive language implicitly recognizes it: "do not oppress one another" when buying and selling, vv. 14, 17: the implication is that the buyer will want to depress the price. He[9] has the whip hand, because the only situation envisaged in which a sale may take place is the seller's economic need, as in v. 25. The attachment of the peasant to his ancestral land is a basic assumption of the whole chapter: he will only sell if he has to. The result of such forced sales in normal conditions is a reduction of the price below the full market value.[10]

However, as I shall show in more detail later on, the text assumes an essentially classless society, where among Israelites impoverishment and inequality are temporary accidents arising from the changes and chances of harsh physical conditions. If this type of society is presupposed, there is no reason why people should not behave in the ways that the text demands. The conviction of its impracticality mainly depends on classical economics' construct of the rational subject who always behaves so as to maximize material benefit. Such a person would certainly not buy a fifty-year lease for the price of even forty-two crops, or lend his feckless neighbor food for a year at zero interest. But the rational subject does not exist: he (he always is a he) is a fantasy of Enlightenment individualism. Real people are motivated by a range of considerations, and especially by what is accepted as the done thing in their society and by the need to maintain the social relationships that are important to them and therefore as much in their interests as material profit. Given a society where the dominant sentiment was a conviction of the equal

---

8. Fager, *Land Tenure*, 104–5. [This is shown in detail in Lefebvre, *Jubilé*, 351–52.]
9. It is clear that the subjects assumed by the text are adult males—of that more later.
10. Westbrook, "Price Factor," 100–101.

value of all the members, it would not be inconceivable for people to act in accordance with that, even against their material interests.[11]

In any case, the laws in section B of the chapter represent a widely accepted morality of social action, found in prophets and wisdom writings as well as in the Torah. True, it is a morality frequently ignored or violated, otherwise we should not hear so much of it; but I do not find it impossible to conceive that the common sentiment in its favor would induce most well-off people who cared for their neighbors' opinion—as in an honor-oriented society everyone does—to give at least an impression of acting in accordance with it.[12]

Subjects and Objects of the Law

To whom, then, are these words addressed, and whom do they concern? Who is expected to implement them, or at least to listen to them, and who may be affected by them? The formal audience here (v. 2) is the Israelites. It is Israel that must proclaim the jubilee, and it is the whole people that must, each individually, return to their native place and possess once more their allotted fields. It is, however, sufficiently clear that once we get down to details it is only the secure possessors of property who are in a position to ensure that the law is obeyed. In v. 14 an attempt is made at a balanced and reciprocal statement: "When you sell property to your neighbor, or buy from your neighbor, do not oppress one another." But already in the next verse the pretense that the seller is in any position to "oppress" the buyer has been dropped: vv. 15–16 are formulated exclusively from the point of view of the buyer, who is warned to ensure that the price corresponds to the number of crop years he may expect from the property before the jubilee.[13]

And as one goes through the following laws in Section B it is always and inevitably the case that the addressee, the "thou" who is the subject of the law, is the secure proprietor who is in a position to help his "brother"

---

11. [In a number of publications, Faust has argued that various material features of the Iron Age I in the highlands, and to a large extent IA II in the kingdoms of Israel and Judah as well—undecorated pottery, the so-called "four-room house," burial by simple inhumation, and the lack of royal inscriptions—are indices of a society valuing equality and simplicity rather than hierarchy and elaboration. See, e.g., Faust, "Decoration versus Simplicity"; *Israel's Ethnogenesis*, 33–117.]

12. [The conviction that ancestral land is in principle inalienable is an ancient and deeply rooted one: this chapter provides a theological basis (Lev 25:23) and a practical means of implementing it (Houston, *Contending*, 196, referring to Lefebvre, *Jubilé*, 395–96).]

13. This is purely relative; there is no indication of what a just price might be absolutely; see Soss, "Old Testament Law."

(vv. 25, 35, 39, 47) who has fallen on evil days. The language of "brotherhood" is important.[14] Although the kind of compassionate actions mandated in section B are the prime responsibility of the family, "your brother" actually means "your fellow-Israelite," for "your brothers" in 25:46 is explained as "the Israelites"; and that is clearly what the similar language in Deuteronomy means.[15] But there is a tension in the use of this motif: the law uses language demanding in principle that people treat each other as equals, as "brothers," but at the same time envisages a situation of inequality, which may be expected to continue until the jubilee: this is particularly clear in vv. 35 and 40. But the jubilee, in theory, offers a term to the situation of inequality. The chapter does not say with Deut 15:11 that "the poor will not cease from the land"; for the return of everyone to their אחזה/*ahuzza*, their ancestral holding (v. 41), marks the end of the state of need that required the sale of the land or of its holder (vv. 28, 40, 54). Division of YHWH's people into sellers and buyers, patrons and clients, masters and servants marks the period between jubilees; at the jubilee each one returns, takes up his holding, and the nation once more becomes equal. At that point the poor cease from the land.

Is this, however, a true picture of what the text envisages? Universal equality? Norman Habel, for one, is clear that it is not. "The society is not truly egalitarian in the modern sense of the word. Laborers, servants, immigrants and urbanites are excluded from gaining the same level of social standing as landholding peasants and priests ... the rural workers at the bottom of the order remain dependent on the landed peasant farmers."[16] But while the text is perfectly explicit on the subject of foreign slaves and the גרים/*gerim* or resident aliens, who have no right to be redeemed, nor do they have ancestral land, so that they have nowhere to return to at the jubilee, it does not admit the existence of rural Israelite workers without an ancestral holding. In the real world there may have been a class of landless laborers and permanent slaves who could show no connection with any ancestral land. But if so this text does not admit it, even though the domination of the countryside by an urban landowning elite and the reduction of its inhabitants to slaves or laborers is frequently surmised to be the essence of the situation to which it is addressed.

On the other hand, it is clear as could be that foreigners and resident aliens, though not a class, since they may include masters as well as slaves, are yet a group without any of the rights of the trueborn Israelite. They may

---

14. It is unfortunately eliminated in the NRSV.
15. See above, chapter 2, 25–28, for a detailed discussion of this feature.
16. Habel, *The Land*, 112.

be enslaved in perpetuity and worked as slaves, whatever precisely that may mean. Yet we may reasonably suppose that they included people who had lived in Judah for generations and knew no other home. We certainly cannot speak of a truly egalitarian society in such conditions. It is also clear enough that even among Israelites this justice only applies between adult males, who are the possessors of land. Women and children are entirely invisible. Now it is strongly argued by, for example, Wright[17] that the adult male subject of the law is not functioning as an individual but as a family head, and the land to which he returns serves as the livelihood for an entire family unit, including all his dependents.[18] This may be true; but it is an uncomfortable fact that the Israelite peasant would sell his children, particularly his daughters, into slavery before he would abandon his land, let alone sell himself (see Neh 5:5).

The limits of the justice of the jubilee are beginning to become clear. It is a specifically nationalistic justice that applies only between "brothers," that is Israelite adult males. Further, with the important exception of the jubilee provision itself, justice depends on the fortunate recognizing their responsibilities to the less fortunate. Justice, between jubilees, is a gift of the superior to the inferior, not wrested by the weak from the strong. It is a matter of choice, however strongly demanded by the "law": the decision by the moneyed relative to redeem his cousin from bondage; the generous support of the impoverished peasant by the patron who lends without interest, or more realistically gives without the expectation of repayment, or takes him on as an indentured servant rather than gaining full value from him as a slave; the choice by the purchaser to pay, generously, the full price recommended. In a word, we are dealing with patronage, normally perhaps patronage within a kinship group,[19] but patronage all the same.[20]

Now, patronage is not to be despised. It is a relationship that can give great security to the client, and that unlike the tax-funded welfare state supplies a motive to the patron to act generously. Job 29 is a view of patronage from the patron's point of view: "When the ear heard, it commended me, and when the eye saw, it approved" (v. 11); "I sat as a chief, I lived like a king among his troops" (v. 25). The prestige gained by acts of generosity, the power flowing from a troop of grateful clients, in a word, honor: the patron did in fact get a great deal back for his apparently uncompensated outlays.

---

17. Wright, *God's People*, 124–25.

18. Cf. also Bendor, *Social Structure*. [The reason for the difference between the slave laws of Exod 21:2–11 and Deut 15:12–18 and Lev 25:39–55 is that the first two apply to dependents, but Lev 25 to family heads (Lefebvre, *Jubilé*, 307–14).]

19. Bendor, *Social Structure*, 236–40.

20. [See now Houston, *Contending*, 44–48.]

But it is anything but equality, and clearly not what is in the mind of radical theologians when they commend the jubilee as the Old Testament ideal of social justice. It is the jubilee itself, the radical return, that is the key to this, so it is this we need to examine.

Who Benefits from the Jubilee?

What we have already said should have begun to clarify whose justice the jubilee is. The group that would clearly benefit from the implementation of the measure, if it ever were implemented, would be the peasantry, the landholding families of Israelite villages. It would not benefit those without recognized title to land: those identified in the text as "the aliens residing with you" (v. 45). We have no means of knowing what proportion of the population these were, but it was clearly not negligible, in view of the frequency with which the *ger* is mentioned in the literature. It would also not benefit, but positively disadvantage, the ruling groups or merely more wealthy farmers mentioned so frequently as exploiting the peasants and seeking to gain control of their land and their persons. This is the straightforward interpretation of the text's implications.

More devious ideas are not lacking; the idea, for example, that the fifty years of the jubilee are related to the fifty years of exile and that the law's object is to legitimate the repossession of Judah by the exiles. Habel points out in its support that the sequel in chapter 26 promotes "the myth of the empty land" which enjoys its sabbaths.[21] It is impossible to disprove, but I am skeptical that it is of more than marginal significance. The context is concerned with impoverishment, not with deportation, and the Near Eastern parallels also underline the economic context of measures of this kind.

The World of the Text and Social Reality

Another approach to establishing the ideological conditioning of a text is to ask what it leaves out, what aspect of social reality is concealed or distorted. And we have already touched on this. The text's picture of the class structure of Israel is deficient. Essentially there are three social groups, none of which are classes: the landholding Israelites, the *gerim*, and the Levites. Poverty and landlessness, which are the motive of the whole system, are in this text

---

21. Habel, *The Land*, 113. Cf. also Levine, *Leviticus*, 274. [The theory depends on the widespread assumption that the Holiness Code is post-exilic, accepted also by me (*Contending*, 34, 192), but recently strongly contested (e.g., by Milgrom, *Leviticus 17–22*, 1361–64).]

not a condition, not a state of life, but a process, an event: "If your brother becomes impoverished . . . ." It is a temporary misfortune of individuals that will last at most fifty years. None of the Hebrew nouns or adjectives meaning "poor" appears in the chapter. Of course, the dramatic setting affects the presentation: "When you enter the land I am giving you . . ." (v. 2). The projected system of the jubilee, if it operates as intended, will prevent poverty from ever becoming the permanent lot of a class. We start from scratch and we exclude class formation from the word go.

But this does not correspond to the facts at any likely period of the text's composition. Descriptive texts on the agrarian situation, for example Nehemiah 5, suggest the existence of a relatively small ruling class, which Nehemiah calls "the nobles and the officers,"[22] who were exploiting the mass of the peasantry who were falling into debt. And on the other hand Hebrew writers generally take for granted that even small proprietors were able to draw for labor on a pool of landless people, men and women, by no means all of whom were *gerim*, whether as slaves or day-laborers at minimum wages.

Despite the constant complaints against the utopianism of the chapter, attention has rarely been given to this truly utopian feature, as it surely is. What is usually called utopianism is in reality no more than impracticality. A distinction should be drawn between the two. A utopia is a fictive world, particularly a fictive social world. If the jubilee regulation is believed unlikely to work in a real society, that does not make it part of a utopia unless the society in which it does work is also described: there are plenty of unworkable regulations in real societies. Leviticus 25 at least knows that people get poor, fall into debt, and want to sell up. Its world is in this sense recognizable. The text seems to mediate between the deep-rooted conviction of the inalienability of the peasants' land and the reality of impoverishment in the cash economy.

Nevertheless, the society portrayed in Leviticus 25 is not a reality. But the fact is that a society like it is necessary for the jubilee to work. A class society would successfully resist the attempt to transform it every fifty years. For like all societies, class society has an ideology which persuades its members that it has to be like that. In contrast, as we have seen, riches and poverty in Leviticus 25 are temporary accidents, and nothing hinders people's return to the original conditions.

---

22. החרים והסגנים. The terms are notably different from those in use in earlier times, e.g., Isaiah's זקני עמו ושריו (Isa 3:14).

We arrive at the paradoxical conclusion that the jubilee may not be impractical, but it is utopian. And it projects a utopia because of the character of the justice that it proposes.

The Key Values

The key values by which the whole system is guided, I suggest, are these:

(a) The proper ordering of society is to be found in the past. In this belief Leviticus is at one with the ancient Near East generally;[23] but it expresses the idea in a way distinctive of the Old Testament. When the Israelites entered Canaan, they received just allocations of land; but the misfortunes of some and the advantage taken of them by others have led inevitably to the loss of this original just ordering. The task of the lawgiver is to ensure that this original justice is restored. This is not a progressive belief, but a conservative one: justice is not a thing of the future to be striven towards by eliminating the distortions and abuses of the past, as French revolutionaries or Marxists believed, but is to be found by rescuing the old order from the encroachments of modernity, from the dynamic forces of the market and capital accumulation. It is not necessary to this belief that the old just order should really have existed, needless to say.

(b) The system values the attachment of the rural population to the soil, and not just of the population generally to the soil in general, but of this man or family to this piece of ground. "Everyone shall return to his own possession"; Naboth refuses Ahab's offer of another vineyard better than his own, because his own belonged to his ancestors. No one should underestimate the strength of this sentiment in any peasant population. In the Highland clearances in the early nineteenth century, the witnesses tell of occasions when people had the roofs of their miserable huts burnt over their heads rather than leave them. And the sentiment underlies the strength of resistance to Israel from Palestinian people who were driven from the homes of their ancestors in 1948.

It should be noted that although some have argued that the jubilee has its origin in a communal system of landholding,[24] there is no trace of this in the text, which takes individual landholding, presumably through inheritance, for granted. But valuing the individual's possession of his own plot on behalf of his family is not the same thing as believing that the individual has an indefeasible property right, including the right of alienation, that the

---

23. [Cf. above, 57.]

24. Cf. Weinfeld, *Social Justice*, 178, and literature noted above in chapter 3, 50, n. 61.

community ought not to interfere with. On the contrary, the text denies this in its theory of divine ownership, and specifically denies that anyone can acquire property rights over land other than his ancestral land.

(c) It is in keeping with the particularity of this attachment that poor relief is envisaged as taking place through patronage rather than through a state system or even a locally organized one. To our minds [in the UK], leaving it to whoever has a mind to it to relieve the necessities of the poor is a hit-or-miss arrangement that comes under the heading of charity rather than justice. The Bible does not recognize this distinction;[25] and certainly the biblical writers would find the impersonality of our system intolerable. Not only this chapter, but the Hebrew Bible generally, assumes that there is always a particular person whose responsibility it will be seen to be to keep the destitute from starving, to put it no higher. This finds concrete expression in the designation of the fellow-Israelite as "your brother"; but more narrowly, the right of redemption gives not merely a right but a responsibility to the family, acting through the next of kin, to relieve a person in straits.

(d) In general these particularities in the concept of justice exclude any abstract egalitarianism. The sons of Israel are a community of equals, and none of them is permitted to acquire overwhelming wealth or power over the others; but it does not occur to Hebrew writers to present equality of income or capital as a good. It is better for Naboth to retain the land of his fathers, however wretched it might be and however many mouths he has to feed, rather than having the land constantly redivided for the sake of equality.

What of the idea of "liberty," as it is often translated, דרור/*deror* in the Hebrew (v. 10), which is to be "proclaimed to all the inhabitants of the land"? This word is found elsewhere in the specific context of release from slavery (Jeremiah 34) or from deportation (Isa 61:1). It is not a right of self-determination as we might conceive it, but is an act of deliverance from subservience to take one's place in this community of equals. Liberty and equality are not so defined that they conflict with each other as in our modern political culture, partly because the third ideal of the French revolution, fraternity, holds them together.

(e) Fager is surely correct to see in the statement of YHWH's ownership of the land in v. 23 the ultimate moral basis of the jubilee legislation, "the cornerstone of the jubilee," as he puts it.[26] And along with this principle go the theological motive clauses which declare that the Israelites, whom YHWH delivered from Egypt and to whom he gave the land of Canaan, belong to him: "they are my slaves, whom I brought from the land of Egypt." The immediate

---

25. [Cf. below, chapter 12.]
26. Fager, *Land Tenure*, 116.

object of both assertions is very similar. No one can acquire absolute rights over YHWH's land or YHWH's people. They are in the position of tenants on his land, and cannot call it their own. It must fulfill—and so must they—YHWH's purposes alone. One can distinguish here a metaphor derived from the subject matter of the chapter, and a rhetorical aim. The metaphor is of God as patron, who stands in the same relation to the people of Israel as they, or their better-off representatives, may from time to time stand towards their own impoverished brethren, except that this relationship is permanent. Note the echo between "aliens and tenants"[27] in v. 23 and "an alien and a tenant"[28] in v. 35. As YHWH has graciously delivered his people from slavery in Egypt and enabled them to live before him, so they are required to deliver their own kin from slavery to live with them.

The rhetorical aim is to persuade the audience that they have no right to appropriate for themselves what YHWH has claimed for himself. Neither land nor people is to be used for personal profit, which is what sale in perpetuity implies. To quote Fager: "If the land is to be used exclusively for God's purposes, it may not be used to further the economic interests of any person or class of persons. The land may not become a commodity to be bought and sold in order to enrich a few wealthy individuals."[29] Nor, one may add, may the people. Fager neatly expresses this by saying that the land must provide the means of life, and not, through exploitation, produce the means of death.

One may now appreciate why the text has to project a utopia. Its understanding of justice is entirely discordant with society as it currently exists.

Conclusion

It is now possible to sum up what we have discovered and suggest possible answers to our initial question. There are quite clearly features of the worldview of this chapter that tie in very closely with the worldview of many Third World countries: the attachment of families to their land, the preference for personal models of justice, the alien nature of Enlightenment models of liberty and equality. In that the object of the text is not to enforce a particular system of land tenure and reform, but to instill principles of justice, we need not be too concerned about its utopian character. The limited scope of the justice it proclaims must counsel caution, though

---

27. גרים ותושבים
28. גר ותושב
29. Fager, *Land Tenure*, 117.

where the jubilee is being used as a simple metonymic symbol for its most positive aspects, this can perhaps be ignored.

The most difficult questions are raised by precisely these positive aspects. The tendency of the market to deepen inequalities is challenged by the principle that Leviticus inherits from the *mīšarum* tradition, that such processes can be halted or put into reverse. The attraction of the jubilee for the debt-remission campaign is its promise of a new start unencumbered by debts, in full possession of one's land and person, just as severely indebted countries today dream of a new start free of debt and unencumbered by IMF structural adjustment programs and the stranglehold of the multinationals. The jubilee suggests that it is possible to go back to the time before such evils overtook them: returning is after all its leitmotiv. But in that its attraction lies in this motif of reversal, returning, a golden age, it is also dangerous. The difficulty with which theologians must wrestle is that going back is not actually possible, and in any case justice does not lie in the past. The only hope of justice is in going forward to a new situation.

However, the deepest value of the symbol lies in the assertion "The land [for this purpose we could translate 'the earth'] shall not be subject to sale in perpetuity, since the earth is mine." The most crying need is for the humble acknowledgement that human beings have no right to absolute possession of the earth or any part of it to do with as they wish: it belongs to a higher purpose.

Chapter 5

The Role of the Poor in Proverbs

(2003)

Anyone familiar with the work of David Clines will be aware that in recent years he has shown an increasing concern for the exercise of critical judgment with regard to the ethics of the Hebrew Bible. I share this concern, but I come at the question from a different point of view, as a Christian theologian concerned to discover in an often morally problematic text aspects that may work as a critique of our lives and attitudes in the modern world.

My particular concern is that of social justice, and more specifically the issue of class, that is, of unequal relations between groups within society that are related to the economic structure. The Hebrew Bible has always been seen as having relevance to this issue because of its frequent words against oppression and in favor of care for the poor. Yet there can hardly be any doubt that the great majority of the Hebrew Bible is the work of social elites and is likely, a hermeneutic of suspicion will maintain, to represent their interests. One approach regards such words as isolated fragments voicing the interests of the oppressed.[1] But as I have argued elsewhere,[2] it is better to regard them as integral to the ideology of the texts, for it is in the interests of the rulers as much as of the ruled to encourage "a decent provision for the poor," which the Tory Samuel Johnson saw as "the true test of civilization."[3] Traditional ideas of social solidarity and generosity, or religious ideas of God as the guarantor of justice, inevitably form part of any ideology that lays claim to universal truth and popular support, but

---

1. Mosala, *Biblical Hermeneutics*, 101–53.
2. Above, chapter 2, 17–20; chapter 3, 36–37.
3. Boswell, *Life of Johnson*, vol. 1, 396. (Year 1770, recollections of Dr Maxwell.)

taken in their full weight may be read as challenging the dominant role of the classes that sponsor it.[4]

This thesis can be illustrated from the book of Proverbs. Here we must have in view two questions, which are related but can be kept distinct. The first is the social background of the writing of Proverbs. Who were the wisdom writers? How did they fit into the society of the time? Whom did they serve? Who were their patrons? When they collected proverbs, such as those in Proverbs 10–29, did those proverbs originate in circles like their own, or are they rather a popular oral literature, and if so in what sort of social background did they originally circulate?

The second is: what attitudes towards wealth and poverty are displayed in this literature? These attitudes are of course very likely to be a function of the social background of the authors or of the people among whom the proverbs circulated, so that one way of investigating the first question might be by answering the second question first, and then arguing that people who had such and such attitudes must have come from such and such a group in society. Thus it might be argued that people who believe that those who live on welfare benefits are all scroungers are likely to come from comfortably off backgrounds themselves. But many of those who hold that view about welfare recipients are themselves among the poorer elements of society. Conversely, while such a view may be popular in the clubs of London's West End, not everyone in the upper middle classes holds it. It seems best, therefore, to tackle the questions separately.

The question of the social background of Proverbs has been dealt with at some length by the late Norman Whybray, who deals separately with the different sections of the book, marked out as they are by differences in literary form.[5] Like everyone else he is clear that the discourses and wisdom poems in Proverbs 1–9 reflect an upper-class urban background.[6] The young man addressed has leisure and money, which he may use wisely or unwisely. There is no reference at all to the poor in these chapters;[7] so although one can safely say that they reflect the experience and values of a wealthy urban elite, one cannot get out of them any reflection on class relationships, except perhaps by way of an argument from silence: there is no instruction, as there is later in the book, to devote part of one's wealth to the relief of poverty.

---

4. Above, chapter 2, 19.
5. Whybray, *Wealth and Poverty*.
6. Whybray, *Wealth and Poverty*, 100–101.
7. Whybray, *Wealth and Poverty*, 102. Actually there is an indirect reference in Prov 6:30: "People do not despise a thief who steals to satisfy his hunger."

Whybray takes all the sentence literature (10:1—22:16 and 25–29) together, and sees it as reflecting the experience and values of people of a middle station in life: modest farming folk—note the many references to an agricultural setting—who are neither rich nor poor, and observe both rich and poor dispassionately, but are constantly threatened by the danger of poverty.[8] This would account, in his view, for the large number of warnings of the sad fate awaiting the lazy.[9] These people are in a situation where they can maintain their modest standard of living only by constant hard work; this is threatened by the lazybones who fails to contribute to the community's hard-won store. The large number of proverbs concerned with the king and the royal court do not show that they originated in the court, for people of any class may be interested in the king.[10] Even the proverbs that commend charity to the poor and condemn oppression are not necessarily addressed to the rich: even the modestly well-off may be asked to help the poor.[11]

But Whybray's and Westermann's views of these chapters have been effectively criticized by Michael Fox and by Mark Sneed.[12] The agricultural setting is in no way dominant;[13] and the court sayings "speak not only *about* kings and courtiers, but *to* and *for* them."[14] Fox quotes Prov 16:10, 14; 25:6-7. He sees the prominence of this theme, with the reference to editorial work by "the men of Hezekiah" in 25:1, as showing that "the court was the decisive locus of creativity."[15] Even if some proverbs circulated among the population, it must certainly have been among the governing cadre of the scribes, associated with the court (of the king or, later, the governor) or the temple, that they were collected and shaped. Sneed defines the scribes simply as an upper-class group, largely on the basis of Ben Sira, who regards a private income as essential to the status of scribe (Sir 38:24).[16] Fox points out that the cadre would include "clerks of high and low degree."[17] But the likelihood is that the highest level of the service were landowners drawing

---

8. Whybray, *Wealth and Poverty*, 31–34. A very similar view is taken by Westermann, *Roots*, at least of a hypothetical older form of these proverbs.

9. Whybray, *Wealth and Poverty*, 38.

10. Whybray, *Wealth and Poverty*, 54–58.

11. Whybray, *Wealth and Poverty*, 35.

12. Fox, "Social Location"; Sneed, "Class Culture." [See also now Fox, *Proverbs 10–31*, 500–503.]

13. Fox, "Social Location," 233.

14. Fox, "Social Location," 235, emphasis original.

15. Fox, "Social Location," 236.

16. Sneed, "Class Culture," 297–99. [For Ben Sira, see now chapter 9 below.]

17. Fox, "Social Location," 236.

income from their estates, not mere hangers-on of the ruling class but themselves members of the economic and social elite.

Sneed also shows that Whybray is wrong to go as he does mainly by the content of the literature to identify its class background. Aristocratic literature as we know it from Egypt has a wide range of interests, including much with a popular appeal; landowners are inevitably interested in agriculture; and the fact that the proverbs appear to view both rich and poor in objective terms is no guide to the standing of the authors. He quotes the Egyptian wisdom writer Amenemope, who was clearly wealthy, but speaks of rich and poor in a very similar style to Proverbs:

> God loves him who cares for the poor,
> More than him who respects the wealthy.[18]

Sneed concludes that there is nothing in Proverbs that requires the authors of the sentences to be humble folk; it is perfectly possible that some of the proverbs have a popular oral origin, but "there is no need to assume this for the bulk of Proverbs."[19]

But if it is accepted that Proverbs as a whole has a broadly upper-class orientation, how is this shown in its attitudes? J. David Pleins's chapter on Proverbs in his massive study of social attitudes in the Hebrew Bible takes a clear line both on the social location of the authors of Proverbs and on their attitude towards wealth and poverty.[20] "This literature is a product of the ruling elite,"[21] "professional functionaries in the monarchic establishment,"[22] who formed the royal civil service and composed literature such as Proverbs as educational textbooks for their apprentices. By this means the young men who are repeatedly addressed in the instruction literature would not only learn to read and write but would also become instructed in the norms and ethics of the world of government and diplomacy, which they aspired to enter. "It is to be expected, then," continues Pleins, "that the values and practices advocated in the wisdom tradition are in accord with the political and economic leanings of the ruling classes."[23]

What are these values and practices? He has already given a broad hint in discussing the Wisdom Psalms in the previous chapter. The authors of

---

18. Amenemope 26.13–14, as in Sneed, "Class Culture," 305.
19. Sneed, "Class Culture," 305.
20. Pleins, *Social Visions*, 452–83; largely anticipated in Pleins, "Poverty."
21. Pleins, *Social Visions*, 457.
22. Pleins, *Social Visions*, 456.
23. Pleins, *Social Visions*, 457.

Proverbs (but not of the Psalms) launch "a veritable attack on the poor."[24] This is strong language. It is slightly qualified in the chapter on Proverbs, but not withdrawn; rather it is backed up by the assertion that in seeking opponents to define their ethical views the one identifiable social group the wise can use is the poor, since the "wicked" or the "fools" are not definable in sociological terms ("the poor as such are the only sociologically defined objects of the wisdom creed's ethical landscape").[25] The role of the poor in Proverbs is to stand as a dreadful warning of the state to which the audience may be reduced if they fail to heed instruction.

The basis for this assertion lies in the repeated statements, both in the instruction and in the sentence literature, that laziness leads to poverty.[26] "The wise see poverty's origins in a lack of commitment to the labors at hand":[27] the poor are responsible for their own poverty. Pleins constantly celebrates prophecy as a foil to the "wisdom creed," on the ground that prophecy in contrast finds the origins of poverty in the exploitative activity of the ruling class.[28]

Pleins is not alone in this estimate of the role of the poor in Proverbs; he depends on a strong tradition in scholarship. He quotes Cornelis van Leeuwen: poverty is "a punishment that one brings upon oneself through one's own fault."[29] He also draws on the work of Kuschke, who argued that the term רש/*rash*, the commonest word for "poor" in Proverbs, was used when referring to "poverty as a self-inflicted evil, as something contemptible,"[30] whereas עני/*'ani* and אביון/*evyon*, which are not as common in this book, implied the rightful claim of the poor to consideration; hence the use of רש/*rash* served to justify existing class divisions.[31]

---

24. Pleins, *Social Visions*, 437.

25. Pleins, *Social Visions*, 465.

26. Proverbs in the sentence literature denouncing laziness appear at Prov 12:11, 14, 24, 27; 19:15, 24; 20:4; 21:5, 25; 22:13; 26:13, 14, 15, 16; 28:19; longer poems on the topic appear at 6:6–11 and 24:30–34, which close with the same couplet. The majority of these warn that lack of diligence will lead to want, though some simply poke fun at the lazy person.

27. Pleins, *Social Visions*, 469.

28. Pleins, *Social Visions*, 470.

29. Leeuwen, *Développement*, 153, as in Pleins, *Social Visions*, 469.

30. Kuschke, "Arm und reich," 44.

31. Kuschke, "Arm und reich," 47. Regrettably, constraints of space make it impossible to discuss here the possible distinctions between the various words translated "poor." [See Houston, *Contending*, 62.]

Is it true that the writers of Proverbs "see poverty's origins" in laziness? Could רש be translated "bum" (in the American meaning of that word), as Pleins half-jokingly suggests?[32]

There is no question that Proverbs very frequently says that laziness begets want. But it is not a logical conclusion from the fact that laziness leads to poverty that poverty, wherever it exists, is caused by laziness. Now there is nothing to prevent the writers from being guilty of such illogicality; and there is much evidence that the connection back from sickness to sin, consequence to cause, was frequently drawn: compare, for example, the line taken by the friends of Job, or the psalms of lamentation which confess sin. But in the sentence literature and Proverbs generally this reverse connection is virtually absent. I have been able to find only one sentence in the entire sentence literature of Proverbs, one verse in six hundred, that deduces conduct from its results: 16:31: "Gray hair is a crown of glory; it is gained in a righteous life"—which is the converse of the frequent observation that righteousness leads to long life. Hence, it is far from demonstrable that the point of the sayings warning of laziness leading to poverty is to hold up the actual poor as a horrid example of what laziness leads to.

Indeed, this is the more unlikely in that the writers know of a number of other possible causes for poverty. "Wealth hastily gained will grow small" (13:11); "A lover of pleasure will suffer want; whoever loves wine and oil will not grow rich" (21:17). The doctrine of retribution so beloved of the wise maintains that the wicked will come to a bad end; a variety of bad ends, one should say, one of which is to fall into poverty: "The wicked earn deceptive wages" (11:18); "The righteous eat their fill, but the belly of the wicked will be empty" (13:25).

But of course it will be pointed out that in citing these verses I have indeed extended the range of the understanding of the origins of poverty in Proverbs, but not altered the basic fact that poverty stands as a dreadful warning: it is generally one's own fault, whether through laziness or through extravagance or as the just retribution for wickedness—in other words, what we might understand as a typically upper-class view of the poor. But there are several reasons why I find this interpretation problematic.

The first, to repeat, is the lack of any sentences reversing the deductive process. There are various ways to get poor, but there are no condemnatory statements about poor people and how they have brought their poverty upon themselves. This is the decisive objection to the view of Kuschke, Pleins, van Leeuwen, and others that the wise despise the poor, "attack" the

---

32. Pleins, *Social Visions*, 469.

poor and so on. The necessary assertions in a literature that is not shy of assertive statements are simply not there.

Secondly, the upper-class bias, which undoubtedly is present in this literature, shows itself in a different way. All the warnings about the dangers that threaten the lazy, the wicked, the pleasure lovers, and all the rest of the damnèd crew who are held up to the reader's gaze apply to the well off. They tell them how they might lose their wealth and join the ranks of the poor. They say nothing about how the poor *as a class* originate. How the well off might become poor is a constant theme of these writers. Why the poor are not well off is not a question that ever occurs to them. A survey of the way in which the poor do appear as subjects of this literature soon demonstrates, as we shall see, that poverty is understood as a given. The poor just are poor; nothing is said about why they are poor. The true limitation of the writers' vision appears in this incuriosity about the structure of society. They do not blame the poor for their own poverty because they are not interested in what causes poverty.

One sentence in Proverbs may make an assertion very close to some in the prophets:

> The land of the poor produces much food, but it is often swept away by injustice [*or* unjustly]. (13:23)[33]

Clearly this does not say that injustice makes a person poor, which in any case does not mean destitute; but it does say that the poor may become destitute through injustice. This is also the implication of the injunctions against oppression of the poor which are also found in the book. But they do not amount to a theory of the origin of class division: on the contrary, they take that as a given.

But the most important reason why we cannot speak of an "attack on the poor" in Proverbs is that the tone of the sentences that speak of the poor is either regretfully objective or positively sympathetic. There is none of the saloon-bar ranting about scroungers and layabouts we might expect from our own experience of upper-class culture (to repeat, the lazy in the proverbs are not members of a class of poor people; they are well-off people who are in danger of becoming poor). The sentence I have just quoted about injustice is a good example of that dry-eyed observation of social facts that

---

33. רב־אכל ניר ראשים ויש נספה בלא משפט. This translation understands ראשים as a spelling of רשים, as it is taken by NRSV, REB, and others, [such as Fox, *Proverbs 10–31*, 570, who, however, translates the verse differently, with some revocalization: "The great man devours the tillage of the poor, and some people are swept away without justice." The point made in the text is not affected.]

gives rise to numerous other sentences that express the fact that the poor are at a serious disadvantage beside the rich.[34]

> A poor man (רש/*rash*) is hated even by his neighbors, but a rich man has many friends (14:20).
>
> The appetite of a worker works for him: his hunger drives him on. (16:26)
>
> A poor man (רש/*rash*) uses entreaties, but a rich man gives harsh answers. (18:23)
>
> A rich man rules over poor people (רשים/*rashim*), and the debtor is his creditor's slave. (22:7)
>
> A wicked ruler over a poor people (עם־דל/*'am-dal*) is a roaring lion or a charging bear. (28:15)

Note that the rich man who gives harsh answers and the creditor who enslaves his debtor are not distinguished from kind rich men or indulgent creditors. The sentences are true of the class as a whole.

It is true, as we have already seen, that the wise are not interested in the origins of the social system, nor are they interested in changing it. But in these sayings we begin to be aware that they have a very good idea of how the system works. Wealth means power, and power is generally used arrogantly. Of that the wise are well aware, and despite the deadpan way in which the facts are presented, a necessary effect of the literary style, they clearly do not approve.

This is shown by their frequent injunctions to their readers to make sure that they behave differently.

> One who closes his ears to the cry of the poor (דל/*dal*) will himself call out and not be answered. (21:13)
>
> The generous man [literally "with a good (or kind) eye," טוב־עין/ *tov-'ayin*] is blessed because he gives of his own food to the poor (דל/*dal*.) (22:9)
>
> One who despises his neighbor is a sinner, but one who is kind to the afflicted (or poor: עני/*'ani*) is blessed. (14:21)
>
> One who gives to the poor (רש/*rash*) has no lack, but one who turns a blind eye gets plenty of curses. (28:27).[35]

---

34. In my translations, I deliberately reproduce the gender bias of the originals, which are written from the point of view of men and addressed exclusively to males.

35. [More comprehensive collections of texts of the above two types may now be found at Houston, *Contending*, 120–21.]

If it were really true that the teaching about laziness implied contempt for the poor as a class, the presence of sayings like these in the same collections would be inexplicable. Sayings in these collections warn the reader not to despise or mock the poor (14:21; 17:5); to interpret other sayings as if they implied contempt for the poor is perverse.

Most significant for my purpose are those sayings that lay a theological foundation for the injunction to be generous to the poor and not to oppress them. Proverbs 14:31 reads, "One who oppresses a poor man (דל/*dal*) insults his Maker, but one who is kind to the destitute (אביון/*evyon*) honors him," and 17:5 is similar: "One who mocks a poor man (רש/*rash*) insults his Maker, and one who gloats over misfortune will pay for it." "The poor man and the exploiter have one thing in common:[36] it is YHWH who gives light to the eyes of both" (29:13). These sayings from the sentence literature root their abhorrence of oppression in the goodness of the Creator. The poor have a dignity that derives from the fact that they are creatures of God; but the oppressor is just as dependent on God for the common goods of life as the poor person.

A slightly different approach is taken by two instructions in the little collection at 22:17–24:34. At 22:22–23, we read, "Do not rob a poor man (דל/*dal*) because he is poor, and do not oppress the afflicted (עני/*'ani*) in the gate, for YHWH will defend their cause and despoil of life those who despoil them." A similar point is made by 23:10–11: "Do not remove an ancient landmark or encroach on the fields of fatherless children; for their Redeemer is strong: he will defend their cause against you." These sayings rest on faith in the activity of God in human affairs and not solely in creation, but by the same token they risk disconfirmation, in the same way as every confident assertion of retribution that this literature makes, when the expected defense fails to materialize, as Job complains: "The earth is given into the hand of the wicked; he covers the eyes of its judges" (Job 9:24).

Pleins emphasizes the fact that the theological basis of the wisdom literature shows no knowledge of the covenant or the distinctive Israelite traditions on which, in his view, prophecy is based, and sees this as a ground for prophetic hostility to the wise. This I doubt. Rooting the call to generosity in creation and our solidarity as human beings is a universalist approach that in no way contradicts the more particularist understanding that relies on the covenant. But as it happens, the warnings against oppression of the poor in the Book of the Covenant in Exodus show a clear relationship to the traditions in Proverbs: compare Exod 22:22–23, "You shall not abuse any widow or orphan. If you do abuse them, when they cry out to me, I will surely

---

36. רש ואיש תככים נפגשו

heed their cry," with Prov 23:10–11 and particularly 21:13. It is very much oversimplifying things to make such sharp distinctions. There is a great deal of cross-fertilization between traditions in ancient Israel, and the plausibility of the teaching of the wise depends to a very large extent on their sharing of a common fund of ethical understanding and theological insight with the population as a whole. This is another point made by Sneed: "The various classes shared most of the same values. Tried and true values had been disseminated throughout ancient Israelite society."[37]

Now, as Sneed emphasizes, this line of exhortation to generosity and kindness to the poor is perfectly characteristic of aristocratic wisdom literature in all ancient cultures. It does not show that the writers were either members of a lower class—we have already dealt with that—or that they had a distinctive solidarity with the poor or one that cut across their generally upper-class interests and concerns. As Sneed says, this would assume "that aristocratic concern for the poor is somehow antagonistic to their self-interest, and this is just not the case."[38]

> Public expression of concern for the poor might have served as a catalyst for peace within the total society. In other words, if the poor feel as though the upper class cares and they see restraint placed on wanton oppression, they may be less willing to revolt.[39]

This is to put it at its lowest. More generously, Kovacs defines this ethic as one of *noblesse oblige*: the wise "are responsible and dutiful citizens who act to uphold the proper social order,"[40] and the proper social order includes the duty of the leaders of society to care for the poor as well as the duty of the poor to respect their leaders and patrons. This means that the inculcation of values shared with the whole of society is a necessary part of the education of those who will take leading positions in it.

It becomes clear, then, that the compilers of the collections in Proverbs 10–31 have typically upper-class attitudes, but share their fundamental social values with the society as a whole. They accept that society is divided into rich and poor: that appears to them to be a given; it has not crossed their mind that it might be changed or that it is the result of human decisions. But they are aware of the destructive effects that this division of society into powerful and powerless may have. And so they attempt to bring

---

37. Sneed, "Class Culture," 306. This point we have seen made in general terms by Walzer (above, chapter 2, 18–19).

38. Sneed, "Class Culture," 302.

39. Sneed, "Class Culture," 303.

40. Kovacs, "Class-Ethic," 178.

up the youth of the ruling classes to be aware of their responsibility towards those who will be in their power, and to treat them in a way that recognizes their common humanity. This would be part of their general responsibility, urged throughout the book, to act moderately and restrain their greed and other passions for the sake of peace in society.[41]

It would appear that there is a serious contradiction in the wisdom teachers' position. They know that rich people treat poor people badly, and say so in more than one place. But their remedy for this is to appeal to individuals to restrain their appetites and be generous. The difficulty is apparent: their solution depends on the very people who are the problem,[42] though maybe that is hidden from them because they are confident of the effectiveness of their own teaching.

However, their approach could be defended were it true, as they claim, that the wicked, which of course includes the oppressors, were restrained by the workings of a cosmos built on the principle of retribution. Oppression could not then get very far, and the current order of society would be reasonably benign. Unfortunately, as Job and Qoheleth both point out, this confidence is an illusion. Job draws a terrifying picture of the sheer brutality of life in the rural slums of Israel in Job 24:

> Out in the fields at night they reap, and they gather the vineyard of the wicked. Naked they spend the night for lack of clothing, and have no covering against the cold.... Yet God pays no heed to their prayer.... God prolongs the life of the mighty by his power. (Job 24:6–7, 12c, 22a)[43]

The principle of retribution fails. But as David Clines has sharply suggested, Job should not really be asking for God to sort out a problem that human beings have created and human beings ought to be able to solve.[44]

But if they are to solve it, simple appeals to generosity are not enough. In any society the key to social relationships may be found in the fundamental religious or philosophical principles that are current. Most significant, therefore, for our purpose in Proverbs are those few texts that ground the appeal to generosity on creation, rather than retribution, on what God and not human beings have made. For if it is true that our common creatureliness

---

41. [This applies as much to Ben Sira as it does to Proverbs: see chapter 9.]

42. This is true also of Deuteronomy's moral appeals: see above, chapter 2, 32.

43. [The translation of these extracts was too heavily dependent on the NRSV in the original edition. I have altered the translation of the first two verses, with the help of Dhorme, *Job*, 358–59; the other two will have to stand, although I am now doubtful whether they are relevant.]

44. Clines, "Quarter-Days Gone," 258.

binds us in solidarity with one another, this takes precedence over any justification for the division of society in a way that gives a few people absolute power over the rest, and the choice of how to use it, the division that the wisdom teachers dumbly accept but do not attempt to justify. "The poor man and the exploiter have one thing in common: it is YHWH who gives light to the eyes of both" (29:13). There is then no justification for any other goods to be monopolized by the one and denied to the other.[45]

---

45. This paper is dedicated to David Clines in appreciation for his thought-provoking scholarship, and especially for his respect, support, and friendship during my seven years as a rather marginal member of the Department of Biblical Studies at Sheffield.

Chapter 6

Was There a Social Crisis in the Eighth Century?

──────── (2004) ────────

1 .The Common View

AGAINST WHAT HISTORICAL BACKGROUND should the texts in the prophetic books of Amos, Micah, and Isaiah be interpreted which denounce acts of oppression committed against the poor, or simply against peasant landholders?[1] There is a *communis opinio* about this in scholarship, which I cannot do better than give in the words of Rainer Albertz, in his *History of Israelite Religion*. I quote Albertz not because he has something distinctive to say, but precisely because he has not, but says what he does have to say very well.

> We do not know precisely what concrete factors sparked off the social crisis at a time of economic boom and political stability after the long Aramaean depression in the reign of Jeroboam II (787–47). As similar phenomena can also be noted in the southern kingdom at this time, it is usually assumed that what we have here is a long-term structural development that already has its roots in the social changes introduced by the formation of the state, which came to a head for the first time in the eighth century. The creation of large estates, from the crown downwards, had made holes in the old Israelite order and had forced aside the egalitarian ideal of the period before the state (Micah 2.1f.). A prosperous stratum of large landowners, officials, military and merchants had set themselves above the traditional small farmers intent only on self-sufficiency (Micah 3.1–9; Isa.

---

1. Minimally defined, these texts are: Isa 1:21–26; 3:13–15; 5:1–7, 8–10; 10:1–4; Amos 2:6–16; 3:9–15; 4:1–3; 5:10–12; 8:4–7; Mic 2:1–5, 6–11; 3:1–4, 9–12. Words for "poor" are not used in the Micah texts, nor in Isa 5:8.

1.23; 3.12, 14), and far outstripped them with market-oriented surplus production. This creeping social development became critical in the eighth century when many small farmers—perhaps because of the population growth and the ongoing division of their businesses as they were handed down from generation to generation—were forced to the brink by the tougher economic conditions. They were less and less in a position to cope with the normal risks of agricultural production from their own resources, and it became increasingly difficult for them to bear the usual burdens of state taxation and forced labour; they were compelled more and more frequently to resort to loans in order to get by. This put large parts of the farming population under such direct pressure from the economically expanding upper class that on a wide front they were driven to dependence on it and became permanently impoverished. The prophets already typify them as a group of the "weak" *(dal)*, "poor" *(ʾebyōn)* and "wretched" *(ʿānāw/ʿanī [sic])*.[2]

But everybody knows all this! Accounts like this appear in every commentary on Amos, and the temptation must be to assume it is true simply by dint of its constant repetition. But serious reasons, though not necessarily conclusive ones, have been put forward for doubting this "incontrovertible" truth, and it behoves the critical investigator to examine them before accepting the *communis opinio* without further ado.

2. Counter-Arguments

I would classify these reasons under three heads. First, there are questions concerning the provenance and reliability of the evidence. Are we really dealing with eighth-century texts? Secondly, there are questions about the interpretation of these texts, assuming that we accept them as being what they claim to be. Do they actually support Albertz's account? Thirdly, there is evidence that definitely comes from the eighth century and may be held actually to disprove that account.

2.1. Are These Eighth-Century Texts?

I begin with questions about the date and reliability of the evidence. The only textual evidence that Albertz cites from the eighth century is the prophetic texts I have already alluded to. He also refers to 2 Kgs 4:1, from an account

---

2. Albertz, *History*, I, 159–60; *Religionsgeschichte*, I, 248–49.

whose final composition is not earlier than the sixth century and which is set in the ninth, or possibly the very early eighth century; Nehemiah 5, which is set and presumably composed in the fifth century; and Exodus 21, which it is not possible to date precisely. The only piece of archaeological evidence he cites—the only piece anyone cites—is de Vaux's preliminary report on discoveries now half a century ago at Tell el-Farʿah North, identified as Tirzah (de Vaux 1955).[3] This is so well known that I need not detail it. The remains certainly date from the eighth century, but whether de Vaux's interpretation is correct is another matter, which will occupy us later.

Obviously, Albertz will not be untypical in this. Almost the only texts in the Old Testament that even purport to be of eighth-century date are the prophets Isaiah, Hosea, Amos, and Micah, so they are the only biblical texts that could be cited to prove a social crisis in the eighth century. That events of this kind happened there can be very little doubt. They are happening to this day in various parts of the world. But by far the most coherent account of them in the Old Testament is Neh 5:2–5. If this text does not prove that a social crisis of this kind happened in the *fifth* century, I do not know the meaning of historical evidence. But to support the hypothesis that such events happened also in the eighth century, we are reliant on the prophetic texts noted above in n. 1 plus the Tell el-Farʿah evidence.

But as we know very well, the idea that we can quote an "eighth-century" prophetic text as evidence for the eighth century is now looking distinctly dodgy. The older picture of the prophetic collections has given place to a thoroughgoing redactional approach, which views each of the collections as the work of creative editors working in the Second Temple era and reducing to order a mass of material, with varied points of view, originating at times spread out over anything from one to three centuries.[4]

Redaction critics are not necessarily "minimalists." Many remain bizarrely confident that they can identify the precise date and origin of every verse. But they tend not to agree with each other. Other scholars have drawn the obvious conclusion, and deny that we can know anything for certain about the origins of anything in the prophetic books, and particularly nothing very much about their date or social background, a point made emphatically by Robert Carroll, when asked to write on just that topic.[5] Carroll's position is well known;[6] and the most recent commentary in English on Amos[7]

3. De Vaux, "Les fouilles."
4. Collins, *Mantle of Elijah*, gives a useful overview.
5. Carroll, "Prophecy and Society."
6. See also Carroll, *Chaos* and *Jeremiah*.
7. Coggins, *Joel and Amos*.

deals with Amos in a very similar way; Coggins treats it as a book of the fifth century, and without denying that parts of it might come from a historical prophet Amos in the eighth, refuses to identify these definitely.

The practical effects of such skepticism operating on texts dissolved by the acids of redaction criticism may be observed on one of the texts relevant to this inquiry. Micah 2:1–2 is a powerful condemnation of landgrabbers who might be supposed to be operating at the time of Ahaz and Hezekiah, when Micah is dated, according to Mic 1:1. However, it has long been observed, for example by Jörg Jeremias,[8] that the oracle of judgment that follows scarcely fits the condemnation that precedes it, and suggests the presence of redactional work. It is announced against "this whole clan";[9] but it seems to mean the whole nation, as in Amos 3:1, as is confirmed by "the land of my people" in v. 4: not the evildoers themselves, as would be appropriate. Further, the expressions "on that day" in v. 4 and "that will be an evil time" in v. 3 suggest that there will be a long gap between the crime and the punishment—also unexpected in a prophetic announcement of divine punishment. By these manipulations the editors of the text make it an announcement by Micah of the exile of Judah in the sixth century. Ehud Ben Zvi adds to this the point that vv. 1–2 are formulated in a quite general way concerning agrarian abuses that occur in every age and have nothing particular to link them to the eighth century. In his view this is deliberate: the words are intended by the text's authors to be capable of multiple application, and are not intended primarily to reproduce Micah's exact words to the eighth-century oppressors.[10]

But the real difference between Jeremias in 1971 and Ben Zvi in 1999 is that whereas Jeremias postulated an eighth-century text for the exilic redactors to work on, and probably thought that this could be used to study eighth-century history, Ben Zvi places the social history of eighth-century Judah among those things "which cannot be learned from this text."[11] Among other reasons, including those already mentioned, one notes his points that "the need to explain Judah's calamity in terms of the wrongdoing in the monarchic period creates by necessity an image of a sinful 'Israel' in the text"; and that "the reconstruction of the history of eighth-century Judah . . . was not a concern of those who shaped the text, nor of those for whom it was shaped."

---

8. Jeremias, "Deutung der Gerichtsworte," 333–35, 349–51.
9. Or family, or however one wishes to translate משפחה.
10. Ben Zvi, "Wrongdoers," 89.
11. Ben Zvi, "Wrongdoers," 99.

And inevitably one must add to these points the fact I have already alluded to that the best securely dated textual evidence for such a social crisis comes from the fifth century. The shapers, to use Ben Zvi's word, of the texts of the prophets could well have been influenced by events much closer to their own times than the eighth century. Can one be certain that they had any eighth-century material before them on this subject at all?

2.2. Interpreting the Evidence

But supposing for the moment that they did, does it actually mean what it has been taken to mean in accounts such as Albertz's? S. Bendor argues in his account of Israelite social structure that it was based on the בית אב / *bet av*, literally "father's house," as the pivotal land-holding entity, which he takes to be the extended family of three or four nuclear families; and that this structure remained intact down to the end of the monarchy, and despite pressures from the state and from creditors the *bet av* generally retained control of its land.[12] We shall look in a moment at the positive evidence he alleges for this. But Bendor is by no means a minimalist, quite the contrary, so he must deal with the evidence that appears to go against his view that he takes to be from the monarchic period.

First, one must understand that he does not see the Israelite village or משפחה/*mishpaha*, or the *bet av* within it, apart from any outside pressures, as an idyllic egalitarian commune. The village was run by the heads of the בתי אבות /*bate avot* (plural of *bet av*), the זקנים/*zeqenim* or elders, who were men of power over their own families and collectively over the village as a whole. There were stronger and weaker, richer and poorer families, and within the *bet av* there were stronger and weaker elements. Some heads of nuclear families had their own plots within the land of the *bet av*, some did not, and weakest of all were the widow and her fatherless children, who had no male to stand up for them, and the *ger* who sought refuge in a *bet av* but had no secure footing within it.

To take first the two texts that speak of the taking over of land, Isa 5:8 and Mic 2:1–2, which have generally been taken to refer to the formation of latifundia through foreclosure on mortgages; on Mic 2:1–2 he argues that "wealthy men of Jerusalem are not needed in order for the fields of Moresheth . . . to be seized. . . . [T]he events take place within the *mishpaha*, . . . its strongman (the head of the *bet av* or the elder of the *mishpaha* or עיר/*'ir* [settlement])" is the culprit. "Within the *mishpaha* he does not even require a corrupt court or an actual sale, but because of his power, he can do it in

---

12. Bendor, *Social Structure*.

the daylight."[13] In Isa 5:8, he interprets "land" (ארץ/*erets*) as the territory of a village or of a *mishpaha*, and the culprits again as the strongmen of the village, who force out the weaker elements and take over their land.[14] Turning to Amos, on 2:6 he argues that the *seller* of the righteous poor cannot be the creditor, but must be the head of the *bet av* who sells for debt a member of the family who *has rights* (צדיק/*tsaddiq*, according to him mistranslated "righteous")[15] in the family land; 8:6 on the other hand denounces the one who buys him.[16] Elsewhere he refers appositely to Isa 50:1, where someone is sold to, not by, a creditor.[17] On Isa 3:13–15, Bendor points out that while "elders" always refers to local leaders, heads of kinship units, שרים/*sarim* (NRSV "princes") does not necessarily refer to royal officials as is usually assumed, but can mean "chiefs" or "leaders" in general, or of local kinship groups in particular (Job 29:9; Ezra 8:29).[18] He would see the verses as accusing powerful local leaders, powerful through their positions in the kinship units, of oppressing the poor of their own locality.

Bendor has, it is clear, given a decidedly different account of matters. For him there is no social crisis in the late monarchy. The social injustices that are denounced by the prophets are a result of the confluence of pressures from the state (and external forces like Assyria) with tensions in the local communities, and the latter had existed and led to inequalities and injustices even before the emergence of the state. This is a reminder that even if we can validate the eighth-century origin of these texts, their interpretation is a precarious matter, and the very worst approach is to assume that the traditional interpretation must be right just because it is so widely assumed.

Moreover, the archaeological evidence from Tell el-Farʿah not only may be but almost certainly has been misinterpreted. The full publication of the excavations, by Chambon in 1984, suggests, at least in Fleischer's interpretation, that de Vaux's conclusions were too hasty, and the significance of the finds much more ambiguous than he had suggested.[19] Although Chambon still describes the houses respectively as "the patrician houses" and "the poor houses,"[20] two of the three so-called "poor" houses are in fact almost as large as the "patrician" ones; the main difference is in the quality

---

13. Bendor, *Social Structure*, 249.
14. Bendor, *Social Structure*, 252–53.
15. Bendor, *Social Structure*, 131–32.
16. Bendor, *Social Structure*, 245–48.
17. Bendor, *Social Structure*, 232.
18. Bendor, *Social Structure*, 257–58
19. Chambon, *Tell el-Farʿah*, 39–44; cf. Fleischer, *Menschenverkäufer*, 393–94.
20. "les maisons patriciennes" and "les maisons pauvres."

WAS THERE A SOCIAL CRISIS IN THE EIGHTH CENTURY? 91

of construction, in which the poor houses continue an earlier tradition of rubble construction and are without foundations, while the patrician ones have two- or three-course foundations and use stones fitted carefully, with hewn stone on the corners. But the three poor houses are an isolated block, they do not constitute a quarter; and though there can be no question that the inhabitants were poorer, there is no way of knowing, as Fleischer points out, what their position in the town was.

2.3. Counter-Evidence

Bendor's one real positive piece of evidence for his sanguine view is in a couple of verses, 2 Kgs 15:19–20, which state that King Menahem of Israel paid for the tribute of 1000 talents of silver, which he had to pay to the king of Assyria, Tiglath-pileser III, here called by his Babylonian throne name Pul, by levying a poll tax of fifty shekels on each גבור חיל/*gibbor-hayil*. This expression is often taken to mean "man of wealth," as in the NRSV. But at 3,000 shekels to the talent the text implies that there were 60,000 such men in the kingdom: they are hardly wealthy men, therefore, and Bendor plausibly argues that these are the heads of each בית אב/*bet av*, however poor, and that their number is evidence of the health of the social system: Israel is still a society of independent families working their own land and paying their own taxes.[21]

When we come to assess all these arguments, we shall see reason to doubt whether this one short text will bear the weight that Bendor wishes to place on it. However, there are more substantial arguments, especially those drawn from the archaeological evidence.

Already in 1982 de Geus was pointing out that the apparent evidence from Tell el-Farʿah was unique; at Tell es-Sebaʿ Level 2 is contemporary with de Vaux's Level 2 at Tell el-Farʿah, and it consists of housing uniform in size.[22] Fleischer surveyed the available evidence in 1989 and came to the same conclusion.[23] We have now a most valuable survey article by John S. Holladay on Israel and Judah down to 750, though in fact on this particular issue taking the story down to the end of the kingdoms. Holladay comes to the same conclusion on a much broader front.[24]

> The pattern of residence in four- and three-roomed houses clearly designed to house livestock, process crops and store

---

21. Bendor, *Social Structure*, 226.
22. De Geus, "Gesellschaftskritik," 53–54.
23. Fleischer, *Menschenverkäufer*, 394–401.
24. [And Faust, *Archaeology*, should now be consulted: see chapter 7.]

> agricultural produce on a family-by-family basis (as opposed to redistributive mechanisms involving communal store facilities) is . . . unvarying from Early Israel down through the late eighth-century highland and Shephelah materials. . . . As far as we . . . know similar residence patterns continued, though less well documented in terms of excavated remains, on down to the final destruction of the Judaean state in 586–582 BCE.[25]

Further, "no residence from Iron II Palestine outstrips the average 'four-room house' by much more than a factor of two, or three at the outside."[26] Where we find smaller houses, they are often squeezed into the courtyard space of larger ones, and Holladay supposes that these would be explained within the *bet av* structure as space found for a house for a son or younger brother on family land within an increasingly crowded fortified village. There is no evidence of one- or two-room hovels or of workers' barracks. Holladay lays stress on the function of these houses as not just residences but, even more, as storehouses, with a capacity in each of more than 15 cubic meters (530 cubic feet). The total storage capacity of a village of 100 houses would be "3.75 times as much as the estimated capacity of the Area G Silo at Hazor and 3.33 times as much as Storage Pit 1414 at Megiddo, the two largest store facilities yet demonstrated for ancient Israel."[27]

What this means, in Holladay's words, is that "Israel was emphatically not a 'redistributive economy,'"[28] that is, one in which all surpluses are controlled by the central power and redistributed to its functionaries and supporters—or even to the population as a whole, though, *pace* Holladay, I do not think anyone has suggested that Israel was a redistributive economy in that extreme sense. It is the peasant houses just described that were "the 'Storehouses of Israel,'" not any government facilities.[29] However, Holladay is quite ready to admit the pressure of debts, tithes, and taxes on the peasant household, and indeed even mounts an argument[30] for increased agricultural specialization, which would be a sign of control over the economy, or of individual farmers, at a level above the peasant family or village. D. C. Hopkins has stressed the importance of diversity as a risk-spreading technique for the highland peasant.[31] For our own purposes, we may state the conclusion

---

25. Holladay, *Kingdoms*, 392.
26. Holladay, *Kingdoms*, 392.
27. Holladay, *Kingdoms*, 393.
28. Holladay, *Kingdoms*, 393.
29. Holladay, *Kingdoms*, 393.
30. Holladay, *Kingdoms*, 389–91.
31. Hopkins, *Highlands*, 213–61.

rather differently: there is no archaeological evidence for any elements of the rural population living in abject poverty, and particularly no evidence for any dramatic change in the conditions of life during the eighth century or at any other period prior to the final downfall of the respective kingdoms.

3. Responses

I shall take the arguments we have reviewed in reverse order, so we begin with the archaeology.

3.1. Responses to the Counter-evidence

It is important to be clear about what Holladay's argument shows and what it does not show. It shows that Israelite peasants continued to build their houses in a traditional style and had the resources to do so to the traditional standard, with their 15 cubic meters of storage space. Excavators can show or estimate the amount of storage space in a house. They cannot show how much of that space was used in any given year. We can tell how much wealth the family was hoping for; we cannot tell how far reality fell short of their expectations.

Moreover, it is not always possible for archaeology to reveal the social relationships subsisting between the inhabitants of these houses. It is not possible to tell how many adjacent houses, or possibly non-adjacent ones, may have belonged to a single *bet av*, so that the relative strength of one *bet av* against another cannot be estimated, nor how that may have changed over time. A peasant might lose his children to creditors, as in Nehemiah 5, and still be living in the same house; he might go on to lose his land, work it as a debt-slave, and hand over a substantial part of the harvest to his lord. He would still need some of that storage space for what was left. There are many forms of dependency that do not require the existence of one- or two-room hovels or workers' barracks.

Further, in any crisis of the kind hypothesized there is always a proportion of the poor who fail beyond dependency into destitution, who become what Gerhard Lenski, in his classic study of social stratification, calls "expendables," "ranging from petty criminals and outlaws to beggars and underemployed itinerant workers."[32] And such people leave no trace of their existence that archaeology can uncover.

Holladay does also note the existence, alongside the traditional villages, of places dominated by a single household, such as ʿIzbet Ṣarṭah, stratum 2.

---

32. Lenski, *Power*, 281.

He suggests that this might be a land grant to a palace retainer.[33] Moreover, in all the general statements he makes about settlement characteristics and residence size, he excepts the capitals and government centers, places such as Samaria, Jerusalem, Lachish, or Megiddo. Thus, Holladay is not to be read as saying that monarchic Israel and Judah remained relatively equal societies. He is only saying that the village communities were relatively equal societies.[34] The ruling classes resident in the capitals and other major centers quite certainly lived on a much grander scale, and some at least of their wealth will have been extracted from the villages.

Moreover, in all the statements he makes about retention of produce in the houses of the people, he excepts taxes, tithes, and debt services. Thus the materials are there in his own article for a conclusion rather different from his repudiation of the idea of a redistributive economy. This conclusion is secure only against an extreme form of redistribution, virtually caricatured by Holladay, in which the individual household retains nothing and waits for state handouts. As I have said, no one has suggested this. There is no question that redistribution was practiced in monarchical Israel and Judah. If they were states, they redistributed; that is what states do. And incidentally, evidence is there in Holladay's article that conclusively disproves the idea that Israel and Judah only became states in the ninth and eighth centuries respectively. What is in question is whether state exactions, as well as the impact of the credit system, increased to such an extent as to compromise the independence and viability of peasant households, as happened in Nehemiah's time.

It is not clear to me that that question is settled by the evidence surveyed by Holladay, and from Judah in the late eighth century there is other evidence that suggests a positive answer. One is the appearance of standardized shekel weights.[35] This implies an increase in monetary transactions as opposed to barter, and probably in the number of exchange transactions overall. The increased monetization of the economy is not good news for subsistence peasants. Whatever payments they must make to the outside world, taxes, loan repayments, payment for goods, are assessed in monetary units mostly after the harvest when the prices of their produce are at their lowest, while loans that they take out are necessarily made when prices are high.

Another is the well-known prevalence of jar handles inscribed למלך/ *lammelek*, "the king's." These finds are confined to late eighth-century contexts. While there are in detail a number of interpretations of this

---

33. Holladay, *Kingdoms*, 391. See Finkelstein, *'Izbet Ṣarṭah*, 12–14, 201. But this is much earlier than the eighth century: Finkelstein, its excavator, dates it to the tenth century.

34. [So also Faust, *Archaeology*, 128–77.]

35. Hopkins, "Bare Bones," 138.

phenomenon, it is unquestionable that it shows that the crown was disposing of large quantities of oil or wine or both, either as taxes or from its own estates; and the four localities also referred to on the handles appear to be central collection points for the produce.[36] This may well be an exceptional measure at the time of Hezekiah's revolt against Assyria, but it illustrates the resources that the crown could command.

This is one of a number of signs of increased specialization in agriculture surveyed by Hopkins,[37] including scores of wine and oil presses, and the isolated farmsteads surveyed by Zwickel in parts of the Shephelah and the fringes of the Judean wilderness dating from the late eighth century, which he interprets as estate farmsteads for the royal domains.[38] Hopkins ascribes the ventures into this specialization to the royal estates, obviously, to royal retainers using their land grants profitably, and to wealthier farmers who could afford the investment required and the increased risk involved. He also notes that village pasture land on the steep hillsides usable for these fruit crops would have been sequestered for this purpose, thus damaging the peasants' ability to spread their own risk.[39]

There seems to be enough evidence to enable us to say that there were latifundia in some areas. But the buildings surveyed by Zwickel are in relatively marginal areas. We can say with reasonable assurance on the basis of the evidence of the villages that village land was never converted into latifundia in the proper sense, the sense the word bears in Roman history, of large tracts worked by slaves, without free peasant inhabitants. That does not mean that the Isaiah and Micah texts on the subject are worthless, but we should be careful how we interpret them. The evidence does not exclude estates being built up out of the former holdings of free peasants who continued to work the land in a state of dependency.

We now turn to Bendor's interpretation of 2 Kgs 15:19–20. This text gives the appearance of being an archival note and therefore has a prima facie claim to reliability. But it does need testing. To support its plausibility, Bendor points to an inscription by an earlier Assyrian king, Adad-nirari III, reporting his exaction of 2,300 talents of silver and twenty of gold from the king of Damascus.[40] But the 1,000 talents is not the only figure that has to be tested for plausibility. In the first place, it is hardly plausible that such a round figure as fifty shekels should bring in exactly the three million

---

36. The most recent discussion is in Fox, *Service*, 216–35.
37. Hopkins, "Dynamics."
38. Zwickel, "Wirtschaftliche Grundlagen."
39. Hopkins, "Bare Bones" 133–34.
40. Bendor, *Social Structure*, 225, following Montgomery, *Kings*, 451.

shekels required, or that Menahem had a precise enough knowledge of his tax base to know that it would. Hence, the figure of 60,000 derived from the data can scarcely be relied on. It could be somewhere close to the truth, but it might be wildly out.

The latest estimate of the population of Palestine in the monarchical period, by Broshi and Finkelstein, suggests a figure for the kingdom of Israel of about 350,000.[41] This is for the total population of the entire area at any time claimed by the kingdom, and we cannot be certain that Menahem controlled the whole of it. If, therefore, the figure of 60,000, or anything near it, is correct, they could not be heads of *bate avot* but of nuclear families. Even so, it is rather on the high side, considering that the population figure includes slaves, paupers, *gerim*, and royal and official families, which were probably both large and exempt. But the smaller the units from which the tax was taken, the less likely it becomes that they could have paid it.

The fifty shekels is the most difficult figure to test. It is unlikely that the text should be understood literally, that every man had to stump up fifty shekels in silver (about 565 grams). Rather, although the tax was denominated in silver, it would have been paid in kind, in agricultural produce. What proportion of a nuclear family's annual requirements might this represent? To answer that, we need to know the exchange rate, the standard prices of staple commodities. The only evidence I know of is the story in 2 Kings 6–7 of the siege of Samaria and the prophecy by Elisha that "by tomorrow wheat flour will be sold for one shekel the seah and barley at a shekel for two" (2 Kgs 7:1). One would assume these prices represent a minimum for a time of plenty. They are, at least the first is, for flour, not for the raw produce, which makes a reliable estimate difficult. The annual dietary requirement for an adult subsisting mainly on bread is between 200 and 300 kilos of wheat, which unmilled would fill about seventeen to twenty-five seahs. However, one must remember that the total produce of a working rural family went to feed their animals as well as themselves. Holladay quotes a minimum figure of 1,800 kilos of wheat and 1,080 kilos of barley for a family of five, based on research on peasant agriculture in modern Iran, where the conditions are comparable.[42] But even so we can safely say that fifty shekels would represent a substantial proportion of their requirements, if paid in grain, and this would be on top of existing taxes and other exactions. Because of the higher value of olive oil and wine than grain it would be easier to pay in these kinds, provided that the family had sufficient available. But all things

---

41. Broshi and Finkelstein, "Population," 54.
42. Holladay, *Kingdoms*, 387.

considered it seems more likely that a tax at such a rate would have been levied on *bet av* heads rather than on householders.

But there cannot have been more than about 20,000 of those at the very most. The text is therefore unlikely to be correct in the implication that the entire tribute was laid off on the *gibbore-hayil*. Menahem may have raised a million shekels or so from this tax, and found the rest in some other way. The text therefore does not give us reliable statistical information about the social structure of the kingdom of Israel in its last years. But I think we can say that, whatever the precise numbers, it would appear, assuming only that the figures of 1,000 talents and fifty shekels are correct, that there was still a reasonably large peasant body subsisting in juridical independence and some way above destitution, such that the state could have some prospects of obtaining a return on an extraordinary tax. Anything more than this is speculation.

3.2. Response to Bendor's Interpretation of the Texts

What are we then to make of Bendor's interpretation of the prophetic texts? He has made a plausible case, and taken on its own it is hard to refute it. However, he has not dealt with all the evidence. The book of Amos contains a great deal more on this subject than the two texts that he deals with, and apart from 2:6–8, whose addressees are unclear, most of it is clearly directed at groups who live in the capital city or are otherwise obviously wealthy or associated with the ruling class. Thus: "Assemble yourselves on Mount Samaria . . . what oppressions are in its midst . . . those who store up violence and robbery in their strongholds" (3:9); "you cows of Bashan who are on Mount Samaria" (4:1); "because you exact taxes from the poor and take from them levies of grain" (5:11).[43] Whether the exactions attacked here are taxes, rent, tithes, or loan repayments, they must be exacted by those who have acquired, legitimately or not, a title to them: tax collectors, landlords, priests, or creditors; and they can also determine by their corruptly used power the outcome of legal cases (v. 12b). The people denounced in 8:4–5, generally referred to as merchants, are certainly not members of the village community, and Marlene Fendler and Rainer Kessler have made a good case that they are actually the same class of people as are addressed elsewhere,

---

43. The word בושסכם in 5:11, translated "you trample" in NRSV, is now widely interpreted (repointed *bošĕkem*) as "you exact taxes," on the basis of an Akkadian verb. Shalom Paul discusses this and other suggestions for its interpretation (Paul, *Amos*, 172–73), and that just mentioned and adopted above certainly seems the most convincing.

large landowners selling, or Kessler would suggest lending, their grain to those with insufficient supply of their own.[44]

Again, while the texts in Micah 2 are filled with difficulties and could be interpreted the way Bendor suggests, Micah 3 is quite unambiguous in addressing "you heads of Jacob and rulers of the house of Israel" (v. 1, and v. 9 is similar). This chapter in plain and furious terms accuses the rulers of Judah of exploiting their people for their own gain, and other elite groups of corruption.

Finally, in Isaiah, even if Bendor's suggestion were to be accepted about 3:14 and 5:8, both texts stand in contexts that are concerned with the rich or with issues of government. This is particularly clear in ch. 5, the better articulated of the two contexts, where 5:8–10 is the first of a series of woes of which several are unambiguously directed at the ruling class.

The conclusion must be that the social criticism in these three prophets is clearly addressed to ruling groups or groups associated with the ruling class in most of the contexts concerned with the issue. This makes it less likely that in the few texts reinterpreted by Bendor a different set of culprits is in view. They thus represent a protest against exploitation by these groups, at a level regarded by the speakers in the text as unacceptable. One must remember that in most societies where there are differences of wealth associated with leadership in the community, the community will bear without complaint exactions that do not exceed traditional levels and that are clearly balanced by benefits received.[45] But when the ruling elite breaks this unwritten compact and threatens to drive its subjects beyond their normal poverty into destitution, or to undermine their ability to maintain their traditional honor and independence, then complaint and perhaps rebellion will break out. These prophetic texts demonstrate that that point had been reached, and if that is how we define a social crisis, and it seems a reasonable definition, then they bear witness to a social crisis. They cannot, however, show on their own that a major transfer of resources had already taken place, resulting in the reduction of the peasant masses in general to dependency or destitution; and the other evidence we have reviewed is rather against that supposition.

---

44. Fendler, "Sozialkritik," 50; Kessler, "Kornhändler." [However, I now prefer Fleischer's proposal that they are crown officials in charge of the urban grain supply (Houston, *Contending*, 64–65; Fleischer, *Menschenverkäufer*, 192).]

45. [Kippenberg, "Entlassung," 75; Houston, *Contending*, 11–12.]

3.3. Reviewing the Setting of the Prophetic Texts

But we have yet to show that these texts date from the eighth century. We must bear in mind Ben Zvi's most persuasive objections, which can easily be extended beyond the texts of Micah that he studies: that the primary object of the editors was not to reproduce eighth-century prophetic speeches, and that it is unlikely that in the transition from the oral to the written medium they would be reproduced accurately; that it was necessary for them to create an image of a sinful Israel; and that they were not themselves interested in reconstructing eighth-century history.

These objections concentrate on the motives and methods of the editors of the texts, and I judge them persuasive in themselves. It is not, I think, possible to argue successfully that the texts are precisely what they claim to be, that is, respectively "the vision of Isaiah the son of Amoz which he saw concerning Judah and Jerusalem"; "the words of Amos which he saw concerning Israel"; and "the word of the LORD which came to Micah of Moresheth which he saw concerning Samaria and Jerusalem." The redaction critics have done their work, and it cannot be undone. However, we may reasonably assume that the editors used material that they believed to represent the words of the prophets under whose name they were writing. Whether they really did has to be shown in each case. Are there features in these texts or their contexts that betray an eighth-century origin and that are unlikely to be the contribution of the editors?

Other contributions to the seminar series in which this chapter was originally given as a paper addressed this question on a broader front in respect of Isaiah and Amos.[46] Hans Barstad, whose contribution on Amos was not included in the resulting volume, argued that the oracles against the nations as a series address a situation that could not have recurred after the eighth century. Damascus was stripped of its independence in 732 BCE, and Israel ten years later. Most of the other states in the series continued to exist in one form or another, but the fact that the series begins with Damascus and ends with Israel is significant. The geopolitical viewpoint of the creator of the series is an eighth-century one. "Israel," we should note, in Amos normally means the kingdom of Israel. The editors were aware of this; that is why when they wished to include Judah they specifically said so, as in the awkward addition to Amos 3:1: "against the whole family which I brought up from the land of Egypt."

These are large-scale features of the text that may be thought to have little direct relevance to the texts we are concerned with. But first of all, the accusation against Israel in Amos 2:6–8 is an integral part of the oracles

---

46. [Cf. Williamson, "Pre-Exilic Isaiah."]

against the nations series, which we have identified as being of eighth-century origin, and its main elements cannot be later than the composition of the series, although it may contain additions. Secondly, some of the other accusations later in the book are addressed, as we have already seen, to the inhabitants of Samaria: in fact, it is precisely the accusations of social injustice in Amos where the connection with Samaria is most deeply embedded. The references to Samaria in the book occur at Amos 3:9, 12; 4:1; 6:1; and 8:14. Only the last of these seems to have no relevance to this issue; Amos 3:9 and 4:1 introduce accusations of oppressive conduct, and Amos 6:1 an accusation of the complacent enjoyment of luxury; Amos 3:12 is in an oracle of judgment. Amos 3:9–11 is an oracle against the city of Samaria itself, "and the tumults and oppressions within it," and the "cows of Bashan" oracle is also closely tied up with the city. Amos 6:1 creates a problem with its parallel mention of Zion, which, as Wolff emphasizes, is contrary to the book's practice elsewhere;[47] yet it makes a far more convincing text than any of the proposed emendations.[48] But even if we suppose the entire oracle, Amos 6:1–7, to be subsequent to Amos (Wolff sees only "at ease in Zion" as secondary), it is still anchored in the pre-722 world, like all these oracles, by its reference to Samaria. Samaria ceased to be the seat of the ruling class of the state of Israel in that year. The references to it in Amos, if they do not bear witness to the composition of these texts before its fall, can only be explained as an elaborate fiction, which I do not choose to regard as a probable explanation of the emergence of prophetic literature.

The book of Isaiah of course includes many references to eighth-century history with every appearance of contemporaneity, but they are probably of limited use for validating the eighth-century origin of the texts we are concerned with, for most of them are in the so-called *Denkschrift* or "memoir," Isa 6:1—9:6 (English 9:7), or in later parts of the book, whereas the denunciations of oppression occur in Isaiah 3, 5, and 10. However, a line of approach similar to the one we took with Amos may work. The careful reader of Isaiah 1–12 will be struck by the rarity with which the name "Israel" is used compared with later prophets, including of course Isaiah 40–55, except in the divine name "The holy one of Israel" and the similar expressions, "the mighty one of Israel" (Isa 1:24) and "the light of Israel" (10:17). "Israel" is used as the name of the northern kingdom in Isa 9:8, 12 and 14 (Heb. 9:7, 11, and 13). Isaiah 10:22 and 11:16 are generally regarded as secondary, even by Wildberger.[49] That leaves four examples. In Isa 1:3, "Israel does not know,

---

47. Wolff, *Dodekapropheton* II, 314–15; =*Joel and Amos*, 269–70.
48. See Paul, *Amos*, 199, n. 2.
49. Wildberger, *Jesaja 1–12*, 413–14, 466–67; *Isaiah 1–12*, 435–36, 489–90.

my people does not consider," and Isa 8:18, "signs and portents in Israel," the whole nation is surely in view, as it obviously is in the phrase "the two houses of Israel" in Isa 8:14, and in the divine titles. The remaining text is Isa 5:7, "the vineyard of YHWH of hosts is the house of Israel, and the men of Judah are his pleasant planting." Isaiah's usage elsewhere should now convince us that the parallelism here does not imply that "Israel" is being used as a synonym for Judah, as so often happens in later prophets, but rather probably refers to the northern kingdom, as in Isaiah 9, or at least includes it, as in Isa 8:14. On this point I disagree with Wildberger. Gray seems in two minds about it, and other commentators I have consulted do not refer to the problem.[50] I would thus argue that the usage of this national name mainly reflects the pre-722 political situation.

But 5:7 of course is the central text for Isaiah's social message. It does not refer to evil doings in general. The pairing of משפט/*mishpat* and צדקה/*tsedaqa*, as a hendiadys in prose or in parallelism in verse, is a standard expression for what we call social justice.[51] It is what kings are expected to provide for the poor of their kingdoms: see for example Psalm 72 or Jer 22:15. And this is what was missing in the vineyard of Israel-Judah. Editorially, the parable of the vineyard has been placed next to the woes, which specify this lack in detail, and the first of these is the accusation against those who accumulate land. Naturally we cannot argue from this juxtaposition that because Isa 5:7 can be traced to the eighth century Isa 5:8 must also be of that date. But I have shown, I believe, that the early chapters of Isaiah contain material with a social concern dating from that century, and that is perhaps all that can be asked.

The same may be true of Micah. The text here does use "Israel" in a way I have suggested Isaiah does not, in referring to the Jerusalem governing circles as "chiefs of the house of Israel" (Mic 3:1, 9). But there is an oracle against Samaria (Mic 1:5–7), and Mic 3:12 is quoted by the elders in Jer 26:18. Here we touch on an issue mentioned by Williamson in connection with Isaiah, in the volume from which the present chapter is drawn.[52] It will hardly cut any ice with the minimalists, since if the Jeremiah account is itself from the Second Temple period, the prophecy that it quotes

---

50. Wildberger, *Jesaja 1–12*, 171–72; *Isaiah 1–12*, 184. Gray, *Isaiah 1–27*, 87. [Williamson, *Isaiah 1–5*, 342–43, argues that the term is inclusive and "Judah" is a closer specification.]

51. Weinfeld, *Social Justice*, 25–44. But Miranda had already pointed this out long before (*Marx and the Bible*, 93, with all the Old Testament passages listed at 107, nn. 35, 36), referring in his turn to earlier, unnamed, exegetes. [See also chapters 3, 40–41, and 10, in the present volume.]

52. [Williamson, "Pre-Exilic Isaiah," 191–95.]

could be so also, presumably. But any possible account of literary history that made the Micah text post-exilic would be so strained and convoluted as to be untenable. The minimum conclusion from Jer 26:18 is that the traditionists who wrote the story, probably in the sixth century, had a text of Micah at their disposal, which they understood to be of Hezekian date. And it surely must be earlier than the fall of the city, from the argument from unfulfilled prophecy. It is not true (yet) that Jerusalem ever became a ploughed field or a wooded height (Mic 3:12). Thus the prophecy is formulated in a way that would not naturally have occurred to anyone familiar with Jerusalem's condition after its fall.

We may add that Ben Zvi's argument à propos of Mic 2:1-5 may be countered by another of Williamson's arguments about Isaiah.[53] Where redactional activity is demonstrated by a change in the point of view within a passage, there must be a diachronic process. The presupposition of the addition, if it is one, of "on that day ..." in v. 4 is that the nucleus of the text dates from before the fall of Jerusalem.

We conclude therefore that the books of Isaiah, Amos, and Micah contain material dating ultimately to the eighth century which bears witness to a marked deterioration in social conditions and relationships in the latter half of that century at the latest.

4. Why the Eighth Century?

However, this deterioration was not severe enough, or more likely not continued long enough, owing to the annihilation of the kingdom of Israel and the catastrophic curtailment of the territory of Judah, to leave any direct material evidence. Hence we should try to support this conclusion by asking whether there are any discoverable reasons why such a deterioration might have occurred just at this time.

There are in fact more than one. We can suggest both internal and external pressures working in combination. Fleischer suggests that an important factor was overpopulation resulting in people trying to squeeze a living from smaller and smaller patches of land, which would, of course, make them more vulnerable to exactions.[54] Traditional ways of dealing with this problem would include forming new settlements within the land, expanding into new land, particularly across the Jordan, emigration, enlisting as mercenaries with foreign armies, or indeed the army of Israel, and drifting to the cities in the usually vain hope of bettering oneself. Some of

---

53. [Williamson, "Pre-Exilic Isaiah," 195-96.]
54. Fleischer, *Menschensverkäufer*, 370-85.

these avenues always remained open; but others closed down over time, and it is particularly relevant to observe that the expansion southwards of the Aramean kingdom of Damascus in the late ninth century cut off much of the land available for settlement. Jeroboam's reconquest of this area should have eased the situation. But contrary to the view expressed by Albertz (see above) and endlessly recycled in introductions to Amos, this reign shows no evidence of increased prosperity. De Geus points out that there is no evidence of new monumental building in Israel or Judah after the end of the ninth century, and there is continued stagnation in pottery styles down to the end of the kingdoms.[55] More recently, a state of stagnation or decline in the eighth century has been confirmed for Hazor by its excavator Amnon Ben-Tor.[56] Despite Fleischer's suggestion that there was no particular further need for monumental building,[57] none of this suggests a burgeoning economy. It is easy to see why the economy might be in decline. The rise of Assyrian power in the west explains almost everything, as de Geus suggests.[58] It demanded both higher expenditure on defense and, as under Menahem, an outflow of precious metals and other valuables in tribute. Micah 2:1-2 may reflect specific confiscatory measures taken by Hezekiah's government to prepare for war against Assyria.[59] The resources had to be extracted from the only ultimate source of wealth in an agrarian commonwealth, the wretched cultivators of the soil.

This scenario accounts far more convincingly for their increased exploitation than the standard picture of burgeoning prosperity. There is one quite general reason for this. As Lenski shows, ruling classes in agrarian societies always strive to secure the whole of the agricultural surplus, that is, what is left after the cultivators have met their basic needs.[60] Hence a rise in the level of exploitation beyond this would need to be induced by specific factors such as a rise in external demands made upon the ruling class, and therefore would not necessarily lead to a rise in the net income of the latter.

But there may also be a quite specific reason, peculiar to this time and area. It is quite possible, as Holladay suggests with detailed evidence in support, that the kingdoms for some time met their expenses to some or

---

55. De Geus, "Gesellschaftskritik," 54–55.
56. [Ben-Tor, *Hazor*, 166: "In comparison to the state of the city in the ninth century BCE, in the eighth century one sees the beginning of decline."]
57. Fleischer, *Menschensverkäufer*, 400.
58. De Geus, "Gesellschaftskritik," 55–56; [so also Ben-Tor, *Hazor*, 166.]
59. Wolff, *Dodekapropheton* II, 44; *Joel and Amos*, 74–75.
60. Lenski, *Power*, 266–71.

a large extent by tolls on the transit trade through Palestine.[61] But towards the end of the ninth century in Israel, rather later in Judah, first pressure from Damascus and then the Assyrians' seizure of control over the trade would have led to declining revenues from this source. At the same time, it became necessary to start paying tribute to Assyria. The only remaining source of finance was agricultural production, and taxes levied on it must have started to increase at this point, quite apart from extraordinary taxes like Menahem's poll tax. The more prosperous families would have been able to deal with the threat by specializing in higher value crops, especially oil, as we have seen. The less prosperous ones were faced with a serious and sometimes desperate situation that they could only deal with through the suicidal course of going into debt to their patrons, whether these were the heads of their own village or city-based landowners or officials. The failure of many of these to deal justly or humanely with those who had thus placed themselves in their power led to the protests that received permanent expression in the texts we have been studying.

We thus reach the conclusion that the eighth century in Israel and Judah offered the right conditions for the development of economic pressure on the peasantry sufficiently severe to be seen as unjust and denounced on that ground by texts in Isaiah, Amos, and Micah, some of which can be linked to that century. Such conditions certainly recurred on more than one later occasion, and were perhaps even more severe in the fifth century; hence we cannot date any specific text in these books to the eighth century simply on the grounds of its subject matter. But there *was* a social crisis in the eighth century.

---

61. Holladay, "Kingdoms," 383–86.

Chapter 7

Exit the Oppressed Peasant?

*Rethinking the Background of Social
Criticism in the Prophets*

(2010)

Introduction

IT IS AN ALMOST universally held assumption in the study of ancient society that where we hear of social oppression the principal victims will be the peasants, the subsistence farmers and agricultural workers of the countryside who formed the great majority of the population in nearly all ancient societies, while their oppressors will be largely found in the cities. This is certainly true of the models that have been used to explain the social oppression mentioned in the Hebrew Bible and denounced in the Prophets. I recently examined a number of these models.[1] The assumption is made the structural backbone of the "rent capitalism" model taken by Oswald Loretz from the geographer Hans Bobek and popularized in English by Bernhard Lang.[2] What is described here is characteristic of modem Middle Eastern societies, at least until recently: a dichotomy of society between the productive rural peasants who work the land as tenants and an unproductive urban bourgeoisie who live by extracting the maximum possible surplus as landlords from the production of the peasants. Though other models do not make this urban-rural split their foundation, they effectively incorporate it. Kippenberg's theory of the development of "ancient class society" locates the initial driving force in the attempt by an aristocracy to secure the fruits of the labor of the peasants for themselves by the use of credit. The aristocrats are not necessarily city-based, but in view of the complete absence of large country houses in ancient Palestine they must have been if the theory

---

1. Houston, *Contending*, 1st ed., 21–46; 2nd ed. (= *Contending* hereinafter), 26–48.
2. Loretz, "Rentenkapitalismus"; Bobek, "Hauptstufe"; Lang, "Social Organization."

is correct.³ The most popular model, certainly among American scholars, has been that of Gerhard Lenski's "agrarian society," in which the sole or only significant source of wealth is the labor of the rural cultivators, while their surplus (not less than 50 percent of total production) is redistributed from them by and to a governing class based principally in the cities, including the ruler and his officials, and often also an aristocracy.⁴

While in the first edition of *Contending for Justice* I devoted much care to attempting to identify the mechanisms of social oppression in the society of Israel and Judah and the elements that bore responsibility for it, I gave virtually none at all to identifying its *victims* as a class. I accepted the universal assumption as thoroughly as anyone. There is, however, evidence for the monarchic period that casts doubt upon the idea that the main victims were the cultivators, and that they were stripped of their entire surplus. This includes King Menahem's poll tax (2 Kgs 15:19–20), which was levied on all "men of substance" (גבורי חיל/*gibbore-hayil*) at a level and in numbers suggestive of substantial untapped surpluses in the rural economy,⁵ as well as the archaeological record of rural villages, where the size and quality of the dwelling houses gives no indication of impoverishment at any time down to the falls of the respective kingdoms.⁶

It is an illustration of the hold of the assumption on me that in an earlier article I set myself to explain this evidence away.⁷ A more interesting example comes from the first edition of my book,⁸ where I showed that the biblical text assumes that the characteristic relationship between rich and poor is that of patronage, and concluded that the most pervasive mechanism through which the poor were exploited was the abuse of this relationship. But it is essential to patronage that it is a face-to-face relationship.⁹ How then can this mechanism be invoked to explain the exploitation of people in villages by people in cities, who would rarely meet? Yet that is what I tried to do, by elaborating an image of a ruling class that included wealthy representatives of rural society as well as state officials based in the provinces. What I failed to notice is, for example, that the poor man in Deut 15:7–11 is "in one of your gates," that is to say in a *city*, for Deuteronomy uses "gates" by synecdoche for "cities," and although עיר/*'ir* in Biblical Hebrew can refer

---

3. Kippenberg, "Typik."
4. Lenski, *Power*, 189–296.
5. See above, chapter 6, 95–96.
6. Holladay, "Kingdoms," 392–93; and below in more detail.
7. Chapter 6 above.
8. Houston, *Contending*, 1st ed., 42–46.
9. Eisenstadt and Roniger, *Patrons*, 48–49.

to a settlement of any size, only real cities have gates. What exactly might be meant by a real city we shall come to in a moment.

In a series of articles, Avraham Faust has surveyed the results of the excavations of all types of settlement in Israel and Judah during the monarchical period in order to establish the nature of the society that inhabited them, and has summed up his conclusions in a recent book in Hebrew.[10] Most references here will be to his English-language articles.[11]

The result of Faust's researches is to establish a striking dichotomy in the society of monarchical Israel and Judah between cities and villages;[12] but although this conclusion in itself is in accord with the consensus, the dichotomy is of a rather different character than has been hitherto assumed. First, it is necessary to clarify what is meant by "village" and "city." "Cities" have been the object of the bulk of archaeological excavation work in the past, in that they form tells, which have attracted the attention of excavators, because the settlement has been rebuilt again and again on the same site, suggesting the perceived importance of having a city on that site. They are protected by defensive walls, which forces up the density of settlement. In Faust's view their defining social characteristics are social stratification and economic specialization.[13] Although they vary considerably in their significance as administrative and military centers, they are all characterized to a greater or lesser extent by the presence of the state, which will be evident at least in the defensive wall, a work beyond the capacity of the local community.[14]

Much less work has been done on the rural villages of this period, as their presence is not immediately evident on the ground, although they must have housed the great majority of the population. Many of the excavations that have been done have been salvage operations in advance of development. A village typically contains a few dozen dwelling houses, together with installations for the processing of agricultural products, such as a threshing floor and an oil press, and storage facilities. They are usually bounded by a

---

10. Faust, *Israelite Society* (2005). [See now his English-language version, Faust, *Archaeology*, which incorporates most of the material in the articles referred to in the following notes.]

11. For what follows, see also, in rather more detail, Houston, *Contending*, 19–25, which also depends on Faust. I should like to express my personal appreciation of Avi Faust's generosity in making the results of his research available to me, in reading and commenting on drafts of this essay and other work, and in guiding me to sources in the archaeological literature.

12. Faust, "Differences."

13. Faust, "Settlement," 44.

14. Fritz, *City*, 117.

wall of sorts, but not one that could withstand a siege, often incorporating the outer wall of the outermost houses.[15]

Faust's conclusions are based primarily on the size and quality of houses in these different types of settlement, and to a lesser extent on other finds. Most of the houses in both cities and villages are based on the traditional "four-room" type. In Israelite villages[16] these are of a generous size, with a ground area generally in the range 115 to 130 square meters; and it is clear that they also had a second story. Faust interprets the size of the houses, and the fact that they vary very much in the extent to which the rooms are subdivided, as an indication that each was the residence of an extended family, which would have been the work unit as well as the living unit.[17] Further, there is no sufficient difference in the size and quality of the dwelling houses, either within one site or between different sites of this type, to suggest any serious degree of social stratification. Of course, this does not exclude some differences of wealth. Thus, even if the villages of Israel were not equal societies, they show every sign of being egalitarian in outlook. This is underlined from a different aspect by the fact that the boundary wall, the storage facilities and installations such as oil presses do not belong to individual houses, but appear to have been constructed and operated communally.[18]

The quality of the houses in these villages, and the capacity of the storage facilities, suggest that they were prosperous, and that their work generated surpluses that were largely retained in the village and did not go to enrich a landlord.[19] Although they would certainly have had to pay taxes, these would have been at a level that they were capable of paying out of their surpluses. Faust's work with Ehud Weiss on the economy of the Levant in the seventh century suggests that these villages successfully competed in a regional market by specializing in particular products.[20]

A very different social picture is presented by the contemporary cities. Here the dwelling houses in general are smaller than in the villages. A study of Hazor VI revealed many houses with a ground area of about

---

15. Faust, "Rural Community," 26–28.

16. A different picture is presented by certain villages in the northern valleys, which Faust interprets as ethnically different from the majority population. For Faust, they show marked signs of being part of public or private estates. (Faust, "Ethnic Complexity"; *Israelite Society*, 256–83; [*Archaeology*, 230–54.]) [Further details in chapter 8 below, 122–23.]

17. Faust, "Differences," 243–47.

18. Faust, "Rural Community"; *Israelite Society*, 142–92; [*Archaeology*, 128–77.]

19. Faust, "Rural Community," 31–32.

20. Faust and Weiss, "Judah, Philistia."

seventy square meters, some larger, some smaller, and only a couple of comparable size with village houses, one of them a luxurious structure of 160 square meters, of good construction, with all its walls freestanding.[21] Faust divides the houses into three groups: the few houses of this kind that can be described as luxurious, a large group of quite modest four-room houses, in the seventy-square-meters range, and some poor structures that are smaller and not built on any regular plan, but simply squeezed into any available patch of land. He concludes that most of these, with the exception of the luxurious houses, would have been inhabited by nuclear families, so that there would be a substantial difference in basic social structure from the villages. The wide variation in the size and quality of the houses also shows a high degree of social stratification. Contrary to my earlier assertion that the situation uncovered by de Vaux at Tell el-Farʿah North had not been reproduced elsewhere,[22] it is now clear that this degree of variation is common in cities. They contained: a wealthy ruling elite, who were able to preserve the extended family structure; a middle class of lower officials, shopkeepers, service workers, and so forth, as well as farmers, as the cities all had land attached to them; and the poor who had been unable to find a secure foothold in the system, including the fatherless, widows, and aliens so frequently mentioned. Many of these would scrape a living as hired laborers; others, in attempting to maintain an independent existence, would have fallen into debt-slavery.

Most cities were founded on the basis of existing settlements, which had been selected for development by the state for administrative and strategic reasons.[23] This intervention appears to have normally led to a very rapid breakdown in the traditional social structure, as the traditional rule by the "elders," or heads of the extended families, was replaced by state control, and state officials settled with their families, while poorer elements flooded in to take advantage of the wealth and opportunities provided by the new foundation. The co-operative ethos of village society would have generally enabled the farming families to withstand the shock of hard times, and not require recourse to the moneylender, or at least to discharge their debts without disaster. But the new conditions of the cities gave rise to a more individualistic ethos and thus exposed everyone in humble circumstances, including the original farming population, to far greater risk of debt and exploitation. Thus, the evidence seems to suggest that the process of social stratification generally assumed for the ninth and eighth centuries indeed

---

21. Faust, "Socioeconomic Stratification."
22. Chapter 6 above, 91.
23. Fritz, *City*, 14.

took place, but rather than covering each kingdom as a whole, it was a piecemeal process that took place within each city, and so spread little by little across the land, until it was temporarily brought to a halt by the Assyrian and Babylonian conquests.

This sketch applies to conditions under the monarchy. On the other side of the caesura of the devastations and deportations, it is likely that things were different.

To an extent, Faust's view is vulnerable to the same criticisms as I have made of Holladay's similar understanding of the strength and security of the rural economy.[24] An analysis based on the size and quality of buildings can only give a picture of social relationships over the long term. It cannot take account of sudden or rapid changes in absolute or relative wealth. As I said there, the size of storage facilities shows us what surpluses farmers expected to house; it does not show us what surpluses they actually had. Nor does it reveal the relationships of power between village families, at least in the short term. Some social differences could be hidden within houses built in happier days. It is possible that there were quite rapid social changes in the second half of the eighth century, especially under the impact of the Assyrian demand for tribute, and it is not clear that the archaeological record can rule this out. But in truth, the double picture given by Faust makes such reservations less necessary; for the society of the cities is likely to offer a perfectly adequate context for all, or nearly all, that we know or think we know about inequality, patronage, and oppression in the period of the monarchy—subject to the detailed interrogation of individual texts, which we shall come to.

A deeper weakness of Faust's treatment of social relationships in the period of the monarchy is that he treats urban and rural society quite separately, virtually as independent worlds that had little or nothing to do with each other. But it is obvious that this cannot be true. Village residents must have been subject to tax and tithe and military service, and in Judah to the corvée. The cities were nourished on their produce, whether they were requisitioned as tax or bought in the market. Such flourishing communities as are depicted in Faust's picture of the villages would have produced a surplus of population, and it is clear that not all children of the village could have stayed there. There were various shifts to which those who left could have resorted. They could have founded new villages or enlisted for mercenary service; but many would have left for the cities. It is likely that many of the destitute people to whom Deuteronomy urges generosity were incomers from the villages, so that the oppressed peasant may not after all need to

---

24. Chapter 6 above, 93–94.

leave the stage: he or she is there in the city, being "pushed aside in the gate" (Amos 5:12), perhaps literally;[25] this is in addition to the fact that the cities contained farming populations vulnerable to exploitation. Of course, there may also have been upward mobility. The official class must have been recruited from somewhere. Moreover, at least some of those who found their way to the cities may not have left their villages of their own accord. The eldest son of a father had an advantage in the inheritance, and it is likely that the further down the birth order a son was, the more likely he was to be subject to pressure to leave.[26]

In brief, the concept of social stratification must cover the entire society, not merely individual settlements. None of Faust's evidence challenges the view that the villages, as well as the lower classes of the cities, were subject to the official class, and that the balance of redistribution did not favor them. What it does is to refine our understanding of how redistribution operated in societies like those of the Hebrew kingdoms, which, it is evident, were not fully mature agrarian kingdoms, but developing towards that condition: that is, that the consequent inequity is more pronounced within the cities than between the cities and the villages, and evidence for it is more obtrusive in the cities. This may have a bearing on how we understand prophetic texts, which is the object of this essay. I will here make the initial working assumption that most of the texts on this subject in Isaiah 1–12, Jeremiah, Ezekiel, Amos, Micah 1–3, and Zephaniah are of monarchical date.

Faust himself has attempted to address this question.[27] However, he spends relatively little time on the texts themselves, and gives specific attention only to Jeremiah. His general point is that the prophets, with some minor exceptions, worked in cities, mostly Jerusalem and Samaria, and engaged with the reality before their eyes, which was one of extreme social stratification. Here I should remark that stratification is not the same thing as oppression, or at least, not the same thing that the prophetic texts identify as oppression. What the prophets denounce is specific acts of exploitation, expropriation, corrupt justice, and violence.[28] The importance of a stratified society is that by making some of its members weaker than others it invites the unscrupulous to commit such acts and enables them to succeed.

Faust is interested in possible exceptions to the rule that the prophets worked in the cities, because, he hopes, it may enable him in addition to provide textual evidence to support his conclusion from the archaeological

25. [See Faust, *Archaeology*, 103–4, and below.]
26. Bendor, *Social Structure*, 175–90.
27. Faust, "Prophetic Social Criticism"; [*Archaeology*, 265–66.]
28. Houston, *Contending*, 86–93.

evidence that there was no social stratification in the villages. He relies on work by Benjamin Uffenheimer,[29] who claims to be able to distinguish oracles uttered by Jeremiah while still in Anathoth, before settling in Jerusalem, from those delivered in Jerusalem, in that the latter use images from city life rather than only rural life and the wilderness. The former make no mention of social evils but are exclusively concerned with apostasy and idolatry. It was when he moved to the city that he came across such evils as the oppression of the poor.

I have not been able to test this case in detail, since I have not had access to Uffenheimer's work, and Faust gives only one brief quotation from it. However, it does not immediately inspire conviction. The images in Jeremiah's poetry are predominantly taken from nature and rural life in all parts of the book where the poetry occurs. But at the same time, Jerusalem is frequently the backdrop of the prophecy, whereas Anathoth never is, perhaps not even in Jer 11:21–23, for the men of Anathoth could have come to attack Jeremiah in Jerusalem. Further, the book is so dominated by the image of Jeremiah as prophet to the city before its fall that the suggestion that parts have a background in Anathoth is impossible to demonstrate convincingly, possible though it may be thought to be. It may readily be granted that the few Jeremian passages denouncing social oppression (Jer 2:34; 5:20–29; 7:1–7; 22:13–19; 34:8–22) are at home in an urban context, though, for example, the victims of Jehoiakim's corvée (22:13) are almost certain to have included people from rural areas. But that the very many passages denouncing apostasy include some where the culprits are villagers is undemonstrable. The address is invariably to the nation as a whole, which suggests a capital-city point of view.

In what follows I limit myself to texts that clearly deal with oppression of the poor. I shall identify texts that are explained better if the victims are understood as city-dwellers, and those where definitely agrarian distress seems to be referred to. It should not necessarily be concluded in the latter case that the victims are villagers, for all cities, as I have noted, retained agricultural land worked by peasants or others who lived in the cities. The majority of texts, however, do not present features distinct enough to enable a judgment. On this basis, it may be possible to arrive at an estimate of how well Faust's theory accounts for the prophetic texts on this subject.

---

29. Uffenheimer, "Urbanization." [I regret that in the original publication of this essay I mistakenly gave Uffenheimer's name as Oppenheimer, misreading the Hebrew spelling.]

2. Amos

Turning first to Amos, there is one text that immediately leaps to the eye after the foregoing discussion. "Gather on the hills of Samaria and see the great tumults *within* it [Samaria], and the oppressions *within its midst*" (Amos 3:9). The oppression is "within" Samaria, which would be taken most naturally to mean that the victims as well as the perpetrators are in Samaria.

Another text in Amos that is most naturally taken of goings-on in an urban context is Amos 8:4–6, the denunciation of the grain dealers. I formerly favored the theory of Kessler and Fendler that the dealers here are actually landowners selling their own surplus crops.[30] But the only strong reason for preferring this is simply that this apparently enables the setting to be a rural one. In fact, most grain dealing would have taken place in the city markets, probably under state control, and conceivably as a crown monopoly.[31] Poor city residents who did not have their own land, as well as farmers specializing in wine or oil production, would have had to rely on them for their food supply, and would have had to go into debt if they could not afford it: and this is how they could be "bought" by the dealers, as v. 6 asserts. The similar reference to commercial sharp practice in Mic 6:9–12 is explicitly located in a "city" (v. 9), presumably Jerusalem.

Again, there is more than one reference to the "gate" in Amos: 5:10, 12, 15 all mention the gate. "Who turn aside the poor in the gate" could be meant literally, because poor people in cities actually lived there, according to Faust.[32] "They hate him who reproves in the gate" and "Establish justice in the gate" have the court in the city gate as their setting: and this probably means the court of a royal judge rather than the court of the elders generally favored by commentators.

Of course, this is not to say that the victims of oppression in Amos are never peasants. "You take a levy of grain from him" (5:11), whatever the nature of the levy, suggests a victim who has grain to be levied. But, as I have pointed out, peasants did live in the cities, though they were not the only poor inhabitants.

The remainder of the texts in Amos are not clear enough to contribute much to this discussion, but their interpretation may well be affected by it. The poor people oppressed by the "cows of Bashan on the hill of Samaria," rather than being the producers of the wine that the wives of the officials and

---

30. Houston, *Contending* 1st ed., 64; cf. Kessler, "Kornhändler"; Fendler, "Sozialkritik," 42.

31. [Fleischer, *Menschenverkäufer*, 192.]

32. Faust, *Israelite Society*, 113–16 [= *Archaeology*, 103–4. More on this in chapter 12 below, 195.]

courtiers demand, could well be persons more immediately in the eye of a visitor to the city, the debt-slaves and laborers who served them personally. (They would probably also have had chattel slaves, but these would not be described as "poor.") However, Samaria's wine was probably produced quite locally—some of the Samaria ostraca refer to place names that we know from the Bible as clans of Manasseh—and it is not impossible that at least some of the vineyards in the vicinity of Samaria were owned by members of the governing cadre and run with hired labor or debt slaves.[33]

At all events, it would be difficult to show that any text in Amos concerning social injustice requires any other geographical context than Samaria and its environs.

3. Isaiah

In a similar way, most of the texts attacking social oppression in Isaiah and Micah allow or indeed require Jerusalem as their geographical context. I will discuss Isa 5:8-10 and Mic 2:1-5, the sole prophetic texts mentioning the seizure of land, later.

Isaiah 1:21-26 concerns the administration of justice in the courts in Jerusalem ("How the faithful city has become a harlot!"), and accuses the judges, who are royal officials, of corruption, and denounces their consequent failure to protect widows and orphans, who of course stand by convention for all vulnerable and unprotected victims of oppression. In ordinary circumstances it is likely that such complainants would take their cases to the nearest royal court. Such courts would have existed in all the fortified cities (2 Chr 19:5), and we should assume that the victims of judicial corruption in Jerusalem lived in the city or its immediate neighborhood. Some of them might be country people, but most, in view of the size of the city, would be townspeople. The context is very similar in Isa 10:1-4, where widows and orphans again appear as the victims of official maladministration. In this case, the officials seem to be accused of getting their hands on the disputed property themselves, which may suggest that it is not a question of poor families here. In this case, there is no specific reference to Jerusalem, but it seems likely that the officials are Jerusalem-based. It is possible that disputes within village families that came to court did offer an avenue by which officials on the make could insinuate themselves into village property. But the archaeological evidence suggests that if this happened it was not on a large scale, except perhaps in the vicinity of Jerusalem, as we may see below.

33. [See Fox, *Service*, 211-12.]

A nationwide situation is again in view in Isa 3:13–15, but the victims, apart from being poor, are not further identified. The accusation "you have despoiled [or trampled] the vineyard" is taken metaphorically by most commentators, in the light of the parable in Isa 5:1–7, and I would tend to agree with this, though Blenkinsopp thinks it is possible to understand it literally at the same time.[34] It is equally true in Isa 5:1–7 itself that the accusation is too general for a precise pinpointing of the victims, though the perpetrators are surely likely to be the same governing classes as are denounced in Isa 3:13–15.

The post-exilic passage Isaiah 58 is mainly exhortation rather than denunciation, but it includes the specific accusation "you drive all your workers" (v. 3a). Then the exhortations in vv. 6–7 imply the prevalence of unfree workers and of destitute people. Where? Everything else we know about Trito-Isaiah suggests that the writers were based in Jerusalem, and nothing about this lengthy passage gives any hint of a rural or agrarian setting. It seems reasonable to suppose that this diatribe is addressed to people who employ slaves in Jerusalem. The homeless people whom they are expected to take into their homes are also obviously wandering the streets of Jerusalem. Homelessness in most ages and places is an urban problem.

4. Micah

Micah 3 has a very clear setting in Jerusalem. Verses 1 and 9 address the "heads of Jacob and commanders of the house of Israel." The accusation that follows in vv. 2–3 is cast in sensationally horrific terms, but in itself it is too highly metaphorical to be referred to any specific acts of oppression. Light is cast on it by v. 10, "who builds Zion with blood and Jerusalem with iniquity." This is an unmistakable reference to the corvée.[35] Kessler compares a whole range of texts speaking of kings "building" various cities, that is to say, fortifying them, or, recalling the discussion above, turning them from villages into real cities.[36] In the late eighth century Hezekiah would have been strengthening the fortifications of Jerusalem to withstand Assyrian attack. The conscripts could well have included contingents of villagers. The chapter attacks the mistreatment of the people, including probably rural people, by their government in the name of "security."

---

34. Blenkinsopp, *Isaiah 1–39*, 200. [Chaney, "Whose Sour Grapes?" takes the two passages to allude to the forced conversion of village land for specialized agriculture for export; see Houston, *Contending*, 41, for a critique.]

35. Cf. below, chapter 8, 120.

36. Kessler, *Micha*, 163–65.

However, it does not have to do with the oppression of peasants as land holders or the seizure of their land.

We have already seen that Mic 6:9–12 (probably post-exilic) is set in an urban context. How does this square with vv. 14a and 15, where the addressees are warned of their failure in every kind of agricultural enterprise? This can be regarded as the cliché of the "futility curse," found in several biblical and extra-biblical texts, without any necessary close relationship to the actual work of the addressees.[37] Even so, it is not unreasonable to suppose that wealthy Jerusalemites at all periods had agricultural property, probably mostly in the neighborhood of the city.

Oppression of peasants as such is, however, the concern of the earlier passage in Mic 2:1–5. The key verse describing the outrages, v. 2, is comparable to Isa 5:8. There is no question that these verses describe the seizure, on whatever pretext, of agricultural land. That it is land used for agriculture is underlined by the judgment pronounced in Isa 5:10. In a different way Micah is equally clear: he speaks of "a man and his inheritance," that is, a family head and the family holding. Both texts accuse unspecified people of seizing houses and land—and turning out families—on unspecified pretexts. Here surely we have the oppression of the peasantry by the rich in order to enlarge landholdings, perhaps through the manipulation of credit, as set out in relatively clear terms in Neh 5:1–5. This is how most commentators interpret the verses. Wolff especially, but other commentators as well, argue that Micah has events in his home town of Moresheth-Gath in view.[38] We do not know whether Moresheth-Gath was a village or a city at this time. In fact, we do not even know where it was precisely, so there is little light available to shed on our question in this direction. It could be true that Micah began prophesying in his home town and then travelled to Jerusalem, only to find conditions even worse there. But there is nothing to indicate the locality of the exploitative activities in Micah 2.

I should like to suggest the alternative possibility that both the Isaiah and Micah texts, which are closely parallel, are set in Jerusalem, and yet speak of the oppression of peasants, in the traditional sense. How can this be? Jerusalem in the late eighth century was for the time and the region a large city, of, on Faust's estimate, between 17,500 and 40,000 inhabitants.[39] It was surrounded by a thickly populated rural area, which was different in

---

37. Hillers. *Micah*, 82; Kessler, *Micha*, 280–81.

38. Wolff, *Micah*, 74. Wolff refers somewhat differently to "members of the royal court, officials, military commanders, and soldiers—groups who were part of a permanent occupation" who "would have taken charge of farms and comfortable homes." This appears to imply simple confiscation.

39. Faust, "Settlement," 111.

its settlement pattern from most of the country. Isolated farmsteads were densely scattered on the north, west, and south of the city; apparently there were several hundred of them.[40] They occupied a band about four kilometers wide.[41] These farmsteads are also found in other parts of the country at this period,[42] but the density is much greater in this area.[43] This would point to the intensive cultivation of the whole area. The east side of the city was used for grazing. Some of the farmsteads are well built, suggesting the personal presence of a proprietor with his family, while others are very small, like small city houses, suggesting that they were owned by an absentee landlord and worked by hired labor, or possibly by debt or even chattel slaves.[44]

It is obvious enough that this pattern of settlement and cultivation responds to the needs and pressures of the rapidly expanding population of the city. But what was the social mechanism—Marxists would call it the mode of production—through which this novel mode of rural settlement and agriculture was instituted? Bear in mind that farmers, and especially peasant farmers, are generally deeply conservative, and that the clan-based type of nucleated settlement had been entrenched in the highlands of Judah and Benjamin for at least 300 years. There were doubtless many traditional villages within easy reach of Jerusalem's markets. They may have been unable to respond effectively to the opportunities of profit in the growth of the city, perhaps especially because traditional village-based agriculture required a large area outside the bounds of the cultivated land to be given over to grazing. But there were those who knew how to take advantage of this commercial opportunity. Some of them would have been based in the city, possibly including those officially responsible for its food supply. According to Hopkins, farmsteads reflect "the penetration of the countryside by the managerial arm of the city-based administration."[45] It was certainly easier for people who had become accustomed to the more individualistic culture of the city to develop this more efficient mode of exploitation of the land, but doubtless there were also those in the villages who took the plunge into consolidating their holdings and living on them. In this way we may account for the larger and more obviously independent farms. In so far as farms were established by those in the city with access to capital, the obvious step was to buy land. If there was reluctance to sell, there were

---

40. Faust, "Farmstead," 100; "Settlement," 102–3.
41. Faust, personal communication.
42. Faust, "Farmstead." [See now also Faust, *Archaeology*, 148–59.]
43. [Cf. now Faust, *Judah in the Neo-Babylonian Period*, 39–48.]
44. Faust, personal communication.
45. Hopkins, "Farmsteads."

ways of overcoming it, and it is this that is presumably referred to by the Isaiah and Micah texts. Although the story of Naboth's vineyard (1 Kings 21) is doubtless legendary, it may well reflect the kind of social situations that arose in this process. Persistent peasant claims could be swept aside, whether through the manipulation of credit described by Nehemiah, or perhaps through less roundabout seizures.

Isaiah is typically hyperbolic in his expression of the result; the mirage of *latifundia* in Judah largely arises from taking Isaiah's hyperbole literally. And the impression cannot be avoided in both passages that a few scandalous cases may have been seized on in a process that may well have proceeded for the most part to the superficial satisfaction of seller as well as buyer. However, as the "jubilee" complex of laws in Leviticus 25, as well as 1 Kings 21, indicates, a deep-seated objection to the treatment of inherited land as a commercial investment persisted, and the Holiness writer gave it theological expression.[46]

5. Zephaniah and Ezekiel

I mentioned the Jeremiah passages earlier. There remain two other passages of ostensibly late seventh- to early sixth-century date to deal with. It hardly needs demonstration that Zeph 3:1-5 deals with conditions in the city. Ezekiel 22:23-29 appears to be based on the Zephaniah passage, and is most naturally interpreted of Jerusalem, though it is addressed as a "land" rather than a city. One verse here requires comment, v. 29, which speaks of the "people of the land" as the oppressors of the poor and the alien. I discussed this expression above, and adopted the view that it refers to wealthy provincial landowners who have made their home in the capital.[47] I would modify this identification now by adding that it is likely that they had acquired their wealth as citizens of walled cities by expropriating the local peasantry. Thus they would have reached their present status by doing what Ezekiel accuses them of doing.

6. Conclusion

I think I have shown that the hypothesis is plausible at the very least that prophetic accusations of social injustice have a background primarily in the capital cities of Samaria and Jerusalem, and that both oppressors and victims mostly resided in those places, or nearby. These prophetic texts

---

46. [See chapter 4 above.]
47. Chapter 3, 52; see also *Contending*, 43.

offer a moral evaluation, of course from a committed and some would say prejudiced viewpoint, of a process of rapid social change in the fortified cities of monarchical Israel and Judah. They cannot be used to challenge archaeological evidence that this process, during the monarchical era, touched rural areas only to a limited extent, except in the immediate hinterland of the capitals.

Chapter 8

Corvée in the Kingdom of Israel

Israelites, "Canaanites," and Cultural Memory

(2018)

1. Introduction

STATES IN THE ANCIENT Near East used levies of forced labor from their subjects, the corvée, to work on all their large-scale public works. There are a number of references to this in the Hebrew Bible, and there is a technical vocabulary for it. I shall be discussing below such references in the account of Solomon's reign and the division of the kingdom, and in Judges, chapter 1. Apart from these, and apart also from the obscure reference to Issachar's corvée service in the blessing of Jacob (Gen 49:15), the context of the references is the kingdom of Judah. They are: 1 Kgs 15:22, where king Asa "called together all Judah, with no exemptions"[1] to use the stones from Baasha's abandoned fortress of Ramah to build defenses at Geba and Mizpah; Micah's accusation (Mic 3:10) against the rulers, that they had built or were "building Zion with blood and Jerusalem with wickedness"; and Jeremiah's condemnation of Jehoiakim (Jer 22:13) for "building his house without right and his upper chambers with injustice, making his neighbor work for nothing and not giving him his wages." The prophetic accusations should probably both be taken as pejorative references to the corvée rather than to the abusive use of wage labor.[2]

---

1. אין נקי

2. For Micah, see Kessler, *Micha*, 163–65, against e.g., McKane, *Micah*, 112. For Jeremiah, Bright (*Jeremiah*, 145) speaks of "conscripted labor"; but Jones (*Jeremiah*, 289) implies it is a matter of failure to pay wages due, and Carroll denies Jer 22:13–15a were originally about a king at all, necessarily therefore not a reference to the corvée (*Jeremiah*, 427). But in the light of the Micah text, from an oracle that was known to the editors of Jeremiah (Jer 26:18–19), the verse should be seen as criticizing the use of the corvée for an essentially private rather than public purpose.

However, as far as I am aware there is no direct reference to the use of the corvée in the kingdom of Israel from Jeroboam I on, as distinct from the largely or entirely legendary account of Solomon. There is, of course, less material on Israel than on Judah in the Hebrew Bible, but it does include a very hostile view of the Omride dynasty in Kings. None of the numerous denunciations of injustice in Amos—from a later period—appear to have the corvée in view. Yet it is certain that the Omrides at least must have used it. They were responsible for extensive building works all over the kingdom. There are the palaces and defense works of Samaria and Jezreel and a number of fortresses on the borders; and the recent lowering of the radiocarbon dates for Iron IIA—which I do not intend to discuss here—brings even more of the archaeological record into their period.[3] Writers who are interested in the subject have normally assumed that Omri and his successors must have conscripted the labor of their Israelite peasant subjects to erect these works. Thus, e.g., Chaney says that Omri "follow[ed] in the footsteps of Solomon," and refers to "increased corvée" exacted from the highland peasantry as a result of his wars.[4]

The tradition that we find in 1 Kings 12 suggests, on the contrary, that Israelite peasants did not expect to have to provide corvée labor. But is there any historical value to this tradition? Where, if that is so, did the kings of Israel find such labor? Naʿaman points to Mesha of Moab's reference in his inscription to the use of prisoners of war for public works, and suggests that Omri's extensive conquests would have gained him large numbers of prisoners of war for use in the building of Jezreel.[5] This, however, would have been a wasting asset. A more enduring source of labor would have been the non-Israelite portion of the Israelite kings' subjects, those who had been subject to Canaanite city states particularly in the Jezreel and upper Jordan valleys, and had later become subject to Israelite rulers. In an earlier publication,[6] I suggested briefly that the kingdom may have drawn on this source in order to avoid using the labor of their Israelite subjects. It is the object of this article to demonstrate the probability of this hypothesis in detail. It will explore the Israelite tradition on the subject, understood as cultural memory, in relation to the historical reality of ethnic diversity in the kingdom of Israel, as demonstrated archaeologically.

---

3. Finkelstein, *Forgotten Kingdom*, 85–105.
4. Chaney, "Systemic Study," 71–72.
5. Naʿaman, "Excavation of Tel Jezreel," 122–24.
6. Houston, *Contending*, 39.

2. Ethnic Diversity in Israel

It will be convenient to begin by showing that there were distinct ethnicities in ninth- to eighth-century Israel, and that it was likely that the state discriminated in favor of one and against others.

Finkelstein, noting the "settlement and cultural continuity" in the northern valleys between Late Bronze and Iron I, which was maintained in the rural areas even after the destruction of the Iron I cities, infers that there was a population in the valleys ethnically distinct from the highland areas where the kingdom was based.[7]

Faust aims to demonstrate such a distinction by highlighting contrasting cultural traits in the two respective areas that appear in the archaeological record of the Iron II period.[8] He refers to three excavated sites, one in the foothills of Carmel, one in the Beth-Shean valley, and one on the eastern shore of the Sea of Galilee. It could be argued that, because none of them are properly speaking in the Jezreel valley, they are hardly characteristic of the area. But what is important is that none of them are in the highlands.

Faust lays most stress on the plan of the dwelling house, arguing that "almost all the houses known in Israelite cities and villages were of" the so-called four-room house type, including as a sub-type the "three-room house,"[9] without denying that this type is also exemplified sporadically elsewhere.[10] His use of the word "Israelite" here is ethnic not political, and it assumes what needs to be proved. I take it that by "Israelite" he means "highland." But in the three valley sites referred to the houses are not of this type. A study of the plans of the houses in these villages shows that they are clearly different from those characteristic of villages in the highlands.[11] Some have only one room; others have two or more rooms en suite, which is a feature excluded by the so-called "four-room" plan. It is not relevant for our purposes that the four-room plan may be used elsewhere or in Iron I, especially in the Transjordan,[12] for we are only concerned with the contrast between highland and lowland within the territory of the kingdom of Israel in Iron Age II.

Faust draws attention to numerous other features,[13] including the lack of walls round these rural settlements of the valleys, which are regular in highland settlements; the presence of cultic buildings or rooms at two of

---

7. Finkelstein, *Forgotten Kingdom*, 110.
8. Faust, *Archaeology*, 230–54, esp. 241–47; cf. earlier Faust, "Ethnic Complexity."
9. Faust, *Archaeology*, 215.
10. Faust, *Archaeology*, 218–19.
11. Faust, *Archaeology*, 236, 238, against 214.
12. See, e.g., Routledge, "Seeing through Walls."
13. Faust, *Archaeology*, 241–47.

the sites, invariably absent in Iron Age highland villages;[14] the smaller size of the houses, suggesting nuclear rather than extended family occupation; the presence of pig bones at one site; and the presence of imported pottery, also absent in the highlands, and not only at rural sites. Even though we are able to identify only such cultural elements as are capable of leaving archaeological traces, these are sufficient to delineate a culture different from that of the highlands.

But are we constrained to define the difference as ethnic?[15] This is not a matter that can be decided by a checklist of distinctions. Distinctions such as the ones just listed may characterize groups defined in other ways, for example by class, caste, or occupation. Ethnic distinction is subjective, something defined by the groups themselves, who perceive themselves as belonging to different peoples or nations, and take certain cultural markers as recognized signs of the difference. But as Routledge points out, the observer may note other differences, resulting from differences in behavior, that are not understood by the actors themselves as ethnic markers.[16] It is only if we have the words of the actors that we can be sure that a particular cultural boundary is regarded as ethnic, and for an ancient people that means texts;[17] in this case biblical texts, as no relevant epigraphic evidence survives from the kingdom of Israel. Of the above list, the only one referred to in the Bible is abstinence from pork (Lev 11:7: "the pig... shall be unclean *to you*"), and that text, certainly in its present form, comes from a later period.[18] Other texts, however, confirm that the geographic boundary between highland and lowland was seen to be correlated with an ethnic one, notably those in Joshua 16 and 17 and Judges 1, which are discussed below. Ethnic distinction is often, though by no means always, correlated with political boundaries; in this case it would presumably be related to a former political boundary, now erased by conquest.

It is no objection to the identification of ethnicity as a factor in the diversity of populations in Israel that ethnic Israelites may have been of local

14. Faust, "Archaeology of the Israelite Cult."

15. See the discussions in Faust, "Archaeology of the Israelite Cult," 230–33, Mc-Guire. "Study of Ethnicity," and Routledge, "Seeing through Walls," 63–65.

16. Routledge, "Seeing through Walls," 64.

17. McGuire, "Study of Ethnicity," 163; Faust, *Archaeology*, 233.

18. Some of the prophetic denunciations of "idolatrous" cults may be related to the presence or absence of shrines in residential areas: see perhaps especially Jer 7:16–19. But they are not connected in such passages with ethnic distinctions—that the prophets were attacking "Canaanite" cults is a scholarly conceit extrapolating from Deuteronomic texts, e.g., Deut 7:1–6; 12:29–31. The reference to walled and unwalled settlements in Lev 25:29–31, brought forward by Faust, *Archaeology*, 241, is likewise not concerned with ethnic distinctions.

origin, contrary to their myths of origin. There are other examples where people of similar origins have begun to define themselves as belonging to separate peoples: for example Northumbrian Angles living on either side of the border between England and Scotland.

But does it follow from this that the people of the lowlands were discriminated against? An older scholarly position, identified for example with Alt, held that the establishment of the monarchy led to the rapid integration and indeed promotion of the "Canaanite" element in the population. It was not absorbed into the Israelite tribes, but into the territories of David's administration, with the same rights and duties as Israelites.[19] Indeed, with Solomon's establishment of a chariot force, the *Schwergewicht*, the predominance in the kingdom, began to shift towards the Canaanites, and this ultimately led to the restoration of the old cultural and political dominance of the plains over the hills.[20]

But Alt does not clearly *identify* the signs of this dominance, and there is much evidence against it. The supposedly Solomonic chariot force first appears in history at the battle of Qarqar in the reign of Ahab.[21] But it is just at this period, in the mid-ninth century, that contemporary evidence begins to appear that the god of Israel is YHWH: witness, for example, the reference to YHWH of Samaria at Kuntillet ʿAjrud,[22] or the Yahwistic names that begin to appear in the Israelite dynasties. Ahab's three known children all have Yahwistic names. Now, there is an interesting passage in 1 Kgs 20:23, 28, where the Arameans before the battle of Aphek are represented as arguing that Israel's god is a god of the hills, and therefore could be defeated in a battle on level ground. This surely reflects a consciousness in the author that the heartland of YHWH's worshippers was the highlands. In what is most important in culture, the advantage remains with the hills.

The more recent archaeological evidence surveyed by Faust suggests a more complex reality.[23] The kingdom deepened its power and extended its reach in the country in large part by building and developing cities, and these were mainly in the lowlands.[24] Such places as Megiddo and Hazor were old Bronze Age cities rebuilt and made regional centers of influence. Among these, Hazor's residential quarters are sufficiently exposed to make it clear that it was a multi-ethnic settlement, in which the elite, those with the largest

19. Alt, *Kleine Schriften*, II, 52.
20. Alt, *Kleine Schriften*, II, 53.
21. Miller and Hayes, *History*, 292, 308–10.
22. יהוה שמרן [Davies, *Hebrew Inscriptions*, 81 (8.017).]
23. Faust, *Archaeology*, 258–68.
24. Cf. Fritz, *City in Ancient Israel*, 13–14; Houston, *Contending*, 38.

and best-built houses, were highlanders, to judge from their house plans.[25] Thus it would seem that Israelites had moved into the conquered areas to take control of them on behalf of the state. It is in *this* sense that the cultural and political dominance of the plains was restored, being exercised by people of highland origin living in the plains. Certainly, some of the old lowland elite could have been accepted into official and other leading positions, but in doing so they would have adopted aspects of Israelite culture.

Alongside this, we find in the non-Israelite villages of the same areas public buildings, a feature normally absent in highland villages, apart from grain silos and the like, and Faust suggests that "the villages . . . served as outposts of the city or palace, and the public buildings belonged to it."[26] Villages forming parts of crown estates are common enough elsewhere in the Near East, as Faust points out. Alternatively, they could be seen as being under a type of feudal or prebendal control. This is in marked contrast to the highland villages, which show no signs of elite dominance, and do show signs that they retained surpluses.

Enough has been said to suggest that the lowland villages, as distinct from the cities, and as distinct also from the ethnically different highland villages, show clear signs of a subordinate position in the state of Israel. It does not require arguing that these ethnically subordinate villagers were subject to corvée demands; what I need to show now is that the cultural memory of Israel, as embodied in the biblical texts on Solomon and the succession to Solomon, serves to justify, and therefore for us to demonstrate, Israelites' exemption from it.

3. Cultural Memory in the Biblical Tradition

I am here using "cultural memory" in the sense developed by Jan Assmann, of a commonly accepted narrative of the past that determines and confirms customs and attitudes of the present.[27]

a. Solomon in Kings

The principal narrative concerned is 1 Kgs 12:1–20, the account of Israel's rejection of the rule of Rehoboam, to be discussed below. But texts in the account of Solomon also require examination. First Kings 5:27 (English versions 5:13) states that Solomon "raised a levy (מס/*mas*) from all Israel of

25. [See Faust, *Archaeology*, 46–55, for Hazor.]
26. Faust, *Archaeology*, 242.
27. Assmann, *Cultural Memory*.

30,000 men" to work on supplies for his building projects, and this must be the presupposition for the later account. But a much interpolated passage in 1 Kings 9 contradicts this. "This is the account of the levy that king Solomon raised..." begins v. 15, and after a meandering account of his building projects and Pharaoh's conquest of Gezer, the passage returns to the matter of the levy in vv. 20–21: "All the people that were left of the Amorites, the Hittites, the Perizzites, the Hivites, and the Jebusites, who were not of the Israelites, their descendants who were left after them, whom the Israelites were not able to put to the *herem*, Solomon conscripted as forced laborers, as remains the case today."[28]

Many commentators regard the statement in ch. 9 as a late apologetic attempt to clear Solomon's name of the odium of being responsible for the practice of imposing forced labor on the people of Israel; the language and ideology are clearly Deuteronomistic.[29] The statement in 5:27, on the other hand, has generally been regarded as more reliable, particularly because it is apparently presupposed by the narrative of the rejection of Rehoboam in ch. 12. But even if 9:20–21 is late, it is likely to reflect a traditional view of the odiousness of the corvée, as Würthwein sees.[30]

There has been an attempt, now it seems abandoned, to make a distinction between מס/*mas* simple, as at 5:27, and מס־עבד/*mas-'obed* as at 9:21, thus removing the contradiction. This goes back to Bachmann in 1868,[31] who defined מס/*mas* as the responsibility of free citizens to supply labor from time to time, while מס־עבד/*mas-'obed* defined a permanent state of slavery resulting from conquest and the loss of independence. All Israel had to perform corvée when required, but the Canaanites were subjected to a permanent servile state. Mendelsohn championed this distinction, arguing for an institution of state slavery, and in one form or another a distinction is accepted by Noth, and Gray in his second edition.[32] But in view of the variation in the vocabulary the distinction cannot be sustained. The עבד/*'obed* in 1 Kgs 9:21 is omitted in 2 Chr 8:8; and while it is stated in 1 Kings 9 that the non-Israelites were levied as מס־עבד/*mas-'obed*, the statements about the same peoples in Judges 1, which we shall look at shortly, use מס/*mas* alone.[33]

---

28. ויעלם שלמה למס־עבד עד היום הזה. As Rainey has shown ("Compulsory Labour Gangs," 200), the term מס refers to the personnel, "forced laborers," "levy," not to the custom or institution of the corvée.

29. E.g., Montgomery, *Kings*, 137, 205, 209; Cogan, *I Kings*, 309.

30. Würthwein, *Erster Buch der Könige*, 113.

31. Bachmann, *Buch der Richter*, 141–42.

32. Mendelsohn, "State Slavery," esp. 17; Noth, *Könige*, 217; Gray, *I & II Kings*, 155.

33. A late addition (not in the Old Greek) in Josh 16:10 uses מס־עבד

The only leading commentator to take a view diverging from the consensus in favor of 5:27 is Noth.[34] He argues that in 9:20–21 it is possible to distinguish a Deuteronomistic redactional stratum from an underlying text (*Grundschrift*), which read "All people who did not belong to the Israelites Solomon conscripted for servile forced labor, and this is still the case today." Noth views the underlying text throughout 9:15–23 as having an official character, shared by this reconstructed text of vv. 20–21, whereas 5:27 is part of a Deuteronomistic or post-Deuteronomistic passage. Thus, Noth reverses the usual view, and asserts that there are no adequate grounds to question the historicity of 9:15–23.[35]

In view of the dubious historical status today of the whole narrative of the United Monarchy, it is meaningless to dispute over the historicity of statements about Solomon's rule. But we may ask about the origin and function of such statements in their contemporary context. And that Noth could be right in seeing the original context of the basic text in 9:20–21 as much earlier than the Deuteronomists is suggested by two points: the clause "who did not belong to the Israelites" is redundant in its present context and not found alongside any other uses of the list of the former nations, which in whatever selection or order is a Deuteronomistic cliché; and עד היום הזה /*'ad hayyom hazze*, "until this day," is standard in aetiological statements and implies that this state of affairs is current. This points to an origin from the kingdom of Israel, even if it does not conclusively prove it. A writer aware of current practice in restricting the corvée to non-Israelites traces it back to Solomon.

b. Judges 1 and Parallels

It coheres with this that in Judges 1, gathering a number of traditions about the tribes, some of which are found in a probably more original form in the tribal allocations in Joshua, pre-Israelite populations that the tribes could not conquer are stated to have been conscripted as מס/*mas*, forced labor. Joshua 17:11–13, with its parallel in Judg 1:27–28, is the most illuminating of these. The tribe of Manasseh is said to have failed to dispossess a list of cities in the northern lowlands, including Beth-Shean, Megiddo, Taanach, Ibleam, and Dor, each with "its daughters," i.e., its dependent villages. "But when the Israelites grew strong, they put them to

---

34. Noth, *Könige*, 216–18.
35. Noth, *Könige*, 218.

forced labor, but they never dispossessed them"[36] (Josh 17:13).[37] The parallel observations in Josh 16:10 and Judg 1:30, 33, 35 all say that the tribes in question themselves put the Canaanites to forced labor (unless "the hand of Joseph" in Judg 1:35 really means the power of the kingdom of Israel). But this cannot have been the case. Corvée can only be imposed by a state, not by a mere tribe. "When (the children of) Israel grew strong" in effect refers to the foundation of the state. These texts reflect a current or at least recent reality of forced labor in the kingdom being done by non-Israelites, and refer it to tribal action, unrealistically, but in line with Israel's cultural memory of being a tribal people. Members of free Israelite tribes do not do forced labor, they have it done for them.[38]

In the context of the tribal allocations in Joshua, these texts explain in the light of the cultural memory of conquest how it is that much of lowland Israel was not in fact occupied by Israelites. In the Judges context, they serve to indict the tribes other than Judah, from a Deuteronomistic point of view, of failure in their God-imposed responsibility of driving out the previous population: "could not dispossess" in Josh 17:12 is replaced by "did not dispossess" in Judg 1:28.[39] But neither context requires the reference to the corvée, which I suggest reflects another and earlier context.

c. 1 Kings 12:1–20

In contrast, the narrative of the succession to Solomon in 1 Kgs 12:1–20, as we have seen, implies what is stated by 5:27 (13), that Solomon imposed corvée on "all Israel." The word מס/*mas* is not used, but the words in v. 4, "your father laid a harsh yoke on us, but if you now lighten the hard service your father imposed[40] and the heavy yoke which he laid on us, we shall serve you," make it virtually certain, as commentators have generally agreed, that the reference is to corvée service. The logic of the narrative implies that after rejecting Rehoboam as king because he refused their modest request for a lightening of the load, Israel would not have accepted anyone else as king who did not agree to at least a lightening of the service, and no doubt preferably a complete remission, even though this is not stated explicitly in connection with their election of Jeroboam (v. 20).

---

36. והורש לא הורישו
37. Judg 1:28 has ישראל, Israel, in place of בני ישראל, the children of Israel.
38. Compare 1 Sam 8:11–18, and Crüsemann, *Widerstand*.
39. O'Connell, *Rhetoric*, 50–72.
40. מעבדת אביך הקשה

I have stated the hypothesis that this narrative is cultural memory. But the question arises, *whose* cultural memory? Is it indeed the memory of Israel, explaining the fact that unlike the non-Israelite population they are exempt from the royal labor service, or is it not rather the memory of Judah or Jerusalem, explaining why the house of David does not rule Israel? Most commentators in fact see the account as written from the point of view of Jerusalem. It begins by assuming that the approval of Rehoboam's kingship by the people is a formality (v. 1),[41] and ends by asserting "so Israel is in rebellion against the house of David down to this day" (v. 19). In v. 16 the cry appears "What part have we in David? And we have no share in the son of Jesse. To your tents, Israel!" This had almost word for word been uttered previously by that villain ("man of Belial") Sheba the son of Bichri (2 Sam 20:1) to launch his rebellion. Uwe Becker argues, following Wellhausen, that this is a literary reprise, showing that the account here is written from the same Jerusalem-based point of view as the account of Sheba's rebellion.[42] Noth, however, diverging from the consensus as before, does not agree that any literary dependence need be assumed between the two passages, regarding the saying as one emerging among the "north Israelites" and then circulating and becoming well known.[43]

Becker performs a redaction-critical dissection of the passage, arguing that the verses dealing with Jeroboam, his rebellion, flight, return, and call to the throne (i.e., 11:26, 40; 12:2 [part], 20a, 25) are an account readable on its own, and that 12:1, 3b–19, the account of Rehoboam's failure, is a subsequent insertion; but it is not from a pre-Deuteronomistic source, for it presupposes the notice of Rehoboam's assumption of power in Jerusalem in 11:43.[44] It is dependent on 5:27–32, of course, the passage that asserts Solomon levied corvée on all Israel, but also, according to Becker, on 9:15–23, which contradicts it, since that passage takes the same ethical position on the corvée. Further, according to Becker, the mise-en-scène of the account, the gathering of "all Israel" to Shechem to confirm Rehoboam's kingship, is modeled on the two elections of David as king in Hebron, by Judah (2 Sam 2:4) and Israel (2 Sam 5:1–3), and these also are the work of a late Deuteronomistic or post-Deuteronomistic redactor, based on the chronological notices in the first edition of the Deuteronomistic history. It takes place at Shechem because there the disastrous story of Abimelech's kingship played itself out. The account is an *"Ätiologie der Zweistaatlichkeit,"* an explanatory

---

41. Becker, "Reichsteilung," 216.
42. Becker, "Reichsteilung," 216–17; Wellhausen, *Composition des Hexateuchs,* 279.
43. Noth, *Könige,* 276.
44. Becker, "Reichsteilung."

story of Israel's division between two states. No specific north-Israelite character (*Prägung*) is detectable.[45]

Becker's account suffers from defects inherent in redaction criticism as a method. It is under-theorized, that is, not supported by any idea of the social environment of the redaction process—contrast the work of David Carr;[46] and it relies on a series of only moderately probable deductions, which cumulatively result in a much less probable conclusion.[47] In particular, Carr notes how insecure readability is as a criterion for the original existence of a reconstructed strand of narrative (such as Becker's Jeroboam text); and that it is precarious to argue for the dependence of one text on another on the basis of isolated characteristics.[48] In the present instance, there is no verbal resemblance at all between 1 Kings 12 and the various texts that Becker says it must depend on, except for v. 16. What we can say is that the base texts of both 1 Kgs 9:20–21 and 1 Kgs 12:1–20 reflect a tradition that corvée service is unacceptable for Israelites. A literary connection is not required. And it is also clearly the case that 1 Kgs 5:27 and 1 Kgs 12:1–20 are parts of the same story: but that should not lead to the conclusion that one depends on the other, only that they belong together.

Daniel Fleming, whose book is aimed at teasing out whatever in the Hebrew Bible originates in text or substance in the kingdom of Israel, agrees with Becker that the account as it stands is written from Judah's point of view, but disagrees that the account has no specifically (north-)Israelite character. It focuses on "aspects of a collective or collaborative leadership that would align with the pervasive tradition observed as central to Israel in various biblical writings."[49] Rehoboam negotiates not with Jeroboam as a leader, but with Israel as a collective. This is clear from the Old Greek text of 1 Kgs 12:3, 12, which has no reference to Jeroboam, and should be regarded as original. It should be said, however, that something similar is said of political practice in Judah in those three places in 2 Kings (14:21; 21:24; 23:30) where "all the people of Judah," or "the people of the land," a collective, however it may be defined, identify and place on the throne the successor to an assassinated king. But I am not convinced by Becker's alternative of a model found in the accounts of the election of David. Here there is no popular assembly: elders and members of the Israelite tribes travel to Hebron to anoint David, rather

---

45. Becker, "Reichsteilung," 216.

46. Carr, *Writing; Formation*.

47. Carr, *Formation*, 139–40.

48. Carr, *Formation*, 113–14, 138–44.

49. Fleming, *Legacy of Israel*, 111; Fleming refers particularly to the account of the rise of Omri in 1 Kings 16.

than requiring him to come to them. And to refer to Judges 9, which concerns Shechem as a city and not Israel, seems perverse in view of the frequent appearance of Shechem as a place of assembly for Israel.

But this is not the most decisive consideration. The decisive point is that while the story is *told* from the point of view of Judah, or at least Jerusalem, the *story itself*, that is, the basic plot, without the episode of Rehoboam's seeking counsel, is one that seems far more likely to have originated in Israel. Supposing the story were developed or composed in Jerusalem, that would have been at the expense of the reputation not merely of the inept Rehoboam but of Solomon, a king who is celebrated in the Deuteronomistic history; even in the section devoted to his sin, the sin in question is the typical Deuteronomistic theme of religious apostasy rather than the cruel exploitation of his compatriots. It seems unlikely that, after the memory of Solomon's greatness had been established, a later Jerusalem-based contributor would have arbitrarily blackened it. But if the story already existed, it could have been appropriated in an ambiguous way to condemn the Israelites for seizing such a pretext to rebel and to celebrate the memory of Solomon's wise advisers who could have averted the disaster if his foolish son had heeded them.[50]

But the people of Israel had nothing invested in the reputation of the house of David. We have already argued that the odiousness of the corvée reflected in this passage is likely to have been an Israelite tradition, and the odium is here inextricably associated with that house.

There is an important further question to answer. There are two different ways in which cultural memory may be applied in Assmann's theory: as *foundational* memories, which purport to relate key events of the past that explain, support, and justify the present institutions and customs of society, and *contra-present* memories, which represent past events as enshrining an ideal that is a challenge to the present situation and may justify revolt against it—Assmann offers the example of the story of David treated as the foundation of messianic belief in the late Second Temple period.[51] Which of these, for Israelites towards the end of their monarchy, is the story of Israel's revolt against Rehoboam? Is it, as I have suggested, a foundational memory, on which is founded the exemption of Israelites from the corvée; or is it a contra-present memory, encapsulating a grievance against a continuing trespass on the rights and dignity of free Israelite tribesmen?

The evidence marshaled in the earlier part of this chapter should, I think, incline us to the former alternative. Israelite kings, unlike Judean

---

50. Cogan, *I Kings*, 351, following Liver, "Book of the Acts," 96–99.
51. Assmann, *Cultural Memory*, 62–69.

ones, had easy access to an alternative source of labor, one that was probably inured to centuries of exploitation in this manner by their own kings;[52] and I consider that 1 Kgs 9:20-23 (with Noth), along with texts in Judges 1, should be taken as serious evidence that they were treated in a discriminatory manner.

An additional or alternative possibility is that the tradition worked as a contra-present memory for Israelites resident in Judah after 722 BCE and observing, or even being subject to, corvée there. It could be that it was in that situation that the memory of the corvée became associated with the house of David and the story of Rehoboam's rejection arose, or at least was elaborated.

But as a foundational memory the story would have resonated with the dominant foundational memory of the kingdom of Israel, the story of the deliverance of Israel from forced labor in Egypt. This is generally agreed to belong to Israel originally rather than Judah, and van der Toorn has described it as Israel's "charter myth."[53]

The sequel bound up with that memory, the conquest of Canaan, is now often seen as ethically and theologically problematic.[54] The answer that the genocide of the Canaanites was not a historical reality, unsatisfactory in any case, must now face what I have here argued *was* a historical reality: the subjection of non-Israelites to discriminatory treatment, including forced labor on the kingdom's projects.

---

52. Chaney, "Systemic Study," 60-61.
53. Toorn, "Exodus"; cf. Albertz, *History of Israelite Religion*, I, 141-42.
54. See, e.g., Prior, *Bible and Colonialism*; Warrior, "Native American Perspective."

Chapter 9

The Scribe and His Class

Ben Sira on Rich and Poor

(2013)

Introduction

IN 2006, I PUBLISHED a book-length examination of the ideologies and theologies of social justice in the Old Testament, with a revised edition in 2008.¹ That work made no reference to the book of wisdom of Ben Sira, despite the fact that more may be found there on the related topics of social justice, money, work, and the relations between rich and poor than in any book of the Hebrew Bible: perhaps about 170 verses. This chapter is a first essay towards repairing this considerable omission.²

My method in *Contending for Justice*, which I will adopt here, relies on an understanding, however precarious, of the social dimensions of the rhetoric. From what class position does the author or authors speak? How do they understand the social position of their audience? How does this affect the way in which the text presents or criticizes class relationships?

An extensive and important study of Ben Sira's teaching on generosity appeared in 2010, and this takes into account his social setting, although its starting point lies in his theology of retributive justice, cosmic

---

1. Houston, *Contending*.

2. All references use the chapter and verse numeration found in Rahlfs, *Septuaginta*, which is normally the same as that in the English versions. Where there is more than one system in use, Ziegler (*Sapientia*) places these numbers in parentheses. The text of the Hebrew manuscripts of Ben Sira is quoted from Beentjes, *Book of Ben Sira*, often with the siglum of the MS quoted. "G" refers to the Greek text. References to the Hebrew Bible are to the Hebrew numeration.

or divine.³ Benjamin Wright and Claudia Camp have similar concerns to mine, but they are interested in the supposed conflicted social status of the scribe as a problem for Ben Sira himself, which is not my topic here.⁴ Both these works cover much of the same ground as this essay. Gregory's views are fairly close to mine, but I shall have frequent occasion to question those of Wright and Camp.

The social position of the scribe is in many ways a determinant of how and to what end he works,⁵ and thus may be relevant to many or even all of the biblical writings: Ben Sira's presentation of the life and activity of the scribe (38:24—39:11) is the only one we have from the biblical period, and it has inevitably contributed much to our own picture of the scribe in Second Temple Judah. Ben Sira's image of his society and his position as a scribe within it may not be quite how we might wish to conceive them, but is certainly the first step towards such a conception. We may not necessarily assume that Ben Sira is typical of scribes even in his own generation, let alone at other periods, but what he says must be strongly indicative. However, for my purpose in this chapter this will not matter much.

Ben Sira's Livelihood and Social Position

For my purpose, the most important statement in this entire passage is the first, in 38:24: "The wisdom of the scribe depends on the opportunity of leisure; only one who has a minimum of business⁶ may exercise the profession of the wise."⁷ The following portraits of the peasant and a number of artisan trades is intended to stress the utter impossibility of people with such demanding manual trades finding the time for the study required to be an expert scribe. Schrader suggests that the keyword of the passage is שקידה/sheqida (38:26), translated in the Greek as ἀγρυπνία (38:26, 27, 28,

---

3. Gregory, *Signet Ring*.

4. Wright and Camp, "Who Has Been Tested?"

5. I do not use inclusive language where to do so would give an impression false to the reality of Ben Sira's patriarchal society.

6. Or "toil, hardship, trouble" (so Schrader, *Leiden*, 121: "*Mühsal, Plage*"). "Business" is given by *DCH* for עסק in agreement with G's πρᾶξις.

7. In the first line I have used the NRSV translation, which follows the Greek: B's חכמת סופר תרבה חכמה has been interpreted as meaning that the profession of the scribe serves to increase human wisdom (Skehan and Di Lella, *Wisdom of Ben Sira*, 445; Schrader, *Leiden*, 120); but this does not make a good parallel with the b line, where B and G are in agreement. The context shows that the final word [יתחכם]/σοφισθήσεται means "exercise the scribal profession" rather than simply "become wise."

30),[8] i.e., "wakefulness," "staying up late," which appears at the conclusion of the portrait of each trade.[9] Seeing that they have to stay up late to finish their work, they would have no time for evening classes!

But if leisure, and therefore a private income, is a requisite for the profession of scribe, at least in Ben Sira's opinion, the question must be raised, "What was the source of Ben Sira's own income?," as he does not answer this question himself. It has often been asked, but never conclusively answered.[10] A number of possibilities, not mutually exclusive, have been suggested. I must stress that in contrast to what is commonly done, we cannot argue from Ben Sira's moral attitudes to his social position. That is, we cannot argue, for example, that, because he warns of the danger of riches and shows sympathy for the poor, he was not rich. Mark Sneed has shown in relation to Proverbs how such stereotypes have skewed argument; in fact, aristocratic writers commonly show sympathy for the poor and urge the giving of alms as *noblesse oblige*.[11]

Wright and Camp assume, rather than arguing, that Ben Sira, his students, and scribes generally form part of a "retainer class" that is "in the employ of the rich and powerful and dependent on them for livelihood."[12] Certainly there is ample evidence that this was one way in which scribes could gain a living. In Ben Sira's book this is suggested by the extensive material advising students how to behave in the company of the great and warning them against the dangers of association with rich persons, for example at 13:1-13 (compare also 39:4a). But it is an unnecessary deduction that all scribes must have been in such employ, or that none had their own sources of income. The passage just cited suggests indeed that even if this had been Ben Sira's experience, at the time of writing he is free to make such comments. The assumption is particularly called in question by the work on education done by Helge Stadelmann and David Carr, who show how central the temple and its priests were to education in Second Temple Judah.[13] If many scribes at this period were priests, they would have been largely supported by the tithes and other perquisites. While they may have served richer or more powerful members of the community, they were not necessarily dependent on them.

8. There is no Hebrew text available after v. 27a.
9. Schrader, "Beruf," 124.
10. See Reiterer, "Recent Research," 35-37.
11. Sneed, "Class Culture"; cf. also Kovacs, "Class-Ethic." See chapter 5 above, 76.
12. Wright and Camp, "Who Has Been Tested?" 163. See Horsley, *Scribes*, where the concept is developed.
13. Stadelmann, *Ben Sira*, 19-39; Carr, *Writing*, 201-14.

Wright and Camp appear to assume that the priestly order as a whole were the rulers of the Jewish community, and even speak of the priestly class, served by the scribal class. This recalls Tcherikover's sharp distinction between the priests and the scribes, which perhaps reads a later situation back too far into the past.[14] In reality, it was only a small group of wealthy priests, surrounding the high priest, who exercised power. The rest of the order probably lived quite modestly, and that there were priests whose primary role was that of study and education as described in 39:1–3, 8a seems probable. Carr characterizes this as a work of "education-enculturation," in which the social elite were educated through the primarily oral study of central cultural texts; at this period, on Ben Sira's showing, the Torah would have taken first place (39:1a–b, 8b). Both Stadelmann and Carr argue that Ben Sira himself was of priestly family.[15]

There are other possibilities canvassed by some. That he received teaching fees is possible: see 51:23 and 51:25.[16] The rabbis later absolutely declined this means of support, but unlike Ben Sira they engaged in trades. He may have been an official, but would such a position offer sufficient leisure?[17] A more likely possibility is that he was a landowner living on his rents, or with slaves tilling his land.[18] It is also possible that a wise and generous patron, someone in the mold of the high priest Simon, whom Ben Sira so obviously admired (50:1–21), encouraged a gifted man to develop himself and gave him the time to do so.

It should be clear from this range of possibilities, none of which can be altogether ruled out, that an entire argument, such as Wright and Camp's, based on the assumption that scribes as a profession and Ben Sira in particular had no independent means of support, must be fallacious. I believe that it is very likely that Ben Sira, who shows great interest in the priesthood, was himself a priest, though he may well have supplemented his income with service to the magnates at some time in his career.

If that were so, Ben Sira's main source of income would have been the priestly perquisites. These were required by the Torah, but in practice were voluntary: this is why he would need to encourage his readers not to neglect them (7:29–31). They were also fixed: they could not be arbitrarily increased, so that Ben Sira would have had no interest in ways of squeezing more income from the land. His means may well have been quite modest. But they

---

14. Tcherikover, *Hellenistic Civilization*, 124–25.
15. Stadelmann, *Ben Sira*, 12–14; Carr, *Writing*, 207.
16. Gordis, "Social Background," 85–86; Stadelmann, *Ben Sira*, 27–34, rejects it.
17. Kieweler, *Ben Sira*, 55.
18. Wischmeyer, *Kultur*, 43, n. 31.

would have been secure, and his entire income would have been derived from the land, whether or not he himself owned any.

Ben Sira's Audience

What of his audience? The injunctions in his book seem to be addressed to persons in a fairly wide range of economic conditions, not including the lower classes. The teaching on credit in chapter 29 is addressed both to those who may be asked for a loan (29:1–2a) and to those who are compelled to borrow (2b–3). If the emphasis on giving alms and paying wages promptly (4:1–10; 7:32–33; 34:18–22) implies a well-to-do audience, in 33:31–33 he addresses someone who has one slave only, not a situation of excessive comfort in the ancient world.[19] Stadelmann defines his audience as "in general of the upper middle class."[20] What might that mean in second-century BCE Jerusalem? Besides priests like (very likely) Ben Sira himself, one might point to officials, small landowners and merchants. But recalling Sneed's point, we should not think that Ben Sira was not also addressing the rich simply because he criticizes rich men and does not identify himself with them.

Carr has a rather different view. He says that scripture was used in Ben Sira's world "first and foremost by *and for* [my emphasis] priestly education-enculturation."[21] Ben Sira teaches "elite leaders." He concludes from 38:24 that "Ben Sira's 'wisdom' was intended for the small minority who had the time to master higher instruction." This would imply that his teaching was solely for those who wished to become fully equipped *Schriftgelehrten*, "learned in the scriptures," like himself, and that these would be drawn exclusively or mainly from the priesthood. Stadelmann's view that there were two levels of education in his school seems to me to be inherently more probable. He argues that in 37:19–26 *Volkserziehungstendenzen* (tendencies towards popular education) are detectable.[22] All have the capacity for wisdom, but not all are able to develop a full working knowledge of Israel's Scriptures. Ben Sira's ideal is one of a *Volkserziehung* which is influenced by Hellenism, but will equip the people to withstand it. Carr has a similar idea, but he does not see it as operative at this period.[23]

---

19. Following the reading אחד; G's εἰ may then be an error for εἰς.
20. Stadelmann, *Ben Sira*, 35–36.
21. Carr, *Writing*, 202.
22. Stadelmann, *Ben Sira*, 296.
23. Carr, *Writing*, 202.

Ben Sira's Social World

Ben Sira's social world is a strikingly urban one.[24] The patronizing depiction of the peasant in 38:25–26 is almost the only reference to the occupation followed by the great majority of people in Judah.[25] Those whom he refers to as "rich" are likely to be aristocratic landowners (who would be city-dwellers), high officials, and leading priests. Much less wealthy and certainly without power are lower officials, ordinary priests, small traders, and the artisans portrayed in 38:27–30; in the lowest place among the free population day laborers and beggars—those who are without any secure livelihood; and slaves. That he ignores the peasantry means that he ignores the fact that his own life and that of his students, friends, and neighbors depends on the labor and anxiety and the frequent indebtedness and hunger of those who produce what he lives on. Despite his sensitivity on many topics, this issue never enters his moral world.

Wright and Camp assert that those whom Ben Sira calls "poor," who may be in need of alms, are distinct from the "utterly destitute."[26] Their grounds for this distinction are far from clear. Earlier they had discussed 29:21–22, 28 and 40:28–30. 29:22 says (according to the Greek text—no Hebrew is extant) "Better the life of a poor man under his wooden roof than sumptuous delicacies in the house of another." 40:28–30 is Ben Sira's warning against begging as a way of life. Wright and Camp comment: "The one whom Ben Sira calls 'poor' has something at least—a roof, some bread or clothing. The kind of destitution that leads to begging is a worse situation than being in poverty."[27] But there is no evidence that the designation "poor"[28] would not have included beggars. The text must be seen in context. The advantage of the poor man under his own roof lies in his dignity. The passage 29:21–28 has nothing to do with begging or destitution. The practice warned against here is taking up semi-permanent residence in the house of another, perhaps a friend or relative, the life of the "poor relation," who may in fact not be "poor" in the straightforward sense, but who takes advantage of connections to lead a more comfortable life, at the price of the cumulative humiliations that Ben Sira catalogs.

---

24. Wischmeyer, *Kultur*, 38–43.

25. עבדה in 7:15 (A) may or may not imply specifically γεωργία as given in G. One should not be misled by Gregory's repeated reference to "the peasant" in his translations in *Signet Ring*, influenced by Horsley. This translates דל. There is no reason to suppose that this word either denotes or invariably connotes a peasant; it means a poor person, and there would have been such in the city as well as in the surrounding countryside.

26. Wright and Camp, "Who Has Been Tested?" 162.

27. Wright and Camp, "Who Has Been Tested?" 160.

28. Whether עני, דל, or אביון

In the first place in Ben Sira's world stand the rich. But the rich man[29] is usually mentioned with criticism or severe reservations. Like the sages of Proverbs, Ben Sira does not identify himself with the rich.[30] He acknowledges that riches carry honor, a key value for him, but argues that even a poor man may be honored for his good sense (10:30–31). Oda Wischmeyer tries to show that Ben Sira draws a sharp distinction between the rich and powerful on the one hand, who are officials and merchants, and the true nobility, the μεγιστᾶνες/*megistanes*, on the other, whose wealth is derived from inherited land: the wealth of the latter, she suggests, is never referred to, they have unquestioned honor (e.g., 10:24), and they are never included in Ben Sira's strictures on the conduct of the wealthy.[31] For example, Wischmeyer would wish to argue that the warnings against being used by a rich man in 13:1–13 do not apply to the aristocrats. But however likely it is that a conservative teacher like Ben Sira had more respect for an old aristocracy than for *nouveaux riches*, I do not think her case has a secure basis in the text. The word μεγιστάν/*megistan* in G represents several different words in the Hebrew text, and most of them may also be represented by other Greek words, so that lexically it is hard to maintain such a distinction. In any case, it is doubtful that there were rich merchants and *nouveaux riches* in second-century Jerusalem. Archaeological evidence does not suggest at present that the thriving commercial economy presupposed by Hengel[32] extended to Judaea.[33] However, there is evidence in the text for a higher level of commercial activity than that implied by the Hebrew Bible. In 8:12 lending to a more powerful person is advised against, which shows that there was a demand for credit for other purposes than the relief of need.

Ben Sira is convinced that it is all but hopeless to expect a trader to have clean hands (26:29—27:3). But this moral perception contrasts with his acceptance of financial dealings of various sorts by the "wise" (42:5–7). Wischmeyer appropriately compares Cicero's evaluation in *de officiis* 1.150ff.[34] Understandably, those financial activities necessary for the carrying on of a well-to-do household are morally approved by the well-to-do.

On the other hand, when it is a question, for Ben Sira and others in his station in life, of being made use of by the rich for their own

---

29. עָשִׁיר or πλούσιος.

30. Cf. Houston, *Contending*, 120, 123.

31. Wischmeyer, *Kultur*, 52–53.

32. Hengel, *Judaism and Hellenism*, 32–55; cf. Collins, *Apocalyptic Imagination*, 24–26.

33. Horsley, *Scribes*, 67.

34. Wischmeyer, *Kultur*, 46.

purposes—and that is exactly how he describes it in 13:4: "As long as the rich [man] can use you he will enslave you, but when you are exhausted he will have nothing to do with you"[35]—he has a clear vision of their lack of scruple, deceit, and injustice.

Wright and Camp, however, comment:

> Ben Sira is no social critic. He does not blame the rich for creating the circumstances that oppress the poor, nor does he advocate any measures, other than almsgiving, that would redress the economic disparities that he sees before him. . . . Ben Sira is not engaging in the kind of social critique that the biblical prophets are.[36]

Every one of these statements betrays a misunderstanding or a misreading of one kind or another. "He does not blame the rich." A close reading of 13:15–19 points to the contrary. Ben Sira's meaning is here conveyed through a series of ironic similes that progressively reinforce each other. The apparently innocent opening remark that every creature associates with its own kind, and likewise with humans, introduces a series of examples that may purport to illustrate this remark, but actually lead up to the devastating comment that "the poor are the grazing ground[37] of a rich man" (13:19). Each example involves a pairing, and in each pairing one member is a predator and the other the prey. "How should a wolf associate with a lamb? Likewise an unjust person with an innocent one" (13:17).[38] Well, everyone knows the way wolves associate with lambs! And the Bible uniformly sees the unjust and the innocent in the same light. "Can there be peace between a hyena and a dog? Can there be peace between a rich person and a poor one?" The purported theme of segregation by kind has already dropped away to reveal the true subject: the hostility between rich and poor. And what form does that hostility take? "The food of the lion is the wild asses of the wilderness; so are the poor the grazing ground of a rich man." The parallelism is inescapable. The rich man is successively compared to a wolf, a hyena, and a lion. The rich are predators, exploiters of the poor. In this context, the comment at 13:24 is surely also ironical: "Wealth is good, so long as no iniquity is involved, while poverty is bad, in the estimate of arrogance." The rich are

---

35. Skehan's translation (Skehan and Di Lella, *Wisdom of Ben Sira*, 249). "Rich" cannot be used as a singular noun in English, so I have added "man." The idea of a female employer, however rich, would not have crossed Ben Sira's mind.

36. Wright and Camp, "Who Has Been Tested?" 161.

37. מרעית.

38. The Hebrew displays the regular contrast of רשע and צדיק ; see above, 43.

frequently characterized as "arrogant" or "proud."[39] 31:8–11 underlines how rare it is to find an honest rich man.

If this is not blame, what would be blame in a book of wisdom? To expect something like a prophetic accusation is to forget the constraints of genre.[40] In any case, the prophets themselves have decided limitations as social critics. No more from prophets than from sages do we get "measures . . . that would redress the economic disparities that" they see before them.[41] And it is also untrue that almsgiving is the only positive action that Ben Sira recommends. As we shall see, he has students whom he expects to become judges, and he warns them to ensure that they defend the poor against their oppressors (4:7–10). Strangely, Wright and Camp devote some attention to this passage later, yet here they seem to have forgotten it.[42]

What I have said so far suggests only that Ben Sira's moral vision coincides with the class interests of himself and his likely audience. But this is by no means all that he has to say. As with Proverbs, his social teaching has two sides to it: a descriptive side depicting the cruelty and injustice of the rich towards those who are at their mercy; and a directive side that aims to ensure that the disciples of the wise do not follow the example of the rich but rather behave with justice and mercy.

Compassion for the Poor

Ben Sira's first major treatment of the topic of behavior towards the poor is in 4:1–10. As in Proverbs, the hearer is assumed to be one who is not counted among the poor any more than the rich: the poem is concerned with how he is to respond to the pleas of poor people. It falls into two parts: vv. 1–6 are negative, while vv. 7–10 give positive instructions.[43] The first part is remarkable for the intensity of the emotional tone. The poor person is "bitter in spirit"[44] and "oppressed."[45] The conclusion is the characteristically biblical warning that the scorned supplicant will cry out and God will hear

39. זד (10:22 (A); 11:9; 35:18); גאה (10:14; 11:30).
40. But Corley (*Ben Sira's Teaching*, 136–37) notes the echoes of Zeph 3:3 and Ezek 22:27 in the image of the wolf.
41. Houston, *Contending*, 96.
42. Wright and Camp, "Who Has Been Tested?" 166.
43. Beentjes, "Sei den Waisen," 56.
44. מר נפש (v. 1), מר רוח (v. 6), both signifying emotional bitterness.
45. מדכדך. In v. 3a Di Lella reads אל תחמיר מעי דך in A, "do not stir up the bowels of the oppressed," Skehan and Di Lella, *Wisdom of Ben Sira*, 166. I have not seen Di Lella, *Hebrew Text*. Beentjes, *Book of Ben Sira*, 24, has a lacuna in place of the verb. G paraphrases.

(cf. Exod 22:22). The Greek text refers to "his creator," while the Hebrew text in A gives "his Rock," which is graphically similar to the likely Hebrew behind the Greek.[46] Both thoughts are biblical, the first in Prov 17:5, for example, the second in the Psalms.

While vv. 1–6 may be primarily concerned with responding to the material need of the poor with alms, Beentjes in his study of this poem shows that the second half has a rather different focus.[47] Verse 8, according to G, enjoins the hearer to give a gracious hearing and answer to the poor. But Beentjes argues that the Hebrew construction in A is not the normal Hebrew for "return his greeting," as given by Skehan;[48] and other versions are similar; rather the sense is "restore (the state of) *shalom* to him."[49] In other words, deliver him from oppression; which is also the theme of v. 9.[50] At the end of v. 8 Ben Sira uses one of his favorite words, ענוה/*'anawa*, "humility" (3:17; 4:8; 10:28; 13:20; 45:4). It expresses the reverse of that arrogance that he so deplores in the rich. 13:20 says this explicitly: "humility is an abomination to pride." 3:17 (A) says that if you behave with humility, "you will be loved more than one who gives gifts." Plainly it does not refer to one's bearing before superiors but before inferiors, meeting them on their own level, not putting on airs, and above all giving them what they need. In line with this is the advice in 18:15–18 not to use harsh words when giving alms—such, one might suggest, as calling the recipient a lazy scrounger as you shove your ungracious gift into his hand.

The final promise in the Hebrew text of A goes beyond the cautious paraphrase in G and has striking biblical echoes which Beentjes explores in detail.[51] "God will call you his son, give you his favor, and deliver you from the pit." It is the king who in the Hebrew Bible is called the son of God (e.g., 2 Sam 7:14; Ps 2:7; 89:28); and the work of delivering the poor from oppression is traditionally assigned to the king, as in Ps 72:12–14.[52] Thus in this second part of the poem Ben Sira has in mind a disciple who is a judge (this is explicit in v. 9). His responsibility is the biblical one of delivering the poor from oppression and protecting the fatherless and widows. He might fail in this through absorbing the social assumptions of the oppressing class,

---

46. G's ὁ ποιήσας αὐτόν presupposes יוצרו; A has צורו.
47. Beentjes, "Sei den Waisen," 57–64.
48. והשיבהו שלום; Skehan and Di Lella, *Wisdom of Ben Sira*, 163.
49. "*und gebe ihm (die Lage von)* שלום *zurück.*"
50. Beentjes, "Sei den Waisen," 57–59.
51. Beentjes, "Sei den Waisen," 60–62.
52. On this see chapter 3 above, and chapter 10 below, 156–66; also Houston, *Contending*, 139–50.

which would make "right judgment disgusting" to him,[53] or through arrogance: he is warned against both.

Ben Sira therefore presents a biblically informed appeal to the educated and well-to-do citizen, who may be called on to exercise the office of a judge, to exercise this, as well as his private use of wealth, to the benefit of the poor and oppressed, the widow and the fatherless. But it is obvious that in doing so he would not relinquish his class position and power. I have commented elsewhere on this tension in various parts of the Hebrew Bible.[54]

Yet Ben Sira's emphasis on humility makes me set a query against the judgment of Schrader, commenting on the exclusion of the artisans from the pursuit of wisdom in 38:24–30, that Ben Sira "has clearly left behind him the Deuteronomic–Deuteronomistic ideal of the people of God as a community of brothers."[55] After all, the Deuteronomic *locus classicus* for this ideal, Deut 15:7–11, itself accepts the permanent existence of a class of poor in the heart of God's people, who must be helped, yet are still "your brothers."[56] Moreover, Ben Sira himself names the recipients of alms as "a brother and a friend" (29:10), surely meaning the same as in Deuteronomy.[57] And on the other hand, though the word ענוה/*'anawa*, "humility," does not occur in Deuteronomy, the idea does; for example, in the instruction to creditors not to go into the debtor's house to collect a pledge, but to wait outside for it to be brought to them (Deut 24:10-11). Ben Sira's teaching is profoundly shaped by the Torah, which takes first place in his curriculum.[58]

It is therefore necessary to comment at this point on Wright and Camp's startling view that Ben Sira's "compassion, and his application of the law's demands" does not reach the "utterly destitute"; they refer to "his failure to include those at the very bottom of the economic ladder in his moral calculus of wealth and poverty."[59] This depends in part on the distinction between the merely poor and the destitute, which we have already seen to be lacking in foundation in Ben Sira's text; but also on their view of his comments on begging in 40:28–30. It is worth giving the text in full. The corrected text of B[60] may be translated:

53. 4:9 A: ואל תקוץ רוחך במשפט יושר
54. Houston, *Contending*; also chapters 2, 3, and 5 above and 10 below.
55. Schrader, "Beruf," 130; my translation.
56. As argued above, chapter 2, esp. 30; Houston, *Contending*, 185–86.
57. Gilbert, "Prêt," 183.
58. [I dissent with respect from my late friend Roger Tomes's opinion that "Ben Sira was not a profound student of the Hebrew Scriptures" ("Education of Ben Sira," 171, cf. 164.)]
59. Wright and Camp, "Who Has Been Tested?" 162.
60. Beentjes, *Book of Ben Sira*, 71; see Skehan and Di Lella, *Wisdom of Ben Sira*, 464, 467.

> My son, do not live a beggar's life: it is better to die than to beg.
> One who looks to another's table—that is no life!
> To one of sense such delicacies are disgusting, and a torture to the stomach.
> To the brazen begging is sweet—but it burns like fire within!

Wright and Camp rightly observe that "Begging seems to constitute a kind of social death in Ben Sira's eyes that is as horrifying to him as actual starvation." To beg is shameful (cf. Luke 16:3): it is a total loss of honor, a central value in Ben Sira's moral universe, and therefore the "person of sense" will have a natural revulsion against taking it up as a way of life. But to deduce from this that he had no compassion for beggars or the destitute and would feel justified in refusing them alms is quite arbitrary. On the contrary, it is a point of honor for the honorable man to succor the destitute (Job 29:15-16). Nowhere does Ben Sira say that a beggar need not be given alms. See 4:4: "Do not reject the plea of a poor person" (דל/*dal*), which can only be thought irrelevant to begging if it is maintained that the word can only mean a property-owning peasant, a view I have already rejected. Moreover, this is the only place in 4:1-10 where דל/*dal* is used, while עני/*'ani* appears thrice.

Lending and Borrowing

When Ben Sira comes to discuss credit in the poem of 29:1-20, the strophe on lending, 29:1-7, treats the issue from the point of view of the borrower (2b-3) as well as the lender (1-2a). In contrast, every reference to credit in the Hebrew Bible assumes that the reader/hearer or subject will be the lender. This shows that for Ben Sira the borrower will not necessarily be the poor person in desperate straits assumed by, for example, Deut 15:7-11. As we have seen, there was some demand for credit for other purposes than the relief of need. This should be borne in mind in what follows.

Lenders are assured that if they lend for the relief of need (2a) they will be fulfilling the commandments (1b). The lender is ὁ ποιῶν ἔλεος (1a), "one who shows *eleos*." There is no Hebrew text available for this chapter, but the phrase must be the equivalent of עשה חסד, "doing *hesed*."[61] Compare 46:7b (B), about Joshua: as this example shows, the phrase does not simply mean "one who does a kindness," as translated by Skehan[62]—this yields a mere truism—but one who is faithful to his commitment, in 29:1 one of compassion.[63]

---

61. Skehan and Di Lella, *Wisdom of Ben Sira*, 369.
62. Skehan and Di Lella, *Wisdom of Ben Sira*, 368.
63. See below in chapter 10, 155-56.

But the rest of the strophe is concerned with repayment. The borrower is exhorted to repay promptly (2b), especially because he or she is more likely to get a loan again in that case (3b). The following verses depict in vivid and amusing terms the antics of a debtor unwilling or unable to repay, and the unhappy consequences of default. Gilbert comments severely that Ben Sira's point of view is that of the rich man who makes the advance, and that he does not realize that the borrower may be genuinely unable to repay. "His sense of social responsibility is quite narrow," he comments.[64] He draws an unfavorable contrast with Luke 6:34–35, where disciples are exhorted to lend without expecting repayment.

This criticism takes account neither of the immediately following context, nor of the fact we have noted, that the borrower is not necessarily poor. It is precisely because he knows that a truly poor borrower may not be able to repay a loan that Ben Sira follows this depiction with the exhortation to have patience with a poor person (29:8a).[65] Ben Sira thinks it is better to give, without expecting repayment, than to lend and still not get your money back. If lending is for genuine need, it is an act of *hesed* and fulfills the commandments. But assuming the plea is from a ταπεινός (this word in G usually represents דל/*dal*, "poor"), why engage in the pretense of a contract of loan? Rather "lose your money" for a "brother or friend" (v. 10); precisely the teaching of Deut 15:7–11, which Ben Sira knew well, as well as of Luke 6:34–35, which he did not. Lending is liable to make enemies (29:6d–f), while giving will defend you against enemies (29:13).

In 12:1–7 the disciple is enjoined not to lend to the wicked. This has nothing to do with making a distinction between deserving and undeserving poor.[66] The wicked in the Bible are regularly oppressors, and here one is warned not to give weapons to them (12:5 in A).[67] In these conditions, it makes sense for Ben Sira to express reservations about lending, while seeing alms as an absolute requirement for the needs of the poor, called צדקה/*tsedaqa*, "justice" (e.g., 3:30),[68] and understood as commanded by the Torah.

---

64. Gilbert, "Prêt," 187: "Son sens social est assez étroit."
65. πλὴν ἐπὶ ταπεινῷ μακροθύμησον.
66. Morla Asensio, "Poverty and Wealth," 162, in accusing Ben Sira of "selfish prudencialism [*sic*]," evidently makes this mistake.
67. G misunderstands לחם in כלי לחם as "bread".
68. [See chapter 12 below.]

Justice, Human and Divine

The teaching of Ben Sira is aimed at the formation in the disciple of the virtue of justice. In my discussion of this virtue as understood in the Hebrew Bible, which is closely similar to Ben Sira's understanding, I argued, referring to MacIntyre's definition of a virtue, that this virtue is required for the practice of patronage within a particular kind of society, which I called a benevolent hierarchy.[69] It is clear that this is the kind of society assumed by Ben Sira. It is also clear that unless it is benevolent, that is, unless its more powerful or wealthier members exercise this virtue, it will not promote the welfare of its members. The difficulty arises, exactly as in the Hebrew Bible, that, according to Ben Sira's observation, the most powerful and wealthy members of his society are very far from exercising it.[70]

It did not lie within the horizon of Ben Sira's practical wisdom to resolve this tension by proposing a new and more equal ordering of society. But the theological motivations that he offers for doing justice embrace a potential resolution. In the first place, he lays emphasis on the fear of God and the observance of the commandments. But he also speaks frequently of the consequences of obedience and disobedience. Like Proverbs, he speaks often enough of an unspecified link between act and consequence, as in 29:11–13. But more often than in Proverbs, the link is attributed to the just action of God. Hengel comments that "the firm connection between human action and divine retribution runs through the work of Ben Sira like a scarlet thread and gave it to a large degree its polemic force."[71]

Thus, in 4:6 we found the Torah theme of God's attention to the cry of the oppressed: "When one bitter in spirit cries out in his pain, his Rock will attend to his cry" (the text of A; my translation). Conversely v. 10 expresses the favor and salvation that the obedient will receive from God. In 35:11–24 the theme of God's action to deliver is developed into an entire poem. "The Lord is a God of justice[72] [so Isa 30:18], with whom there is no respect of persons" [so Deut 10:17] (35:12 B[73]).[74] The cry of the poor pierces

---

69. MacIntyre, *After Virtue*, 187; Houston, *Contending*, 132–34.

70. From a different point of view, Tcherikover, *Hellenistic Civilization*, 145–51, sketches the tension well.

71. Hengel, *Judaism and Hellenism*, 143.

72. כי אלהי משפט הוא; G has misdivided the words to give the banal ὅτι κύριος κριτής ἐστιν.

73. 35:15 in Beentjes, *Book of Ben Sira*, 61.

74. Wright and Camp, "Who Has Been Tested?" 160, think Ben Sira is "walking a rather thin line" between God's impartiality and God's especial listening to the prayers of the oppressed. On the contrary, these emphases support each other. "Respect of persons" (λαμβάνειν πρόσωπον/נשא פנים) is the corrupt regard to personal connections,

the clouds, "and will not cease till God takes action and the righteous judge does justice" (35:16–18).[75] Thus Ben Sira resolves the tension between his moral teaching and the state of society by faith in a continuous divine rectification of affairs. Without this faith the kind of society Ben Sira takes for granted cannot be squared with his ethics.

Wright and Camp, however, argue that the faith of Ben Sira in God's retribution is far from confident:

> [Ben Sira] lacks the comfort level of the Proverbs sages, their confidence in the observable moral order of the world and their place in it ... although Proverbs admits that the divine will may supercede [sic] human plans, the earlier book is much more wedded to a theologized logic of material retribution than is Ben Sira.[76]

They seem to be relying for this observation on such remarks as those in 11:10–28 about the transitoriness of riches and the swift and seemingly arbitrary changes of fortune that can be brought about by God:

> Ben Sira seems to want to have his cake and eat it too. He knows the world does not work according to the divine justice his tradition leads him to expect, but he tries desperately to make himself and his readers believe it is so.[77]

But it must be questioned whether such texts as 11:12–13, 14, 18–19, 21–22 in fact suggest that "God seems to give wealth and take it away in morally random ways," as Wright and Camp assert, or that Ben Sira "does not notice" the incongruity with such verses as 11:17 which maintain the traditional doctrine of the reward of piety.[78] Ben Sira is indeed fully aware of the evidence that may be held to cast doubt on the doctrine of retribution, but the point of the texts about change of fortune is that despite all appearances in the course of life, in the end a person will receive God's due reward for good or ill, as is stated emphatically in vv. 27–28. This is no different from what Job's friends maintain. It is hard to see that Ben Sira is uncertain about this, however implausible the idea may appear to us—or indeed to the author of Job or to Qoheleth.

---

usually with the powerful, which denies a fair hearing to others, especially the oppressed. Failure to recognize this has led to misunderstanding of texts in the Hebrew Bible also: see Houston, *Contending*, 114–15, 218–19.

75. My translation of v. 18 in B; this is v. 21b in Beentjes.
76. Wright and Camp, "Who Has Been Tested?" 162.
77. Wright and Camp, "Who Has Been Tested?" 170.
78. Wright and Camp, "Who Has Been Tested?" 162.

Whether the eschatological continuation of the poem in chapter 35 in vv. 19–24 is due to Ben Sira himself is disputed. It identifies the injustice being suffered by any individual oppressed person with the general injustice of oppressive foreign rule over God's people, which he will put an end to in due course. It is widely held that this, along with the prayer that follows in 36:1–17, is an addition of Maccabaean age. Middendorp makes a case for this, largely dependent on the vocabulary.[79] His methodology has been questioned by Maria Carmela Palmisano.[80] Vocabulary depends to a large extent on the subject and the genre. The question is whether it is plausible that Ben Sira would have essayed this kind of writing, not an easy question in the abstract. Kieweler mentions Ben Sira's claim in 39:6 that the scribe may be inspired with "a spirit of understanding," suggesting this points to a "mixture of wisdom and prophecy."[81] Since the social developments in Jerusalem that Ben Sira found most troubling were encouraged by the Hellenistic rulers, it would not be surprising that he should pray for God's people to be delivered from them, and difficult to believe that he could have been perfectly comfortable with their rule. Kieweler rightly urges that he shows no sign of supporting the Hellenizing reform movement of the early second century, and the arrogant rich whose manipulative ways he warns against took the lead in this.[82] Middendorp argues that 36:8 appears to echo Daniel (11:27, 35), with a distinctive use not only of קץ/*qets*, "end," but also of מועד/*mo'ed*, "appointed time";[83] but Palmisano shows that the allusion is likely to be to Hab 2:3.

Conclusion

The work of Ben Sira is deeply rooted in a vanished social situation, and sharply marked not only by his own social position but also by his personal prejudices, as for example against women or against foreigners of various kinds, or indeed against the activity of commerce; and his remarks on the treatment of slaves, which I have not been able to deal with here, are contradictory and often harsh. Wright and Camp may be right in arguing that he finds his situation to some extent conflicted, though I do not

---

79. Middendorp, *Stellung*, 125–32.

80. Palmisano, *Salvaci, Dio!*, 25–44. Marböck, "Sir. 38,24–39,11," 79, also cites Schrader, *Leiden*, 87–93; Marböck himself withholds judgment. See also Collins, "Ecclesiasticus," 690a.

81. Kieweler, *Ben Sira*, 57.

82. Kieweler, *Ben Sira*, 63.

83. Middendorp, *Stellung*, 128, 131.

agree with them that his teaching is affected by a need to keep in with the powerful: his contempt for those who use their power to control and manipulate is clearly expressed.

And I hope that this discussion will have shown that Ben Sira's prejudices do not include one against those less fortunate than himself. But, in a similar way to those who express themselves on this subject in the Hebrew Bible,[84] his compassion for the poor and vulnerable and his urging of those in a position to do so to defend their rights does not extend to any questioning of the order of society as such. He perpetuates the belief perceptible everywhere in the Hebrew Bible that if only the members of society would act in obedience to the law of God and as their position requires of them, there would be peace and justice in society, and that if they do not, judgment awaits them.

Is there then any permanent value in Ben Sira's work? I believe there is. It lies in his perceptions, often psychologically penetrating, of what life is like in an inescapably unequal society—and if the inequality of our own society is not inescapable it is certainly deeply rooted—and how it may be possible nevertheless to act therein with justice, compassion, and humility towards those with less of the world's goods and power than ourselves.

---

84. Cf. Houston, *Contending*.

Chapter 10

Doing Justice

*The Phrase "Justice and Right"
in the Hebrew Bible*

─────────── (2017) ───────────

Introduction

A STUDY OF THE preaching of Martin Luther King Jr reveals that "easily his favorite verse from either testament" was Amos 5:24, which in the KJV reads "But let judgment run down as waters, and righteousness as a mighty stream."[1] More recent versions have generally replaced "judgment" with "justice." One wonders why they have not also replaced the old-fashioned word "righteousness," which is nearly as misleading as "judgment." In my translations below, I have generally used "right" or "the right," except where it appears to designate a personal quality.

King is not the only reader whose attention has been arrested by Amos's impressive simile, nor is he the only campaigner for social justice who has expressed the nature of the social change they have been seeking in the two abstract nouns that form the subject of this sentence: justice, משפט/*mishpat* and right(eousness), צדקה/*tsedaqa*. But far from being distinctive of Amos, the linkage of these two terms is very common, with between fifty and sixty examples, which include at least 12 percent of all occurrences of משפט/*mishpat* and no less than a third of all occurrences of צדקה/*tsedaqa*.[2] Precision is impossible, because there are several texts that have approximations to this usage: in the opposite order, or using צדק/*tsedeq* instead of צדקה/*tsedaqa*, or with the words in the plural, and it is not always clear whether they should be counted as examples of this idiom. The list below includes all

---

1. Bartlett, "Let Justice Roll Down," 10.
2. *DCH* under the two respective words; Miranda, *Marx and the Bible*, 108–9, nn. 35–38.

cases where משפט/*mishpat* is used with either צדקה/*tsedaqa* or צדק/*tsedeq*, in either order, and in the singular, excluding cases where either word is used in the plural, which often gives a different nuance.[3] The only exception I have allowed is Ps 72:1, where the versions (Greek and Syriac) give the singular, though admittedly this may be due to the influence of the standard expression. I think it is probable, however, that Ps 103:6, where both words are in the plural, does reflect the common expression: "YHWH performs right acts, acts of justice for all who are oppressed."[4] One text (Ps 50:6) yields the expression through a probable emendation.

It is of course quite typical of Hebrew poetry to use two rough synonyms in so-called synonymous parallelism. But it is much less common for a word-pair of this kind to be used not only in parallelism, but also as a single phrase, linked by "and." But this is true of this pair of words. Of the fifty-nine texts I have listed, thirty-two speak of "justice *and* right," most often משפט וצדקה/*mishpat utsedaqa*, both in prose and in poetry,[5] and the other twenty-seven use the words in parallelism.[6]

It is clear from this evidence that the linking of these two words is more than a poetic trope. It is a common idiom, and it is widely accepted that rather than each word having a separate meaning the two words taken together express a single idea.[7] Commonly, this figure of speech, in which two linked words express a single idea, is referred to as *hendiadys*. Although everyone uses this word, including me in previous publications,[8] it is inaccurate. H. W. Fowler, in his *Modern English Usage*, once the "Bible" of all good writers, defines it thus: "The expressing of a compound notion by giving its two constituents as though they were independent and connecting

---

3. Gen 18:19; 2 Sam 8:15 (= 1 Chr 18:14); 1 Kgs 10:9 (= 2 Chr 9:8); Isa 1:21; 1:27; 5:7, 16; 9:6 (Eng. 7); 16:5; 28:17; 32:1, 16; 33:5; 56:1; 58:2; 59:8-9a, 14; Jer 4:2; 9:23 (Eng. 24); 22:3a, 13, 15b-16; 23:5; 33:15; Ezek 18:5, 19, 21, 27; 33:14, 16, 19; 45:9; Hos 2:21 (Eng. 19); Amos 5:7, 24; 6:12; Ps 33:5; 36:7 (Eng. 6); 37:6; 50:6, if emended (אלהי משפט for אלהים שפט [BHS]); 72:1, 2; 89:15 (Eng. 14); 97:2; 99:4; 106:3; 119:121; Job 8:3; 29:14; 37:23; Prov 1:3; 2:9; 8:20; 16:8; 21:3; Eccl 3:16; 5:7a.

4. עשה צדקות יהוה ומשפטים לכול עשוקים

5. Gen 18:19; 2 Sam 8:15 (= 1 Chr 18:14); 1 Kgs 10:9 (= 2 Chr 9:8); Isa 9:6 (Eng. 7); 33:5; Jer 4:2; 9:23 (Eng. 24); 22:3a, 15b-16; 23:5; 33:15; Ezek 18:5, 19, 21, 27; 33:14, 16, 19; 45:9; Hos 2:21 (Eng. 19); Pss 33:5; 89:15 (Eng. 14); 97:2; 99:4; 119:121; Job 37:23; Prov 1:3; 2:9; 21:3; Eccl 5:7a.

6. Isa 1:21; 1:27; 5:7, 16; 16:5; 28:17; 32:1, 16; 56:1; 58:2; 59:8-9a, 14; Jer 22:13; Amos 5:7, 24; 6:12; Ps 36:7 (Eng. 6); 37:6; 50:6; 72:1, 2; 106:3; Job 8:3; 29:14; Prov 8:20; 16:8; Eccl 3:16.

7. E.g., Miranda, *Marx and the Bible*, 93; Weinfeld, *Social Justice*, 25; Williamson, *Isaiah 1–5*, 135; Houston, *Amos*, 35-36.

8. E.g., Weinfeld, *Social Justice*, 25; Houston, *Amos*, 35.

them with a conjunction instead of subordinating one to the other."[9] He gives as common examples in English: "nice and warm" instead of "nicely warm," "try and do better" instead of "try to do better," and "grace and favor" instead of "gracious favor." Expressions like "assault and battery" and "stand and deliver" do not fit the definition because "their two parts are on an equal footing and not in sense subordinate one to the other." "Justice and righteousness" would appear to be this kind of figure, words indivisibly joined and expressing one idea, but equal to one other.

By no means all writers, however, treat these words as expressing a single idea. For example, J. L. Mays in his commentary on Amos says that while *mishpat* refers to justice in the courts, *tsedaqa* is the source of that justice.[10] Hans Wildberger says about Isa 1:27: "if the first term [משפט/*mishpat*] basically refers to the extrinsic activities connected with the administration of justice, the second term [צדקה/*tsedaqa*] deals with the intrinsic relationships which are commanded for those who relate to others within a particular community."[11] While this might be plausible in reference to these particular cases, it would be impossible to argue the same for the many cases where the two words are linked by "and," and stand on the same footing in the sentence. In those instances they are most frequently (in nineteen out of thirty-two cases) the object of the verb עשה/*'asa*, to do: kings and others *do* justice and right, and the two objects cannot plausibly be given distinct referents, especially as sometimes one or the other word serves on its own to express what seems to be much the same thing: for example, Jer 5:1: "anyone who does *justice* (משפט/*mishpat*)"; Ezek 18:22, 24: "his right conduct (צדקתו/*tsidqato*) which he has done," in a context that speaks repeatedly of "doing justice and right."

I have suggested that in this idiom the wide semantic range of each of the two words is restricted by its partner.[12] The range of משפט/*mishpat* covers rule, judgment, justice, custom, law, legal decision, and more, while the connotations of צדקה/*tsedaqa* include right order, just conduct, generosity, prosperity, salvation, and victory. But משפט/*mishpat* when linked with צדקה/*tsedaqa* would refer specifically to *just* rule, laws, and customs, while צדקה/*tsedaqa* in its turn would be restricted to the sphere of government and society, including the divine government of the world. The complete expression, looked at along with the range of contexts in which it occurs,

---

9. Fowler, *Modern English Usage*, 245.
10. Mays, *Amos*, 91–93.
11. Wildberger, *Isaiah 1–12*, 64.
12. Houston, *Amos*, 35.

may be taken, as has generally been seen,[13] to refer to just rule, to God's just ordering of the world, and in the human realm to just social and political relationships, or what we would call social justice, the virtues of the just society: just and generous relationships, honesty and integrity, freedom from corruption and violence, and the legal, political, and religious means by which these may be ensured.

My ultimate object in this paper is to inquire what accounts for the distribution of the idiom in the Hebrew Bible: of the fifty-nine texts that I have listed, only one is in the Torah and four in the historical books; thirty-three in the prophets, of which fourteen are in Isaiah; eleven in the Psalms; and ten in the wisdom literature. In particular, why is it so rare in the Torah and so common in Isaiah and the Psalms?

Justice for the Poor

The first step to an answer is to look in more detail at the referents, contexts, and associations of the pairing. The earliest work to my knowledge to study it in any detail was José Miranda's unjustly neglected *Marx and the Bible*.[14] His remarks do not appear to be cited by Weinfeld or any other subsequent writers, except me. It could be that the work's appearance in the context of the liberation theology movement, its polemical tone and overstatements, and the name in its title, which would have been a red rag to a bull in certain quarters, account for its neglect in what is usually termed mainstream biblical scholarship. According to Miranda:

> even the most supernaturalistic exegetes recognize that *ṣᵉdakah umišpaṭ* [sic] ("justice and right") is the most clearly technical term that the Old Testament uses to signify justice for the poor and oppressed, social justice. . . . The nonspecialized reader has only to read [the passages in which the term appears] to establish that indeed "justice and right" or "right and justice" (*mišpaṭ uṣᵉdakah*) means justice for the poor and needy.[15]

Miranda does not identify the previous exegetes who recognized this, and I have not been able to find out who they were; a desultory scan of some commentaries published earlier than 1971, when Miranda wrote, does not turn them up. We have already noted that Mays on Amos (1969) does not even recognize the expression as a standard idiom, and that would be

---

13. Weinfeld, *Social Justice*, and other works noted above.
14. Miranda, *Marx and the Bible*, 93–97 and 108–9, nn. 35–38.
15. Miranda, *Marx and the Bible*, 93.

true of others as well. H. H. Schmid in his seminal work on the concept צדק/*tsedeq* treats examples of the expression simply as variants of צדק/*tsedeq*, though he does note that the phrase עשׂה משׁפת וצדקה/*'asa mishpat utsedaqa*, "to do justice and right," is frequent in texts expressing the royal ideology; see below.[16]

Certainly, many of the contexts in which it appears do refer to justice for the poor: so clearly, for example, in Psalm 72.[17] The opening verses use variations of the formula twice, then as the psalm proceeds the king's responsibility is defined as being to give judgment for the poor and rescue them from oppression: vv. 4, 12–14. Again, in the well-known verse Isa 5:7, with its paronomasia, "and he looked for justice, and behold, bloodshed, for right, and behold, a cry of distress,"[18] "bloodshed" and "a cry of distress" surely refer to the fate of the oppressed; and, to return to Amos, in the context of prophetic denunciations of the oppression of the poor the expression occurs as a parallel word-pair three times (5:7, 24; 6:12), in each case to bewail the destruction or absence in Israel of "justice and right." However, no more than fifteen cases of the expression (plus Ps 103:6) refer explicitly and primarily to justice for the poor or oppressed: the other nine of these are Isa 16:5 (the context is the appeal of Moabite refugees for asylum—could this verse be part of their appeal?),[19] 32:1 (see v. 7), 58:2, the three cases in Jeremiah 22, Ezek 45:9, Job 29:14, and Eccl 5:7a. In the seven cases in the parables of Ezekiel 18 and 33, where the surface meaning describes the conduct of an individual, the treatment of the poor, especially the person's debtors, certainly takes a prominent place, but this appears as part of a broader picture of principled or unprincipled behavior. As the idiom is used to introduce the whole detailed list of conduct in each case, it must have a wider reference than simply justice for the poor.

Further argument is needed to associate the other uses of the expression with justice for the poor, and to some extent this is provided by Moshe Weinfeld, in his work *Social Justice in Ancient Israel and the Ancient Near East*.[20] This book is exclusively devoted to the analysis of this expression, and others that he holds to be equivalent or related, and investigates the associations of the idiom in detail. It is especially valuable for its detailed research into the Near Eastern parallels to both the linguistic expression

16. Schmid, *Gerechtigkeit als Weltordnung*, 85.

17. See chapter 3.

18. ויקו למשׁפט והנה משׂפח לצדקה והנה צעקה

19. Rather than an irrelevant eschatological prophecy—so Wildberger, *Isaiah 13–27*, 143. [The point is argued in an unpublished paper by Fleur Houston.]

20. Weinfeld, *Social Justice*. See also Weinfeld, "Justice and Righteousness."

and the institutional and legal forms in which "justice and righteousness" is often embodied. Weinfeld amasses a large amount of evidence both from the Hebrew Bible and from the ancient Near East, particularly cuneiform texts from Mesopotamia.

Weinfeld expresses his basic understanding of this expression on the first page of his introduction.[21] Though he does not refer to Miranda, he is fundamentally at one with him in understanding the main thrust of the expression as to do with relieving the misery of the poor by combating oppression, as expressed in Ps 72:12–14. (Weinfeld calls the expression a "concept," but I am cautious about identifying verbal locutions with mental concepts.) He asserts that the passages in which it occurs do not refer "only to formal judicial proceedings" (despite the use of the term משפט/ *mishpat*). Rather, the "concept" is "more associated with *mercy and lovingkindness* or . . . with the context of ameliorating the situation of the destitute, . . . the latter cannot be aided by righteous judgements [*sic*] in court alone, but by the elimination of exploitation and oppression on the part of the oppressors."[22] Even more clearly a little later in the book he states: "the concept refers primarily to the improvement of the conditions of the poor, which is undoubtedly accomplished through regulations issued by the king and his officials, *and not* by offering legal assistance to the poor man in his litigation with his oppressor."[23] The assertion that the expression has nothing to do with litigation in court is dubious, as we shall see; whether there were in Israel or Judah "regulations issued by the king and his officials" with this effect we shall investigate.

Two key aspects of Weinfeld's analysis are highlighted in his introductory remarks. One is that "justice and right" are frequently associated not only with words such as מישרים/*mesharim*, which means much the same thing (the conventional translation is "equity"), but also with the word חסד/ *hesed*, which he translates "kindness," often in the word-pair חסד ואמת/ *hesed we'emet*.[24] Unfortunately his understanding of the biblical sense of the word חסד/*hesed* is defective. It comes to mean kindness or charity in later Hebrew, but in the Bible the notion of acting in pursuit of a pre-existing commitment, whether as a relative or a patron or a covenant partner, is essential to it: "steadfast love" is the characteristic rendering of the NRSV.[25]

21. Weinfeld, *Social Justice*, 7.
22. Weinfeld, *Social Justice*, 7; emphasis in the original.
23. Weinfeld, *Social Justice*, 35; emphasis mine.
24. Weinfeld, *Social Justice*, 29. Weinfeld oversaw the translation of his work from Hebrew himself, although he thanks two friends for assistance with it (ibid., 5).
25. Clark, *The Word Hesed*, 267.

חסד ואמת/*hesed we'emet* is a word-pair similar to the one we are discussing in combining two quasi-synonyms, for אמת/*emet* in this context means "truth" in the sense of truth to a commitment, faithfulness. The expression occurs mainly in reference to God and his commitment to his people or indeed to his creation,[26] e.g., at Ps 89:15 (Eng. 14), "Right and justice are the foundation of your throne; steadfast love and faithfulness go before you."[27] However, it is also found in connection with government on earth, for example at Isa 16:5: "A throne will be established *in steadfast love*, and a ruler will sit on it *in faithfulness* in the tent of David, pursuing *justice* and quick to act in *right*."

This does not mean that kindness, generosity, and charity are not part of the connotation of our expression. They very clearly are in a passage such as Ezekiel 18 or Isaiah 58, as in a more political connection in Psalm 72: see vv. 13 and 14: "He (the king) has pity on the poor and the needy, and saves the lives of the needy . . . precious is their blood in his sight." Weinfeld is correct to argue that doing justice and right does not denote some legalistic process of correction, but implies doing good to the poor in whatever way is available (among other things, as we shall see).

The Justice of the King

Looming larger in Weinfeld's book is his assertion that the theme of justice and righteousness is predominantly associated with the king: that as well as denoting a character trait that may be attributed to God (e.g., Ps 33:5), or to the king (Ps 72:1), or a social ideal associated with government as in Isa 9:6 (Eng. 7) or 16:5, it is applied practically to "just dealing in the social sphere," and above all denotes a *task* that is part of the king's responsibility.

A whole series of texts demonstrate the royal associations of this idiom. They are not all of monarchic date; many of them would generally be regarded as postdating the monarchy, but they either look back to the monarchy as their narrative setting, or look forward to an ideal or eschatological king of the future. For example, Ezek 45:9 exhorts the "princes of Israel" to execute "right and justice," צדקה ומשפט/*tsedaqa umishpat*, in place of חמס ושד/*hamas washod*, "violence and extortion." The text is looking back to the monarchic period and finds its example a bad one. But according to 2 Sam 8:15, "David did justice and right for all his people"; and the Queen of Sheba tells Solomon "Blessed be the LORD your God, who has . . . made you king to do justice and right" (1 Kgs 10:9). The association

---

26. Cf. Weinfeld, *Social Justice*, 204.
27. צדק ומשפת מכון כסאך חסד ואמת יקדמו פניך

with the monarchy is particularly clear in Jeremiah, where five of the seven texts in our list speak of the king's duty of doing justice.[28] The connection is less clear in Isaiah, but see 9:6 (Eng. 7), 16:5, and 32:1; all of these texts are ideal or eschatological in character. It is worth mentioning also Job 29:14, where Job adopts a virtually royal persona. Many of these texts speak of the king *doing* justice and righteousness. It is then something that is not merely a general ideal, but a specific responsibility. The case of Psalm 72 is peculiarly important, since this probably represents the Davidic dynasty's own self-presentation, emerging as it does from the Jerusalem temple, which in the monarchic period was effectively the royal chaplaincy. They presented themselves, as did the kings of Mesopotamia and elsewhere in the ancient Near East,[29] as kings with a care for the poor and a concern to repress their exploitation: "justice and right" is a responsibility that they purport to have taken on with the utmost seriousness.[30]

Yet of our fifty-nine attestations of the expression in various forms, only fifteen or sixteen have an explicit connection with the king. Probably as many define a socio-political ethos but without mentioning any king. This is true of those in Amos and at least nine of the fourteen texts in Isaiah (1:21; 1:27; 5:7; 32:16; 33:5; 56:1; 58:2; 59:9, 14); Jer 9:23 (MT [Eng. 9:24]), and, in the Writings, at least Ps 99:4, Eccl 3:16 and 5:7. The great majority of these texts are post-monarchic in date, of course. But a few are generally seen as dating from the monarchy: the three in Amos and Isa 1:21 and 5:7, and probably Jer 9:23; the date of Psalm 99 is disputed, but in any case it celebrates God, not any king, as the direct source of "justice and right." It is possible to make the assumption in these cases that it is the king whom the original hearers of the text would have held to have the earthly responsibility for "justice and right," and hence that they might detect indirect allusion to a failure by the king to exercise his responsibility.[31] This is likely in Isaiah, where explicit criticism of the king is avoided (except in ch. 7), even where government policy is directly attacked, as in Isa 30:1-17 and 31:1-3. The reason it is absent from Amos, apart from a single possibly secondary verse (7:9), is less clear. Perhaps the Judean prophet and his Jerusalem-based editors did not expect kings of Israel to do "justice

---

28. Possibly six, if Weinfeld (*Social Justice*, 47) is right in emending Jer 9:23aβ after 1 Sam 2:10 LXX, השכל וידע יהוה ועשה חסד משפט וצדקה בארץ (This is a retroversion from Weinfeld's English, "understanding and knowing YHWH, and establishing kindness, justice and righteousness in the land"; I have not seen his Hebrew.)

29. Fensham, F. Charles. "Widow, Orphan and the Poor in Ancient Near Eastern Legal and Wisdom Literature." JNES 21 (1962), 129-39.

30. See above, chapter 3, 37-57; Houston, *Contending*, 139-50.

31. Or the absence of a responsible monarch altogether. Compare chapter 11, 188.

and right." Some texts, moreover, portray YHWH as acting in royal fashion to establish "justice and right" in Israel.³² Psalm 99:4 expresses it most explicitly: "justice and right you have done in Jacob."³³ See also Isa 28:17; 32:16; 33:5; Hos 2:21 (Eng. 19). This is a point to which we shall return.

Thus the idea that "justice and right" in society is to be protected or advanced by sovereign action, if not by the earthly king then directly by God, is widespread in the Hebrew Bible. Weinfeld, however, develops the argument primarily through comparison with ancient Near Eastern parallels. It is a very ancient understanding of the king's responsibility, especially in Mesopotamia, that he should temper the harshness of relationships in an evolving or established class society, relationships between rich and poor, powerful and vulnerable, creditor and debtor, rulers and ruled. Weinfeld shows that our expression is the equivalent of the Akkadian *kittum u mīšarum*, "truth [or right] and justice," and especially that the phrase "to do justice and right" refers to activities by kings analogous to those undertaken by Mesopotamian kings in defense of social order and justice. He devotes attention in particular to the decrees of *mīšarum*, justice, or *andurārum*, freedom or liberation, issued from time to time by Mesopotamian kings, proclaiming to their subjects, or certain of their subjects, relief from taxes, conscript labor, and military service, cancellation of debts and deliverance from enslavement for debt.³⁴ They would be issued by a king on his accession in particular, and sometimes on subsequent occasions. They are attested especially for the Old Babylonian dynasty, in the second quarter of the second millennium BCE; but, as Weinfeld shows, such institutions and such ideas were widely distributed in time and space.³⁵

In Weinfeld's view this administrative activity, this publication of decrees of justice and liberation, is what is meant by "doing justice and right," and this is what was expected of kings, whether or not they did it.³⁶ Moreover, when the text says that such-and-such a king—David, Solomon (at least according to the queen of Sheba!), Josiah—"did justice and righteousness," this means, according to Weinfeld, that they did actually engage in such specific acts of social amelioration. He had already argued in an earlier work, and repeats in this one, that 2 Sam 8:15–18 is derived from "a state document of the Davidic period" (vv. 16–18 go on to list the principal ministers in David's government),³⁷ and v. 15 "refers to acts

---

32. See chapter 11 below.
33. משפט וצדקה ביעקב אתה עשית
34. Weinfeld, *Social Justice*, 25–44.
35. Weinfeld, *Social Justice*, 77.
36. Weinfeld, *Social Justice*, 45–74.
37. Weinfeld, *Deuteronomy and the Deuteronomic School*, 153–54; *Social Justice*, 46;

of liberation performed by David upon his ascent to the throne, and it reflects a practice known to us from Mesopotamia: the establishment of *mīšarum* upon coronation."[38] In the same passage of his earlier book he argues that those kings who are described in the book of Kings as having done right in the eyes of YHWH must have done the same. This argument is unsatisfactory, and is not repeated in his later work. Unlike the statement that David "did justice and right," the assessment of each of the Hebrew kings in the book of Kings comes from the hand of the Deuteronomistic redactors of the book, and there is nothing to suggest that this was an aspect of the royal responsibility that interested them. Wherever the assessment goes into detail, the main concern is invariably the purity of the cult, and usually nothing else is mentioned.

According to Weinfeld, it can be deduced from 1 Kings 12 that an edict establishing "justice and right" is what the people of Israel demanded of Rehoboam on his accession, for such decrees included alleviation of the corvée.[39] Weinfeld does not, however, speculate on what this might have meant for Jeroboam and those who succeeded him on the throne of the northern kingdom. In all probability it was more than the throne of any of them was worth to impose any corvée on ethnic Israelites.[40] But, as I have argued elsewhere,[41] they had an alternative, referred to several times in the biblical text, to conscript non-Israelites in the conquered regions of the kingdom. I have also argued that it is possible that no taxes were raised in ethnically Israelite areas of the kingdom before Menahem imposed an extraordinary poll tax to raise money for the Assyrian tribute (2 Kgs 15:20).[42] This would not necessarily render decrees of justice and right redundant in the kingdom, but it may explain why criticism of the government as such, and certainly of any corvée, is absent in Amos. Contrast Mic 3:1-4, addressed to the government of Judah, a kingdom inhabited by a single ethnic group, apart perhaps from nomadic tribes in the Negev that were

---

he adds here that the authenticity of the document "is not to be doubted."

38. Weinfeld, *Social Justice*, 47.

39. Weinfeld, *Social Justice*, 54, n. 29; 84.

40. This is an obvious deduction from the mere existence of the account in 1 Kings 12, regardless of its historicity. [See chapter 8 above.] Fleming, *The Legacy of Israel*, 109-13, agrees with others that it "is told from Judah's point of view" (110), but argues that it accords with what we know of Israel's political ethos.

41. Houston, *Contending*, 38-39; cf. Josh 9:21; Judg 1: 28, 30, 32, 33; 1 Kgs 9:20-21; and Faust, *Archaeology of Israelite Society*, 230-54, esp. 248-50 and 252-54. [See now chapter 8 above.]

42. Houston, *Amos*, 64.

difficult to control, so that the government, if it wished to impose tax and corvée, had to do so on its own people.

Weinfeld links Israelite kings' "doing of justice and right" with the Mesopotamian decrees primarily through comparison of vocabulary: for example he compares Ps 72:2, 4 and Jer 22:3 with various formulae, particularly in the prologue to the Code of Hammurabi; Isa 11:4, where the eschatological king slays the wicked with his breath, is interpreted of a decree.[43] Sometimes this argument appears overpressed. For example, Ps 72:5a, where he argues for an original text "they will see him as the sun,"[44] is compared with various Akkadian passages speaking of the king shining forth as the sun.[45] But this fails to make sense of the rest of the verse.[46] Again, Weinfeld says that the words "then it was well [with him]" in Jer 22:15–16 "can . . . be explained" by way of phrases in the cuneiform texts about the king "doing good" to the people.[47] The parallels are fairly weak, and hardly demonstrate the case. Better supported is his observation that in Ezek 45:8–17 and 46:16–18

> the prophet demands the very actions that were the central components of the *mīšarum* and *andurārum* in Mesopotamia: the preservation of the patrimony by establishing the year of liberty (45:8, 46:16–18), cancellation of taxes and levies (45:9), the organized collection of tithes and priestly-dues [sic] (45:13–17), and the establishment of weights and measures (45:10–12)

—all this, of course, prefixed by the demand to "do justice and right" (45:9).[48] But Weinfeld is surely in error in comparing the phrase there חמס ושד הסירו/ *hamas washod hasiru*, "remove violence and robbery," to "destroy evil and evildoers" in Akkadian.[49] The "violence and robbery" that the princes are to remove is their own, as indicated by the opening remonstrance "Enough!" (רב לכם/*rav lakem*).

---

43. Weinfeld, *Social Justice*, 48–50.
44. יראוהו עם שמש
45. Weinfeld, *Social Justice*, 51–53.
46. The widely accepted emendation יאריך fits much better. See also chapter 3 above, 40, n. 16.
47. Weinfeld, *Social Justice*, 54–55. He argues that the parallels show that the first of the two appearances of the sentence is in the correct location (the second is a dittography), but the correct wording is with לו as in the second, referring to "the poor and needy person": "then it went well with him [the poor person]."
48. Weinfeld, *Social Justice*, 55.
49. Weinfeld, *Social Justice*, 56.

Thus, while a certain degree of "parallelomania" has led Weinfeld to overpress the evidence in some cases, it can be safely admitted that he is correct in making the general case that ancient Judah (the case for [northern] Israel is less clear) shared a common tradition with the Mesopotamian kingdoms in which the king was expected, and admitted the responsibility, to defend the poor and repress exploitation, and that this responsibility was expressed in the phrase עשה משפט יצדקה/'asa mishpat utsedaqa, which has Akkadian parallels.[50] But it is not nearly so clear that this responsibility was regularly exercised through decrees and never through judicial action; still less that the ideological prominence of the responsibility was always matched by its practical and effective exercise.

On the former question, as we have seen, Weinfeld understands this royal responsibility as exercised exclusively through the king's administrative function, in virtue of which he publishes decrees. Jackson argues that his judicial function, responding to pleas and adjudicating disputes, either in his own person or through appointed judges, is equally important as a means of implementing social justice.[51] Weinfeld, Jackson observes, appears to regard judicial activity as a matter of applying legal rules in modern fashion, whether or not it results in genuine justice, so that justice can only be achieved by edict.[52]

Weinfeld's understanding of judicial practice appears to be the same as Otto's so far as Mesopotamia is concerned.[53] Otto draws a sharp and in my opinion unjustified distinction between the situations in Mesopotamia and

50. Lemche has argued that of the two main designations in Akkadian for such decrees, both of which have counterparts in Hebrew, *mīšarum* must be an early loanword in Hebrew (as מישרים) because it is not used after the end of the Old Babylonian dynasty; but on the other hand דרור is borrowed from the Assyrian form *durārum*, without the prefix *an-*, during the time of Judah's vassalage to Assyria, c. 734–c. 622 BCE. דרור is used both in reference to the royal decree imposing the covenant releasing debt slaves in Jer 34:8, 15 and as the content of the jubilee declaration in Lev 25:10. The institutions of the sabbatical and jubilee years, he says, "depend on social thought which originated late in Israel." (Lemche, "Andurarum," 22; cf. "Manumission.") If that is the case, it would be unlikely that kings would be issuing such decrees earlier in the history of Israel and Judah. However, Lemche has overlooked the phonological evidence. Why should *durārum* have become דרור? The rounding of the long *a* is characteristic of Canaanite dialects, but that phonological change took place far earlier than the eighth century, and did not continue into later times: compare *tartān* and *rab-šāqeh*, words that presumably were really borrowed in the eighth or seventh century. (I accept that the Masoretic vocalization is much later, but a pronunciation with ō would have acquired a *mater lectionis*.) I would deduce that the word, and therefore no doubt some form of the institution, had long been known in the southern Levant.

51. Jackson, "Justice and Righteousness," 244–54.

52. Weinfeld, *Social Justice*, 35.

53. Otto, *Theologische Ethik*, 81–94. See also Otto, "Programme"; "Gerechtigkeit im Land."

monarchic Judah,[54] unjustified because he does not compare like with like. In Mesopotamia, he suggests, the need for such decrees lay in a tension between law, i.e., contract law, *Vertragsrecht*,[55] and justice, whereas in Judah the law embodied justice in itself. In Hammurabi's code, the king recognizes his divinely imposed responsibility for social justice in the Prologue and Epilogue, "to demonstrate justice (*mīšaram*) within the land, to destroy evil and wickedness, to stop the mighty exploiting the weak, . . . to improve the welfare of my people,"[56] but the laws themselves are not formulated with respect to the Prologue and Epilogue. The way in which the king exercises his responsibility for justice is not by law, but by decree. The decrees take priority over law and, retrospectively only, nullify it. "The establishment of justice therefore nullifies the applicable law retrospectively and on a single occasion."[57] The last words underline that the decrees do not affect the continuing operation of the law in the future. Biblical law, on the other hand, requires "the permanent solidarity of the economically stronger party with the weaker,"[58] grounded theologically in the actively expressed compassion of YHWH himself, "for I am compassionate" (Exod 22:26, English versions 27). Thus, "Whereas in Mesopotamia law and justice could only be reconciled by an occasional nullification of the law, in Judah the dealing of the compassionate God with humanity is the foundation of an ethic of compassion."[59] It is difficult to see this theological assessment as a historical judgment, which would imply that acts of "justice and right" were redundant in Judah; for it compares the practical enforcement of contracts in Mesopotamia with the ideal conception of justice in the biblical codes. These can only be understood in their literary context as covenant law, which certainly demands an "ethic of compassion" from its readers and hearers, but, as Jackson stresses, is not addressed to the judges.[60] Jackson suggests that so far from law being in tension with justice in Mesopotamia, royal decrees may have been significant in creating or modifying ideas

---

54. Otto assumes that the Book of the Covenant is of Judean origin, though this can hardly be taken for granted; cf. Fleming, *Legacy of Israel*, 114, n. 1.

55. Otto, "Programme," 42–44.

56. Richardson, *Hammurabi's Laws*, 28–31.

57. Otto, *Theologische Ethik*, 88. ("Die Durchsetzung von Gerechtigkeit setzt also geltendes Recht rückwirkend und einmalig außer Kraft.")

58. Otto, *Theologische Ethik*, 88; ("die permanente Solidarität des wirtschaftlich Stärkeren mit dem Schwächeren,")

59. Otto, *Theologische Ethik*, 89. ("Können in Mesopotamien Recht und Gerechtigkeit nur durch eine zeitweise Außerkraftsetzung des Rechts miteinander vermittelt werden, so begründet in Juda das Handeln Gottes als des Barmherzigen mit den Menschen ein Ethos der Barmherzigkeit.")

60. Jackson, "Ideas of Law," 187–88.

of justice applied by judges: "these judges are expected to apply, in the very act of adjudication, the same concept of social justice which the king applies in the proclamations."[61] Ultimately, as argued by Finkelstein,[62] such concepts might become enshrined in the codes, as for example in the law requiring the release of debt slaves after three years in *CH* L117,[63] though Jackson surely goes too far in saying that the codes "contain provisions which, if made effective, would render the *mesharum* acts unnecessary."[64]

In attempting to make concrete the idea of the king's "doing justice and right" through his judicial function, Jackson brings forward the examples of the cases brought before David in 2 Samuel 14 by the wise woman of Tekoa with her fictional sons, one of whom has killed the other, and by the two harlots before Solomon in 1 Kings 3.[65] In each case the king decides the case in virtue of his presumed supernatural endowment of wisdom ("like the angel of God," 2 Sam 14:17; "the wisdom of God was with him," 1 Kgs 3:28) in an unexpected but evidently just way. When the king of Israel restores the estate of the Shunemite woman, Elisha's patron (2 Kgs 8:6), he is doubtless using his discretion to override both the actual appropriation of the estate and the custom that allowed no share of a man's estate to go to his widow (cf. Num 27:8-11). In each case, justice in the sense of משפט וצדקה/*mishpat utsedaqa* is applied through the royal discretion or through the king as the fount of mercy. But none of these examples has directly to deal with the defense of the poor against exploitation and oppression, even though Jackson makes the point that widows and prostitutes both belonged to powerless or oppressed classes, "lacking their natural, familial protectors," and in a private communication points out that in all three cases the suppliant or appellant is a woman.

These examples are "literary constructions designed to celebrate a role attributed to the king."[66] They illustrate that the king was understood to have the power to decide what was just regardless of custom or expectation. But that is no proof that he regularly did so. The critique of the practice of law in e.g., Isa 5:23; 10:1-4 is sufficient to indicate that the defense of the poor and vulnerable was not to be expected from the royal judges in monarchic

---

61. Jackson, "Justice and Righteousness," 246.

62. Finkelstein, "Ammiṣaduqa's Edict," 103.

63. Richardson, *Hammurabi's Laws*, 78-79.

64. Jackson, "Ideas of Law," 186; cf. "Justice and Righteousness," 254, appealing to Finkelstein, "Ammiṣaduqa's Edict"; but I cannot find this statement there. All Finkelstein says is that the law-codes contained provisions derived from the same kings' earlier *mišarum* acts.

65. Jackson, "Justice and Righteousness," 249-51.

66. Jackson, private communication.

Judah, at least in Isaiah's time. Jeremiah preserves the memory of Josiah as a truly just king, who "did justice and right" and "judged the cause of the poor and needy" (Jer 22:15–16); but quite apart from the *parti pris* we might detect in a prophet whose main support came from the family of Shaphan,[67] what is there to indicate that Josiah was more than a shining exception?

The Justice of the King: Ideology and Reality

The judicial decisions of the king or his judges, as well as his occasional decrees, might be expected and represented to be in favor of the poor and against the oppressor, but it does not follow that they were usually or even often so in reality.

It is clear from such a text as Psalm 72, which almost certainly derives from the monarchic-period Jerusalem temple, that is from the royal chaplaincy, that the king's supposed concern and action for the poor was an important part of the dynasty's self-presentation.[68] This is in ironic contrast with the central role of the development of state institutions and state-led urbanization in social stratification and the formation of an exploiting class.[69] Such ideological propaganda cries out for ideological criticism, and I responded to the cry in my article of 1999, a discussion somewhat abbreviated in *Contending for Justice*.[70] I suggested that it was likely that there was a certain degree of such activity, although the evidence was limited, if only because it would have been in the royal interest. Kings would gain favor with the populace by deciding cases in favor of the oppressed; by remitting taxes and labor service; and by compelling creditors to cancel debts owed to them. At the same time they would be cutting down threats to their own power by undermining rival centers of power in the faction-ridden ruling class.[71] (We should note that debts were not so much means of monetary enrichment for creditors as instruments of power, enabling them to gain slaves and dependents.[72]) But the claims in Psalm 72, I concluded,[73] conceal the king's interest behind the pretext of

---

67. Chapter 3 above, 47.

68. Jackson, private communication; Houston, *Contending*, 139–50.

69. Dearman, *Property Rights*; Nurmi, *Die Ethik unter dem Druck*; Houston, *Contending*, 35–43, 49.

70. Chapter 3 above; *Contending*, 143–50.

71. Chaney, "Debt Easement," 129–30; chapter 3 above, 52. Cf. Gottwald, "Expropriators."

72. Boer, *Sacred Economy*, 158–61, and literature mentioned there at n. 24, esp. Finley, "Debt-Bondage," 153–56.

73. Chapter 3, 53.

his personal concern for the poor (vv. 12–14), and displace his exploitative activity onto foreign nations (vv. 9–10).

It is undoubtedly also true of the Mesopotamian kings' decrees that the sedulously cultivated representation of their concern for social justice was at the very least an exaggeration. Roland Boer points out that it is misleading to describe *mīšarum* decrees as abolishing debts and giving people their freedom: rather, debts were cancelled partially and selectively, and the effect was "to shift labor from one type of dependency to another"; not to free them, but to put them "back into their previous status."[74] It is easy to compare such edicts with the measures of debt relief and liberation in the Torah (see below); but these naturally express the ideal and give little impression of the complexity and compromise of measures in a really existing polity. The evidence in Weinfeld's work, as distinct from his conclusions, does give an impression of this complexity. Moreover, remission of debts and taxes was not targeted specifically on the poor, whatever claims may have been made, but rather benefited a wide range of people, some of them quite well off.

All this would also have been true of similar edicts in Judah and/or Israel, if any. The one such edict that we know anything of, the liberation of debt-slaves by covenant under Zedekiah reported in Jeremiah 34, was manifestly inadequate, since the whole point of the passage is that the liberation was nullified as soon as the immediate emergency had passed (assuming that the purpose was to make them available for military service in the siege):[75] "they went back afterwards and took back the slaves that they had released and enslaved them once more" (Jer 34:11). The retrospective character of the measure, shared with all the Mesopotamian decrees, made it powerless to affect future action.

We may reasonably conclude that the justice asserted in the phrase משפט וצדקה/*mishpat utsedaqa* in royal propaganda such as Psalm 72 was more a matter of ideology than reality. But even ideally, justice as projected in Psalm 72 and in most of the other places where the expression is used is a top-down affair, as I have pointed out. The king "decides when justice has been breached, and how it is to be restored."[76] The exploited are not given a chance to decide for themselves how society ought to be ordered. Establishing "justice and right" makes no long-term difference to the structure of society or the distribution of wealth, and it is certainly

---

74. Boer, *Sacred Economy*, 160, quoting the decree of Lipit-Ishtar in the translation of Renger, "Royal Edicts," 145.

75. Cf. Weinfeld, *Social Justice*, 152, n.1; Jackson, "Justice and Righteousness," 239, n. 79; but note also Chavel's doubts, "Let My People Go!," 71–73 (see above, 48, n. 48).

76. Chapter 3, 56.

true of the Mesopotamian decrees that they were not meant to make any such change. As Dominique Charpin expresses it, "The rules of the game were not changed, they simply proceeded to a new deal."[77] Justice was not a future goal to which one might or might not make progress: it was an ideal to be found in the past, a return to origins.

To sum up this part of the argument: משפט וצדקה/*mishpat utsedaqa*, rather than always expressing a merely general idea of social justice, has a specifically political connotation and, in texts written in the monarchic period or referring to it, frequently or even usually refers to acts of justice supposed to be undertaken by the king. It originated as an element in the royal ideology, and in several places this is still evident. The boast of "doing justice and right" must be understood as an ideological claim that represents such acts, whatever their real effect, as the fulfillment of the age-old expectation of the just king who defends the poor against oppression.

However, the majority of the biblical texts on the subject, as we shall see, do not participate in this ideology, because they are not issued by the dynasty and do not represent its self-understanding or self-presentation.

The Justice of God

An essential aspect of the ideology is its religious motivation. As is almost universally the case, the direction of affairs by the king is justified on the grounds that the king represents the powers of the cosmos. Weinfeld comes oddly late in his book to the question of the divine exercise of "justice and righteousness."[78] We have already noted that it can be understood as bestowed by God on the ruler (Ps 72:1), and also that God may be imagined as establishing it among his people, or in the whole earth, in royal fashion (e.g., Isa 33:5). It is indeed a characteristic of God himself in, e.g., Ps 33:5a, "He loves right and justice," or 89:15 (Eng. 14), "Right and justice are the foundation of your throne"; further Jer 9:23 (Eng. 24). Weinfeld's treatment of this theme makes God's "justice and right" analogous to the king's "justice and right," and he identifies three realms where it is exercised: in Israel, among the peoples of the world, and in creation.[79]

Now while it is true that the way in which God's action is conceived theologically is inevitably based on an analogy with human action, and that the biblical understanding of God, including God's justice, is formed

---

77. Charpin, "Le 'bon pasteur," 113. ("Les règles du jeu n'étaient pas changées, on procédait seulement à une nouvelle donne.")

78. Weinfeld, *Social Justice*, 179–214.

79. Weinfeld, *Social Justice*, 183.

to a great degree by the analogy of monarchy, analogy is not the only way in which God's justice relates to kingly justice in the Hebrew Bible. For it is clear that the king's "justice and right" is represented as *derived* from God's: Ps 72:1 alone shows that, and in Isa 9:6 (English 9:7) it seems likely to me that the implied subject of "to establish and support it" (להכין אתה ילסעדה) is God rather than the newly announced king, especially in view of the final line of the verse: "The zeal of YHWH of hosts will accomplish this."[80] The king's justice exists because God is just. Likewise, where God is said, as in many examples in Isaiah and the Psalms, to establish "justice and right" among the people, without specific mention of the king, or in the world, it is evident that this means among other things that "justice and right" will be done by people on earth: see for example Isa 1:27, 28:17, 33:5, Ps 99:4.[81] God is acknowledged as the source of the hoped-for justice on earth. In fact, these two relationships of analogy and derivation form a reciprocal movement between them. God is understood to act to establish "justice and right," as human rulers ought to, and this action of God results in justice exercised by human beings.[82]

In Isa 59:9 and 59:14, on the other hand, God's "justice and right" is withheld because of people's failure to seek justice. These sentences cannot be simply truisms: the prophet cannot just be saying that there is no justice in Judah because people are not doing justice. Rather, the point is that they do not receive the gift of justice on earth from God because they have failed to make their own conduct consistent with it. Justice in society is, it seems, the gift of God, but it may be rejected or ruined by the injustice of human beings.

I believe the best way of explaining the relationship of royal justice, and all human justice, to divine justice is by way of H. H. Schmid's concept of "justice as world order."[83] Schmid's work concerns the word צדק/*tsedeq* and other words from the same root, including צדקה/*tsedaqa*, rather than the dual expression that we are studying, which he treats as a variant with a function particularly in the royal ideology. He shows that the ideologies

---

80. *Contra* Wildberger, *Isaiah 1-12*, 385, 405, and Weinfeld, *Social Justice*, 57-58.
81. Cf. chapter 11 below.
82. Cf. Jackson, "Law and Religion," 193.
83. Schmid, *Gerechtigkeit*. Schmid's thesis is dismissed by Jože Krašovec, *Justice de Dieu*, 15-17, on the grounds that his citations are taken out of context, that his conclusions do not follow from them, and, unkindest cut of all, "que l'auteur a vu dans la notion de justice l'ordre cosmique avant d'avoir commencé l'analyse" (15: "that the author saw cosmic order in the notion of justice before beginning the analysis."). I can only say that this does not seem to me to be true of Schmid's argument in greater measure than of any other large academic thesis.

of ancient Near Eastern societies in general, including Israel, centered on a concept of world order—in Akkadian this is known as *kittum u mīšarum*, in Egypt as *ma3ʿat*. This world order is controlled ultimately by the supreme or creator god, but on earth it is the king who is responsible for ensuring its maintenance. In Israel, he argues, pretty convincingly, the sense of צדק/*tsedeq* and its derivatives, which in themselves just mean "what is right, just or correct," or action that is right or just, is "directed towards" the same sense of a world order that is created and directed by YHWH, while the king is responsible as God's delegate for order on earth, so that they refer to what conforms to the divine order of the world. He shows that this group of words plays a role in six distinct spheres of life: in law, in wisdom, where צדק/*tsedeq* and צדקה/*tsedaqa* refer to what is morally right, in nature, where they refer to fertility and resultant prosperity, in war, where צדקה/*tsedaqa* often means "victory," in the cult, where they designate correctly offered sacrifices, and in kingship. And in many examples from other ancient Near Eastern societies it is precisely the first five of these spheres of life that appear as areas of the king's responsibility.

Now, when the general idea of what is right and just indicated by צדק/*tsedeq* and צדקה/*tsedaqa* is specifically qualified by combining them with משפט/*mishpat*, it points, as we can see from our examples, to the right order of society, originally as directed by the king, which conforms with right world order, and is ultimately the gift of God. It is clear that in this right order of society relations between the classes of society are of central importance: it is essential to right order that the poor are not oppressed, no more by the state itself than by their creditors or patrons, and maintain the freedom and dignity that belongs to them as members of their communities: ideologically, this is the significance of decrees of liberation. In its origin the idea of world order as ordained by God expresses the royal ideology. But it did not remain corralled in that ideological pen, as we shall see.

Justice in the Prophets

We can now get a better grasp of the meaning of that famous utterance in Amos 5:24. "Justice and righteousness" should "roll like water" because it is the gift of God, and only at a secondary stage the work of kings and other human beings. Koch's conception that justice and righteousness in Amos are like a "fluid," that they "pour out healingly like a river over the people," sent down from above by YHWH,[84] takes the metaphor too literally, but I believe correctly interprets the structure of Amos's theological ethics. And

---

84. Koch, *The Prophets*, vol. 1, 58.

as two other sayings of Amos complain, using a different metaphor, in Israel this divine flow is obstructed by the refusal of those with power to behave justly. Both 5:7 and 6:12 imply that justice is something that exists outside of those denounced, which they have ruined or destroyed: "you have *turned*[85] justice into poison, and the fruit of righteousness into wormwood" (6:12; 5:7 is similar). In 5:24 the complaint is that by thinking to honor God in the liturgy rather than by protecting the poor, they have prevented justice from flowing. As I would translate: "take away from me the noise of your songs, and let me not hear the music of your lutes, *so that* justice may run like water, and righteousness like a never-failing stream."[86]

More instances of the usage we are studying occur in the book of Isaiah than in any other. An important early essay of John Barton suggests why this should be so.[87] Barton sets himself in this essay to elucidate the ultimate ground or base assumptions of Isaiah's ethics, and shows convincingly that, in Isaiah's understanding, "The universe forms an ordered whole in which each creature should know its place; and God's place, if we may speak so, is supreme."[88] He notes of Isa 3:1–12, where both the "social decay" of eighth-century Judah and its punishment by God end in anarchy, that it seems "to imply an ethical system which sets a very high value on the received order of society."[89] Even more sharply in a later essay, which extends his observations to the whole of the book of Isaiah, he notes that "Isaiah's vision of society is of a stable, aristocratic state, in which the poor are protected by an attitude of noblesse oblige on the part of the ruling classes, and property-owning males are given their 'rightful' preeminence. Humility towards God goes hand in hand with respect for the long-established orders of society."[90]

The convergence between Barton's observations and Schmid's is very noticeable. Barton noticed it himself, but at that point downplayed it, being dubious about connecting his own observations with צדקה/*tsedaqa*, and noting that this word is not all that common in Isaiah 1–39 compared

---

85. הפכתם

86. Cf. Joosten, *Verbal System*, 148; Waltke and O'Connor, *Biblical Hebrew Syntax*, 563. [I argue the case fully for taking the verse as a clause of purpose in Houston, "Folly at Bethel."]

87. Barton, "Isaiah of Jerusalem." Barton refers in the title of his article to "Isaiah of Jerusalem," meaning only to examine the ethics of the eponymous prophet himself, but noting that few of the relevant passages in Isa 1–39 are (or were in 1981!) controversial from a literary-critical point of view.

88. Barton, "Isaiah of Jerusalem," 8 (87–88 in reprint [a], 136 in reprint [b]).

89. Barton, "Isaiah of Jerusalem," 10 (89 in reprint [a], 137 in reprint [b]).

90. Barton, "Ethics in the Book of Isaiah," 70; 148 in reprint. Cf. Barton, *Ethics in Ancient Israel*, 116.

with Deutero-Isaiah.[91] (Recently, he has more clearly embraced Schmid's conclusions.)[92]

Although צדקה/*tsedaqa* may be relatively uncommon in Isaiah 1–39, it occurs repeatedly in connection with משפט/*mishpat*; out of twenty instances of צדק/*tsedeq* or צדקה/*tsedaqa* in Isaiah 1–39, thirteen may be said to be linked with משפט/*mishpat*: although there are only ten in my list, Williamson adds 26:9, which I have excluded because משפט/*mishpat* is used in the plural, and suggests that in two other texts (Isa 11:4 and 32:17 [twice]) there is an implicit link.[93] On the other hand, these words are never associated in Isaiah 40–55: there, צדק/*tsedeq* or צדקה/*tsedaqa* is rather—and repeatedly—set in parallel with words from the root ישע/*y-sh-'*, bringing it into the semantic field "salvation," "victory," etc.[94] This is a point to which we shall return.

Characteristic then of Isaiah 1–39, or rather 1–33,[95] is a usage of צדקה/*tsedaqa*, "the right," directed towards a conception of the divine order that embraces the supremacy of YHWH and the traditional order of society. The protection of the poor, but also other aspects of justice and right dealing in society, are indicated by the combination of צדקה/*tsedaqa* with משפט/*mishpat*, and they characterize, or rather, should and will characterize, the kingship and the hill of Zion, which is its seat. Thus in Isa 1:21–28 they are said to have been the characteristics of Zion in former times, in contrast with its present violence and corruption and lack of protection for the vulnerable, represented by widows and orphans (v. 23b). In v. 27 it is through משפט/*mishpat* and צדקה/*tsedaqa* that it will be redeemed.[96] Zion is their locus again at 28:17, where they sweep away "the refuge of lies," and at 33:5. They explicitly characterize the coming or eschatological king and his government in 9:6, 16:5, and 32:1; compare also 11:4.

All this is not unexpected in a prophetic book that is generally understood as standing close to the Davidic house and its concerns. The book of Psalms shares with Isaiah its closeness in its origins to the Davidic house and its political and religious entourages. Zion is a leading theme in both of them. It is true that in the Psalms, the phrase is applied chiefly to God, and largely in psalms that are likely to be post-monarchic. But liturgical language

---

91. Barton, "Isaiah of Jerusalem," 13–14 (140 in 2003 reprint).
92. Barton, *Ethics in Ancient Israel*, 94–126, esp. 94–100.
93. Williamson, *Isaiah 1–5*, 135, n. 49.
94. See, besides the commentaries, Krašovec, *Justice de Dieu*; Houston, *Contending*, 211–14.
95. I am grateful to Professor George Brooke for this correction.
96. See Williamson's discussion of the construction here: *Isaiah 1–5*, 156–58.

is conservative, and here we see the inheritance, I would suggest, of a characteristic usage in the royal sanctuary of the God who authorizes and inspires the royal practice of justice, as stated in Psalm 72.

But in Isaiah, it is important to observe that despite the social conservatism of the text, justice and right are never seen as being characteristic of the actual royal administration, whether present or past (depending on views of the redactional status of the particular text): it is a hope for the future, not a reality of the present corrupt times. At most, Isa 33:5 might be interpreted differently, which says that YHWH "filled" or "has filled" Zion with justice and right. But in the broadly eschatological context of these final chapters of Isaiah 1–33, this must be understood as being once again a future expectation. To quote Leclerc's study of justice (משפט/*mishpat*) in Isaiah, "The city that once was filled with justice and righteousness (1:21b) has been restored to that condition, apparently not through human agency (1:27) but through YHWH's own act on its behalf."[97]

Moving to the last eleven chapters of Isaiah, we find much less emphasis upon royal justice, whether present or to come. In Isa 56:1 and 58:2 it is a demand laid upon the people as a whole, while in 59:9 and 59:14, as we have seen, it is the gift of God, which they cannot receive because they have failed to respond to the demand. The theology here is very similar to that in Amos. But the theme of royal justice is not entirely absent from these chapters. In Isa 61:1-2, the idiom of "justice and right" does not appear, but we find the tradition of release, דרור/*deror*, which should be seen as going back to the royal decrees, as exemplified in Jer 34:8. The words of proclamation are placed on the lips of an imagined royal personage, as Weinfeld has seen,[98] though few of the commentators see it, persisting in thinking that the prophet is speaking in his own person. The combination of the gift of the Spirit of YHWH and anointing is decisive (see 1 Sam 16:13), yet Westermann, who points out the parallels, refuses to draw the obvious conclusion.[99] The connection with the jubilee legislation, pursued by Zimmerli, is less direct.[100]

Thus, in Isaiah "justice and right" has been transformed from the function it exercises in the royal ideology, where it is the alleged gracious act of the divinely legitimized king, into an ideal that calls all existing powers into question for their failure to ensure justice in society, and can only be a

---

97. Leclerc, *Yahweh is Exalted*, 84.
98. Weinfeld, *Social Justice*, 141; cf. Houston, "Today, in Your Very Hearing," 45–46.
99. Westermann, *Isaiah 40–66*, 365–66. John Goldingay tries to have it both ways, speaking of "a prophetic king, or rather . . . a kingly prophet," *Isaiah 56–66*, 291.
100. Zimmerli, "Das 'Gnadenjahr des Herrn.'"

reality as God's eschatological gift, upon the future king or upon the people. In this way the motif has been freed from the matrix of the royal ideology and operates independently as a prophetic and theological idea with a critical and eschatological function. This transformation not only occurs in new uses of the expression, but also influences the way in which earlier uses are read. The traditional understanding of Psalm 72, found not only in versions such as the LXX, the Vulgate, or the KJV, but also in the spelling of some verbs in the MT as indicatives rather than jussives (see vv. 2, 4), is as a prophecy rather than a prayer.[101] Here "justice and right," rather than the substance of a prayer for the current Judean ruler and society, has become the promised policy of the messianic king.

Justice and the Individual

In a number of texts משפט וצדקה/*mishpat utsedaqa* refers to the *individual* virtue of justice, for example in some late psalms (Pss 36:7 [Eng. 6]; 37:6; 106:3; 119:121), and in the wisdom literature: Prov 1:3; 2:9; 16:8; 21:3. In 16:8 the wisdom context suggests the individual application, although taken on its own it could have a social reference, and 21:3 could apply to a king, but in the context is probably not intended to apply to kings exclusively. Job 29:14 belongs here also, though I have already referred to it above in connection with royal justice because of the virtually royal persona here adopted by Job. We shall see shortly that the difference between these two usages is not as great as might be thought. Qoheleth, however, clearly still uses the expression with a social reference (Eccl 3:16; 5:7). The other main context for this individual usage is in Ezekiel, where in the parable of ch. 18 it defines the conduct of the just man (so gendered in the text): v. 5, "when a man is just and does justice and right"[102] (cf. 19, 21, 27); similarly in 33:14, 16, 19. Although the context of this usage is Ezekiel's critique of the exiles' attempt to blame their fathers' generation for their plight, and the generations of individuals represent generations of the nation, the individuals of the parable are realistic enough, if schematic.

The one text in the Torah where it is used, in Gen 18:19, appears to fall into the same category, but the case is not so simple; we shall come back to this.

The expression is unlikely, in my opinion, to have acquired this individual connotation in a monarchic society with the tradition of royal justice that we have explored. The wisdom sentences of Proverbs 10–29 are

101. Above, chapter 3, 38-39 and n. 12.
102. ואיש כי יהיה צדיק ועשה משפט וצדקה

notoriously difficult to date, and some would wish to put Prov 16:8 and 21:3 in the monarchic period. But none of the other examples of the individual usage are earlier than the sixth century, and I see no reason to regard these as exceptions. It is rather the case that this typically royal idea has been transferred (Schmid says "democratized,"[103] but this is hardly the right word) to the individual patron who is responsible for the welfare of many less powerful people and "executes true justice between members of the community" (Ezek 18:8), another distinctly kingly function. "Most of the entries in Ezekiel's list relate to the exercise of power by kings and others in positions of authority." [104] Weinfeld prefers to downgrade the social significance of the final phrase: "it is not the passing of a verdict in a court which is being referred to, but rather, the preservation of . . . right social relationships between a man and his fellow."[105] In this he is followed by Mein, who emphasizes the domestic context of ethics among the exiles.[106] I am not convinced; I see no reason why the exiles should not have set up formal though unofficial means of settling disputes among themselves.

Weinfeld appears to see the connection of these texts with the removal of the monarchy, but muddies the issue by referring to a number of texts with a setting in the monarchic era in this connection, including Isa 5:7, Jer 4:2, and Amos.[107] While it is true that the conduct of individuals affects the welfare of society in all ages, the idiom under consideration plainly refers in these texts to the ethos of the entire society, not to particular responsibilities of individuals, and the same is true of the texts from Trito-Isaiah (Weinfeld says "Second-Isaiah"), which Weinfeld discusses in this connection.

Absence in the Torah

The most obvious question for this study, and its initial impulse, is why this expression should be so infrequent in the Torah, seeing that one of the central themes of the moral teaching of the Torah is the maintenance of justice in the society of Israel, with the protection of the poor. There are only two possible attestations, one in Gen 18:19, where YHWH expresses his purpose with Abraham "that he may instruct his sons and his house after him to keep the way of YHWH and *to do justice and right,* משפט וצדקה/*mishpat utsedaqa*";

---

103. Schmid, *Gerechtigkeit*, 127.
104. Block, *Ezekiel Chapters 1–24*, 568.
105. Weinfeld, *Social Justice*, 220.
106. Mein, *Ezekiel and the Ethics of Exile*, 197–98.
107. Weinfeld, *Social Justice*, 221, 216–19.

and the other, in a less typical form, in Deut 33:21.[108] I have not included the latter in my list of examples, because of the plural, and its most likely meaning is "he [Gad] executed YHWH's justice, and his statutes with Israel" (cf. NRSV), suggesting probably retributive rather than social justice.[109]

We begin by asking whether there were other opportunities to use the expression in the Torah, and the answer must be: of course!

In the first place, we need to consider those measures in the Torah that would have a similar effect to *mīšarum* decrees, and can be shown to have close genetic relationships to them.[110] These are the Deuteronomic *shemitta* or remission of debts (Deut 15:1–3) and the jubilee in Leviticus 25. These passages in the Torah fulfill essential aspects of "justice and right": the remission of debts, the return of mortgaged property, the release of debt slaves, and their return to their home and family. We must also include here at a somewhat greater remove the law providing for the freedom of debt slaves after six years (Exod 21:2–6; Deut 15:12–18), which like Law 117 in the Code of Hammurabi has a prospective rather than retrospective effect, making a permanent claim on the behavior of the possessors of slaves.

Weinfeld argues that the remission and the jubilee are "functionally speaking, identical to the Mesopotamian *mīšarum* and *durāru(m)*."[111] He goes on to show a series of correspondences in terminology and content between the Pentateuchal texts, especially Deut 15:2–3, and the Mesopotamian decrees.[112] The use in Lev 25:10 of the noun דרור/*deror* ("liberty"), the direct equivalent in form and meaning of the Akkadian *(an)durārum*, is the most obvious similarity; and the instruction in that verse that ". . . everyone shall return to his own family" recalls conceptually the Sumerian equivalent of *(an)durārum*, AMA-AR-GI4, literally "return to mother."[113] In Deut 15:2 the writer is quoting an older text, interrupting the parenetic second-person style and proclaiming the remission of debts, whose style suggests it is a

---

108. צדקת יהוה עשה ומשפטיו עם ישראל

109. So, e.g., McConville, *Deuteronomy*, 472. Nelson (*Deuteronomy*, 392), appears to agree with Weinfeld (*Social Justice*, 180) that the phrase occurs "in connection with the Lawgiver," but this only means that the Song is attributed to Moses.

110. For what follows, cf. Weinfeld, *Social Justice*, 152–78; Otto, "Programme," 51–63; Lemche, "Manumission," 56–57; Kaufman, "Social Welfare Systems," 281.

111. Weinfeld, *Social Justice*, 156.

112. Weinfeld, *Social Justice*, 157–65. However, in Deuteronomy 15 the older law embedded in the typically Deuteronomic second-person exhortation is confined to v. 2. The following verse takes up the vocabulary but reverts to the second person. See above, chapter 2, 23–24.

113. Weinfeld, *Social Justice*, 159; middle syllable rendered there as -ra-.

legal text.[114] It is thus clear that an earlier tradition lies behind the Torah provisions for release. Otto argues in relation to the Deuteronomic law that the earlier tradition in question is the provision for the sabbatical year in Exod 23:10-11, where the verb שמט/*shamat* occurs in relation to the seventh year, and that the law is formulated in conscious opposition to neo-Assyrian decrees of *durārum*, deliberately avoiding the word דרור/*deror*, which only comes into use once there was no longer any influence from Assyrian power.[115] But in view of the evidence surveyed above, it seems probable that there was a native tradition of royal decrees that used both the word דרור/*deror* and the phraseology of Deut 15:2.

However, it is easy to see that there are fundamental differences between these Torah provisions and royal decrees. The first is their periodicity. Edicts of *mīšarum* were typically published on the accession of a king, an irregular and unpredictable event, and sometimes irregularly thereafter. It is a frequent complaint against the jubilee law that creditors would be able to predict and discount the jubilee in advance; and the Deuteronomic text shows itself aware of a similar objection to the *shemitta*: "Be careful not to entertain in your heart the wicked thought, 'The seventh year, the year of release, is near . . . ,' and not to begrudge your poor brother your giving" (Deut 15:9). In both cases the text must fall back on exhortation (Deut 15:7-11; Lev 25:14-17),[116] relying on the doubtful commitment of the individual to "justice and right."[117] Weinfeld argues that the institution of the jubilee as a regularly recurring proclamation of release was older than the monarchy, and was weakened by the predominance of the monarchy.[118] But although it is perfectly possible, indeed likely, that village plots were redistributed regularly in tribal Israel,[119] only a national authority could command such a measure over the country as a whole. Any possible tribal institution could have had little to do with the Mesopotamian tradition.

The second difference is related. It concerns authority and enforcement. *Mīšarum* decrees were issued under the authority of the king, and enforced by royal officers. The Torah provisions carry the sole authority of YHWH (through Moses in the case of Deuteronomy), and contain

114. Mayes, *Deuteronomy*, 247-48. Stylistic details in Weinfeld, *Social Justice*, 162-66. Cf. Houston, *Contending*, 181, n. 55. Otto regards vv. 1-2 as forming an integral Deuteronomic unit: "Programme," 53-54; this is stylistically improbable.

115. Otto, "Programme," 51-63.

116. Note the use here of the second person singular in a plural context.

117. Chapter 2, 29-30; Houston, *Contending*, 186, 188, 197.

118. Weinfeld, *Social Justice*, 177. Cf. also Milgrom, *Leviticus 23-27*, 2242.

119. Lemche, *Early Israel*, 196-98; Boer, *Sacred Economy*, 72-74; and literature noted above in chapter 3, n. 61.

no practical provisions for enforcement, only the ultimate sanction of YHWH's blessing or curse in Leviticus 26 and Deuteronomy 28. It is the community that is to put the provisions into effect, and their observance is up to the conscience of the individual. Otto rightly observes in relation to Deut 15:1–10 that it is "not the rules of a legal institution, but an ethical program."[120] He goes on to suggest that the authors would have regarded this "ethical program" as superior to the Assyrian *durārum*, whose effect could be nullified by a simple clause in a contract.[121] This judgment seems to overlook the fact that the *shemitta* could be, and from the first century BCE was, nullified in the same way, by the *prozbul* (not mentioned in Otto's article). The fact is that the effectiveness of all law rests in the last analysis on consent, regardless of what measures may be taken to enforce it. The absence of consent rendered the Assyrian edicts no more than propaganda for the justice of the king. Sadly, a similar fate overtook the *shemitta*, even though efforts were made to enforce it; while the jubilee remained nothing more than an ideal, though an influential one.

I have argued in relation to the jubilee law that the apparently utopian character of the text is relativized once one understands that, rather than mandating a specific administrative procedure, it projects a "narrative ideal of justice" (adapting to a different context an expression of Jackson's).[122] The text's purpose is not to administer, but to persuade. These texts, in a word, are not decrees ordaining justice, but education in justice. Is it possible that this is why the tag "justice and right" is absent? The difficulty with this suggestion is that though these texts do not represent royal administrative justice, they are in complete harmony with the broader ideal of social justice signified by the use of the expression in the prophets. The simple explanation is that the expression is generalizing, and is not required as a heading for individual provisions.

This explanation will not apply where there are series of commandments of a social character, restraining creditors in the exercise of their power and assumed rights, warning judges against bias and corruption, and making simple provision for the needs of the landless and vulnerable, as in Exod 22:20—23:12 or Deut 24:6–22. Here and generally, apart from the few provisions for communal institutions (the third-year tithe in Deut 14:28–29 may be mentioned besides the jubilee and the year of release), the teaching on social justice concerns individual responsibility, including much of the text

---

120. Otto, "Programme," 55: "nicht Gesetz einer Rechtsinstitution, sondern ethisches Programm."

121. Otto, "Programme," 56, 59. He shows (43) this does not apply to the Old Babylonian *mišarum*, which provided for the breaking of tablets.

122. Chapter 4, 61; Jackson, *Wisdom-Laws*, 25 and passim.

of Deut 15:1–11 and Leviticus 25. But as we have seen, Ezekiel and the wisdom writers can refer to individual responsibility under the rubric of "justice and right," so there seems to be no reason in principle why it could not have been used in these texts: why, for example, the teaching in the Book of the Covenant should not begin at Exod 22:20 (Eng. 21) "You shall do justice and right," rather than abruptly with "An alien you shall not oppress." One would have thought this would have been entirely appropriate as a superscript for these series. The one text that does use it, Gen 18:19, may indeed foreshadow this teaching, in that Abraham's "children and his house after him" is no doubt intended to embrace all generations of Israel, and may be interpreted as serving as an anticipatory superscript for the teaching on justice.[123]

I would explain this phenomenon by positing a crucial distinction between other works and the Torah. The Prophets, Former and Latter, the Psalms, and some other of the Writings preserve the memory of Israel and Judah as a kingdom or kingdoms, and it is here that the expression is at home. In contrast, the ideal Israel of the Pentateuch is constituted as a *non-monarchical* society. The passage on the king in Deut 17:14–20 permits but does not mandate the appointment of a king, and assigns him no positive functions. It is all about what the king is not to do. Certainly it does not say that the king is to do "justice and right," although in the older tradition that is above all what the king is to do. The ideal Israel of the Torah is capable of organizing itself as a people under God with no earthly head, given that Moses' role is temporally limited, Aaron's is restricted to the cultic realm, and Joshua's function will be largely military. This acephalous conception of Israel is appropriate, of course, to the situation of real-life Judeans and Samarians[124] as self-organized communities under Persian rule, the more so as the Torah has an official character as literature published by the leaders of the community and intended as foundational to its self-understanding, identity, and organization.

What I wish to suggest is that the idiom משפט וצדקה/*mishpat ut-sedaqa*, at the time of the final redaction of the Torah, would still have retained its associations with the native royal ideology, and so would not have been appropriate in this work constituting Israel as a non-monarchic, acephalous community, and presenting teaching on measures of social justice to be implemented by the community, not by kings. It is true that Ezekiel and the wisdom writers had redirected its application to the private individual; but to be more precise, to an individual with public functions as a patron. The term even in this context retained a hierarchical flavor:

123. So Miranda, *Marx and the Bible*, 93–97.
124. [See Houston, "Between Salem and Mount Gerizim."]

"justice and right" is done by God to his people, by kings to their subjects, and by patrons to their clients, in any case on earth by men (always men) of at least relative wealth and power to those with less or none of either. The use of this expression would obscure the primary goal of the teaching of the Torah on social justice: to point to the responsibility of Israel *as a community* under God to live as a just society.

Abraham in Genesis 18 fulfills the role of father and therefore patron for his children and his household. But what about the blocks of teaching I have referred to above which are obviously addressed to the individual in precisely the hierarchical position that I have just sketched? Would it not have been reasonable to use the idiom there? It is just here that the Torah shows how far it diverges from the ancient royal ideology of social justice as a gift from the superior. Precisely here, where the situation of economic inequality between members of the society is most palpable, the texts may be taken as implying their equality in social and simply human terms, regardless of whether this implication is intended. In Deuteronomy and Leviticus 25 they refer to the economic inferior as אחיך/*ahika*, "your brother," assimilating the situation to that of the ancient village kinship community.[125] The Book of the Covenant, making the point more unobtrusively, uses רעך/*re'eka*, "your neighbor" (Exod 22:25 [Eng. 26]), but emphasizes the shared humanity of creditor and debtor.[126] The idiom משפט וצדקה/*mishpat utsedaqa*, with its royal or hierarchical associations, would have obscured this point. To be sure, as I have emphasized in my studies of all these passages, this implication makes no difference to the economic inequality that is the presupposition of them all, and these communal measures, even if effectively implemented, and these moral teachings, even if obeyed, would do little more than prevent it from getting worse.[127] Class division remains: the difference the Torah makes is that society is divided with a bad conscience, and more important, that its teaching survives, preserved by its religious canonization, to inspire future generations to more effective action against poverty and inequality.

It may still be asked why it should not have appeared all the same in the *narrative* of the Pentateuch, referring to God's function in ruling and judging Israel and ordering their society aright. I have already suggested that the Deuteronomistic historians were simply uninterested in this aspect of the king's, and therefore presumably God's, responsibility. But what of the

---

125. Chapter 2 above, 27–30; Houston, *Contending*, 184; cf. Perlitt, "Ein einzig Volk von Brüdern."

126. Otto, *Theologische Ethik*, 84–86; Houston, *Contending*, 112–14.

127. Houston, *Contending*, 117–18, 185–90, 199–203.

Torah? It is important here that the central narrative of the Torah concerns YHWH's deliverance of Israel from oppression in Egypt. This action has been characterized by liberation theologians as the exercise of justice for the oppressed, indeed as the classical paradigm of such action. Miranda, for example, says of Exodus 3 that YHWH's determination to deliver Israel is motivated solely by their cry of distress, and that "it seems to me that we must completely exclude the possibility that Yahweh's 'descent' to 'deliver' in Exod 3:7–9 should be attributed to the fact that it is 'my people' who cry out."[128] If this were so, this act would be the prime example of the divine exercise of "justice and right," delivering the poor and oppressed impartially for the sake of a just society. I have argued against Miranda's view on the simple grounds of the prominence of references to the personal and even family relationship of YHWH and Israel.[129] And Levenson has mounted a more detailed argument against liberationist construals of the exodus, employing this among other arguments. "The point is not that it is Israel's *suffering* that brings about the exodus, but that it is *Israel* that suffers."[130]

The significance of this particularism here lies in the fact that while acts of particular and general deliverance can both claim to represent the "righteousness of God," only impartial and general justice, as ideally furthered by kings, can be called משפט וצדקה/*mishpat utsedaqa*. In *Contending for Justice* I considered both kinds of justice as representing ideas for the justice of God on the social models respectively of the king and the patron.[131] We saw above that in the book of Isaiah, the use of צדקה/*tsedaqa* with משפט/*mishpat*, common in 1–33 and 56–66, is not found in chs. 40–55, where it is replaced by uses with words from the root ישׁע, *y-sh-ʻ*, and it is clear that the reason for this is the different roles that YHWH plays in the different parts of the book. In 40–55 he is the deliverer of Israel, and it is his particular and partial justice that is in play. And it is this aspect that is in evidence, predominantly, in the Torah, as it is in Deutero-Isaiah.[132]

However, because of the specificity of the narrative and the limited use of poetic reflection, there would be little opportunity for a generalizing description such as צדקה/*tsedaqa* or צדק/*tsedeq*. Indeed, neither of these words is found in the Torah in reference to the action of God, except in Deut 33:21. The celebratory hymn in Exod 15:1b–17, the Song of the Sea, uses ישׁועה /*yeshuʻa*, "victory" (v. 2), but without a parallel, as the poetic style of the piece

---

128. Miranda, *Marx and the Bible*, 89.
129. Houston, *Contending*, 209–10.
130. Levenson, "Exodus and Liberation," 152; italics in the original.
131. Houston, *Contending*, 205–19.
132. I am grateful once again to George Brooke for pointing out this parallel to me.

does not employ parallelism to any great extent. But the Song of Deborah does use the phrase צדקות יהוה/*tsidqot YHWH*, "the victories of YHWH," using the plural of צדקה/*tsedaqa* (Judg 5:11).

The truth may simply be that narrative, and especially the style of narrative generally employed in the Hebrew Bible—"historicized fiction," or alternatively "fictionalized history," as it is called by Alter[133]—is not receptive to the use of a phrase which is generalizing in character, bureaucratic in origin, and poetic in its use as a split parallel pair.

Conclusion

There was of course nothing arbitrary in Martin Luther King's choice of Amos 5:24 among the nearly sixty examples of "justice and right" in the Hebrew Bible as his "favorite verse" on which to preach. The most obvious reasons are that it is an exhortation (or, in my view, to be more precise, a final clause attached to an exhortation), and that it is prophecy, appealing to a man who saw himself as a prophet.[134] But at a deeper level it makes sense that he should use as a sermon text a verse exhibiting the decoupling of the phrase by the prophets from the royal ideology to describe the ethos of a whole society; for the small number of other exhortations, in Jeremiah 22 and Ezekiel 45, are explicitly addressed to kings. What King longed for, along with others who have fought for social justice throughout the ages, was not justice as a privilege dispensed by the ruling class to its grateful recipients—even though that is what he initially demanded, in the form of the Civil Rights Act—but a society so structured that justice was its essence. The phrase משפט וצדקה/*mishpat utsedaqa* too often designates the former, even though it carries the potential to imply the latter. The Torah therefore, when embodying its vision of a society imbued with solidarity across differences of wealth in legal or ethical terms, avoids the use of a phrase too deeply associated with the hierarchies of kingly rule.

---

133. Alter, *Art of Biblical Narrative*, 24–25.
134. Bartlett, "Let Justice Roll Down."

Chapter 11

The Psalms of YHWH's Kingship

The Divine King Executes Royal Justice

(NOT PREVIOUSLY PUBLISHED)

Psalms 93–100 as a Sequence

In this short chapter I want to show how Psalms 96 to 99 in their context are a continuous sequence artistically arranged and showing YHWH acting to establish "justice and right" on the pattern of the ideal earthly king, as seen in previous chapters of this work.[1]

Reading a series of psalms as a sequence is today hardly novel. It is obvious that the order of the Psalter is not random, even if there is still controversy over such large-scale hypotheses of organization as that of Gerald Wilson.[2] Gelston, for example, says that "there is no attempt at a final editing of the complete Psalter; it seems simply to have grown by accretion."[3] Fortunately for my present purpose I do not need any theory of the ordering of the entire Psalter, though I shall make some use of one of Wilson's most important hypotheses. That the Psalms from 93 to 100 have been intentionally placed together is obvious, though many scholars have been puzzled by the presence of the lament Psalm 94 in this series, which otherwise, apart from the second half of Psalm 95, consists entirely of praise. This particular puzzle, as we shall see, is soluble. I offer here a way of understanding the specific order of these psalms, especially those in the central core of so-called enthronement psalms (better, "psalms of YHWH's kingship"), Psalms 96–99. It may not matter whether this ordering is intentional; I suggest it is at least aesthetically convincing, if not also rhetorically. My proposal is close to that of Jonathan Magonet, who argues

---

1. See above, chapters 3 and 10.
2. Wilson, *Editing*.
3. Gelston, "Editorial Arrangement," 167.

"for a coherent sequence, one that celebrates and sets out to define the implications of YHWH's kingship for Israel and for the peoples of the world, with righteousness and justice being the principal features."[4]

Wilson argues that the end of Book 3 with Psalm 89 marks the most important break in the Psalter.[5] The covenant with David has been highlighted by the presence of royal psalms at what Wilson calls the "seams" between books, at 2, 72, and 89. Here we see it repudiated by YHWH, who has cast the throne of his anointed servant to the ground and wrapped him in shame (Ps 89:45–46 [44–45]). The main thrust of the Psalter then turns from the kingship of David and his heirs to the kingship of God.[6] The somber commencement of Book 4 in Psalm 90 expresses the need to take refuge in YHWH alone in view of the sinfulness of humanity and the shortness of life, and the theme of refuge in YHWH is developed in the rather more upbeat Psalms 91 and 92. Wilson makes 94 also part of this group, and suggests that the reversal of the logical order of Psalms 94 and 93 "provides an interlocking mechanism by which the Yhwh-*mālak* group (with its 'frame' [Psalms 95 and 100]) is bound together with the preceding group of Psalms 90–92 and 94."[7] This is clarified by the following diagram from Wilson's article.[8]

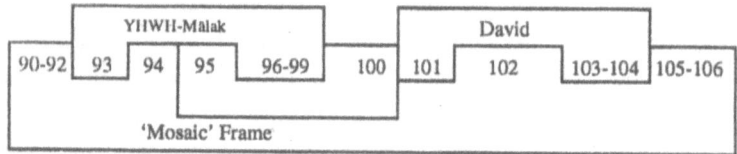

Justice in Psalms 93–100

But YHWH's ability to protect and save is developed fully in the celebration of YHWH's kingship that occupies the following sequence. The main thesis that I wish to maintain in this paper is that the primary function of divine kingship in these texts, in line with the ideology of earthly kingship, is the

---

4. Magonet, "On Reading Psalms," 168.

5. Wilson, *Editing*, 214–28; "Shaping the Psalter," 75.

6. It must be pointed out, however, that the theme of the kingship of YHWH is by no means absent in Books 1–3: see, e.g., Ps 22:29 (28); indeed, as we learnt in chapter 3 concerning Psalm 72, the earthly kingship depends on it. And conversely the Davidic kingship is taken up again as a theme in Books 4 and 5: Psalms 101, 110, 132, and 144 are all royal psalms.

7. Wilson, "Shaping the Psalter," 75.

8. Wilson, "Shaping the Psalter," 76. Reproduced by permission.

exercise of justice, defined more precisely as the saving or protective justice that the weak depend on to protect them from the oppression of the strong. However, two forms of justice can be traced in these psalms. The one is the universal, impartial justice of the divine king. This is the primary theme, appearing at the climaxes of Psalms 96 and 98 and eventually in a different application in Psalm 99. But crisscrossing this is the partial and particular justice of the national god who defends and saves his people from their enemies. I have distinguished these two forms in my *Contending for Justice* and argued that as the former is pictured on the analogy of earthly kingship, the latter takes up the analogy of the patron who defends and assists his client in return for allegiance and tribute.[9]

As far as earthly kingship is concerned, the classic text is Psalm 72, which I dealt with in detail in chapter 3. Here the king's universal rule and privileges are requested on the grounds that "he rescues the poor when they cry, the wretched, and those who have no helper." We also saw that the means by which he would have been expected to rescue them was by decree or by judicial action, and that "to do justice and right" (or "righteousness")[10] was the standard expression in Hebrew for this category of justice (e.g., 1 Sam 8:15). This justice finds its source, as Ps 72:1 says plainly, in YHWH: "YHWH, give your justice[11] to the king, and your righteousness to the king's son." The standard expression עשׂה משׁפט וצדקה/*'asa mishpat utsedaqa* appears in Ps 99:4, and the verse 97:2 plainly alludes to it, as Zenger notes;[12] an allusion in 94:15 is less certain. However, Psalm 99 goes on to speak of YHWH giving laws (v. 7). But of all this more in due course.

If this sequence of psalms dates, as a structured sequence, from a time after the fall of Jerusalem, as seems likely even apart from Wilson's hypothesis,[13] it is a significant complement to the position taken by the editors of the Torah discussed at the end of the last chapter. We saw that they generally avoided the use of the tag "justice and right," and my proposal was that owing to their reconceiving Israel as an acephalous and egalitarian community, a term associated with a monarchic and hierarchical society was no longer appropriate. In broadly the same period and circumstances the editors responsible for the Psalms apply it without reserve to the action of God. The community that acknowledges no earthly lord, apart from the foreign lords

---

9. Houston, *Contending*, 204–19.
10. See above, chapter 10, 150–53.
11. The MT has משׁפטיך plural, but it is singular (τὸ κρίμα σου) in the LXX.
12. Hossfeld and Zenger, *Psalmen 51–100*, 680.
13. See, e.g., Tate, *Psalms 51–100*, 505; Hossfeld, *Psalmen 51–100*, 664, etc., notwithstanding Day's arguments for a pre-exilic date for the individual psalms, "How Many Pre-exilic Psalms?" 234–40.

imposed upon them against their will (cf. Deut 17:15b; Neh 9:36–37), here acclaims YHWH as its king. The close connection of divine and human kingship that we studied in detail in the last chapter is broken with the collapse of the Judean monarchy. It is another question how the divine kingship, deprived now of its earthly vice-regent, is conceived of as expressed in practice. I will return to this question at the end of the chapter.

Following the sequence through in order, I note the following. I do not intend to detail all the numerous connections between these psalms: this has been done comprehensively by Howard,[14] as well as among commentators most thoroughly and perceptively by Tate[15] and Hossfeld and Zenger.

Psalm 93 makes no overt allusion to the justice of YHWH: but the first verse speaks of the establishment of the order of creation: "the world stands firm, not to be shaken." YHWH's majesty, and therefore the order he has created, is proof against the raging of the primeval waters. And the order of creation is the underlying basis of "justice and right" as it comes to expression in human society, as we again noted in the last chapter.[16] This is expressed in a subtle chain of allusions noted by Magonet:[17]

> 93:1c–2: the *world* stands firm ... your *throne* stands firm.
>
> 96:13 he judges *the world* in justice
>
> 97:2 justice and judgment are the base of *his throne*

Psalm 94 is complex in genre and structure, but fundamentally it is a lament for the absence of precisely that category of justice, social justice as we would call it, in human society, specifically in Israel: "Your people, YHWH, they crush, and your estate they abuse. Widow and sojourner they kill, and orphans they murder." But it asserts that divine wisdom teaches that YHWH will not abandon his people. Verse 15 asserts, reading literally, "for unto right will justice return."[18] Alter's translation is "For justice will join with judgment."[19] The text asserts that the two elements of the

---

14. Howard, *Structure*.
15. Tate, *Psalms 51–100*.
16. Above, 167–68.
17. Magonet, "On Reading Psalms," 168. In the Hebrew:
93:1c–2 תכון תבל ... נכון כסאך
96:13 ישפט תבל בצדק
97:2 צדק ומשפט מכון כסאו

18. כי עד־צדק ישוב משפט. Many argue that instead of צדק, "right," we should read צדיק, "the just person," in line with Symmachus and the Syriac. It is an easier reading, which is precisely why we should reject it, following one of the oldest principles in textual criticism, *difficilior lectio potior*.

19. Alter, *The Hebrew Bible*, vol. 3, 226.

standard expression, justice and right, belong together and ultimately will be together. It is certainly possible to separate them, and the text implies that the current situation is that they are indeed separated: law without justice is the curse of every society under oppression. Zenger quotes from Jan Assmann the sentence "'Saving justice' saves not only from injustice but also from law."[20] This is said in reference to Egypt, but it applies to the ancient Near East in general. The psalm asserts that what God gives, and what kings ought to give, is משפט וצדקה/*mishpat utsedaqa*, justice *with* right, judgment *with* justice. The sequel in the psalm sequence asserts that this is what God as king comes to establish.

On this particular front Psalm 95 does not advance us very far, as, though it acknowledges YHWH as king, it does not speak of his justice, but primarily of his creation of the world, in a less mythopoeic vein than Psalm 93, and his rejection and punishment of any skeptical attitude among his people. It prepares us for the full celebration of YHWH's kingship, expressed primarily in his justice, which is to follow in the next four psalms.

This core group forms an artistically arranged series. Two psalms, 96 and 98, that begin "Sing to YHWH a new song!" alternate with two, 97 and 99, that begin "YHWH reigns!" Psalm 96 includes the latter phrase as a quotation from Psalm 93 in v. 10; it is worth noting here that Psalm 98 mentions the kingship of YHWH ("sound loud before the king, YHWH") at a structurally similar position, in v. 6. In both psalms this leads up to the final series of commands to the natural world to celebrate YHWH's coming in judgment.

There is no explicit mention of Israel in Psalm 96, though YHWH's own people must be the implied audience for most of the imperatives, including the praise of YHWH and the evangelizing of the nations (v. 3). Howard suggests that in Psalms 97 and 98 attention switches between Israel and the nations in chiastic fashion: in Psalm 97 we have the nations first, then Israel, in Psalm 98 Israel followed by the nations.[21] Finally, in Psalm 99 the focus is on YHWH's own people almost throughout; the peoples mentioned in vv. 1-2 fade out rapidly. This feature is then broadly symmetrical, thus:

Ps 96	Ps 97A	Ps 97B	Ps 98A	Ps 98B	Ps 99
nations	nations	Israel	Israel	nations	Israel

20. Hossfeld and Zenger, *Psalmen 51-100*, 680, from Assmann, "Idee vom Totengericht," 11. "Die 'rettende Gerechtigkeit' rettet nicht nur vor Unrecht, sondern auch vor Recht." It is impossible to reproduce the play on words in English. It could also be translated "'Saving righteousness saves not only from injustice but also from justice."

21. Howard, *Structure*, 177-78.

But how do the nations and Israel relate respectively to YHWH's exercise of judgment? All the psalms proclaim YHWH as the *universal* king; all at least refer to "the peoples" or "the nations" as witnesses of his glory, justice, and salvation or as objects of his judgment (first in Ps 96:10 and 13). His justice therefore is universal, and this is what the final strophe of Psalm 96 asserts, echoed in that of Psalm 98 in similar wording, calling on the natural world to rejoice in his coming for judgment. That rejoicing is called for makes it plain that the judgment spoken of is not punitive: it is rather "justice and right." We must wait until Ps 99:4 for that precise phrase, but two expressions in Psalm 96 announce the same idea. In v. 10 we read "he will judge the peoples with equity."[22] And the last verse announces that the judgment of the world and peoples will be "in justice and in his faithfulness," בצדק ו . . . . באמונתו/*betsedeq we . . . be'emunato*. We may compare the association of צדק/*tsedeq* and משפט/*mishpat* with אמת/*emet*, "truth" or "faithfulness," in such texts as Ps 89:15 (14) and Isa 16:5, for the latter is a word from the same root, and with much the same meaning, as אמונה/*emuna*. YHWH's judgment of the peoples will be an expression of equity and justice, and of his faithfulness to his commitment, or indeed to justice itself. The lament of Psalm 94 is here being answered for the nations, but not yet for Israel, in comprehensive fashion: under YHWH as king the peoples will experience their deliverance from oppression.

Marcel Krusche makes the important point that the rejoicing of the natural world implies that with the coming of YHWH to judge, the elements of the natural world—heaven, earth, and sea, open country and forest—are not simply the observers of the judgment, but its objects alongside the nations.[23] They cease to be dangers to humanity. "YHWH makes the world a place where not only the peoples live with another in peace, but also nature exists in harmony with human beings."[24] I would argue that they thus experience the establishment of "justice and right," the just ordering of society extended to the cosmos, an ordering that the Priestly account of creation depicts in Genesis 1 as established at the outset, and in Gen 6:11-13 as disrupted. This disruption is not repaired after the flood but only suppressed (Gen 9:1-3); the violence of the natural world is kept in check by the fear of humanity, but harmony is not restored. This theme will be fully explored in our final chapter, chapter 13.

22. ידין עמים במישרים. The Hebrew מישרים is probably derived from Akkadian *mišarum*.

23. Krusche, *Königtum*, 118-26.

24. Krusche, *Königtum*, 126, my translation. "JHWH macht die Welt zu einem Ort, an dem nicht nur de Völker miteinander in Frieden leben, sondern auch die Natur in Harmonie mit den Menschen steht."

Magonet says that "in the context of the sequence, Psalm 97 makes concrete the closing 'chorus' of Ps 96."[25] Is this correct? After the initial announcement of YHWH's kingship and call to the "isles" to rejoice, the psalm depicts a theophany, in which for our purposes the key expression is that the foundation of his throne is צדק ומשפט/*tsedeq umishpat* (v. 2). There is no significant difference between this expression and the commoner משפט וצדקה/*mishpat u tsedaqa*, and there is an echo with צדק/*tsedeq* in v. 6. YHWH is to exercise his kingship by judging in justice. In v. 8 Zion is glad, and the "daughters of Judah" rejoice "because of your judgments (משפטיך/*mishpateka*), YHWH." We must reckon with the possibility that these "judgments" consist in the putting to shame in the preceding verse of the worshippers of idols, and do not therefore contribute to the theme we are exploring. But v. 10 certainly requires attention. "He guards the lives of his faithful. From the hand of the wicked he saves them." This is a further answer to Psalm 94's lament. Oppression is eliminated from YHWH's people. But is this an expression of "justice and right"? The difficulty here is that, as I said in the last chapter, "only impartial and general justice, as ideally furthered by kings, can be called משפט וצדקה/*mishpat utsedaqa*."[26] Here YHWH's attention to "his faithful" is as the national god, perhaps even the god of a narrower group than the nation.[27] This must be characterized as the justice of the patron. Moreover, the establishment of justice in the natural world is absent here.

The point is developed much more explicitly in the first half of Psalm 98. "YHWH has made known his victory (ישועתו/*yeshuʿato*), and in the eyes of the nations he has revealed צדקתו/*tsidqato*." (Ps 98:2) The last word—צדקה/*tsedaqa* with a suffix meaning "his"—may be understood in different ways, e.g., KJV, NIV "his righteousness," REB "his saving righteousness," NRSV "his vindication." Alter's translation "his bounty" is a bold departure, but not unjustified in view of the diversity of the word's connotations. The nations may see it, but they are not the beneficiaries. "He has remembered his kindness and his faithfulness to the house of Israel" (v. 3a). Strongly recalling Deutero-Isaiah, whichever the direction of influence, these words express YHWH's exclusive, partial, patronal justice towards Israel. "All the ends of the earth have seen"—but not experienced!—"the victory of *our* God" (v. 3b). The linkage of צדקה/*tsedaqa* not with משפט/*mishpat* but with ישועה/*yeshuʿa*, "victory," is characteristic of Deutero-Isaiah. Just

---

25. Magonet, "On Reading the Psalms," 169.

26. Chapter 10 above, 179.

27. Cf. Kraus, *Psalms 60–150*, 260; Briggs, Charles Augustus. *A Critical and Exegetical Commentary on the Book of Psalms* (ICC). 2 vols. Edinburgh: T & T Clark, 1907; Tate, *Psalms 51–100*, 520, though he does not say so explicitly.

as its linkage with משפט/*mishpat* narrows the sense of צדקה/*tsedaqa* to the legal and political, so its linkage with ישועה/*yeshu'a* directs its sense towards the military and economic.

But after making this point, the psalm moves back to the same acclamations, in almost the same words, as in Psalm 96, of YHWH's arrival to judge the whole earth in justice. "He judges the world in justice (בצדק/*betsedeq*) and the peoples in equity (במישרים/*bemesharim*)" (v. 9).

So far we have seen two divergent concepts of justice alternating in line with the ethnic focus of the texts. But in the final psalm of the group the two are in a sense brought together. In v. 2, firstly, the two ethnic loci are brought together in a way so far unexampled in the series: "YHWH is great in Zion, and he is high above all the peoples."

I see v. 4 as the key text. Its first sentence is the most difficult in the whole sequence. The translation I endorse is that of the REB, "The king in his might loves justice."[28] And this is immediately followed by twin expressions of the understanding that YHWH has acted to establish true justice, not this time in the world as a whole but specifically in Israel. "It is you[29] who have firmly founded righteousness (or equity—מישרים/*mesharim*), it is you who have done justice and right in Jacob." The latter sentence[30] is the almost precise equivalent of the statement about David in 2 Sam 8:15. The understanding of YHWH's action in justice is modeled on that of kings, and in such a text as Psalm 72 is seen, conversely, as the source from which the king's justice is derived. There, YHWH is prayed to bestow his justice on the king, and at the same time to grant that king universal dominion. Here, the human mediator has vanished, and the deity becomes solely and directly responsible for the reign of justice.

But whereas in the preceding psalms this statement about YHWH's impartial action to remove oppression was referred to the world as a whole, while Israel was favored with victory and vindication or "bounty" as

---

28. ועז מלך משפט אהב. This is not the place to discuss all the suggested construals and emendations of these four words, but some possibilities can be dismissed. They are unlikely to be linked with v. 3, as that concludes with words that are generally recognized as a refrain (cf. vv. 5 and 9). And the king in question in this context is surely bound to be YHWH, and not the king in Jerusalem. Alter renders "And with a king's strength he loves justice." I am not sure how he is construing the syntax, but this does not seem very far from the REB rendering "The King in his might loves justice," in which עז מלך, "the might of the king," may be being understood as a metonymy for "the mighty king." This seems the simplest solution. Clearly משפט here is pregnant with the sense of צדקה: not merely justice but righteous justice.

29. The repeated use of the subject pronoun אתה should not be ignored: there is an implied contrast, presumably with any human claim to have done justice.

30. משפט וצדקה ביעקב אתה עשית

YHWH's exclusive client, here in Psalm 99 Jacob, that is Israel, becomes the specific, though of course not exclusive, site of YHWH's impartial action to remove injustice and establish equity.

Two seemingly divergent tracks have proved to be in fact convergent, and the psalm goes on to praise YHWH for instituting through Israel's founding fathers the practical means to give expression to justice. We saw in previous chapters that Babylonian kings established "equity" by decree rather than by law, retrospectively cancelling debts and taxes, and that this would be true also for kings of Judah.[31] But there is little doubt that in Ps 99:7 the "precepts," עדת/'*edot*, and "statute," חק/*hoq*, given by YHWH to Moses, Aaron, and Samuel are laws, which they are said to have kept—indeed, this is the commonest type of context in which these words occur. It seems likely that many of the laws in the ancient Near Eastern codes are scribal expressions of the social justice embodied in the decrees, through the mediation of judicial decisions in individual cases.[32] In the Torah this seems to be true of such texts as the Deuteronomic release of debts and the Jubilee of Leviticus. And the post-monarchic era in which this sequence of psalms was put together, and many of its individual psalms are likely to have been composed, was also that of the composition of the Torah. In a broader sense forbearance and vengeance, the themes of v. 8, are also aspects of justice.

The praise of YHWH's justice is complete. All that remains is for the purely expressive praise, Psalm 100, which recalls much of the terminology and expression of the first part of Psalm 95, to create with the latter a frame round the core kingship psalms to underline their thematic unity, as Howard argues.[33]

Divine Justice

We may wish to ask in what context the text expects this divine justice to be realized. Is it an expectation for the immediate future, for a community struggling to be reborn after devastation and exile, as perhaps Ps 97:8 might suggest: "Zion heard and rejoiced, and Judah's villages exulted, because of your judgments, YHWH"? I posited above, along with the majority of other interpreters,[34] that the present arrangement is post-exilic. It would go back no earlier than to the restored temple in the late sixth or fifth century. Yet at this time the community was firmly under the control of an imperial power

---

31. Chapter 3, 45–53; chapter 10, 156–66.
32. See above, chapter 10, 162–63.
33. Howard, *Structure*, 175.
34. Krusche, *Königtum*, 126, n. 130.

from which little in the way of "justice and right" was to be expected (see, e.g., Neh 9:36–37). The hope for such a just re-ordering of the world and of conditions in "Israel" in particular had to rest on faith rather than on experience, and meanwhile functions as a critique of current conditions—yet reaching far beyond any hypothetical release from "slavery" to the imperial power—and at the same time an assurance to those who saw themselves as "slaves" of their ultimate liberation.

It is remarkable that in this situation the composers or editors of the psalm sequence were able repeatedly to call the nations to see and acclaim YHWH's glory and the victory he had given to his people, to denounce their gods as "ungods" (so Alter: אלילים/*elilim*, 96:5, 97:7), and to proclaim his judgment of the entire world. Are they thinking of an indefinite eschatological future, as was formerly the most widely accepted interpretation? This may well be suggested by the conclusions to Psalms 96 and 98, which depict the joyful restoration of harmony between human beings and the natural world, otherwise found in the Hebrew Bible perhaps only in Isa 11:6–9. Or is the judgment rather seen as realized in the liturgical present, as Mowinckel thinks?[35] On the other hand, Ps 99:6–8, as we have just noted, sets YHWH's establishment of justice in Jacob firmly in the past, though of course this past is understood to determine the character of the present.

There can never be any certainty over the origin of these psalms or of their present arrangement, or over the intentions and expectations that brought them into being. But if we view them as an existing literary, liturgical, and canonical work, all of these contexts are potential contexts for any particular performance of the sequence or reflection on it. This is because it is in the nature of liturgical language, indeed of poetic and imaginative language in general, to admit multiple realizations according to the reader's or performer's own context. Believers today may meditate on these psalms, sing them or perform them in some way, in expectation of fulfillment, whatever the context. For Christians they are an unfolding of the faith expressed in the prayer "Thy kingdom come, thy will be done on earth as it is in heaven." Does this function ideologically to reconcile them to the present situation of disharmony and injustice?[36] This must depend on their personal attitudes and the theological stances of their community. Many perhaps are thus reconciled; but others are rather emboldened by the scriptural depiction of God's eschatological victory and establishment of "justice and right" to fight against all that undermines and threatens peace and justice.

---

35. Mowinckel, *Psalmenstudien* II; *Psalms in Israel's Worship*, 109–16.
36. Cf. Houston, *Contending*, 219–22.

Chapter 12

"To Share Your Bread with the Hungry"

Justice or Charity?

(2018)

1. Prologue

It is a commonplace in modern Christian advocacy for development charities to argue that giving to the poor, at least in a constructive manner rather than merely as a stopgap, is "not charity but justice." I take this to mean that it is not a voluntary act of benevolence, but an obligation. So understood, it is not only a modern idea. There are famous sayings by Christian preachers of the fourth and fifth centuries that categorize almsgiving as the exercise of justice, in that it is simply giving the poor what is due to them. So Basil of Caesarea: "The bread you are holding back belongs to the hungry; the coat you keep in your wardrobe belongs to the naked; the shoes moldering in your house belong to the barefoot; the money you are hiding underground belongs to the needy. So you are doing wrong[1] to all those whom you were in a position to help."[2] That this may be more than a rhetorical flourish is suggested by John Chrysostom, who tells those with inherited wealth that if they go far enough back they will find their wealth arises from some injustice.[3] To share one's bread with the hungry is no voluntary charitable act, but a restoration to the poor of what belongs to them.[4]

---

1. ἀδικεῖς.
2. Basil, "On the Saying of the Gospel," 277.
3. John Chrysostom, "In Epistulam I ad Timotheum," 562–63.
4. For the whole issue, see Anderson, *Charity*.

2. In the Hebrew Bible: Under the Monarchy

While almsgiving is in these sources argued to be justice, if we look at the issue from the perspective of the Hebrew Bible, we find that a far wider concept of justice or righteousness has been progressively narrowed to that of almsgiving or "charity." I shall argue in this chapter that this development results from social changes over the whole period of the Old Testament, and is only complete in the deutero-canonical writings. I shall be using concepts in economic anthropology; initially the well-known trio of modes of exchange postulated by Karl Polanyi and refined by Marshall Sahlins: reciprocity, redistribution, and exchange.[5] But for the analysis of almsgiving itself I find more helpful the recent work of David Graeber in his fascinating work *Debt, the First 5,000 Years*. (This is only one way of approaching the question: I have in my *Contending for Justice* used a more sociological analysis of the underlying development.)[6]

In writings usually supposed to be from the monarchic period (leaving out of account the virtually undatable wisdom sentences in Proverbs), we do not find the feeding of the hungry and the clothing of the naked as even an *aspect* of justice. The prophets' condemnations, for example, are not directed against those who have failed to feed the hungry or clothe the naked, but against more active wrongs. This idea first appears in Ezekiel and Trito-Isaiah (see section 4 below). The book of the covenant, likewise, apart from the sabbatical injunctions, is concerned to counsel against active injustice: "you shall not exploit . . . you shall not oppress . . . do not act like a moneylender, do not impose interest . . . return [the pledge] before sunset . . . do not pervert the justice due . . . do not accept a bribe" (Exod 22:21—23:9). Deuteronomy, which we shall come to in a moment, is rather different.

Why should this be? In peasant society it is unusual for individuals to be left to starve. There is a strong tendency for households to help one another when in difficulty, if only because of "the hard-headed realization that some aid to one's neighbor may simply be a form of insurance against the rainy day."[7] In monarchic Israel and Judah this tendency may well have been strengthened and formalized through the institution of the משפחה/ *mishpaha*, a real or fictive kinship group that often embraced all or most of the inhabitants of a village.[8] "Generalized reciprocity," to use Sahlins's rather unwieldy term—"indefinite reciprocity" would be better—would

---

5. Polanyi, "Economy as Instituted Process"; Sahlins, "Primitive Exchange."
6. Houston, *Contending*, 18–51.
7. Wolf, *Peasants*, 80.
8. Bendor, *Social Structure*, 67–86; Faust, *Archaeology*, 170–75.

have applied, as usual, between kin, especially with gifts of food.⁹ But this is not what we generally understand by "charity." Giver and receiver are equals and members of the same community, and in the medium term each expects to give and receive more or less equally. Famine, if it came, would affect everyone equally, and could not be relieved by individual charity. It is in line with this that רָעָב/*ra'av* in texts set in the monarchic era almost without exception refers to a disaster affecting the community rather than to personal suffering: famine rather than hunger.¹⁰

However, possibilities were emerging in the later monarchy which could lead to the destitution of an individual or a nuclear family. This is suggested by Deuteronomy's emphasis on the *personae miserae*. The גֵּר/*ger*, or resident alien, and the Levite would have fallen outside the circle of solidarity within which reciprocal relations could be assumed.¹¹ The parallel emphasis on widows and the fatherless suggests, however, a much narrower circle, confined to the stronger members of one בית אב/*bet av* or extended family, as Bendor suggests.¹² But I regard this radical restriction as unlikely in the village setting. It is much more likely in the developing urban sector sponsored by the steadily increasing power of the state, where the same sense of solidarity would not have existed in the community as a whole, and where there are clear signs of social stratification.¹³ Here there would be some who could not rely on any regular source of income. Besides the widow and orphan, there were perhaps young male incomers from a countryside that could not support all the souls it produced.¹⁴ These would be the most likely candidates for destitution and hunger. The command in Deuteronomy to pay a wage laborer before the sun goes down (Deut 24:14–15) is an index of the precarious livelihood of some in the cities of the late monarchy, probably, as well as later.

Some institutions might protect those exposed to the danger of destitution. The institution of patronage probably existed, giving people some security of livelihood in return for their support of the patron in the power negotiations of the elite.¹⁵ The relationship of patron and client is, ideally,

---

9. Sahlins, "Primitive Exchange," 174–202.
10. Similarly other words from the same root. See *DCH*, vol. 7, 514–15.
11. Cf. Sahlins, "Primitive Exchange," 178–81.
12. Bendor, *Social Structure*, 183–96.
13. Nurmi, *Ethik unter dem Druck*; Faust, *Archaeology*, 114–17.
14. See chapter 7 above.
15. Wolf, *Peasants*, 86–87; Simkins, "Patronage"; Houston, *Contending*, 44–48; Domeris, *Touching the Heart of God*, 80–94.

one of balanced reciprocity, where the return should be made at a level recognized as equivalent and in a limited period of time.[16]

It is, of course, not only the poor who are the objects of patronage. Mephibosheth eats "at David's table" (2 Sam 9:11), four hundred and fifty prophets of Baal and four hundred prophets of Asherah "at Jezebel's table" (1 Kgs 18:19), one hundred and fifty people every day "at my [Nehemiah's] table" (Neh 5:17–18). In each case the object of the provision is to reward the recipients for their support and to ensure their loyalty. It is a prudent object for a ruler to bind influential people to their support, and they can do so through redistribution; it is one of its principal objects. Those who do not have access to the levers of redistribution may still be able to use wealth they have gained through redistribution or in other ways for a similar object, and the poor, because of their neediness, are the most likely to respond as required. The command in Deuteronomy to invite to the sacrificial feasts at Weeks and Booths "the Levite who is within your gates, the alien, the fatherless child and the widow who is in your midst" (Deut 16:11, 14) may be an attempt to extend the "generalized reciprocity" of the village to those who might fall outside it, especially in the urban setting; but it can easily be read as a theological validation of patronage.[17]

The permanent imbalance of power between patron and client means that an unscrupulous patron can easily manipulate the relationship, for example through loans, to bend the client to his will and to obtain labor service from his family or himself. Balanced reciprocity thus degenerates into the oddly titled "negative reciprocity," which is no reciprocity at all, but sheer exploitation, provoking the condemnations of an Amos or an Isaiah.[18] What the relationship does not lead to, however, is destitution. Labor power was valuable to the patron, and was worth a meal or two a day.

Moreover, the monarchy, despite its leading role in the development of a stratified society, was conceived to be an institution repressing such injustice. "Justice and righteousness," משפט וצדקה/*mishpat utsedaqa*, was the responsibility of the ruler (e.g., 2 Sam 8:15, 1 Kgs 10:9, Isa 9:7).[19] The king was expected to implement this responsibility by repressing the exploitation of the poor (Ps 72:12–14) and by countering violent class relationships with violence against the oppressor through administrative and judicial means.

---

16. Sahlins, "Primitive Exchange," 202–6.
17. Houston, "Rejoicing before the Lord."
18. Domeris, *Touching The Heart of God*, 94; see Sahlins, "Primitive Exchange," 177.
19. See for full discussions chapters 3 and 10 above, with the literature mentioned there.

It is possible that the Israelite states also used their power of redistribution to assist the destitute. There are in many Israelite and Judean cities large buildings near the gate where the small finds are of a domestic character rather than what one would expect in a public building.[20] Faust links this phenomenon with the frequent mention of the gate in connection with the poor (e.g., Amos 5:12), and suggests that these buildings were provided as accommodation for the homeless. He considers that the state only provided accommodation, and the residents had to rely on alms. However, it is not impossible that they also received basic rations, as the authorities would be doing the same for the city garrison. It may be therefore that in the socially divided cities a primitive welfare system reduced the need for personal alms.

3. Deuteronomy

It is clear already that Deuteronomy witnesses to an evolving urban culture where people were exposed to the danger of destitution in a way unheard of in the countryside. Nothing represented explicitly as almsgiving is mentioned in the law code, Deuteronomy 12–26, but in 10:18–19 we find the reminder that "YHWH loves the alien (גר/ger) and provides food and clothing, and you shall love the alien, since you were aliens in the land of Egypt." But two passages in the code are relevant: the law of the third-year tithe in 14:28–29, and the immediately following seventh-year debt remission, more precisely the exhortation in 15:7–11.

The third-year tithe provides for the storage of provisions for the needy, specified as the Levite, the alien, the widow, and the fatherless. But this is not almsgiving, because it is to be done as a community, not as individuals. It is a redistributive institution rooted no doubt in the solidarity of the village, but to be applied also in the urban situation.

The following passage, Deut 15:1–11, although its main subject is another community institution, the seventh-year debt release, does address the positive responsibility of the individual. The patron is urged not to hesitate to lend to his needy client even when the year of release is approaching and the loan will be cancelled before it has been repaid. (I have given reasons elsewhere to suppose that the remission is a cancellation rather than a suspension.)[21] In that case, the so-called loan will be

---

20. Faust, *Archaeology*, 101–9 and literature mentioned on 101. Such buildings have been found at Beersheba, Tirzah, Beth-shemesh, Mizpah, Hazor, and Arad, among other places.

21. Above, chapter 2, 24–25; cf. Chirichigno, *Debt-slavery*, 272–75.

effectively a gift. But to refuse to lend is implicitly seen as oppressive. The patron is thus forced to choose between committing injustice and sharing his bread with the hungry.

But what the text emphasizes is not that the disbursement is effectively gratuitous, but, implicitly, that the relationship is one of equality. The suppliant is in the gendered language of the text "your brother," "your poor and needy brother." The community is seen in the image of a family.[22] So on the one hand, the transaction is characterized as a loan, not a gift, and on the other it is made a family affair. There is a hidden contradiction here. We do not usually make loans to family members; in the tribal village we expect unconditional help, and in fact the debtor *is* getting a gift, if not an unconditional one. So why maintain the fiction of a loan? This is not too difficult to see: charity is humiliating—even now—for it underlines the inequality, the poverty, the low status of the recipient compared with the donor. If it is humiliating now, how much more so in a society saturated in the honor-shame complex? But as Graeber argues, even though as long as the debt subsists the debtor is subordinate to the creditor, once the debt is paid, or—might one add?—once it is cancelled by higher authority (not by a gracious creditor), a relationship of equality is restored.[23]

In fact, Sahlins's classification of forms of exchange is inadequate to the analysis of charitable giving. Under the sobriquet of *noblesse oblige*, Sahlins classifies gift-giving to the poor, which expects no return, under the heading of generalized reciprocity, the same heading as neighborly help within the village.[24] But the power relationships are entirely different in the two cases. Intuitively this looks like a misfile, curiously similar to the deliberate ideological mystification of Deuteronomy 15. This is where Graeber's recent, entirely different analysis of "the moral grounds of economic relations" becomes valuable.[25] He classifies them under three heads that do not correspond in any simple way to the Polanyi trio. They are "communism," "exchange," and "hierarchy." "Charity" is a hierarchical relationship, one that, as Graeber points out, "operates by a principle that is the very opposite of reciprocity."[26] But how, in that case, can it be *justice*? As Graeber points out, "reciprocity is our main way of imagining justice."[27] How can it be justice unless, like Basil and John Chrysostom, we formulate

---

22. Above, chapter 2; cf. Perlitt, "Ein einzig Volk von Brüdern."
23. Graeber, *Debt*, 120–22.
24. Sahlins, "Primitive Exchange," 176.
25. Graeber, *Debt*, 90–126.
26. Graeber, *Debt*, 110.
27. Graeber, *Debt*, 114.

it as the return to the poor of what belongs to them, or as a loan to God that God will duly return?

4. Sixth Century and Later

It is not any particular social structure or form of exchange that made "charity" in its simplest sense—the feeding of the hungry and the clothing of the naked—a necessity, but the breakdown of *all* social structures. The Assyrian and Babylonian invasions, the fall of the kingdoms, the deportation of elite groups, and the institution of imperial rule, led to radical changes in the economy and society, in modes of oppression, and therefore in ideas of social justice.[28] In the first place, the violence, devastation, and disruption of the invasions in themselves must have created large numbers of hungry and homeless people. Ezekiel's "four judgments, the sword, famine, wild beasts, and pestilence" (Ezek 14:21) are no figure of speech, but the reality in a land suffering major invasion. Secondly, the consequent collapse of social institutions and the entire infrastructure meant that the old social structures of the rural community could not survive.[29] The משפחה/*mishpaha* disappears, eventually to be replaced by the new institution of the בית אבות/*bet avot*, "fathers' house," which probably originated among the deportees, and was less, or not at all, based on kinship.[30] Thirdly, the imperial powers imposed heavy taxes (Neh 5:4, 14); indeed, even before the annexations their demands for tribute had led to increased burdens on the cultivators (2 Kgs 15:19–20). The lack of co-operative institutions and the increased financial burdens meant that at least from the Persian period onwards the existence of the rural population would have been more precarious and more exposed to rapacious creditors, as Nehemiah 5 shows. Fourthly, the disappearance of the native monarchy and the beginning of imperial rule made it impossible to appeal to the king's responsibility of "justice and righteousness."[31]

Thus, it should be no surprise that what is veiled in Deuteronomy is openly admitted in all later writings. In the prophetic literature it is precisely in the sixth century and after that we first hear of the obligation of private individuals to "share their bread with the hungry." Giving to the poor to relieve hunger is urged or praised in e.g., Ezekiel 18: it is a mark of the צדיק/

---

28. Domeris, *Touching the Heart of God*, 128–50, discusses changes in the economy between the seventh and first centuries, and identifies the sixth century as the main watershed.
29. Faust, *Judah*, esp. 106–8.
30. See Smith, *Religion of the Landless*, 93–126.
31. See chapter 10 above, 156–66.

tsaddiq, the just man (so gendered), as well as refraining from exploitative practices, such as charging interest and retaining pledges, to "give his bread to the hungry and to clothe the naked" (v. 7); similarly in Isaiah 58, the release of the oppressed (here perhaps persons in debt bondage) goes along with the exhortation that has provided my chapter title:

> [the fast that I desire]
> Is it not to share your bread with the hungry, to take home the homeless poor,
> when you see the naked, to cover them, and not to hide yourself from your own flesh and blood? (Isa 58:7)

Compare Ps 112:9a, and especially Job 31:16-20, where Job's oath of clearance asserts his generosity to the destitute: "if I ate my piece alone, and the orphan did not share it" (v. 17).

In Job 29, on the other hand, Job's praise of his own justice (vv. 12-17) concentrates on his kinglike defense from exploitation of the poor, the widow, the orphan, the blind, and the lame, in terms reminiscent of Psalm 72.[32] Nehemiah, similarly, can be seen acting in this way in Nehemiah 5, of course to his own advantage, pursuing his quarrel with the Judean upper class by making them restore what they have gained from their peasant debtors. Texts from this period are still able to represent persons with power as actively delivering the poor from oppression.

In the period subsequent to the Hebrew Bible, however, this active defense of the vulnerable against injustice, whether by kings or patriarchs, tends to drop out of view, for native rulers able to act like Nehemiah no longer exist. At the same time a market economy is developing, and more of the country is absorbed into royal and other large estates, often owned by foreigners, with the cultivators reduced to tenants or sharecroppers. Neither of these developments was to the advantage of the peasants unable to compete with the power of the great estates, and the numbers of the desperately poor are likely to have increased.

So we reach the position sketched at the beginning of this paper, in which the connotations of צדקה/*tsedaqa*, justice or right, are almost reduced to that of almsgiving: sharing one's bread with the hungry and clothing the naked are repeatedly mentioned, and in Tobit the burial of the dead. I say "almost reduced": Ben Sira expects his students to exercise justice not only by giving alms, but also in their activity as judges by judging fairly for the poor (Sir 4:7-10).[33]

---

32. See chapter 3 above; Houston, *Contending*, 126-31.
33. See chapter 9 above, esp. 142-43.

5. Retrospect: The History of "Justice"

We have seen that in the monarchic period, the dual character of society, the royal urban sector and the communal rural sector, is paralleled by two co-existing concepts of social justice: the royal tradition of "justice and right" and the communal tradition appealed to in Deuteronomy.[34] The texts prescribing the institutions of debt release and (possibly) third-year tithe, and also the jubilee in Leviticus, could be versions of royal administrative decrees, denuded of their enforcement mechanisms by the fall of the monarchy.[35] But, as we have seen, the ideological context in which they are presented is an attempt to recreate on a national scale the mutual support between real or fictive kin in the pre-exilic village משפחה/*mishpaha*, which in Graeber's terms is "communistic."[36] On the other hand, in the royal ideology it is the king who is responsible for enforcing social justice, so that individual charity, however necessary in reality, does not need to be mentioned.

In the Persian period individual, hierarchical, non-reciprocal charity becomes firmly entrenched as a requirement of justice, even if other aspects are still important and rulers can still act as defenders of the poor. In the Hellenistic period צדקה/*tsedaqa* comes to be applied primarily to almsgiving. Ben Sira alludes to the Deuteronomic tradition of solidarity (Sir 4:7–10; 29:10); the older traditions are not dead.[37] But by and large, almsgiving or works of mercy have become the main expression of justice.

6. Conclusion

Has justice then at the end of the process been reduced to "charity," that is, a voluntary expression of benevolence within a hierarchical structure, or is almsgiving actually justice, that is, the discharge of a reciprocal obligation, a debt, to one's neighbor or to God? Whatever ideology writers of the Hellenistic and later periods apply to it, it cannot be said that any of them view it as voluntary. It is not presented as a matter of choice. It is an obligation, and the virtue of justice, so understood, consists in responding to

---

34. Cf. Nurmi, *Ethik unter dem Druck*, 368–74; Cook, *Social Roots*, 143–80. Neither of these writers, however, recognizes the role of the monarchy in maintaining social justice, even as an ideological fantasy.

35. See above, chapter 3, 53; chapter 10, 174–76. Also Kaufman, "Social Welfare Systems," 281, and Morrow, *Scribing the Center*, 101. Weinfeld, *Social Justice*, 157–68, attributes the utopian character of these texts to the literary rather than the historical context.

36. Graeber, *Debt*, 94–102.

37. Chapter 9 above, 145.

human need.[38] For Ben Sira (29:1, 9, 11) it fulfills the commandments. It is an obligation, but of that (to us) paradoxical kind exemplified also by the Hebrew חסד/*hesed*, which refers to the discharge of obligations incurred in a personal relationship, whether familial, covenantal, or patronal: but how and when to discharge them is a personal choice.[39] Almsgiving is therefore understood as justice.

But it is surely a profoundly inadequate understanding of justice. In the first place, it is non-reciprocal and hierarchical. In the second place, it can only alleviate, not annul, the misery caused by injustice, even if it is said to restore what is owing to the poor because of injustice. To eliminate injustice, political structures are necessary, and they must be used in the interest of the poor (the royal ideology put into practice); or even better, the poor must take charge of their own destiny, as the liberation theologians have long argued, and so make real the Deuteronomic ideal of solidarity.

---

38. Cf. Houston, *Contending*, 132–34.
39. Clark, *The Word* Hesed; Houston, *Contending*, 45.

Chapter 13

Justice and Violence in the Priestly Utopia

Reflections on Genesis 1 and 6–9 in the Shadow of the Environmental Crisis

(2011)

Introduction

Perhaps the only developed and consistent theory of the relations between God, human beings and their environment in the Bible is that sketched by the so-called priestly writer (P) in chapter 1 (with 2:1–3) and parts of chapters 6–9 of Genesis. This would account for the considerable amount of attention these chapters, especially the first, have attracted in the debate on the Bible, Christianity, and the environment. In particular, discussion has focused on the blessing on human beings in Gen 1:28 (with the corresponding divine statement of intention in v. 26). This reads, according to the Hebrew text: "Be fruitful and multiply, fill the earth and subdue it; and rule over [or 'govern'] the fish of the sea, the birds of the air, and every living thing that crawls [or 'moves'] upon the earth."[1]

In what must be one of the most influential short papers in the history of the humanities, the historian Lynn White Jr. argued over fifty years ago that a large share of the responsibility for the already looming environmental disaster was borne by the way this text had been applied in the history of Western Christianity to justify the increasing exploitation of the earth and its creatures.[2] The Bible here had evidently authorized humankind to take control of the earth and its creatures and to use them

---

1. Verse 26 has "and the beasts and all the earth" after "birds of the air"; and the LXX adds this in v. 28. The beasts are needed to complete the picture, but not "all the earth," which has already been mentioned.

2. White, "Historic Roots."

for their own benefit; theologians argued that the earth had been created for the good of humankind, and farmers and engineers and industrialists over the centuries acted on that presupposition, with increasingly damaging effects on the health of ecosystems and the diversity of species. From a different point of view, Norman Habel has argued more recently that the text on the creation of human beings in Gen 1:26–30 is an interruption in the consistent and beautiful story of the emergence of "Earth" (he treats this word as a proper name, with a capital letter and no article), which violates its spirit by imposing upon Earth a hierarchical dominance that devalues Earth and its creatures.[3]

White's article stirred much criticism: see, for example, Barr or Houston.[4] Biblical scholars in particular argued, and generally agree, that the text in question does not mean what it was taken to mean. As I argued, Gen 1:28 could not imply that human beings were being given permission to exploit the earth and its creatures, for two main reasons: first because the position they were being given was one of kingship, and the Old Testament never authorizes kings to use their positions to benefit themselves, and denounces them when they do so: rather they exist to benefit their subjects; and secondly because v. 29 indicates that human beings need special permission, over and above the grant of "dominion," even to use plant produce for food, let alone exploit the earth in any other way.[5]

But in 1999 Peter Harrison pointed out that these criticisms of White were misplaced.[6] It did not matter what the text originally may have meant; what mattered, what influenced history, was "what the text was taken to mean at certain periods of history," and "how it was taken to sanction a particular attitude toward the natural world."[7] However, he went on to show that this specific text, on human dominion, had not in fact been taken in that way in the Middle Ages, which White saw as the key turning point in the rise of exploitative doctrines and practices in Western Europe.[8] In the church fathers and the early medieval period it had been allegorized: the beasts to be kept under control were the human passions; later the point became one of intellectual mastery of the world. (Barr had made a similar point with a slightly different emphasis.)[9] Only in the seventeenth century

---

3. Habel, "Geophany."
4. Barr, "Man and Nature," 15–30; Houston, "'And let them have dominion.'"
5. Houston, "'And let them have dominion,'" 166–67.
6. Harrison, "Subduing the Earth."
7. Harrison, "Subduing the Earth," 89.
8. Harrison, "Subduing the Earth," 89–95.
9. Barr, "Man and Nature," 23–24.

did the text begin to be taken literally, and used to legitimize agriculture, colonization, and the clearing of virgin land: activities understood as the restoration of the human dominion lost with Adam's fall.[10] But this reading of the text emerged just at the time that an anthropocentric view of the universe was being questioned.[11] Thus the reign of the literal sense of the text over doctrine and practice was quite limited, virtually confined to the seventeenth century, according to Harrison.

Today, few of the leaders of politics, commerce, and industry, who have the greatest influence on the way in which human activity impacts on the environment, would think of justifying their activities by reference to this text, and any influence it may have over them is at most extremely indirect. For those who do read it, the question is not how the text has in fact influenced the thinking and activity of people in the past, but how, or whether, it ought to influence ours. The issue is not reception history, but hermeneutics. Thus the "original meaning" comes back into the frame. Those who read the text are bound to be interested in what it "really means"; but they also want to know how it should now be interpreted. The remainder of this paper thus falls into two parts: on exegesis and on hermeneutics.

Exegesis

Any attempt to apply Genesis 1 to life has to take into account the fact that the world which is declared "very good" in Gen 1:31 is not the world that presently exists. I am putting it strongly, of course: no new creation is required after the flood, and most of the elements of that world continue to exist; but the relations between them are profoundly transformed, according to the priestly account. This is acknowledged, for example, by Terence Fretheim, who uses the heading "Genesis 9:1—11:26—A New World Order."[12] In Gen 1:29–30 God assigns food to humans and animals respectively. Humans are to eat seeds and fruit, animals are to have the green stuff of the plants. Nothing is said about animal food for either group. It is true that it is not specifically prohibited, and some have taken this as a loophole to argue that it is not excluded.[13] But human beings are specifically permitted to eat flesh in Gen 9:3, implying, as most agree, that it was previously out of bounds.[14]

---

10. Harrison, "Subduing the Earth," 96–103.
11. Harrison, "Subduing the Earth," 103.
12. Fretheim, "God and the World," 83.
13. E.g., Calvin, *Genesis*, 99–100; Dequeker, "Green Herbage."
14. See, e.g., Westermann, *Genesis 1–11*, 163–64; Harland, *Value*, 150.

Thus, the world brought into being by God's word of creation and blessing is a world without predation and without violence—so, for example, von Rad in his Genesis commentary and more recently William P. Brown.[15] Humanity carries out its function of "government" of the animals by natural authority, not by coercion: this is demonstrated by Noah, who models this function to perfection, as Peter Harland, Brown, and Fretheim all suggest.[16] The animals simply "come" to Noah (Gen 7:9), without, it seems, needing to be driven or coerced.

Violence enters this world and totally wrecks it: "The earth was wrecked before God; the earth was filled with violence; and God looked at the earth and saw that it was wrecked, because every living thing [literally 'all flesh'] had wrecked its way on the earth" (Gen 6:11–12).[17] I have translated כל בשר/kol basar, "all flesh" as "every living thing," although some influential commentators, including Westermann, think it only refers to humanity.[18] However, this is not the majority view, and it should be noted that "all flesh" means "every living thing" at every one of the numerous times it occurs in the flood account that follows.[19] "Violence," חמס, the Hebrew word used in 6:11–13, has been defined as "criminal oppression of the unprotected by those mightier than they."[20] Animals therefore must have been preying on one another, and indeed attacking human beings, to follow the hint of 9:5, and human beings have also been practicing violence: the sequel in 9:3–6 implies that this has included eating animal flesh and attacking each other.[21] Gardner interprets "have wrecked their way" by way of 1:28–30: each group has disregarded the divine commands given here.[22]

The priestly writer does not himself say how this could have happened. On some views of the history of the Pentateuch, the priestly writer incorporated the so-called J (non-priestly) narrative into his own, and in that case the story of Cain and Abel (Gen 4:1–16) would have indicated an origin for violence among human beings. Cain's violence is repeated and magnified in his descendant Lamech (Gen 4:23–24). Bernhard Anderson

---

15. Von Rad, *Genesis*, 59; Brown, *Ethos*, 46–52.
16. Harland, *Value*, 197; Brown, *Ethos*, 55; Fretheim, *God and the World*, 52.
17. Anne Gardner ("Ecojustice," 119–20) uses "destroy" for שחת instead of the traditional "corrupt," to emphasize the verbal link with v. 13 and the sense of physical damage. I think "wreck" works better.
18. Westermann, *Genesis*, 416, following Hulst, "Kol Basar."
19. Westermann, *Genesis*, 416; Gardner, "Ecojustice," 121.
20. Gunkel, *Genesis* (English), 143.
21. Gunkel, *Genesis* (English), 148.
22. Gardner, "Ecojustice," 121.

takes this line.²³ But Anderson also describes the events in Genesis 3 and 6:1–4 as violence; both cases are rather dubious, certainly as regards the present text of Genesis.

An alternative, but much more speculative, view has been put forward by Philip Davies.²⁴ He takes the J passages, following Blenkinsopp,²⁵ to be a supplement to P in Genesis 1–11, rather than an earlier document, and believes that the J passage Gen 6:1–4 as it now stands is a deliberate bowdlerization of an account of the descent of rebel "sons of God," or angels, much more like the story of the Watchers in the Book of Enoch (1 Enoch), one of the most important extra-canonical apocalyptic books, which offers two variant versions of this evidently old story. Here we are told:

> the women became pregnant and gave birth to great giants ... the giants turned against (the people) in order to eat them. And they began to sin against birds, wild beasts, reptiles, and fish. And their flesh was devoured the one by the other, and they drank blood. And then the earth brought an accusation against the oppressors. And Azaz'el [one of the angels] taught the people (the art of) making swords and knives, and shields and breastplates. ... And the people cried and their voice reached unto heaven. (1 En. 7:2, 4–6; 8:1)²⁶

According to Davies, P's original story of the irruption of violence into God's good creation was something similar to this, derived from the same source as the Enoch story, and it has been censored and reduced to unintelligibility by the author of J, in order to promote against this a view of sin as purely human in origin. This is as described in Genesis 2–4, and summarized in Gen 6:5–7, J's explanation for the flood, where the word אדם/*adam*, humankind, occurs four times.

Whatever the origin of this universal violence, it is the reason why, as God tells Noah (Gen 6:18), "I am bringing the flood on the earth to destroy everything which has the breath of life from under the sky." Yet the fresh start thus given the world is not a start over again from the original point. The charge given to humans through Noah in 9:1–7 differs in significant ways from the original one in 1:28–30: "The fear of you and the dread of you shall be upon every beast of the earth ... into your hands they are delivered. Every moving thing which lives may be food for you; along with the green herbs, I give you everything" (Gen 9:2–3). They are to control animals by force and

23. Anderson, "Creation," 163–64.
24. Davies, "And Enoch."
25. Blenkinsopp, *Pentateuch*, 93.
26. Isaac, "1 Enoch," 16.

fear, not by their recognized authority. The last sentence is mistranslated in all the modern versions.[27] God cannot be saying "as *I gave you* the green herbs, so I give you everything" (the words italicized are not in the Hebrew), because he did not give them the green herbs in the first place: they were for the animals (1:29–30).[28] The sense is that humans are given control over all food resources, including those on which the animals feed, as well as being permitted to eat them. It seems that the relations between people and animals have been permanently altered: the flood has enabled a new start, but not the restoration of the primeval world.

If the blessing in Genesis 9 may be said to reflect the world as it is, that in 1:28–30 could be said to express the divine intention for the world: it is the cosmos in the mind of God, the ideal, the priestly utopia. If P places it at the start of creation, the Isaianic tradition places it in the ideal future. Here the rule of the shoot from the stump of Jesse, the ideal king, who rules in justice and destroys oppressors, is figured in the peace that reigns in the animal world: "The wolf will dwell with the lamb, and the leopard will lie down with the kid, . . . a lion will eat straw like cattle, and a baby will play over an adder's den, . . . they shall not hurt or destroy in all my holy mountain, for the land will be full of the knowledge of YHWH as the waters cover the sea" (Isa 11:6–9). It is the authority of the messianic king, as well as the knowledge of God, that creates this peaceful world.

I would suggest that the function that humanity is to discharge in relation to the animals in Gen 1:28 can be understood, at least in part, along the same lines. They are told to "govern" the animals. The Hebrew verb רדה/*rada*, usually translated "rule" or "have dominion," has been mined for various connotations according to the attitude of the interpreter to the text as a whole. Some assert that it implies harsh control, on the basis of a supposed original meaning "tread down."[29] It refers to the use of slaves in Lev 25:43, 46. Others take it in quite the reverse sense: Norbert Lohfink refers to another possible original meaning "lead to pasture," so that the command is to domesticate the animals; and Erich Zenger develops this into the picture of the human being as "shepherd of the animals," "who is to lead and protect the 'house of life' pastorally and competently."[30] But talk of "original meanings" should have been banished from exegetical discussion

---

27. [But see Alter, *Hebrew Bible*, vol. 1, 32.]

28. Harland, *Value*, 150.

29. E.g., Westermann, *Genesis*, 158–59. But as Lohfink points out ("Subdue," 11), its alleged use in Joel 4:13 of treading the winepress is quite uncertain: רדו may just as well be derived from ירד, "go down." As this would otherwise be the only place where רדה had this meaning, this seems more likely.

30. Lohfink, "Subdue," 12; Zenger, *Gottes Bogen*, 96.

long ago.³¹ The word in every case means "rule," "govern," "control," but not necessarily implying harsh control, which is expressed with qualifying words, as in Lev 26:43, 46, 53; Ezek 34:4. It is not distinctively applied to kings, but when it is, it appears usually to refer to rule over foreigners and enemies (1 Kgs 5:4 [English 4:24]; Isa 14:6; Pss 72:8; 110:2); and as it also applies to the control of slaves and conscript labor, its connotations are far from pastoral, in the modern sense of that word. But there are features of the context that serve to exclude the implication that human beings are to exploit the earth and other creatures for their own purposes. Brown has four points.³² I would select just two.

On the one hand, human beings are created in the image of God. The discussion of the meaning and implications of this assertion is ancient and extensive and seems impossible to resolve.³³ It cannot be adequately summarized here. But Westermann has a useful wide-ranging survey, from which two interpretations emerge as the frontrunners.³⁴ Westermann himself adopts the interpretation that "God has created all people 'to correspond to him,' that is so that something can happen between creator and creature."³⁵ This is along the same lines as Barth's view that the human creature's nature as the image and likeness of God means that a human being can be addressed by God as "you," and is an "I" who is responsible before God.³⁶ This lays all the emphasis on the relation between humanity and God; yet in the text the statement that humanity was created as the image of God is most closely linked with the attribution to them of dominion over the earth. The only other place in the Old Testament where the idea is given significance is in Gen 9:6, where it is the motivation for the avenging of human blood. Human beings have a dignity in virtue of their creation in God's image, which means they cannot be destroyed with impunity.

The other view interprets humanity made in the image of God as representing God to the earthly creation. This view was developed by Wildberger and Schmidt on the basis of Egyptian and Mesopotamian evidence, and is also referred to by von Rad.³⁷ In these ancient Near Eastern cultures kings are referred to as the image of such-and-such a god, representing the god

31. Barr, *Semantics*, 107–60.
32. Brown, *Ethos*, 45–46.
33. See, e.g., Jónsson, *Image*, or Garr, *In His Own Image*.
34. Westermann, *Genesis*, 147–58.
35. Westermann, *Genesis*, 158.
36. Barth, *CD* III/1, 182–85.
37. Wildberger, "Abbild"; Schmidt, *Schöpfungsgeschichte*, 127–48; von Rad, *Genesis*, 58.

to their people. In the same way, humanity as the image of God in Genesis 1 represents the majesty of God to the earth and its creatures. Westermann objects to this. Humans are not an individual like a king, and it is hard to see how they can be a representative. The idea does not fit with the theology of P, which emphasizes that God is transcendent and revealed only in defined holy places. "He could not possibly think of a human being as standing in the place of God on earth."[38] And since there are some ancient Near Eastern passages speaking, like Genesis, of the creation of humans in the image of God, the proper comparison is with these, and not with the texts about kings. The first of these three objections is not strong. It might equally well apply to the notion of humans "ruling" the earth (like a king); but that is obviously in the text. The second is, I believe, based on a misunderstanding. The suggestion is not that God is actually present or revealed in human beings, but that human beings take God's place for this particular purpose. The third has some weight, but cannot be decisive.

I would take the view that the creation of humanity in the image and likeness of God entails the consequence that human beings are able to govern the earthly creation, and implies that in so governing, humanity functions to represent God. This does not in any way exclude the implication that humanity is the counterpart and conversation partner of God, a view that is obviously supported by the Bible as a whole. But following up the former implication, we should deduce that therefore people, exercising the divine prerogative, must be intended to supervise and care for creatures rather than exploiting them.[39]

The other feature of the context that needs to be taken into account has already been referred to: that the needs of human beings are met by a specific divine grant (Gen 1:29), not by the freely chosen use of their power; and this grant does not include any use of animals for food or any other purpose. But if the object of the power granted is not for human beings to satisfy their needs (or wants), what is it?

A central function of government in the Hebrew conception is to check oppression. See, e.g., Ps 72:12-14, as well as Isa 11:4: "He shall vindicate the poor with justice, and decide with equity for the wretched of the land; he shall strike the tyrant with the rod of his mouth, and slay the unjust with the breath of his mouth." Now "violence"—חמס/hamas—is one of the ways in which oppression is conceived in the Hebrew Bible.[40] Therefore, I suggest that the authority of the human governors exists, among other things, to

---

38. Westermann, *Genesis*, 153.
39. Compare von Rad, *Genesis*, 56-58; Brown, *Ethos*, 45-46.
40. See Houston, *Contending*, 67-68, 90, 142.

repress violence among the animals. Lohfink may, however, be right that this is to be done by peaceably taming them: or rather, in this primordial world they are tame to start with.[41]

But once humans have taken to violence themselves, they are no longer able to prevent it from breaking out among the animals, especially if they are themselves wreaking it on them by killing and eating them.[42] This connection is made explicit in the passage from 1 Enoch we looked at above. Thus, they have lost their governing authority. The "fear and dread" inspired in the animals by human beings following Gen 9:2 maintains their government, but is a poor substitute for the charismatic authority bestowed on them by the original blessing. On this conception the permission granted them to eat the flesh of any living thing is a means to enforce their authority. Interpreters in the critical period do not seem to have recognized that Gen 9:2 implies a weakening rather than a strengthening of humanity's original authority; but Calvin, for example, speaks of "this dominion, which, although greatly diminished, is nevertheless not entirely abolished."[43] I think this is a correct perception. Even with the post-flood blessing, humanity is unable to repress violence among the animals; they can only protect themselves and use the animals for their own needs. Genesis 9:5 makes it clear that one of the objects of this dispensation is to protect human beings from the attacks of wild animals.

So the differences between Gen 1:28–30 and Gen 9:1–7 arise from the difference between the ideal and the real, or in theological terms "fallen," worlds. Zenger characterizes the images of humanity presented by them each in the terms of ancient Near Eastern iconography as respectively the "shepherd of the animals"[44] and the "lord of the animals"; but he also tries to minimize the difference, speaking of the original blessing being "supplemented and extended" in Genesis 9.[45] Most interpreters recognize the language of warfare in the phrases "the fear of you and the dread of you" and "into your hands they are delivered." Zenger attempts to avoid this implication by arguing that texts like Deut 2:25 and 11:25, where the Israelites are assured that fear and dread will grip their enemies, have to do with YHWH's clearing away of the nations before them without their needing to fight.[46] I do not find this convincing even in the context of Deuteronomy; the panic

---

41. Lohfink, "Subdue," 12.
42. Gardner, "Ecojustice," 126; cf. Anderson, "Creation," 163–64.
43. Calvin, *Genesis*, 291.
44. Cf. Barr, "Man and Nature," 22.
45. Zenger, *Gottes Bogen*, 90–96; 116; 118.
46. Zenger, *Gottes Bogen*, 118.

spread among the enemies may make it unnecessary to fight, but it is a panic *in* war, not to forestall war. On Zenger's own showing, wild beasts were always regarded as a threat to human life in the world of the Hebrew Bible,[47] hence, they needed to be fought; and his iconographic examples of the "lord of the animals" theme include the reliefs of the king of Assyria hunting lions from his chariot. If this is not war, what is?

But the dispensation also includes a measure to protect animals from wanton and uncontrolled attacks by human beings. Gerhard Liedke speaks of "reciprocal measures of protection."[48] Verse 4 warns that flesh may not be eaten with its blood. The mode of expression is unclear, but the practical meaning is not, since it is a statement, the first in the Bible, of the basic rule of kosher slaughter. What is more difficult to see is its significance in the context, except that it appears to be saying that we may consume animals' flesh, but not their life. Odil Hannes Steck argues that, taken together with the fact that the eating of flesh is by divine permission (v. 3), this takes the killing of animals out of the realm of "violence," i.e., חמס/*hamas*.[49] It is the regulated exercise of a divinely granted liberty, not the private satiation of greed. The later dietary laws given to Israel (primarily in Leviticus 11) place this license further under divine regulation.[50]

As our theme is justice, we need to ask whether and how the priestly author would have seen these two successive dispensations as examples of justice. This cannot be simply answered from what the writer says elsewhere, as justice is not a topos in P. But it seems certain that the dispensation of Genesis 1 would have been seen as expressing the justice of the world order.[51] The author would have been baffled by Habel's criticism. Earth's perfection would have been seen to depend on a government representing the authority of God and ensuring the justice of God. Concepts of justice in the Hebrew Bible, indeed the ancient world as a whole, are rooted in structured relationships.[52] That the mere existence of authority should "devalue" those subject to it, as Habel suggests,[53] would have been found a puzzling idea, especially if the intention of authority is to maintain just relationships among the creatures. So far from speaking "from the perspective of Earth," Habel

---

47. [Cf. chapter 11 above, 186.]
48. Liedke, *Im Bauch*, 145: *wechselseitige Schutzmaßnahmen*.
49. Steck, "Mensch."
50. Houston, *Purity*, 253–58.
51. Cf. Schmidt, *Schöpfungsgeschichte*.
52. Houston, *Contending*.
53. Habel, "Geophany," 47–48.

appears to speak from the perspective of an extreme modern liberalism that is unable to swallow any concept of authority.

The dispensation in Genesis 9 is a more ambiguous matter. But it exists under the sign of God's covenant (Gen 9:8-17), which guarantees its permanence, and may be seen to express God's justice. But from what we have seen, it is certain that justice would now be seen to be absent in the animal world. There is an interesting parallel in Greek literature, in Hesiod, *Works and Days*, lines 277-78: Zeus has decreed "that fish and beasts and winged birds should eat one another, since justice is not with them."[54] What we mean by "the law of the jungle" is the antithesis of justice. However, it seems that the rules in Gen 9:4-6 are intended to ensure that human beings' relationships to each other and to the animal world are governed by law, not by the unregulated greed and exploitation that constitute violence. The rules are minimal, or even symbolic, and are likely to be thought inadequate to constitute justice; but evidently the writer believed this was the nearest approach to justice that was attainable among God's creatures in the world as it is.

Hermeneutics

It will now be clear how problematic any application of these texts must be for us today. On the one hand, the dispensation of Genesis 1 involves a conception of natural life that is wholly mythical. The relationship of creatures to each other in ecology as scientifically understood inevitably includes predation, otherwise the herbivores would destroy all vegetation; and the idea that human beings could control this by the force of their divine blessing seems to invoke magical ideas. The associated "subduing of the earth" probably refers primarily to agriculture,[55] and while this is a more realistic idea, it probably implies that the earth is improved by tillage, the draining of swamps, and so forth, as seventeenth-century interpreters thought;[56] any idea that this (however organic the technology) reduces biodiversity and therefore the "goodness" of a world created with a variety of species, could only emerge in our own day. Still less is the idea of violence having been introduced by fallen angels, if that was indeed P's original idea, acceptable within the modern worldview.

On the other hand, while Gen 9:1-7 is more realistic ecologically, the vast increase in human power enabled by scientific knowledge has, as Liedke puts it, pushed to an extreme the asymmetry of the conflict between

---

54. Hesiod, *Theogony*, 108-11.
55. Brown, *Ethos*, 44; but Lohfink thinks it simply means "take possession."
56. See Harrison, "Subduing," 103.

nature and the human race in a way that the writer, for whom wild beasts continued to be a serious danger to human beings, would have been unable to conceive.[57] The sixth mass extinction of species in geological history has begun, but this one is our responsibility: it demands effective rather than symbolic measures for the protection of nature.

If the literal application of these texts is an impossibility, it is equally impossible for us to use allegory like their early Christian interpreters. It is, however, possible to draw out their theological or ethical significance, and here I wish to concentrate on the ethical:[58] using them as tools to reflect on the choices available to the human race at this time in our relation to other creatures of the earth.

Two factual points have been thoroughly and realistically grasped by the priestly author. One is the inescapable dominance of the human race over the earth. This is simply a fact, which cannot be wished away. The massive brain of our species, its possession of speech, its capacity for innovation and organization, make it inevitable that its will should prevail in relation to the natural world. The ethical conclusion from this is surely not to entertain fantasies of a world without such dominance, but to accept the responsibility which that entails, of making conscious reflective decisions about any action affecting other living creatures and earth systems.

The other is the ingrained violence of the natural world, the incessant competition for space and resources, often expressed in predation and exploitation, which forms the essential backdrop to Darwin's theory of natural selection. Too often environmental campaigners appear to give a sentimental picture of the perfect harmony and balance in the natural world that would exist if only it were not for human greed and meddling. If there is balance in natural ecosystems, it is not harmony, but an equilibrium of competitive efforts; and no balance is ever stable, but constantly changing as species rise and decline. The ethical question is how humans as the overwhelming victors in the evolutionary conflict, having upset all balances, should use their victory.

The ethical stance of the priestly text is against violence in the sense it bears in Genesis 6: the greedy and brutal violation of another's rights, integrity, or life. The objection does not extend to the use of coercion by lawful authority: to describe P as "pacifist," as Zenger does, is problematic.[59] The positive value the text promotes is better described as justice than as non-violence.

57. Liedke, *Im Bauch*, 173.
58. [For theological reflections, see Houston, "Sex or Violence?"]
59. Zenger, *Gottes Bogen*, 117.

Now, the present activity of the human race towards the earth and its creatures is one of sustained, extreme, and progressively destructive violence. We are using our victory to plunder and destroy. Given our capacity for conscious reflection and decision, it is possible for us to turn away from this inborn violence as other forms of life cannot. The mythical reign of divine justice sketched in Genesis 1 is in a sense attainable through us, the responsible representatives of the Creator, provided we embrace the way marked out for us there. Years ago, Liedke coined the slogan "solidarity with creation in the conflict between humanity and creation," to be expressed by "lessening its suffering, relieving its need, reducing violence, and thereby giving it new hope."[60] That task has yet to be seriously undertaken.

---

60. Liedke, *Im Bauch*, 178 (my translation).

Bibliography

Albertz, Rainer. *A History of Israelite Religion in the Old Testament Period.* 2 vols. Translated by John Bowden from *Religionsgeschichte in alttestamentlicher Zeit.* London: SCM, 1994.

———. *Religionsgeschichte in alttestamentlicher Zeit.* ATD Ergänzungsreihe 8/1. Göttingen: Vandenhoeck & Ruprecht, 1992.

Alt, Albrecht. "Micha 2,1–5: γῆς ἀναδασμὸς in Juda." In *Kleine Schriften zur Geschichte des Volkes Israel* Band III, 573–81. Munich: Beck, 1953.

Alter, Robert. *The Art of Biblical Narrative.* London: Allen and Unwin, 1981.

———. *The Art of Biblical Poetry.* New York: Basic, 1985.

———. *The Hebrew Bible: A Translation with Commentary.* 3 vols. Vol. 1: *The Five Books of Moses: Torah.* Vol. 2: *Prophets: Nevi'im.* Vol. 3: *The Writings: Ketuvim.* New York: Norton, 2019.

Anchor Bible Dictionary. Edited by David Noel Freedman. 6 vols. New York: Doubleday, 1992.

Anderson, Bernhard W. "Creation and Ecology." In *Creation in the Old Testament,* edited by Bernhard W. Anderson, 152–71. Issues in Religion and Theology 6. London: SPCK, 1984.

Anderson, Gary A. *Charity: The Place of the Poor in the Biblical Tradition.* New Haven, CT: Yale University Press, 2013.

Aristotle. *The "Art" of Rhetoric.* Edited and translated by John Henry Freese. LCL. London: Heinemann, 1926.

Assmann, Jan. *Cultural Memory and Early Civilization: Writing, Remembrance, and Political Imagination.* Translated from *Das kulturelle Gedächtnis.* Cambridge: Cambridge University Press, 2011.

———. "Die Idee vom Totengericht und das Problem der Gerechtigkeit." In *Gerechtigkeit: Richten und Retten in der abendländischen Tradition und ihren altorientalischen Ursprüngen,* edited by Jan Assmann, Bernd Janowski, and Michael Welker, 10–19. Munich: Fink, 1998.

———. *Das kulturelle Gedächtnis: Schrift, Erinnerung, und politische Identität in frühen Hochkulturen.* Munich: Beck, 2007.

Bachmann, Johannes. *Das Buch der Richter: mit besonderer Rücksicht auf die Geschichte seiner Auslegung und kirchlicher Verwendung,* 1er Band. Berlin: Wiegandt und Grieben, 1868.

Baker, David L. *Tight Fists or Open Hands? Wealth and Poverty in Old Testament Law.* Grand Rapids: Eerdmans, 2009.

Barr, James. "Man and Nature: The Ecological Controversy and the Old Testament." *BJRL* 55 (1972) 9–32.

———. *The Semantics of Biblical Language.* Oxford: Oxford University Press, 1961.

Barth, Karl. *Church Dogmatics,* III/1, *The Doctrine of Creation.* Edited by Geoffrey W. Bromiley and Thomas F. Torrance, and translated by J. W. Edwards, O. Bussey, and Harold Knight, from *Kirchliche Dogmatik,* III/1. Edinburgh: T. & T. Clark, 1958.

———. *Kirchliche Dogmatik,* III/1, *Die Lehre von der Schöpfung.* Zurich: Zollikon, 1945.

Bartlett, Russell S. "Let Justice Roll Down Like Waters: The Model of Hebrew Prophecy in the Ministry of Martin Luther King, Jr." *Journal of the Interdenominational Theological Center* 21 (1993) 10–38.

Barton, John. *Ethics in Ancient Israel.* Oxford: Oxford University Press, 2014.

———. "Ethics in Isaiah of Jerusalem." *JTS* 32 (1981) 1–18. Reprinted in (a) *The Place Is Too Small for Us: The Israelite Prophets in Recent Scholarship,* edited by Robert P. Gordon, 80–97. Sources for Biblical and Theological Study 5. Winona Lake, IN: Eisenbrauns, 1995. (b) *Understanding Old Testament Ethics: Approaches and Explorations,* 130–44. Louisville, KY: Westminster John Knox, 2003.

———. "Ethics in the Book of Isaiah." In *Writing and Reading the Scroll of Isaiah,* edited by Craig C. Broyles and Craig A. Evans, 67–77. Leiden: Brill, 1997. Reprinted as "Ethics in the Isaianic Tradition" in *Understanding Old Testament Ethics: Approaches and Explorations,* 145–53. Louisville, KY: Westminster John Knox, 2003.

Basil of Caesarea. "On the Saying of the Gospel according to Luke, 'I will pull down my barns and build bigger ones.'" *PG* 31, 277.

Becker, Uwe. "Die Reichsteilung nach I Reg 12." *ZAW* 112 (1972) 210–29.

Beentjes, Pancratius C. *The Book of Ben Sira in Hebrew: A Text Edition of All Extant Hebrew Manuscripts and a Synopsis of All Parallel Hebrew Ben Sira Texts.* SVT 68. Leiden: Brill, 1997. Reprinted, Atlanta: SBL, 2006.

———, ed. *The Book of Ben Sira in Modern Research: Proceedings of the First International Ben Sira Conference 28–31 July 1996, Soesterberg, Netherlands.* BZAW 255. Berlin: de Gruyter, 1997.

———. "'Sei den Waisen wie ein Vater und den Witwen wie ein Gatte': Ein kleiner Kommentar zu Ben Sira 4, 1–10." In *Der Einzelne und seine Gemeinschaft bei Ben Sira,* edited by Renate Egger-Wenzel and Ingrid Krammer, 51–64. BZAW 270. Berlin: de Gruyter, 1998.

Belgrave, Kate. "Work Capability Assessments: The Fightback." *New Statesman,* 29 July 2012. http://www.newstatesman.com/blogs/staggers/2012/07/workcapability-assessments-fightback (accessed 2015-12-13).

Ben-Tor, Amnon. *Hazor: Canaanite Metropolis, Israelite City.* Jerusalem: Israel Exploration Society, Biblical Archaeology Society, 2016.

Ben Zvi, Ehud. "Wrongdoers, Wrongdoing and Righting Wrongs in Micah 2." *Biblnt* 7 (1999) 87–100.

Bendor, S. *The Social Structure of Ancient Israel: The Institution of the Family (Beit ʾAb) from the Settlement to the End of the Monarchy.* Jerusalem Biblical Studies 7. Jerusalem: Simor, 1996.

Bird, Phyllis. "Poor Man and Poor Woman: Gendering the Poor in Prophetic Texts." In *Missing Persons and Mistaken Identities: Women and Gender in Ancient Israel*, 67–78. Minneapolis: Fortress, 1997 (1996).
Blenkinsopp, Joseph. *Isaiah 1–39: A New Translation with Introduction and Commentary*. AB 19. New York: Doubleday, 2000.
———. *The Pentateuch: An Introduction to the First Five Books of the Bible*. London: SCM, 1992.
Block, Daniel I. *Ezekiel Chapters 1–24*. Grand Rapids: Eerdmans, 1997.
Bobek, Hans. "Die Hauptstufe der Gesellschafts- und Wirtschaftsentfaltung in geographischer Sicht." In *Wirtschaftsgeographie*, edited by Eugen Wirth, 441–85. Darmstadt: Wissenschaftliche Buchhandlung, 1969.
Boer, Roland. *The Sacred Economy of Ancient Israel*. Library of Ancient Israel. Louisville, KY: Westminster John Knox, 2015.
Boswell, James. *The Life of Samuel Johnson, LL.D.* With an introduction by S. C. Roberts. Everyman's Library 1. 2 vols. London: Dent, 1949 (1791).
Bright, John. *Jeremiah: A New Translation with Introduction and Commentary*. AB 21. Garden City, NY: Doubleday, 1965.
Broshi, Magen, and Israel Finkelstein. "The Population of Israel in Iron Age II." *BASOR* 287 (1992) 47–60.
Brown, William P. *The Ethos of the Cosmos*. Grand Rapids: Eerdmans, 1999.
Broyles, Craig C. "The Redeeming King: Psalm 72's Contribution to the Messianic Ideal." In *Eschatology, Messianism and the Dead Sea Scrolls*, edited by Craig A. Evans and Peter W. Flint, 23–40. Grand Rapids: Eerdmans, 1997.
Brueggemann, Walter. *Theology of the Old Testament: Testimony, Dispute, Advocacy*. Minneapolis: Fortress, 1997.
Butler, Patrick. "Benefit Sanctions Leave Clients Hungry for Months." *The Guardian*, 2 March 2015. http://www.theguardian.com/society/patrick-butler-cutsblog/2015/mar/02/food-banks-benefit-sanctions-leave-clients-hungry-for-months (accessed 2015-12-13).
Calvin, John. *A Commentary on Genesis*. London: Banner of Truth, 1965 (1554).
———. *A Commentary on the Psalms of David*, vol. 2. London: Thomas Tegg, 1840 (1557).
Carney, T. F. *The Economies of Antiquity: Controls, Gifts and Trade*. Lawrence, KA: Coronado, 1973.
Carr, David M. *The Formation of the Hebrew Bible: A New Reconstruction*. New York: Oxford University Press, 2011.
———. *Writing on the Tablet of the Heart: Origins of Scripture and Literature*. New York: Oxford University Press, 2005.
Carroll, Robert P. *From Chaos to Covenant: Uses of Prophecy in the Book of Jeremiah*. London: SCM, 1981.
———. *Jeremiah: A Commentary*. OTL. London: SCM, 1986.
———. "Prophecy and Society." In *The World of Ancient Israel: Sociological, Anthropological, and Political Perspectives*, edited by R. E. Clements, 203–26. Cambridge: Cambridge University Press, 1989.
Chambon, Alain. *Tell el-Farʿah, 1: L'age du fer*. Paris: Éditions Recherche sur les Civilisations, 1984.

Chaney, Marvin L. "Debt Easement in Israelite History and Tradition." In *The Bible and the Politics of Exegesis*, edited by David Jobling et al., 127–40. Cleveland, OH: Pilgrim, 1992.

———. "Systemic Study of the Israelite Monarchy." *Semeia* 37 (1986) 53–76.

Charpin, Dominique. "Le 'bon pasteur': idéologie et pratique de la justice royale à l'époque paléo-babylonienne." In *Les moyens d'expressions de pouvoir dans les sociétés anciennes*, edited by Argo, centre d'études comparées des civilisations anciennes, 101–14. Lettres orientales 5. Leuven: Peeters, 1996.

Chavel, Simeon. "'Let My People Go!' Emancipation, Revelation, and Scribal Activity in Jeremiah 34.8–14." *JSOT* 76 (1997) 71–95.

Chirichigno, Gregory C. *Debt-Slavery in Israel and the Ancient Near East*. JSOTS 141. Sheffield, UK: JSOT, 1993.

Clark, Gordon R. *The Word* Hesed *in the Hebrew Bible*. JSOTS 157. Sheffield, UK: JSOT, 1993.

Clines, David J. A. "Quarter Days Gone: Job 24 and the Absence of God." In *God in the Fray: A Tribute to Walter Brueggemann*, edited by Tod Linafelt and Timothy K. Beal, 242–58. Minneapolis: Fortress, 1998.

Cogan, Mordechai. *I Kings: A New Translation with Introduction and Commentary*. AB 10. New York: Doubleday, 2000.

Coggins, Richard J. *Joel and Amos*. NCB. Sheffield, UK: Sheffield Academic, 2000.

Collins, John J. *The Apocalyptic Imagination: An Introduction to Jewish Apocalyptic Literature*. Grand Rapids: Eerdmans, 1998.

———. "Ecclesiasticus, or The Wisdom of Jesus Son of Sirach." In *The Oxford Bible Commentary*, edited by John Barton and John Muddiman, 667–98. Oxford: Oxford University Press, 2001.

Collins, Terence. *The Mantle of Elijah: The Redaction Criticism of the Prophetical Books*. The Biblical Seminar 20. Sheffield, UK: JSOT, 1993.

Cook, Stephen L. *The Social Roots of Biblical Yahwism*. Studies in Biblical Literature 8. Atlanta: SBL, 2004.

Corley, Jeremy. *Ben Sira's Teaching on Friendship*. BJS 316. Providence, RI: Brown University Press, 2002.

Craigie, Peter C. *The Book of Deuteronomy*. NICOT. Grand Rapids: Eerdmans, 1976.

Crüsemann, Frank. "'. . .damit er dich segne in allem Tun deiner Hand . . .' (Dtn 14,29)." In *Mitarbeiter der Schöpfung: Bibel und Arbeitswelt*, edited by Luise and Willy Schottroff, 72–103. Munich: Kaiser, 1983.

———. *Die Tora: Theologie und Sozialgeschichte des alttestmentlichen Gesetzes*. Munich: Kaiser, 1992.

———. *The Torah: Theology and Social History of Old Testament Law*. Translated by Allan W. Mahnke from *Die Tora*. Edinburgh: T. & T. Clark, 1996.

Crüsemann, Frank. *Der Widerstand gegen das Königtum: die antiköniglichen Texte des Alten Testaments und der Kampf um den frühen Israelitischen Staat*. WMANT 49. Neukirchen-Vluyn: Neukirchener, 1978.

Dahood, Mitchell. *Psalms 51–100: A New Translation with Introduction and Commentary*. AB 17. 3rd ed. Garden City, NY: Doubleday, 1974.

Daube, David. *The Exodus Pattern in the Bible*. Oxford: Oxford University Press, 1963.

Davies, G. I. *Ancient Hebrew Inscriptions: Corpus and Concordance*. Cambridge: Cambridge University Press, 1991.

Davies, Philip R. "And Enoch Was Not, for Genesis Took Him." In *Biblical Traditions in Transmission: Essays in Honour of Michael A. Knibb,* edited by Charlotte Hempel and Judith M. Lieu, 97–107. Leiden: Brill, 2006.
Day, John. "How Many Pre-exilic Psalms Are There?" In *In Search of Pre-exilic Israel,* edited by John Day, 225–50. London: T. & T. Clark, 2004.
Dearman, J. Andrew. *Property Rights in the Eighth-Century Prophets: The Conflict and Its Background.* Atlanta: Scholars, 1988.
Dequeker, Luc. "'Green Herbage and Trees Bearing Fruit' (Gen 1:28-30; 9:1-3)." *Bijdragen* 38 (1977) 118–27.
Dhorme, Édouard [Paul]. *A Commentary on the Book of Job.* Translated by Harold Knight from *Le Livre de Job.* With a preface by Francis I. Andersen. Nashville: Nelson, 1984.
———. *Le Livre de Job.* Paris: Lecoffre, 1926.
Di Lella, Alexander A. *The Hebrew Text of Sirach: A Text-Critical and Historical Study.* Studies in Classical Literature 1. The Hague: Mouton, 1966.
Dictionary of Classical Hebrew. Edited by David J. A. Clines. 9 vols. Sheffield, UK: Sheffield Academic (vols. 1–5); Sheffield Phoenix (vols. 6–9), 1993–2016.
Domeris, William Robert. *Touching the Heart of God: The Social Construction of Poverty among Biblical Peasants.* LHBOTS 466. London: T. & T. Clark, 2007.
Driver, S. R. *A Critical and Exegetical Commentary on Deuteronomy.* ICC. 3rd ed. Edinburgh: T. & T. Clark, 1902.
Dybdahl, Jon L. "Israelite Village Land Tenure: Settlement to Exile." Ph.D. diss., Fuller Seminary, 1981. Ann Arbor, MI: University Microfilms International, 1982.
Eagleton, Terry. *Literary Theory: An Introduction.* Oxford: Blackwell, 1983.
Edzard, D. O. "'Soziale Reformen' im Zweistromland bis ca. 1600 v. Chr.: Realität oder literarischer Topos?" *Acta Antiqua Academiae Scientiarum Hungaricae* 22 (1974) 145–56.
Egger-Wenzel, Renate, and Ingrid Krammer (eds). *Der Einzelne und seine Gemeinschaft bei Ben Sira.* BZAW 270. Berlin: de Gruyter, 1998.
Eisenstadt, S. N., and L. Roniger. *Patrons, Clients and Friends: Interpersonal Relations and the Structure of Trust in Society.* Cambridge: Cambridge University Press, 1984.
Epsztein, Léon. *La justice sociale dans le proche-orient ancien et le peuple de la Bible.* Paris: Cerf, 1983.
———. *Social Justice in the Ancient Near East and the People of the Bible.* Translated by John Bowden from *La justice sociale.* London: SCM, 1986.
Ewans, Martin. *Afghanistan: A Short History of Its People and Politics.* New York: Perennial, 2002.
Fager, Jeffrey A. *Land Tenure and the Biblical Jubilee: Uncovering Hebrew Ethics through the Sociology of Knowledge.* JSOTS 155. Sheffield, UK: Sheffield Academic, 1993.
Faust, Avraham. "The Archaeology of the Israelite Cult: Questioning the Consensus." *BASOR* 360 (2010) 23–35.
———. *The Archaeology of Israelite Society in Iron Age II.* Winona Lake, IN: Eisenbrauns, 2012.
———. "Decoration versus Simplicity: Pottery and Ethnic Negotiation in Early Israel." *Ars Judaica* 9 (2013) 7–18.
———. "Differences in Family Structure between Cities and Villages in Iron Age II." *Tel Aviv* 26 (1999) 233–52.

———. "Ethnic Complexity in Northern Israel during Iron Age II." *PEQ* 132 (2000) 2–27.

———. "The Farmstead in the Highlands of Iron II Israel." In *The Rural Landscape of Ancient Israel*, edited by Aren M. Maeir et al., 91–104. BAR International Series 1121. Oxford: Archaeopress, 2003.

———. *Israelite Society in the Period of the Monarchy: An Archaeological Examination* (Hebrew). Jerusalem: Yad Izhak Ben-Zvi, 2005.

———. *Israel's Ethnogenesis: Settlement, Interaction, Expansion and Resistance*. London: Equinox, 2006.

———. *Judah in the Neo-Babylonian Period: The Archaeology of Desolation*. Atlanta: SBL, 2012.

———. "Social Criticism of the Prophets and the Social Reality in Israel and Judah: An Archaeological Examination." In *Studies in Bible and Exegesis, Presented to Shmuel Vargon*. Vol. 10, 263–79 (Hebrew, English abstract). Ramat-Gan, Israel: Bar-Ilan University Press, 2011.

———. "The Rural Community in Ancient Israel during Iron Age II." *BASOR* 317 (2000) 17–39.

———. "The Settlement of Jerusalem's Western Hill and the City's Status in Iron Age II Revisited." *ZDPV* 121 (2005) 97–118.

———. "Socioeconomic Stratification in an Israelite City: Hazor VI as a Test Case." *Levant* 31 (1999) 179–90.

Faust, Avraham, and Ehud Weiss. "Judah, Philistia, and the Mediterranean World: Reconstructing the Economic System of the Seventh Century B.C.E." *BASOR* 338 (2005) 71–92.

Fendler, Marlene. "Zur Sozialkritik des Amos." *EvTh* 33 (1973) 32–53.

Finkelstein, Israel. *The Forgotten Kingdom: The Archaeology and History of Northern Israel*. SBL Ancient Near East Monographs 5. Atlanta: SBL, 2013.

———, ed. *ʿIzbet Sartah: An Early Iron Age Site near Rosh Haʿayin, Israel*. BAR International Series 229. Oxford: BAR, 1986.

Finkelstein, J. J. "The Edict of Ammiṣaduqa: A New Text." *Revue d'assyriologie et d'archéologie orientale* 63 (1969) 45–64.

Finley, Moses. "Debt-Bondage and the Problem of Slavery." In *Economy and Society in Ancient Greece*, edited by Brent Shaw and Richard Saller, 150–66. London: Chatto and Windus, 1981.

Fleischer, Günther. *Von Menschenverkäufern, Baschankuhen, und Rechtsverkehrern*. BBB 74. Frankfurt am Main: Athenäum, 1989.

Fleming, Daniel E. *The Legacy of Israel in Judah's Bible: History, Politics and the Reinscribing of Tradition*. Cambridge: Cambridge University Press, 2012.

Fowler, H. W. *A Dictionary of Modern English Usage*. 2nd ed. Edited by Ernest Gowers. Oxford: Clarendon, 1965.

Fox, Michael V. *Proverbs 10–31. A New Translation with Introduction and Commentary*. AB 18B. New Haven: Yale University Press, 2009.

———. "The Social Location of the Book of Proverbs." In *Texts, Temples, and Traditions: A Tribute to Menahem Haran*, edited by Michael V. Fox et al., 227–39. Winona Lake, IN: Eisenbrauns, 1996.

Fox, Nili Sacher. *In the Service of the King: Officialdom in Ancient Israel and Judah*. Monographs of the Hebrew Union College 23. Cincinatti, OH: Hebrew Union College, 2000.

Fretheim, Terence E. *God and the World in the Old Testament*. Nashville, TN: Abingdon, 2005.
Frick, Frank S. "*Cui Bono?*—History in the Service of Political Nationalism: The Deuteronomistic History as Political Propaganda." *Semeia* 66 (1994) 79–92.
Fritz, Volkmar *The City in Ancient Israel*. The Biblical Seminar 29. Sheffield, UK: Sheffield Academic, 1995.
Gadamer, Hans-Georg. *Truth and Method*. 2nd ed. Translation of *Wahrheit uund Methode*, 3rd ed. London: Sheed and Ward, 1989.
———. *Wahrheit und Methode*. 3rd ed. Tübingen: Mohr, 1972.
Gardner, Anne. "Ecojustice: A Study of Genesis 6.11–13." In *The Earth Story in Genesis*, edited by Norman Habel, 117–29. Sheffield, UK: Sheffield Academic, 2000.
Garr, W. Randall. *In His Own Image and Likeness: Humanity, Divinity and Monotheism*. Leiden: Brill, 2003.
Gellner, Ernest, and John Waterbury. *Patrons and Clients in Mediterranean Society*. London: Duckworth, 1977.
Gelston, Anthony. "Editorial Arrangement in Book IV of the Psalter." In *Genesis, Isaiah, and Psalms: A Festschrift to Honour Professor John Emerton for his Eightieth Birthday*, edited by Katharine J. Dell et al., 165–76. Leiden: Brill, 2010.
Geus, C. H. J. de. "Die Gesellschaftskritik der Propheten und die Archäologie." *ZDPV* 98 (1982) 50–57.
Gibson, J. C. L. *Canaanite Myths and Legends*. 2nd ed. Edinburgh: T. & T. Clark, 1978.
Gilbert, Maurice. "Prêt, aumône et caution." In *Der Einzelne und seine Gemeinschaft bei Ben Sira*, edited by Renate Egger-Wenzel and Ingrid Krammer, 179–90. BZAW 270. Berlin: de Gruyter, 1998.
Goldingay, John. *Isaiah 56–66*. ICC. London: Bloomsbury T. & T. Clark, 2014.
Gordis, Robert. "The Social Background of Wisdom Literature." *HUCA* 18 (1943) 77–118.
Gorringe, Timothy J. *Capital and the Kingdom: Theological Ethics and Economic Order*. London: SPCK, 1994.
Gottwald, Norman K. "The Expropriators and the Expropriated in Nehemiah 5." In *Concepts of Class in Ancient Israel*, edited by Mark R. Sneed, 1–19. South Florida Studies in the History of Judaism 201. Atlanta: Scholars, 1999. Reprinted in *Social Justice and the Hebrew Bible*, vol. 3, 35–53. Eugene, OR: Cascade, 2018.
———. "Social Class and Ideology in Isaiah 40–55; An Eagletonian Reading." *Semeia* 59 (1992) 43–58. Reprinted in *Social Justice and the Hebrew Bible*, vol. 1, 44–59. Eugene, OR: Cascade, 2016.
———. "Social Class as an Analytic and Hermeneutical Category in Biblical Studies." *JBL* 112 (1993) 3–22. Reprinted in *Social Justice and the Hebrew Bible*, vol. 1, 21–43. Eugene, OR: Cascade, 2016.
Graeber, David. *Debt: The First 5,000 Years*. Brooklyn, NY: Melville House, 2011.
Gray, George Buchanan. *A Critical and Exegetical Commentary on the Book of Isaiah I–XXVII*. ICC. Edinburgh: T. & T. Clark, 1912.
Gray, John. *I & II Kings: A Commentary*. OTL. 2nd ed. London: SCM, 1970.
Gregory, Bradley C. *Like an Everlasting Signet Ring: Generosity in the Book of Sirach*. Deuterocanonical and Cognate Literature Studies 2. Berlin: de Gruyter, 2010.
Guillaume, Philippe. *Land, Credit and Crisis: Agrarian Finance in the Hebrew Bible*. London: Equinox, 2012.

Gunkel, Hermann. *Genesis Translated and Interpreted.* Translated by Mark E. Biddle from *Genesis übersetzt und erklärt.* Macon, GA: Mercer, 1997.

———. *Genesis übersetzt und erklärt.* 3rd ed. HKAT 1, 1. Göttingen: Vandenhoeck & Ruprecht, 1910.

Gunkel, Hermann. *Die Psalmen übersetzt und erklärt.* 4th ed. HKAT 2, 2. Göttingen: Vandenhoeck & Ruprecht, 1926.

Habel, Norman C. "Geophany: The Earth Story in Genesis 1." In *The Earth Story in Genesis*, edited by Norman C. Habel, 34–48. Sheffield, UK: Sheffield Academic, 2000.

Habel, Norman C. *The Land Is Mine: Six Biblical Land Ideologies.* Minneapolis: Fortress, 1995.

Hamilton, Jeffries M. *Social Justice and Deuteronomy: The Case of Deuteronomy 15.* SBLDS 136. Atlanta: Scholars, 1992.

Harland, Peter J. *The Value of Human Life: A Study of the Story of the Flood (Genesis 6–9).* SVT 64. Leiden, Brill, 1996.

Harrison, Peter. "Subduing the Earth: Genesis 1, Early Modern Science and the Exploitation of Nature." *JR* 79 (1999) 86–109.

Hengel, Martin. *Judaism and Hellenism: Studies in their Encounter in Palestine during the Early Hellenistic Period.* Translated by John Bowden from *Judentum und Hellenismus.* 2 vols. London: SCM, 1974.

———. *Judentum und Hellenismus: Studien zu ihrer Begegnung unter besonderer Berücksichtigung Palästinas bis zur Mitte des 2 Jh.s v.Chr.* WUNT 10. 2nd ed. Tübingen: Mohr, 1973.

Henrey, K. H. "Land Tenure in the Old Testament." *PEQ* 86 (1954) 5–15.

Hesiod. *Theogony, Works and Days, Testimonia.* Edited and translated by Glenn W. Most. LCL. Cambridge: Harvard University Press, 2006.

Hillers, Delbert R. *Micah: A Commentary on the Book of the Prophet Micah.* Hermeneia. Philadelphia: Fortress, 1984.

Holladay, John S. "The Kingdoms of Israel and Judah: Political and Economic Centralization in the Iron IIA–B (ca. 1000–750 BCE)." In *The Archaeology of Society in the Holy Land*, edited by Thomas E. Levy, 368–98. New York: Facts on File, 1995.

Hopkins, David C. "Bare Bones: Putting Flesh on the Economics of Ancient Israel." In *The Origins of the Ancient Israelite States*, edited by Volkmar Fritz and Philip R. Davies, 121–39. JSOTS 228. Sheffield, UK: Sheffield Academic, 1996.

———. "The Dynamics of Agriculture in Monarchical Israel." In *SBL 1983 Seminar Papers*, 177–202. SBL Seminar Papers Series 22. Atlanta: Society of Biblical Literature, 1983.

———. "Farmsteads." In *Oxford Encyclopedia of Archaeology in the Near East* II, 306–7. New York: Oxford University Press, 1997.

———. *The Highlands of Canaan: Agricultural Life in the Early Iron Age.* SWBA 3. Sheffield, UK: Almond, 1985.

Horsley, Richard A. *Scribes, Visionaries and the Politics of Second Temple Judea.* Louisville, KY: Westminster John Knox, 2007.

Hossfeld, Frank-Lothar, and Erich Zenger. *Psalmen 51–100.* HThKAT. Freiburg: Herder, 2000.

Hossfeld, Frank-Lothar, and Erich Zenger. *Psalms 2: A Commentary on Psalms 51–100*. Edited by Klaus Baltzer and translated by Linda M. Maloney from *Psalmen 51–100*. Philadelphia: Fortress, 2005.

Houston, Fleur S. *You Shall Love the Stranger as Yourself: The Bible, Refugees and Asylum. Biblical Challenges in the Contemporary World*. London: Routledge, 2015.

Houston, Walter J. *Amos: Justice and Violence*. OTG. Sheffield, UK: Sheffield Phoenix, 2015. Reprinted: Bloomsbury T. & T. Clark, 2017.

———. "'And let them have dominion . . .': Biblical Views of Man in Relation to the Environmental Crisis." In *Studia Biblica I: Papers on Old Testament and Related Themes*, edited by E. A. Livingstone, 161–84. JSOTS 11. Sheffield, UK: JSOT, 1979.

———. "Between Salem and Gerizim: The Context of the Formation of the Torah Reconsidered." *JAJ* 5 (2014) 311–34.

———. *Contending for Justice: Ideologies and Theologies of Social Justice in the Old Testament*. LHBOTS 428. London: T. & T. Clark, 2006.

———. *Contending for Justice: Ideologies and Theologies of Social Justice in the Old Testament*. 2nd, rev. ed. London: T. & T. Clark, 2008. (=Houston, *Contending*)

———. "Folly at Bethel: Amos on Religion." In a forthcoming Festschrift. London: Bloomsbury T. & T. Clark.

———. *Purity and Monotheism: Clean and Unclean Animals in Biblical Law*. JSOTS 140. Sheffield, UK: JSOT, 1993.

———. "Rejoicing before the Lord: The Function of the Festal Gathering in Deuteronomy." In *Feasts and Festivals*, edited by Christopher Tuckett, 1–13. CBET 53. Leuven: Peeters, 2009.

———. "Sex or Violence? Thinking Again with Genesis about Fall and Original Sin." In *Genesis and Christian Theology*, edited by Nathan MacDonald et al., 140–51. Grand Rapids: Eerdmans, 2012.

———. "'Today, in Your Very Hearing': Some Comments on the Christological Use of the Old Testament." In *The Glory of Christ in the New Testament: Studies in Christology in Memory of George Bradford Caird*, edited by Lincoln D. Hurst and N. T. Wright, 37–47. Oxford: Clarendon, 1987.

Houtart, François. *Religion et modes de production précapitalistes*. Brussels: Éditions de l'Université de Bruxelles, 1980.

Howard, David M., Jr. *The Structure of Psalms 93–100*. Winona Lake, IN: Eisenbrauns, 1997.

Hulst, A. R. "Kol Basar in der priesterlichen Fluterzahlung." *OTS* 12 (1958) 28–68.

Isaac, E. "1 (Ethiopic Apocalypse of) Enoch: A New Translation and Introduction." In *The Old Testament Pseudepigrapha*, vol. 1: *Apocalyptic Literature and Testaments*, edited by James H. Charlesworth, 5–90. London: Darton, Longman, and Todd, 1983.

Jackson, Bernard S. "Ideas of Law and Legal Administration: A Semiotic Approach." In *The World of Ancient Israel: Sociological, Anthropological and Political Approaches*, edited by R. E. Clements, 185–202. Cambridge: Cambridge University Press, 1989.

———. "Justice and Righteousness in the Bible: Rule of Law or Royal Paternalism?" *ZAR* 4 (1998) 218–62.

———. "Law and Religion in the Hebrew Bible." In *Law and Religion in the Eastern Mediterranean from Antiquity to Early Islam*, edited by Anselm C. Hagedorn and Reinhard G. Kratz, 189–215. Oxford: Oxford University Press, 2013.

———. *Wisdom-Laws: A Study of the Mishpatim of Exodus 21:1—22:16*. Oxford: Oxford University Press, 2004.

Jameson, Fredric. *The Political Unconscious: Narrative as a Socially Symbolic Act*. Ithaca, NY: Cornell University Press, 1981.

Jenkins, Simon. "Budget 2014: George Osborne, It's Not Your Job to Look after the Very Rich." *The Guardian*, 19 March 2014. http://www.theguardian.com/commentisfree/2014/mar/18/osborne-wealth-gapgovernments-conspire-obscene (accessed 2015-12-13).

Jeremias, Jörg. "Die Deutung der Gerichtsworte Michas in der Exilszeit." *ZAW* 83 (1971) 330-54.

Jobling, David. "Deconstruction and the Political Analysis of Biblical Texts: A Jamesonian Reading of Psalm 72." *Semeia* 59 (1992) 95-127.

John Chrysostom. "In Epistulam I ad Timotheum Cap. IV, Homilia 12." *PG* 62, 562-63.

Jones, Douglas Rawlinson. *Jeremiah*. NCBC. Grand Rapids: Eerdmans, 1992.

Jones, Owen. "The TTIP Deal Hands British Sovereignty to Multinationals." *The Guardian*, 14 Sept. 2014. http://www.theguardian.com/commentisfree/2014/sep/14/ttip-deal-british-sovereignty-cameron-ukip-treaty (accessed 2015-12-13).

Jónsson, Gunnlaugur A. *The Image of God: Genesis 1.26-28 in a Century of Old Testament Research*. CB OTS 26. Stockholm: Almqvist & Wiksell, 1988.

Joosten, Jan. *The Verbal System of Classical Hebrew: A New Synthesis Elaborated on the Basis of Classical Prose*. Jerusalem: Simor, 2012.

Kaufman, Stephen A. "A Reconstruction of the Social Welfare Systems of Ancient Israel." In *In the Shelter of Elyon: Essays on Ancient Palestinian Life and Literature in Honour of G. W. Ahlström*, edited by W. Boyd Barrick and John R. Spencer, 277-86. JSOTS 31. Sheffield, UK: JSOT, 1984.

Kessler, Rainer. "Die angeblichen Kornhändler von Amos viii 4-7." *VT* 29 (1989) 13-22.

———. "Frühkapitalismus, Rentenkapitalismus, Tributarismus, antike Klassengesellschaft: Theorien zur Gesellschaft des alten Israel." *EvTh* 54 (1994) 413-27.

———. *Micha, übersetzt und ausgelegt*. HThKAT. Freiburg: Herder, 1999.

———. *Staat und Gesellschaft in vorexilischen Juda vom 8. Jahrhundert bis zum Exil*. SVT 47. Leiden: Brill, 1992.

Kieweler, Hans Volker. *Ben Sira zwischen Judentum und Hellenismus: Eine kritische Auseinandersetzung mit Th. Middendorp*. BEATAJ 30. Frankfurt am Main: Lang, 1992.

Kippenberg, Hans G. "Die Entlassung aus Schuldknechtschaft in antiken Judäa: Eine Legitimitätsvorstellung von Verwandtschaftsgruppen." In *Vor Gott sind alle gleich: soziale Gleichheit, soziale Ungleichheit und die Religionen*, edited by Günter Kehrer, 94-104. Düsseldorf: Patmos, 1983.

———. *Religion und Klassenbildung im antiken Judäa: Eine religionssoziologische Studie zum Verhaltnis von Tradition und gesellschaftlicher Entwicklung*. 2nd ed. Göttingen: Vandenhoeck & Ruprecht, 1982.

———. "Die Typik antiker Entwicklung." In *Seminar: Die Entstehung der antiken Klassengesellschaft*, edited by Hans G. Kippenberg, 9-61. Frankfurt am Main: Suhrkamp, 1977.

Koch, Klaus. *Die Profeten I: Assyrische Zeit*. Stuttgart: Kohlhammer, 1978.

———. *The Prophets*, vol. 1: *The Assyrian Period*. Translated by Margaret Kohl from *Die Profeten I*. London: SCM, 1982.

Kovacs, Brian W. "Is There a Class-Ethic in Proverbs?" In *Essays in Old Testament Ethics (J. Philip Hyatt in memoriam)*, edited by James L. Crenshaw and John T. Willis, 176–89. New York: Ktav, 1974.

Krašovec, Jože. *La Justice de Dieu dans la Bible hébraique et l'interprétation juive et chrétienne*. OBO 76. Fribourg: Éditions Universitaires, 1992.

Kraus, F. R. "Ein Edikt des Königs Samsu-iluna von Babylon." *Assyriological Studies* 16 (1965) 225–31.

———. *Ein Edikt von Ammi-Ṣaduqa von Babylon*. Leiden: Brill, 1958.

———. *Königliche Verfügungen in altbabylonischer Zeit*. Leiden: Brill, 1984.

Kraus, Hans-Joachim. *Psalmen*, 2. Teilband, *Psalmen 60–150*. BKAT XV/2. 5th ed. Neukirchen-Vluyn: Neukirchener, 1978.

———. *Psalms 60–150*. A Continental Commentary. Translated by Hilton C. Oswald from *Psalmen*, 2. Minneapolis: Fortress, 1993.

Krusche, Marcel. *Göttliches und irdisches Königtum in den Psalmen*. FAT 2/109. Tübingen: Mohr, 2019.

Kuschke, Arnulf. "Arm und reich im Alten Testament mit besonderer Berücksichtigung der nachexilischen Zeit." *ZAW* 57 (1939) 31–57.

Lang, Bernhard. "The Social Organization of Peasant Poverty in Biblical Israel." In *Monotheism and the Prophetic Minority*, 114–27. SWBA 1. Sheffield, UK: Almond, 1983.

Leclerc, Thomas L. *Yahweh is Exalted in Justice: Solidarity and Conflict in Isaiah*. Minneapolis: Fortress, 2001.

Leeuwen, Cornelis van. *Le développement du sens social en Israel avant l'ère chrétienne*. Studia Semitica Neerlandica 1. Assen: van Gorcum, 1955.

Lefebvre, Jean-François. *Le jubilé biblique: Lv 25—exégèse et théologie*. OBO 194. Fribourg: Universitaires, 2003.

Lemche, Niels Peter. "*andurārum* and *mīšarum* . . ." *JNES* 38 (1979) 11–22.

———. *Early Israel: Anthropological and Historical Studies on the Israelite Society Before the Monarchy*. SVT 37. Leiden: Brill, 1985.

———. "The Manumission of Slaves—the Fallow Year—the Sabbatical Year—the Jobel Year." *VT* 26 (1976) 38–59.

Lenski, Gerhard E. *Power and Privilege: A Theory of Social Stratification*. New York: McGrawHill, 1966.

Levenson, Jon D. "Exodus and Liberation." In *The Hebrew Bible, the Old Testament and Historical Criticism: Jews and Christians in Biblical Studies*, 127–59. Louisville, KY: Westminster John Knox, 1993.

Levine, Baruch S. *Leviticus*. JPS Torah Commentary. Philadelphia: Jewish Publication Society of America, 1989.

Liedke, Gerhard. *Im Bauch des Fisches: Ökologische Theologie*. Stuttgart: Kreuz, 1979.

Liver, Jacob. "The Book of the Acts of Solomon." *Biblica* 48 (1967) 75–101.

Lohfink, Norbert. "Poverty in the Laws of the Ancient Near East and of the Bible." *Theological Studies*, 52 (1991) 34–50.

———. "'Subdue the Earth?' (Genesis 1:28)." In *Theology of the Pentateuch: Themes of the Priestly Narrative and Deuteronomy*, 1–17. Edinburgh: T. & T. Clark, 1994.

Loretz, Oswald. "Die prophetische Kritik des Rentenkapitalismus." *UF* 7 (1975) 271–78.

MacIntyre, Alasdair. *After Virtue: A Study in Moral Theory*. 2nd ed. London: Duckworth, 1985.

Magonet, Jonathan. "On Reading Psalms as Liturgy: Psalms 96–99." In *The Shape and Shaping of the Book of Psalms*, edited by Nancy L. De Claissé-Walford, 161–77. Atlanta: SBL, 2014.

Marböck, Johannes. "Sir. 38,24—39,11, Der schriftgelehrte Weise: Ein Beitrag zu Gestalt und Werk Ben Siras." In *La Sagesse de l'ancien Testament*, edited by Maurice Gilbert, 293–316. BETL 51. Leuven: Leuven University Press, 1979.

———. "Structure and Redaction History in the Book of Ben Sira: Review and Prospects." In *The Book of Ben Sira in Modern Research*, edited by Pancratius C. Beentjes, 61–79. Berlin: de Gruyter, 1997.

Marx, Karl. *Grundrisse: Foundations of the Critique of Political Economy (Rough Draft)*. Translated by Martin Nicolaus from *Ökonomische Manuskripte 1857/58*. New York: Random House, 1973.

———. *Ökonomische Manuskripte 1857/58*. In *Karl Marx and Friedrich Engels. Gesamtausgabe* II/1–2. Berlin: Dietz, 1981.

Marx, Karl, and Friedrich Engels. *The Communist Manifesto*. Official English translation, approved by Engels. New York: Monthly Review, 1998 (1848).

Mayes, A. D. H. *Deuteronomy*. NCBC. Grand Rapids: Eerdmans, 1979.

Mays, James Luther. *Amos: A Commentary*. OTL. Louisville, KY: Westminster John Knox, 1969.

McConville, J. Gordon. *Deuteronomy*. Apollos OT Commentary 5. Leicester, UK: Apollos, 2002.

McGuire, Randall H. "The Study of Ethnicity in Historical Archaeology." *Journal of Anthropological Archaeology* 1 (1982) 159–78.

McKane, William. *Micah: Introduction and Commentary*. Edinburgh: T. & T. Clark, 1998.

Mein, Andrew. *Ezekiel and the Ethics of Exile*. Oxford: Oxford University Press, 2001.

Melotti, Umberto. *Marx and the Third World*. London: Macmillan, 1977.

Mendelsohn, Isaac. "State Slavery in Ancient Palestine." *BASOR* 85 (1942) 14–17.

Merendino, Rosario Pius. *Das deuteronomische Gesetz: Eine literarkritische, gattungs- und überlieferungsgeschichtliche Untersuchung zu Dt 12–26*. BBB 31. Bonn: Hamstein, 1969.

Middendorp, Theophil. *Die Stellung Jesu Ben Siras zwischen Judentum und Hellenismus*. Leiden: Brill, 1973.

Milgrom, Jacob. *Leviticus 17–22: A New Translation with Introduction and Commentary*. AB 3A. New York: Doubleday, 2000

———. *Leviticus 23–27: A New Translation with Introduction and Commentary*. AB 3B. New York: Doubleday, 2001.

Miller, J. Maxwell, and John H. Hayes. *A History of Ancient Israel and Judah*. Louisville, KY: Westminster John Knox, 2006.

Miranda, José Porfirio. *Marx and the Bible: A Critique of the Philosophy of Oppression*. Translated by John Eagleson from *Marx y la biblia*. London: SCM, 1977.

———. *Marx y la biblia: Critica a la filosofia de la oppression*. Salamanca: Ediciones Sigueme, 1971.

Montgomery, James A. *A Critical and Exegetical Commentary on the Books of Kings*. Edited by Henry Snyder Gehman. ICC. Edinburgh: T. & T. Clark, 1951.

Morla Asensio, Victor. "Poverty and Wealth: Ben Sira's View of Possessions." In *Der Einzelne und seine Gemeinschaft bei Ben Sira*, edited by Renate Egger-Wenzel and Ingrid Krammer, 151–78. BZAW 270. Berlin: de Gruyter, 1998.

Morrow, William S. *Scribing the Center: Organization and Redaction in Deuteronomy 14:1—17:13*. SBL Monograph Series 49. Atlanta: Scholars, 1995.
Mosala, Itumeleng J. *Biblical Hermeneutics and Black Theology in South Africa*. Grand Rapids: Eerdmans, 1989.
Mouffe, Chantal. "Hegemony and Ideology in Gramsci." In *Gramsci and Marxist Theory*, 168-204. London: Routledge, 1979.
Mowinckel, Sigmund. *Offersang og sangoffer: salmediktningen i Bibelen*. Oslo: Aschehoug, 1951.
———. *Psalmenstudien* II. Kristiania: Dybwad, 1921. Reprint, Amsterdam: Schippers, 1961.
———. *The Psalms in Israel's Worship*. 2 vols. Revised by the author and translated by D. R. Ap-Thomas from *Offersang og sangoffer*. 1962. Reprint, Sheffield, UK: JSOT, 1992.
———. *Psalms Studies*. 2 vols. History of Biblical Studies, 2-3. Translated by Mark E. Biddle from *Psalmenstudien*. Atlanta: SBL, 2014.
Naʿaman, Nadav. "Historical and Literary Notes on the Excavation of Tel Jezreel." *Tel Aviv* 24 (1997) 120-28.
Nakanose, Shigemitsu. *Josiah's Passover: Sociology and the Liberating Bible*. Maryknoll, NY: Orbis, 1993.
Nelson, Richard D. *Deuteronomy: A Commentary*. OTL. Louisville, KY: Westminster John Knox, 2002.
North, Robert. "*Yād* in the Shemitta-Law." *VT* 4 (1954) 196-99.
Noth, Martin. *Könige*, I Teilband. BKAT IX/1. Neukirchen-Vluyn: Neukirchener Verlag, 1968.
Nurmi, Janne J. *Die Ethik unter dem Druck des Alltags: Die Impulse der gesellschaftlichen Änderungen und Situation zu der sozialkritischen Prophetie in Juda im 8. Jh. v. Chr.* Åbo: Åbo Akademis Förlag, 2004.
O'Connell, Robert H. *The Rhetoric of the Book of Judges*. SVT 63. Leiden: Brill, 1996.
Oded, Bustenay. "Judah and the Exile." In *Israelite and Judaean History*, edited by John H. Hayes and J. Maxwell Miller, 435-88. OTL. London: SCM, 1977.
O'Donovan, Oliver, and Joan Lockwood O'Donovan. *From Irenaeus to Grotius: A Sourcebook in Christian Political Thought 100-1625*. Grand Rapids: Eerdmans, 1999.
Osgood, Sylvia Joy. "Early Israelite Society and the Place of the Poor and Needy: Background of the Message of the Eighth-Century Prophets." 2 vols. Ph.D. thesis, University of Manchester, 1992. Ann Arbor, MI: ProQuest Dissertations and Theses, 1992.
Otto, Eckart. "Programme der sozialen Gerechtigkeit: Die neuassyrische (an)durāru-Institution sozialen Ausgleichs und das deuteronomische Erlaßjahr in Dtn 15*." *ZAR* 3 (1997) 26-63.
———. *Theologische Ethik des Alten Testaments*. Theologische Wissenschaft 3,2. Stuttgart: Kohlhammer, 1994.
———. "'Um Gerechtigkeit im Land sichtbar werden zu lassen . . .' Zur Vermittlung von Recht und Gerechtigkeit im alten Orient, in der hebräischen Bibel und in der Moderne." In *Recht-Macht-Gerechtigkeit*, edited by Joachim Mehlhausen, 107-45. Gütersloh: Kaiser, 1998.
Palmisano, Maria Carmela. *"Salvaci, Dio dell'universo!": Studio dell'eucologia di Sir 36H,1-17*. Analecta Biblica 163. Rome: Pontificio Istituto Biblico, 2006.

Paul, Shalom M. *Amos: A Commentary on the Book of Amos.* Hermeneia. Minneapolis, MN: Fortress, 1991.
Perlitt, Lothar. "Ein einzig Volk von Brüdern." In *Kirche: Festschrift für Günther Bornkamm zum 75. Geburtstag*, edited by Dieter Lührmann and Georg Strecker, 27–52. Tübingen: Mohr, 1980.
Pleins, J. David. "Poverty in the Social World of the Wise." *JSOT* 37 (1987) 61–78.
———. *The Social Visions of the Hebrew Bible: A Theological Introduction.* Louisville, KY: Westminster John Knox, 2001.
Polanyi, Karl. "The Economy as Instituted Process." In *Trade and Market in the Early Empires: Economies in History and Theory*, edited by Karl Polanyi, Conrad M. Arensberg, and Harry W. Pearson, 243–69. Glencoe, IL: Falcon's Wing, 1957.
Pons, Jacques. *L'oppression dans l'ancien testament.* Paris: Letouzey et Ané, 1981.
Premnath, D. N. "Latifundialization and Isaiah 5.8–10." *JSOT* 40 (1988) 49–60.
Prior, Michael. *The Bible and Colonialism: A Moral Critique.* Sheffield, UK: Sheffield Academic, 1997.
Rad, Gerhard von. *Das erste Buch Mose.* 4th ed. 3 vols. ATD, 2–4. Göttingen: Vandenhoeck & Ruprecht, 1956.
———. *Genesis: A Commentary.* 2nd ed. OTL. Translated by John H. Marks from *Das erste Buch Mose.* London: SCM, 1963.
Rahlfs, Alfred. *Septuaginta: Id est Vetus Testamentum graece iuxta LXX interpretes.* 2 vols. in one. Stuttgart: Deutsche Bibelgesellschaft, 1935.
Rainey, Anson F. "Compulsory Labour Gangs in Ancient Israel." *IEJ* 20 (1970) 191–202.
Reiterer, F. V. "Review of Recent Research on the Book of Ben Sira (1980–1996)." In *The Book of Ben Sira in Modern Research*, edited by Pancratius C. Beentjes, 23–60. Berlin: de Gruyter, 1997.
Renger, Johannes M. "Royal Edicts of the Old Babylonian Period—Structural Background." In *Debt and Economic Renewal in the Ancient Near East*, edited by Michael Hudson and Marc Van de Mieroop, 139–62. Bethesda, Maryland: CDL, 2002.
Richardson, M. E. J. *Hammurabi's Laws: Text, Translation and Glossary.* The Biblical Seminar 73; Semitic Texts and Studies 2. Sheffield, UK: Sheffield Academic, 2000.
Rodd, Cyril S. *Glimpses of a Strange Land: Studies in Old Testament Ethics.* Edinburgh: T. & T. Clark, 2001.
Rogerson, J. W. *According to the Scriptures: The Use of the Bible in Social, Moral and Political Questions.* Biblical Challenges in the Contemporary World. London: Equinox, 2007.
Routledge, Bruce. "Seeing through Walls: Interpreting Iron Age I Architecture at Khirbat al-Mudayna al-ʿAliya." *BASOR* 319 (2000) 37–70.
Sahlins, Marshall. "On the Sociology of Primitive Exchange." In *Stone Age Economics*, with a new foreword by David Graeber, 168–258. London: Routledge, 2017 (1972).
Sandel, Michael J. *Justice: What's the Right Thing to Do?* London: Allen Lane, 2009.
Schmid, Hans Heinrich. "Creation, Righteousness and Salvation: 'Creation Theology' as the Broad Horizon of Biblical Theology." In *Creation in the Old Testament*, edited by Bernhard W. Anderson, 102–17. Issues in Religion and Theology 6. London: SPCK, 1984.
———. *Gerechtigkeit und Weltordnung: Hintergrund und Geschichte des alttestamentlichen Gerechtigkeitsbegriffes.* BHTh 40. Tübingen: Mohr, 1968.

Schmidt, Werner H. *Die Schöpfungsgeschichte der Priesterschrift*. WMANT 17. Neukirchen-Vluyn: Neukirchener, 1964.
Schrader, Lutz. "Beruf, Arbeit und Muße als Sinnerfüllung bei Jesus Sirach." In *Der Einzelne und seine Gemeinschaft bei Ben Sira*, edited by Renate Egger-Wenzel and Ingrid Krammer, 117–50. BZAW 270. Berlin: de Gruyter, 1998.
Schrader, Lutz. *Leiden und Gerechtigkeit: Studien zu Theologie und Textgeschichte des Sirachbuches*. BBET 27. Frankfurt am Main: Lang, 1994.
Schwantes, Milton. *Das Recht der Armen*. BBET 4. Frankfurt am Main: Lang, 1977.
Scouflaire, Marie-France. "Le pouvoir en Mésopotamie; confrontation de deux pouvoirs à la période paléo-babylonienne, dans le domaine juridique: celui du roi et celui des 'marchands.'" In *Les moyens d'expressions de pouvoir dans les sociétés anciennes*, edited by Argo, centre d'études comparées des civilisations anciennes, 115–30. Leuven: Peeters, 1996.
Seitz, Christopher R. *Theology in Conflict: Reactions to the Exile in the Book of Jeremiah*. BZAW 176. Berlin: de Gruyter, 1989.
Seitz, Gottfried. *Redaktionsgeschichtliche Studien zu Deuteronomium*. BWANT 5.13. Stuttgart: Kohlhammer, 1971.
Simkins, Ronald A. "Patronage and the Political Economy of Monarchic Israel." *Semeia* 87 (1999) 123–44.
Skehan, Patrick W., and Alexander A. Di Lella, OFM. *The Wisdom of Ben Sira: A New Translation with Notes, Introduction and Commentary*. AB 39. New York: Doubleday, 1987.
Smith, Daniel L. *The Religion of the Landless: A Sociology of the Babylonian Exile*. Bloomington, IN: Meyer-Stone, 1989.
Sneed, Mark R. "The Class Culture of Proverbs: Eliminating Stereotypes." *SJOT* 10 (1996) 296–308.
Soss, Neal M. "Old Testament Law and Economic Society." *Journal of the History of Ideas* 34 (1973) 323–44.
Stadelmann, Helge. *Ben Sira als Schriftgelehrter: eine Untersuchung zum Berufsbild des vor-makkabäischen Sōfēr unter berücksichtigung seines Verhältnisses zu Priester-, Propheten- und Weisheitslehrertum*. WUNT, 2nd series, 6. Tübingen: Mohr, 1980.
Steck, Odil Hannes. "Der Mensch und der Todesstrafe in Gen 9,6a." *ThZ* 53 (1997) 118–30.
Tate, Marvin E. *Psalms 51–100*. WBC 20. Dallas: Word, 1990.
Tawney, R. H. *Equality*. With a new introduction by Richard M. Titmuss. London: Allen and Unwin, 1964 (1931).
Tcherikover, Victor. *Hellenistic Civilization and the Jews*. Jerusalem: Magnes, 1959.
Tomes, Roger. "The Education of Ben Sira." In *Interpreting the Text: Essays on the Old Testament, Its Reception and Its Study*, 157–71. Sheffield, UK: Sheffield Phoenix, 2015.
Toorn, Karel van der. "The Exodus as Charter Myth." In *Religious Identity and the Invention of Tradition: papers read at a NOSTER conference in Soesterberg, January 4–6, 1999*, edited by Jan Willem van Henten and Anton Houtepen, 113–27. Assen: Royal van Gorcum, 2001.
Uffenheimer, Benjamin. "Urbanization as a Religious and Social Problem in the Words of the Prophets" (Hebrew). In *Collection of Papers Read at the Twelfth Congress of Historical Studies*, 207–26. Jerusalem: The Israeli Historical Society, 1968.

Van Seters, John. *A Law Book for the Diaspora: Revision in the Study of the Covenant Code.* New York: Oxford University Press, 2003.

Vanderhooft, David. "The Israelite *Mishpaha* in the Priestly Writings, and Changing Valences in Israel's Kinship Terminology." In *Exploring the Long Durée: Essays in Honor of Lawrence E. Stager*, edited by J. David Schloen, 219–35. Winona Lake, IN: Eisenbrauns, 2009.

Vaux, Roland de. "Les fouilles de Tell el-Farʿah près Naplouse—Cinquième campagne." *RB* 62 (1955) 541–89.

Veijola, Timo. *Das 5. Buch Mose Deuteronomium, Kapitel 1,1—16,17.* ATD 8,1. Göttingen: Vandenhoeck & Ruprecht, 2004.

Waltke, Bruce K., and M. O'Connor. *An Introduction to Biblical Hebrew Syntax.* Winona Lake, IN: Eisenbrauns, 1990.

Walzer, Michael. *Interpretation and Social Criticism.* Cambridge: Harvard University Press, 1987.

Warrior, Robert Allen. "A Native American Perspective: Canaanites, Cowboys and Indians." In *Voices from the Margin: Interpreting the Bible in the Third World*, edited by R. S. Sugirtharajah, 235–41. 3rd ed. Maryknoll, NY: Orbis, 2006.

Weinberg, Joel. *The Citizen-Temple Community.* JSOTS 151. Sheffield, UK: JSOT, 1992.

Weinfeld, Moshe. *Deuteronomy and the Deuteronomic School.* Oxford: Clarendon, 1972.

———. "'Justice and Righteousness'—משפט וצדקה—The Expression and its Meaning." In *Justice and Righteousness: Biblical Themes and Their Influence*, edited by Henning Graf Reventlow and Yair Hoffman, 228–46. JSOTS 137. Sheffield, UK: JSOT, 1992.

———. *Social Justice in Ancient Israel and in the Ancient Near East.* Rev. ed. Minneapolis: Fortress, 1995.

Wellhausen, J[ulius]. *Die Composition des Hexateuchs und der historischen Bücher des Alten Testaments.* 2er Druck mit Nachtragen. Berlin: Reimer, 1889. Reprint, Nabu Public Domain Reprints, n.d.

Westbrook, Raymond. *Property and the Family in Biblical Law.* JSOTS 113. Sheffield, UK: Sheffield Academic, 1991.

Westermann, Claus. *Genesis 1. Teilband, Genesis 1–11.* 2nd ed. BKAT I/1. Göttingen: Vandenhoeck & Ruprecht, 1976.

———. *Genesis 1–11: A Commentary.* Translated by John J. Scullion from *Genesis 1. Teilband.* London: SPCK, 1984.

———. *Roots of Wisdom: The Oldest Proverbs of Israel and Other Peoples.* Translated from *Wurzeln der Weisheit.* Edinburgh: T. & T. Clark, 1995.

———. *Wurzeln der Weisheit: die ältesten Sprüche Israels und anderer Völker.* Göttingen: Vandenhoeck & Ruprecht, 1990.

White, Lynn Jr. "The Historic Roots of our Ecological Crisis." *Science* 155 (10 March 1967) 1203–7 (reprinted many times).

Whybray, R. N. *Wealth and Poverty in the Book of Proverbs.* JSOTS 99. Sheffield, UK: JSOT, 1990.

Wikipedia. "Transatlantic Trade and Investment Partnership." https://en.wikipedia.org/wiki/Transatlantic_Trade_and_Investment_Partnership (accessed 2015-10-21).

Wildberger, Hans. "Das Abbild Gottes, Gen 1:26–30." *ThZ* 21 (1965) 245–59, 481–501.

Wildberger, Hans. *Isaiah 1–12: A Commentary.* Translated by Thomas H. Trapp from *Jesaja 1–12.* Minneapolis: Fortress, 1991.

———. *Jesaja 1–12.* 2nd ed. BKAT 10.1. Neukirchen-Vluyn: Neukirchener, 1980.

Williamson, H. G. M., *A Critical and Exegetical Commentary on Isaiah 1–27*. Vol. 1, *Isaiah 1–5*. ICC. London: T. & T. Clark, 2006.
Wilson, Gerald H. *The Editing of the Hebrew Psalter*. SBLDS 76. Chico, CA: Scholars, 1985.
———. "Shaping the Psalter: A Consideration of Editorial Linkage in the Book of Psalms." In *The Shape and Shaping of the Psalter*, edited by J. Clinton McCann Jr., 72–82. JSOTS 159. Sheffield, UK: Sheffield Academic, 1993.
Wischmeyer, Oda. *Die Kultur des Buches Jesus Sirach*. BZNW 77. Berlin: de Gruyter, 1995.
Wolf, Eric R. *Peasants*. Foundations of Modern Anthropology. Englewood Cliffs, NJ: Prentice-Hall, 1966.
Wolff, Hans Walter. *Dodekapropheton II: Joel und Amos*. 2nd ed. BKAT XIV/2. Neukirchen-Vluyn: Neukirchener, 1975.
———. *Dodekapropheton IV: Micha*. BKAT XIV/4. NeukirchenVluyn: Neukirchener, 1982.
———. *Joel and Amos: A Commentary on the Books of the Prophets Joel and Amos*. Hermeneia. Translated by Waldemar Janzen, S. Dean McBride, Jr, and Charles A. Muenchow from *Dodekapropheton II.*. Philadelphia: Fortress, 1977.
———. *Micah, A Commentary*. A Continental Commentary. Translated by G. Stansell from *Dodekapropheton IV*. Minneapolis: Augsburg, 1990.
Wright, Benjamin G., III, and Claudia V. Camp. "'Who Has Been Tested by Gold and Found Perfect?': Ben Sira's Discourse of Riches and Poverty." *Henoch* 23 (2001) 153–74.
Wright, Christopher J. H. *God's People in God's Land: Family, Land and Property in the Old Testament*. Grand Rapids: Eerdmans, 1990.
Würthwein, Ernst. *Das Erster Buch der Könige, Kapitel 1–16*. ATD 11,1. Göttingen: Vandenhoeck & Ruprecht, 1977.
Zenger, Erich. *Gottes Bogen in den Wolken: Untersuchungen zu Komposition und Theologie der priesterlichen Urgeschichte*. SBS 112. Stuttgart: Katholisches Bibelwerk, 1983.
Ziegler, Joseph. *Sapientia Iesu Filii Sirach*. Septuaginta, XII(2). Göttingen: Vandenhoeck und Ruprecht, 1965.
Zimmerli, Walter. "Das 'Gnadenjahr des Herrn.'" In *Archäologie und Altes Testament: Festschrift für Kurt Galling zum 8. Januar 1970*, edited by Arnulf Kuschke and Ernst Kutsch, 321–32. Tübingen: Mohr, 1970.
Zwickel, Wolfgang. "Wirtschaftliche Grundlagen in Zentraljuda gegen Ende des 8. Jh.s aus archäologischer Sicht." *UF* 26 (1994) 557–92.

Author Index

Albertz, Rainer, 85–87, 89, 103, 132n53
Alt, Albrecht, 124
Alter, Robert, 4n9, 4n12, 180, 184, 187, 188n28, 190, 206n27
Anderson, Bernhard W., 204–5, 209n42
Anderson, Gary A., 14n46, 14n48, 191n4
Aristotle, 25n21, 41
Assmann, Jan, 125, 131, 185

Bachmann, Johannes, 125
Baker, David L., 12n41
Barr, James, 202, 207n31, 209n44
Barstad, Hans, 99
Barth, Karl, 207
Bartlett, Russell S., 150n1, 180n134
Barton, John, 169–70
Basil of Caesarea, 191, 196
Becker, Uwe, 129–31
Beentjes, Pancratius C., 133n2, 141n43, 141n45, 142, 143n60
Ben Zvi, Ehud, 88–89, 99, 102
Ben-Tor, Amnon, 103
Bendor, S., 66n18, 66n19, 89–90, 91, 95–98, 111n26, 192n8, 193
Benjamin, Walter, xv
Bird, Phyllis, 42n23
Blenkinsopp, Joseph, 115, 205
Block, Daniel I., 173n104
Bobek, Hans, 105
Boer, Roland, 2n1, 9, 164n72, 165, 175n119

Boswell, James, 73n3
Briggs, Charles Augustus, 187n27
Briggs, Emilie Grace, 187n27
Bright, John, 120n1
Broshi, Magen, 96
Brown, William P., 204, 207, 208n39, 211n55
Broyles, Craig C., 39n15
Brueggemann, Walter, 54

Calvin, John, 38, 54, 203n13, 209
Camp, Claudia V., 134, 135, 136, 138, 140–41, 143–44, 146n74, 147, 148–49
Carney, T.F., 49n52
Carr, David M., 130, 135, 136, 137
Carroll, Robert P., 87, 120n1
Chambon, Alain, 90
Chaney, Marvin L., 18, 48, 49n53, 53, 115n34, 121, 132n52, 164n71
Charpin, Dominique, 10, 56–57, 165–66
Chavel, Simeon, 47–48, 165n75
Chirichigno, Gregory C., 24n17, 24n18, 31n47, 60n4, 195n21
Clark, Gordon R., 155n25, 200n39
Clines, David J.A., 73, 83, 84n45
Cogan, Mordechai, 126n29
Coggins, Richard J., 87n7, 88
Collins, John J., 139n32, 148n80
Collins, Terence, 87n4
Cook, Stephen L., 199n34
Corley, Jeremy, 141n40

AUTHOR INDEX

Craigie, Peter C., 24n17, 24n18, 25n22, 28
Crüsemann, Frank, 20n9, 30, 52, 128n38

Dahood, Mitchell, 41
Daube, David, 23
Davies, G.I., 124n22
Davies, Philip R., 205
Dearman, J. Andrew, 164n69
Dequeker, Luc, 203n13
Dhorme, Édouard, 83n43
Di Lella, Alexander A., 134n7, 141n45, 143n60
Domeris, William Robert, 193n15, 194n18, 197n28
Driver, Samuel Rolles, 24n17, 24n18, 24n19, 28n34, 51n63
Dybdahl, Jon L., 50n61

Eagleton, Terry, 36
Edzard, D.O., 56
Eisenstadt, S.N., 106n9
Engels, Friedrich, 15
Epsztein, Léon, 25n20
Ewans, Martin, 21n11

Fager, Jeffrey A., 63n8, 70, 71
Faust, Avraham, xix, 64n11, 91n24, 107–12, 113, 116, 117, 122–23, 124, 125, 192n8, 193n13, 195, 196n29
Fendler, Marlene, 97–98, 113
Fensham, F. Charles, 157n29
Finkelstein, Israel, 94n33, 96, 121n3, 122
Finkelstein, J.J., 25n20, 163
Finley, Moses, 164n72
Fleischer, Günther, 52n68, 90–91, 98n44, 102, 103
Fleming, Daniel E., 130, 159n40, 161n54
Fowler, H.W., 4n11, 151–52
Fox, Michael V., 75, 79n33
Fox, Nili Sacher, 95n36, 114n33
Fretheim, Terence E., 203, 204
Frick, Frank S., 47
Fritz, Volkmar, 107n14, 109n23, 124n24

Gadamer, Hans-Georg, 3, 55
Gardner, Anne, 204, 209n42
Garr, W. Randall, 207n33
Gellner, Ernest, 30n43
Gelston, Anthony, 181
Geus, C.H.J. de, 91, 103
Gibson, J.C.L., 46n38
Gilbert, Maurice, 143n57, 145
Goldingay, John, 171n69
Gordis, Robert, 136n16
Gorringe, Timothy J., 58
Gottwald, Norman K., 9n35, 36, 48, 49, 50, 164n71
Graeber, David, 6n17, 7n20, 192, 196, 199
Gramsci, Antonio, 19, 30
Gray, John, 49n54, 101, 125
Gregory, Bradley C., 14n47, 133–34, 138n25
Guillaume, Philippe, 7n21
Gunkel, Hermann, 38, 39n14, 204n20, 204n21, 204n22

Habel, Norman C., 65, 67, 202, 210–11
Hamilton, Jeffries M., 13n45, 20n8, 22, 24n17, 25n20, 25n24, 26n26, 28, 29, 30
Harland, Peter J., 203n14, 204, 206n28
Harrison, Peter, 202–3, 211n56
Hayes, John H., 124n21
Hengel, Martin, 139, 146
Henrey, K.H., 50n61
Hesiod, 211
Hillers, Delbert R., 116n37
Holladay, John S., 91–94, 96, 103–4, 106n6, 110
Hopkins, David C., 92, 95, 117
Horsley, Richard A., 135n12, 139n33
Hossfeld, Frank-Lothar, 183n12, 183n13, 184
Houston, Fleur, xxiii, 154n19
Houston, Walter J., 3n6, 4n10, 6n18, 7n22, 9n32, 11n38, 14n47, 31n49, 33n52, 39n13, 56n80, 64n12, 66n20, 67n21, 77n31, 80n35, 98n44, 98n45, 105, 106, 107n11, 111n28, 113n30, 115n34, 118n47, 121, 124n24, 133, 141n41, 142n52, 143,

AUTHOR INDEX

146n69, 146n74, 149n84, 151n7, 151n8, 152, 157n30, 159n41, 159n42, 164, 169n86, 170n94, 171n98, 175n114, 175n117, 177n124, 178n125, 178n126, 178n127, 179, 183, 190n36, 192, 193n15, 194n17, 198n32, 200n38, 200n39, 202, 208n40, 210n50, 210n52, 212n58
Houtart, François, 48
Howard, David M., 184, 185, 189
Hulst, A.R., 204n18

Isaac, E., 205n26

Jackson, Bernard S., 8, 31n50, 46, 60, 161, 162–63, 165n75, 167n82, 175
Jameson, Fredric, 44, 53
Jenkins, Simon, 16
Jeremias, Jörg, 88
Jobling, David, 37, 40n17, 42–43, 44, 50, 53, 54n77
John Chrysostom, 191, 196
Jones, Douglas Rawlinson, 120n1
Jónsson, Gunnlaugur A., 207n33
Joosten, Jan, 169n86

Kaufman, Stephen A., 48n49, 174n110, 199n35
Kessler, Rainer, 50, 52n68, 97–98, 113, 115, 120n1
Kieweler, Hans Volker, 136n17, 148
Kippenberg, Hans G., 21–22, 22–23, 27n32, 30n43, 31n48, 50n61, 51, 98n45, 106n3
Koch, Klaus, 168
Kovacs, Brian W., 82, 135n11
Krašovec, Jože, 167n83, 170n94
Kraus, F.R., 25n20, 46n37
Kraus, Hans-Joachim, 39n14, 187n27
Krusche, Marcel, 38n10, 186,189n34
Kuschke, Arnulf, 77, 78

Lang, Bernhard, 105
Leclerc, Thomas L., 171
Leeuwen, Cornelis van, 77, 78
Lefebvre, Jean-François, 60n4, 63n8, 64n12, 66n18

Lemche, Niels Peter, 47n46, 48n49, 51n61, 51n65, 161n50, 174n110, 175n119
Lenski, Gerhard E., 93, 103, 106
Levenson, Jon D., 179
Levine, Baruch S., 67n21
Liedke, Gerhard, 210, 211–12, 213
Lohfink, Norbert, 28–29, 206, 209, 211n55
Loretz, Oswald, 105

MacIntyre, Alasdair, 146
Magonet, Jonathan, 181–82, 184, 187
Marböck, Johannes, 148n80
Marx, Karl, 1, 15, 16, 49, 50
Mayes, A.D.H., 23n16, 24n17, 28n35, 51n64, 175n114
Mays, James Luther, 152, 153
McConville, J. Gordon, 24n18, 174n109
McGuire, Randall H., 123n15, 123n17
McKane, William, 120n1
Mein, Andrew, 173
Melotti, Umberto, 49
Mendelsohn, Isaac, 125
Merendino, Rosario Pius, 24n17
Middendorp, Theophil, 148
Milgrom, Jacob, 60n4, 67n21, 175n118
Miller, J. Maxwell, 124n21
Miranda, José Porfirio, 5n13, 17n1, 18, 43, 101n51, 150n2, 151n7, 153, 155, 177n123, 179
Montgomery, James A., 95n40, 126n29
Morla Asensio, Victor, 145n66
Morrow, William S., 199n35
Mosala, Itumeleng J., 17, 18n3, 36, 37n6, 48, 50, 73n1
Mouffe, Chantal, 19n6
Mowinckel, Sigmund, 190

Na'aman, Nadav, 121
Nakanose, 30n46
Nakanose, Shigemitsu, 20n9
Nelson, Richard D., 174n109
North, Robert, 24n17
Noth, Martin, 125, 127, 129
Nurmi, Janne J., 164n69, 193n13, 199n34

O'Connell, Robert H., 128n39

AUTHOR INDEX

O'Connor, M., 169n86
O'Donovan, Joan Lockwood, 55n78
O'Donovan, Oliver, 55n78
Oded, Bustenay, 52n67
Osgood, Sylvia Joy, 50n61
Otto, Eckart, 161–62, 174n110, 175, 176

Palmisano, Maria Carmela, 148
Paul, Shalom M., 6n16, 97n43, 100n48
Perlitt, Lothar, 25–28, 29, 178n125, 196n22
Philo of Alexandria, 24n18
Pleins, J. David, 76–78, 81
Polanyi, Karl, 192, 196
Pons, Jacques, 42n25
Premnath, D.N., 52n69
Prior, Michael, 132n54

Rad, Gerhard von, 204n15, 207, 208n39
Rainey, Anson F., 126n28
Reiterer, F.V., 135n10
Richardson, M.E.J., 162n56, 163n63
Rodd, Cyril S., 2
Rogerson, J.W., xxii, 2–3
Roniger, L., 106n9
Routledge, Bruce, 122n12, 123

Sahlins, Marshall, 192, 193n9, 193n11, 194n16, 194n18, 196
Sandel, Michael J., 2
Schmid, Hans Heinrich, 40, 154, 167–70, 173
Schmidt, Werner H., , 207, 210n51
Schrader, Lutz, 134, 143, 148n80
Schwantes, Milton, 38n11, 42
Scouflaire, Marie-France, 53n71
Seitz, Christopher R., 52n67
Seitz, Gottfried, 23n16, 28n35
Simkins, Ronald A., 193n15
Skehan, Patrick W., 134n7, 140n35, 142, 143n60, 144
Smith, Daniel L., 197n30
Sneed, Mark R., 75–76, 82, 135, 137
Soss, Neal M., 64n13
Stadelmann, Helge, 135, 136, 137
Steck, Odil Hannes, 210

Tate, Marvin E., 183n13, 184, 187n27
Tawney, R.H., 33n52
Tcherikover, Victor, 136, 146n70
Tomes, Roger, 143n58
Toorn, Karel van der, 132

Uffenheimer, Benjamin, 112

Van Seters, John, 31n49
Vaux, Roland de, 87, 91, 109
Veijola, Timo, 24n18

Waltke, Bruce K., 169n86
Walzer, Michael, 18–19, 32–33
Warrior, Robert Allen, 132n54
Waterbury, John, 30n43
Weinberg, Joel, 30
Weinfeld, Moshe, 8–9, 11–12, 25n20, 40, 45–47, 48n49, 60n7, 69n24, 101n51, 151n7, 151n8, 153, 154–61, 165, 166, 167n80, 171, 173, 174–75, 176, 199n35
Weiss, Ehud, 108n20
Wellhausen, J., 129
Westbrook, Raymond, 63n10
Westermann, Claus, 75, 171, 203n14, 204, 206n29, 207, 208
White, Lynn, 201–2
Whybray, R.N., 74–75
Wildberger, Hans, 100–101, 152, 154n19, 167n80, 207
Williamson, H.G.M., 99n46, 101, 102, 151n7, 170
Wilson, Gerald H., 181, 182
Wischmeyer, Oda, 136n18, 138n24, 139
Wolf, Eric R., 192n7, 193n15
Wolff, Hans-Walter, 100, 103n59, 116
Wright, Benjamin G., 134, 135, 136, 138, 140–41, 143–44, 146n74, 147, 148–49
Wright, Christopher J.H., 51n62, 66
Würthwein, Ernst, 125

Zenger, Erich, 38n11, 183, 184, 185, 206, 209–10, 212
Zimmerli, Walter, 171
Zwickel, Wolfgang, 50n56, 95

Subject Index

Hebrew words are listed in the informal transliteration used in the main text, Akkadian ones in scholarly transliteration.

(an)durārum, 8–9, 47, 158, 160, 161, 174–75
Abimelech, 129
Abraham, 12, 173–74, 177–78
Afghanistan, 21
agrarian society, 106
Ahab, 69, 124
alien, *see ger*
alms, almsgiving, 13–14, 70, 75, 140–42, 143, 144, 145, 191–92, 195, 198
Anathoth, 112
ancient class society, 105–6
ancient Near East, 7, 40, 45, 60, 67, 69, 120, 125, 154–55, 157–61, 167–68, 185, 207–8, 209. See also Egypt *and* Mesopotamia.
archaeology, 87, 90–95, 103, 106–12, 114, 119, 121, 122–23, 124–25, 139, 195
aristocrats, 105, 106
Asa, 120
Assyria, 91, 103, 104, 110, 176

Baasha, 120
begging, 138, 143–44
bet av, 89–90, 97, 193
bet avot, 197
biodiversity, 211

blessing, 201, 211
blood, prohibition of, 210
borrowing, *see* debt
brother, 12, 25–28, 31, 65–66, 70, 143, 145, 178, 196

Canaanites, 120–32, 159
capitalism, 1–2, 10, 14–16, 48
charity, 13–14, 22, 70, 75, 155–56, 191–200. See also alms
Christianity, 201–2
cities, 105, 106, 107, 108–12, 117, 119, 122, 124, 193, 195–96
class, 36–37, 44, 56, 67–68, 73, 74, 75–76, 133–34, 137–41, 143, 178, 194
communal landholding, 50, 69
corvée, 50, 86, 110, 112, 115, 120–32, 158, 160, 164, 207
court (of the ruler), 75
courts of law, 46
covenant, 61, 81, 162, 165, 182, 211
credit, *see* debt
cultural memory, 125–32

Damascus, 99
David, 38, 47, 129–30, 156, 182
house of, 47–53, 129, 131, 132, 170

SUBJECT INDEX

debt, 7, 10, 12–13, 22, 23–30, 68, 72, 86, 92, 94, 109, 113, 144, 158, 164, 195–96
    remission of, 24–30, 48, 53, 56, 60, 164–65, 174, 189, 195, 199
decree, 45–46, 60–61, 158–66, 175, 189
deror, 47, 70, 171, 174–75
destitute, destitution, 7, 70, 79, 93, 97–98, 110, 115, 138, 143–44, 155, 193, 194, 195
dietary laws, 210
divine right of kings, 54

economic anthropology, 192
education, 135–36
Egypt, 32, 53, 63, 70–71, 76, 132, 168, 179, 185, 207
enthronement psalms, 181–91
environment, 201–213
equality, inequality, 65, 70, 72, 108–10, 149, 178, 196
eschatology, 148, 171–72, 189–90
estates, 75–76, 85, 95, 108n16, 125, 198
ethnic diversity, 122–25
exodus, the 32, 63, 70–71, 132, 179
exploitation, 3, 7–8, 15, 17–18, 21–22, 30, 40, 45, 52, 56, 71, 98, 103, 106, 109, 111, 131, 132, 155–57, 161, 163, 194, 198
    of the earth 201–2, 211, 212
extinction, 212

faction, 18, 53
family, 12, 27, 66, 89, 108, 109, 116, 193–96
farmsteads, 117
flood, the, 205
foreigner, 26
four-roomed house, 91–92, 108, 109, 122
futility curse, 116

gate, 113
ger, 26, 65, 66, 67, 193, 195
go'el, ge'ullah, 51
God, 27, 29, 32, 37, 39, 41, 42, 55, 58, 62, 71, 83–84, 128, 141–42, 143, 146, 148, 169, 177, 178, 187, 197, 199, 201, 204
    and the flood, 205–6
    as creator, 81, 83–84, 168, 203–4, 206
    covenant of, 211
    imitation of, 32
    in history, 81
    image of in humankind, 207–8
    kingship of, 181–90
    law of, 149
    justice of, xv, xx, 3, 4–5, 7, 11, 17, 40, 44, 54, 73, 146–47, 153, 156, 157, 158, 162, 166–68, 170–72, 178–79, 181–90, 210, 211
    on the side of the poor, 36, 37
    sons of, 205
    word of, 17–18
    wrath of, 30
    see also YHWH

Hazor, 124
hegemony, 19, 22
hermeneutics, 2–3, 17–20, 35–37, 55, 73, 133, 211–13
hesed, 144, 155–56, 200
Hezekiah, 115
hierarchy, 14, 64, 146, 177–78, 180, 196, 199–200
highlands of Israel, 121–25
honor, 144, 196
humanity, 201–13
    dominion of, 207, 209–11
humility, 142–43, 149, 169

ideology, 17–20, 36, 44–53, 67, 73, 164–66
inequality, *see* equality.
inheritance, 50–51
Israel (name), 100–101
    kingdom of, 9, 18, 46, 48–49, 91, 94, 96–97, 99–100, 101, 102, 103, 104, 106, 107–12, 119, 120–32, 154, 155, 157, 161, 163, 165, 168, 177, 192, 195
    land of, 63, 70, 72, 83, 92
    people of, 2, 3, 10, 11, 12, 15, 19, 23, 26–27, 28, 33, 34, 44, 45, 48, 50, 61–72, 81, 82, 85, 88, 89, 92, 99, 100–101, 108, 156, 158, 159,

SUBJECT INDEX

166, 168, 173, 175, 177–78, 179,
    184, 185–90, 210
Issachar, 120

J, 205
Jacob, 120
Jehoiakim, 120
Jeremiah, 112
Jeroboam I, 121, 128, 129, 130
Jerusalem, 9, 50, 52n67, 94, 101, 102,
    111, 112, 113, 114, 115, 116,
    116–18, 120, 129, 131, 137, 139,
    148, 157, 164, 188n28
  fall, 183
  See also Zion
Jezreel, 121
Josiah, 20n9, 21, 46–47
jubilee, 12, 13, 47, 48, 53, 58–72, 118,
    174, 175–76, 189, 199
Judah, 9, 18, 23, 25, 45, 46, 47–53, 67,
    88, 91, 94, 98, 99, 101, 102, 103,
    104, 106, 107–12, 117–18, 119,
    120, 128, 129–32, 155, 159,
    161–66, 168, 169, 177, 192
  Second Temple, 134, 135, 138
judges, 114, 141, 161, 162, 176
judicial action, 161–64, 194
justice and right(eousness), *see mishpat utsedaqa*

king, kingship, 3–10, 18, 19, 37–57, 75,
    142, 156–66, 167–71, 176, 177,
    179, 181–90, 199, 202, 206, 208

lammelek jar handles, 94–95
land (of the peasant family), 69
latifundia, 52, 89, 95, 116–18
law, 60, 162–64, 185, 189, 211
  codes, 46, 60, 163
laziness, 77, 77n26, 78
lending, *see* debt
liberty, 70, 71
lowlands of Israel, 121–25

Manasseh, tribe of, 114
market, 198
Marxism, 21
materialism, historical, 36, 50
Menahem, 91, 106, 159

Mesha, king of Moab, 121
Mesopotamia, 7–9, 10, 46, 48, 53,
    56–57, 60–61, 155, 157, 158–56,
    160–63, 165–66, 174–76, 207–8
messianic prophecy, 39, 55–56
mišarum (misharum), 8–9, 24–25, 46,
    47, 60–61, 72, 158, 160, 161,
    165, 174–75
mishpaha, 89–90, 192, 197, 199
mishpat utsedaqa, 4–7, 9, 11–13, 40, 47,
    57, 101, 150–80, 181–90, 194,
    197
mishpat, 152, 171
mode of production, 48, 117
  Asiatic, 49, 50, 53
  tributary, 48–53
monarchy, *see* king
Moses, 175

Naboth, 69, 118
nations, 185
neighbour, 178

Omri, Omrides, 121
oppression, oppressors, 6–7, 10–11, 17,
    18, 22, 34, 35–37, 42, 44, 52, 73,
    79, 81–83, 85, 90, 97, 100, 105–
    6, 110, 111–19, 140, 141, 145,
    146, 148, 185, 197, 204, 206
  deliverance from, 40–41, 43, 44,
    45, 46, 54, 56, 141–43, 154–55,
    164–66, 168, 179, 182–83, 186,
    187, 188, 194, 198, 208
order, 167–70
  of creation, 184
overpopulation, 102–3

P, 201–13
patron, patronage, 30, 66–67, 70, 104,
    106, 146, 173, 177–78, 179, 183,
    193–94
peasants, 63, 65, 67, 69–70, 92–97,
    105–112, 113, 116, 117, 134,
    136, 192–93, 198
poor, the, 75–84, 138–40, 200
  compassion for the, 141–44
  justice for the, 6–10, 28–31, 40–57,
    153–56, 169, 208
poverty, 67–68, 78

price, 63, 64, 96
priests, 136
property, 64, 68–69
prophets, 111–19, 168–72, 180, 192, 197
proverbs (sentence literature), 74, 75, 192
prozbul, 178
Psalter, editing of, 181–90

rada, 206–7
rational subject, 63
reciprocity, 192–93, 196, 200
    negative, 194
redaction criticism, 87–89, 99, 128–29
redemption, 51, 62, 70
redistribution, 49, 92, 94, 194, 195
Rehoboam, 126, 129–131, 159
rent capitalism, 105
retainer class, 135–36
retribution, 81, 83, 147, 174
rhetoric, 37–43, 61–64
rich, the, 75–84, 138–41
ruling class, 97–98, 100, 106, 169, 180

Samaria (city), 6, 94, 96, 100, 101, 111, 112, 114, 118, 121, 124
    (province), 177
scribes, 75, 133–49
Shaphan, 47
Sheba son of Bichri, 129
Shechem, 129, 131
shekel weights, 94
shemitta, 174–76
slaves, slavery, 31–32, 47, 60, 65, 114, 115, 117, 190, 206–7
    release, 31–32, 47, 165, 174
Solomon, 38, 49, 120, 124, 125–27, 128, 129, 131, 156
specialization, agricultural, 94, 95

stratification, social, 107–12

tax, 50, 60, 86, 91–92, 94, 96, 104, 106, 108, 110, 158, 159–60, 164, 197
Tell el-Farʿah, 87, 90–91
Tirzah, 87
tithes, 13, 92, 94
Torah, 12–13, 20, 48, 53, 56, 136, 143, 145, 146, 165, 172, 173–80, 189
tribute, 44–45, 48, 91, 104, 110, 197
tsedaqa, 14, 57, 145, 152, 167–68, 179–80
    see also mishpat utsedaqa
tsedeq, 167–68, 179

utopia, 59, 68–69, 71, 176, 206

villages, 13, 21, 28, 49–52, 90, 94, 106, 107–8, 110–12, 117, 122, 192, 193, 196
violence, 42, 194, 204–5, 208–13

wages, 193
widows (and fatherless), 8, 26, 42n23, 50, 109, 114, 142, 163, 170, 193, 198
wisdom, 73–84, 168

YHWH, 5, 32, 34, 52, 54, 61, 63, 65, 70–71, 84, 124, 158–59, 162, 168, 170, 171, 173–74, 175–76, 179, 180, 195, 206, 209
    kingship of, 181–90
    See also God.

Zedekiah, 47, 165
Zion, 50, 100, 115, 120, 170, 171, 188. *See also* Jerusalem.

Ancient Document Index

Ancient Near Eastern Documents

Amenemope

26:13–14　　76

Old Testament

Where there is a difference between the verse numbering in the Hebrew text and most English versions, the English numbers are placed in parentheses.

Genesis

1–9	201–13
1:1—2:3	201
1	186, 211
1:26–30	202
1:26	201
1:28–30	204, 205, 206
1:28	201, 202, 206–9
1:29–30	203, 206
1:29	208
1:31	203
2–4	205
3	205
4:1–16	204
4:23–24	204
6–9	201
6:1–4	205
6:5–7	205
6:11–13	186, 204
6:18	205
7:9	204
9:1–7	205–6, 209–10, 211–12
9:1–3	186
9:2	209
9:3–6	204
9:3	210
9:4	210
9:5	204
9:8–17	211
18:19	12, 151n3, 151n5, 172, 173, 177, 178
49:15	120

Exodus

3:7–9	179
3:21–22	23
15:1b–17	179
15:2	179
21	87
21:2–11	31n50, 66n18
21:2–6	31, 174
21:1	40n20

Exodus (continued)

21:2	23, 26
21:4	31
21:5–6	23
21:7–11	31
22:20 (21)	177
22:20 (21)—23:12	176
22:20 (21)—23:9	192
22:21–22 (22–23)	81
22:22 (23)	29, 142
22:24 (25)	50
22:25 (26)	178
22:26–27 (27–28)	29
22:26 (27)	162
23:10–11	23, 175
23:11	24n18
38:25–26	45n34

Leviticus

11	210
11:7	123
25	xviii, 3, 33, 47, 48, 58–72, 118, 123, 176–77
25:2–22	60
25:2	64, 68
25:8–22	12, 61
25:8–10	61
25:10	8, 70, 161n50, 174
25:11–12	61
25:13	61
25:14–17	175
25:14	61, 63, 64
25:15–16	61, 64
25:17	62, 63
25:17a	61
25:17b–19	61
25:18	60
25:20–22	61
25:23–55	60, 62
25:23–34	62
25:23–24	62
25:23	64n12, 70, 71
25:24–25	51n65
25:25	12, 27, 62, 63, 65
25:26–27	62
25:28	62, 65
25:29–31	123n18
25:29–30	62
25:30	12
25:31–34	62
25:35–38	62
25:35–37	62
25:35	12, 28–29, 65, 71
25:36	62
25:38	62
25:39–55	66n18
25:39–46	47, 62
25:39–41	62
25:39	12, 65
25:40	65
25:41	65
25:42	62
25:43–46	62
25:43	206, 207
25:45	67
25:46	12, 65, 206, 207
25:47–55	62
25:47–52	62
25:47	12, 65
25:48	12
25:53–54	62
25:54	65
25:55	62
26	67, 176
26:53	207

Numbers

27:8–11	163

Deuteronomy

2:25	209
7:1–6	123n18
10:17	146
10:18–19	195
11:25	209
12–26	195
12–18	20n9
12:29–31	123n18

13:7–12 (6–11)	27	24:10–11	143
14:28–29	13, 176, 195	24:14–15	193
15	48, 58	24:14	26
15:1–18	20–34	25:5–10	27
15:1–11	xviii, 23–30, 176–77, 178	28	176
15:1–10	176	33:21	174, 179
15:1–3	12, 174		
15:1–2	175n114		
15:1	23		

Joshua

9:21	159n41
16–17	123
16:10	126n33, 128
17:11–13	127–28
24:2	49n54

15:2–3	174
15:2	12, 23–28, 24nn17–19, 25, 31, 174–75, 174n112
15:3	12, 25, 26, 174n112
15:4–6	28–29, 30
15:4	28
15:5	28
15:7–11	13, 25, 26, 28–30, 31, 106, 143, 144, 145, 175, 195–96

Judges

1	123, 126, 127–28, 132
1:27–28	127–28
1:28	128n37, 159n41
1:30	128, 159n41
1:32	159n41
1:33	128, 159n41
1:35	128
5:11	180
9	129, 131

15:7	12, 25
15:9	12, 24, 25, 29, 175
15:10b	28
15:11	12, 14, 25, 28, 29–30, 58, 65
15:11a	28
15:12–18	xviii, 3, 31–32, 47, 66n18, 174
15:12	23, 25, 26, 29, 31, 31n49

Ruth

4	51n65

1 Samuel

2:10	157n28
8:10–18	52, 128n38
8:15	183
16:13	171

15:13–15	31
15:13–14	23, 31
15:14	32
15:15	32
15:16–17	23
15:17b	31
16:11	194
16:14	194
16:18–19	60
17:14–20	177
17:15	26
17:15b	184
19:6	27
21:15–17	51
23:21 (20)	26

2 Samuel

2:4	129
5:1–3	129

2 Samuel (continued)

7:14	142
8:15–18	158–59
8:15	5, 9, 47, 151n3, 151n5, 156, 188, 194
9:11	194
14	163
14:17	163
20:1	129

1 Kings

3	163
4–5	49
5:4 (4:24)	49n54, 207
5:27–32 (13–18)	129
5:27 (13)	125–27, 128, 130
9:15–23	127, 129
9:15	126
9:20–23	132
9:20–21	126–27, 130, 159n41
10:9	5, 151n3, 151n5, 156, 194
11:26	129
11:40	129
11:43	129
12	121, 159
12:1–20	125, 126, 128–32
12:1	129
12:2	129
12:3	130
12:3b–19	129
12:4	128
12:12	130
12:16	129, 130
12:19	129
12:20	128
12:20a	129
12:25	129
15:22	120
18:19	194
20:23	124
20:28	124
21	69, 118

2 Kings

1–25	47
4:1	23, 86–87
6–7	96
7:1	96
8:3–6	46
8:6	163
12:1	51
14:21	130
15:19–20	45, 91, 95–97, 106, 197
15:20	159
21:24	52, 130
22:1	51
23	20n9
23:30	52, 130
23:31	52
24:18	52

1 Chronicles

18:14	151n3, 151n5

2 Chronicles

8:8	126
9:8	151n3, 151n5
19:5	114

Ezra

4:10	49n54
8:29	90
8:36	49n54

Nehemiah

2:17	49n54
5	9, 68, 87, 93, 197, 198
5:1–5	23, 116
5:2–5	87
5:4	197

5:5	66
5:14	197
5:17–18	194
9:36–37	184, 190
10:32	24n18

Job

8:3	151n3, 151n6
9:24	81
24:6–7	83
24:12	83
24:22	83
29	66
29:9	90
29:11	66
29:12–17	198
29:14	11, 151n3, 151n6, 154, 157, 172
29:15–16	144
29:25	66
31:16–20	198
31:17	198
37:23	151n3, 151n5

Psalms

2	182
2:7	142
12:5	7
16:5–6	51
18:21–25 (20–24)	43, 54n77
18:28 (27)	7
22:29 (28)	182n6
33:5	5, 151n3, 151n5, 156
33:5a	166
35:10	7
36:7 (6)	11, 151n3, 151n6, 172
37:6	11, 151n3, 151n6, 172
45:8 (7)	43
50:6	151n3, 151n6
72	xviii, xxi, 3, 6–7, 19, 101, 154, 157, 164, 165, 171, 172, 182, 182n6, 183, 188, 198
72:1–17	35–57
72:1–7	40n17, 44
72:1–4	39, 40, 42, 53
72:1–3	39n15
72:1–2	40, 154
72:1	5, 42, 54, 151, 151n3, 151n6, 156, 166, 167, 183
72:2	6, 38, 39n12, 40n20, 41–42, 151n3, 151n6, 160, 172
72:3	40
72:4–11	39n15
72:4	6, 38, 39n12, 40, 154, 160, 172
72:5–17	40
72:5	39, 40n16
72:5a	160
72:6–7	39, 40
72:7	40n17
72:8–17	40n17, 44
72:8–11	38n11, 39, 41
72:8	39n12, 207
72:11	43
72:12–17	39n15
72:12–14	6, 38, 39, 39n12, 41, 42, 53, 54, 142, 155, 156, 194, 208
72:12	38, 41, 44
72:13	39n12
72:15	39, 39n12, 41
72:16	39, 39n12, 40
72:17	39, 39n12, 40n16, 43
72:18–19	37
72:20	37
76:9	7
89	182
89:15 (14)	5, 151n3, 151n5, 156, 166, 186
89:20–38 (19–37)	54
89:28 (27)	142
89:31–34 (30–33)	44

Psalms (continued)

89:45–46 (44–45)	182
90–92	182
90	182
91	182
92	182
93–100	181–90
93	182, 184
93:1–2	184
93:1	185
94	181, 182, 184–85, 186, 187
94:15	183, 184–85
95	185
95:7b–11	181
96–99	181–90, esp. 185–89
96	183, 185, 185–86
96:3	185
96:5	190
96:10	185, 186
96:11–13	186, 190
96:13	184, 186
97	185, 187
97:2	151n3, 151n5, 183, 184, 187
97:6	187
97:7	190
97:8	187, 189
97:10	187
98	183, 185, 187
98:3	187
98:6	185
98:7–9	186, 190
98:9	188
99	183, 185, 188–99
99:1–2	185
99:2	188
99:3	188n28
99:4	11, 151n3, 151n5, 157, 158, 167, 183, 186, 188
99:5	188n28
99:6–8	190
99:7	183, 189
99:8	189
99:9	188n28
100	189
101	43, 54n77, 182n6
101:1	43
101:2	43
101:7	43
101:8	43
103:6	151, 154
106:3	11, 151n3, 151n6, 172
110	182n6
110:2	207
112:9	198
119:121	11, 151n3, 151n5, 172
132	182n6
132:12	44, 54n77
144	182n6

Proverbs

1–31	xix, 73–84
1–9	74
1:3	11, 151n3, 151n5, 172
2:9	11, 151n3, 151n5, 172
6:6–11	77n26
6:30	74n7
8:20	151n3, 151n6
10–31	82
10–29	74, 172–73
10:1—22:16	75
11:18	78
12:11	77n26
12:14	77n26
12:24	77n26
12:27	77n26
13:11	78
13:23	79
13:25	78
14:20	80
14:21	80, 81
14:31	81
16:8	11, 151n3, 151n6, 172, 173
16:10	75
16:14	75

16:26	80	1:1	99
16:31	78	1:3	100–101
17:5	81, 142	1:21–28	170
18:23	80	1:21–26	85n1, 114
19:15	77n26	1:21	5, 151n3, 151n6, 157
19:24	77n26		
20:4	77n26	1:21b	171
21:3	11, 151n3, 151n5, 172, 173	1:23	85–86
		1:23b	170
21:5	77n26	1:24	100
21:13	80, 82	1:27	151n3, 151n6, 152, 157, 167, 170, 171
21:17	78		
21:25	77n26		
22:7	80	3:1–12	169
22:9	80	3:12	86
22:13	77n26	3:13–15	85n1, 90, 115
22:17—24:34	81	3:14–15	50
22:22–23	81	3:14	68n22, 86, 98
23:10–11	81, 82	3:15	52
24:30–34	77n26	5:1–7	85n1
25–29	75	5:7	4, 5, 101, 151n3, 151n6, 154, 157, 173
25:1	75		
25:6–7	75		
26:13	77n26	5:8–10	85n1, 98
26:14	77n26	5:8	52, 85n1, 89, 90, 98, 116
26:15	77n26		
26:16	77n26	5:10	116
28:15	80	5:16	151n3, 151n6
28:19	77n26	5:23	163
28:27	80	6:1—9:6 (7)	100
29:13	81, 84	7	157
31:1–9	47	8:14	101
		8:18	101
		9:6 (7)	5, 11, 151n3, 151n5, 156, 157, 167, 170, 194

Ecclesiastes

3:16	151n3, 151n6, 157, 172
5:7	157, 172
5:7a	151n3, 151n5, 154

9:7 (8)	100
9:11 (12)	100
9:13 (14)	100
10:1–4	85n1, 114, 163
10:1–3	50
10:17	100
10:22	100
11:1–9	56
11:6–9	190, 206
11:4	170, 208
11:16	100
14:6	207

Isaiah

1–66	169–72
1–39	169–71
1–33	170–71, 179
1–12	100

Isaiah (continued)

16:5	151n3, 151n6, 154, 156, 157, 170, 186
26:9	170
28:17	151n3, 151n6. 158, 167, 170
30:1–17	157
30:18	146
31:1–3	157
32:1	11, 151n3, 151n6, 154, 157, 170
32:7	154
32:16	11, 151n3, 151n6, 157, 158
32:17	170
33:5	11, 151n3, 151n5, 157, 158, 166, 167, 170, 171
40–55	100, 170, 179, 187–88
50:1	90
56–66	171–72, 179
56:1	11, 151n3, 151n6, 157, 171
58	115
58:2	11, 151n3, 151n6, 154, 156, 157, 171
58:3	115
58:6–7	115
58:7	198
59:8–9	11
59:8–9a	151n3, 151n6
59:9	157, 167, 171
59:14	151n3, 151n6, 157, 167, 171
61	47
61:1–2	171
61:1	70

Jeremiah

1–52	112
2:34	112
4:2	151n3, 151n5, 173
5:1	152
5:20–29	112
7:1–7	112
7:16–19	123n18
9.23 (24)	151n3, 151n5, 157, 166
11:21–23	112
21	180
22:3	160
22:3a	151n3, 151n5, 154
22:13–19	46, 112
22:13–15	120n2
22:13	112, 120, 151n3, 151n6, 154
22:15–16	6, 9, 160, 163–64
22:15b–16	151n3, 151n5, 154
22:15	101
23:5	11, 151n3, 151n5
26:18–19	120n2
26:18	101–2
32:6–12	51n65
33:15	11, 151n3, 151n5
34	70, 165
34:8–22	9, 112
34:8–11	47
34:8–9	47
34:8	161n50, 171
34:11	165
34:15	161n50
34:19	52

Ezekiel

14:21	197
18	14, 156, 197–98
18:5–9	11
18:5	151n3, 151n5, 154, 172
18:7	198
18:8	173
18:19	151n3, 151n5, 154, 172
18:21	151n3, 151n5, 154, 172
18:22	152
18:24	152
18:27	151n3, 151n5, 154, 172
22:23–31	52
22:23–29	118
22:27	141n40
22:29	52, 118

33:14	151n3, 151n5, 154, 172	5:11	6, 97, 97n43, 113
		5:12	6, 97, 111, 113, 195
33:16	151n3, 151n5, 154, 172	5:15	113
33:19	151n3, 151n5, 154, 172	5:24	4, 150, 151n3, 151n6, 154, 157, 168–69, 173, 180
34:4	207		
45	180	6:1–7	100
45:8–17	160	6:1	100
45:9	11, 151n3, 151n5, 154, 156, 160	6:12	6, 151n3, 151n6, 154, 157, 169, 173
46:16–18	160	7:9–11	5
		7:9	157
		7:17	51
Daniel		8:4–7	85n1
		8:4–6	113
11:27	148	8:4–5	97–98
11:35	148	8:5–6	6
		8:6	90
		8:14	100
Hosea			
2:21 (19)	151n3, 151n5, 158	**Micah**	
		1–7	37n6
Joel		1:1	88, 99
		1:5–7	101
4:13	206n29	2	98
		2:1–5	52, 85n1, 102, 116
		2:1–2	85, 88, 89
Amos		2:2	116
		2:3	88
1:1	99	2:4	88, 102
1:3—2:16	99	2:5	51
2:6–16	85n1	2:6–11	85n1
2:6–8	97, 99–100	3:1–9	85
2:6	6, 23, 90	3:1–4	85n1, 159
2:8	6	3:1–3	50
3:1	88, 99	3:1	98, 101, 115
3:9–15	85n1	3:2–3	115
3:9–11	100	3:9–12	85n1
3:9	97, 100, 113	3:9	98, 101, 115
3:12	100	3:10	50, 115, 120
4:1–3	85n1	3:12	101, 102
4:1	6, 97, 100, 113–14	6:9–12	113, 116
5:7	151n3, 151n6, 154, 157, 169, 173	6:14–15	116
5:10–12	85n1		
5:10	113		

Habakkuk

2:3	148

Zephaniah

3:1–5	118
3:3	141n40

Apocrypha

Tobit

1–14	14

Sirach

1–51	xx, 133–49
3:14	14
3:17	142
3:30	14, 145
4:1–10	137, 141–44
4:1–6	141–42
4:1	141n44
4:3a	141n45
4:4	144
4:6	141n44, 142, 146
4:7–10	141, 142–43, 198, 199
4:8	142
4:9	142
4:10	142, 146
7:10	14
7:15	138n25
7:29–31	136
7:32–33	137
8:12	139
10:14	141n39
10:22	141n39
10:24	139
10:28	142
10:30–31	139
11:9	141n39
11:10–28	147
11:12–13	147
11:14	147
11:17	147
11:18–19	147
11:21–22	147
11:27–28	147
11:30	141n39
12:1–7	145
12:3	14
12:5	145
13:1–13	135, 139
13:4	140
13:15–19	140
13:17	140
13:19	140
13:20	142
13:24	140
16:1	14
18:15–18	142
26:29—27:3	139
29	137
29:1–20	144–45
29:1–7	144–45
29:1–2a	137, 144
29:1	200
29:2b–3	137, 144
29:2b	145
29:3b	145
29:6	145
29:8	14
29:8a	145
29:9	200
29:10	143, 145, 199
29:11–13	146
29:11	200
29:13	145
29:21–28	138
29:21–22	138
29:28	138
31:8–11	141
35:11–24	146
34:18–22	137
35:12	146
35:16–18	146–47
35:18	141n39
35:19–24	148
36:1–17	148
36:8	148
37:19–26	137

38:24—39:11	134
38:24-30	143
38:24	134, 137, 75
38:25-26	138
38:26	134-35
38:27-30	138
38:27	134-35
38:28	134-35
38:30	135
39:1-3	136
39:1	136
39:4	135
39:8	136
40:28-30	138, 143-44
42:5-7	139
45:4	142
46:7	144
50:1-21	136
51:23	136
51:25	136

Pseudepigrapha

1 Enoch

7-8	209
7:2	205
7:4-6	205
8:1	205

New Testament

Luke

6:34-35	145
16:3	144

Rabbinic writings

Mishnah

Shebiit

10.1	24n18
10.3	25

Philo

de Septennio

8	24n18

Greco-Roman writings

Aristotle

Ἀθηναίων Πολιτεία
(*Constitution of Athens*)

	25n21

Rhetoric

16-17	41

Hesiod

Theogony

108-11	211n54

Early Christian writings

Basil of Caesarea

"On the Saying of the Gospel according to Luke, 'I will pull down my barns and build bigger ones.'"

PG 31, 277	191

John Chrysostom

"In Epistulam I ad Timotheum Cap. IV, Homilia 12."

PG 62, 563-63	191

www.ingramcontent.com/pod-product-compliance
Lightning Source LLC
Chambersburg PA
CBHW030614230426
43661CB00053B/1982